American Sociology
and Pragmatism

American Sociology and Pragmatism

Mead, Chicago Sociology, and Symbolic Interaction

J. David Lewis and Richard L. Smith

The University of Chicago Press
Chicago and London

The University of Chicago Press, Chicago 60637
The University of Chicago Press, Ltd., London

J. DAVID LEWIS is assistant professor of sociology
at the University of Notre Dame.
RICHARD L. SMITH is assistant professor of sociology at the College of Charleston.

Library of Congress Cataloging in Publication Data

Lewis, J David.
   American sociology and pragmatism.

   Bibliography: p.
   Includes index.
   1. Sociology—United States.   2. Chicago school
of sociology.   3. Symbolic interactionism.
I. Smith, Richard L., joint author.
HM22.U5L48   301'.0973   80-15489
ISBN 0-226-47697-9

Contents

Tables

Foreword

Sociology developed, over the millennia, from folk generalizations to philosophical inquiry, to become in the nineteenth century an academic subject, and finally, near the end of the century, the beginnings of a science. The transition to the last stage was centered at the then new University of Chicago. In the past few years scholars have shown a growing interest in this development. The present study, by J. David Lewis and Richard L. Smith, is an advance in our understanding of that transition, and, as the title indicates, gives particular attention to the influence of the American pragmatic philosophers—especially to George Herbert Mead and the type of social psychology that has come to be known as symbolic interactionism.

Lewis and Smith provide a thorough and painstaking metatheoretical analysis of the major American pragmatists—Peirce, James, Dewey, and Mead—and then extend this analysis to the science of sociology as it developed at Chicago. There is a particularly searching examination of the influence of Mead on Chicago sociology, including a historical reconstruction of Mead's personal relationships with Chicago faculty and graduate students. The authors find both influence and inconsistency at Chicago, as well as some present-day misconceptions about the importance of its influence.

The University of Chicago opened in 1892,

and Albion Small, president of Colby College, was invited by Chicago's president, William Rainey Harper, to join the university and head a department of history. Small, however, suggested that he undertake to create a department of sociology, and Harper, receptive to innovations, agreed to this. Small soon brought in two exceptionally able men, William I. Thomas and George E. Vincent; Harper, without consulting Small, appointed Charles Richmond Henderson to complete the original department. Within the next few years a large number of colleges and universities followed the Chicago example.

President Harper intended to create a great university in the heart of the Midwest. With major financial support from John D. Rockefeller, as well as several wealthy residents of the city of Chicago, he was able to attract an outstanding faculty. So, in the year of its founding, the University of Chicago took its place in the front rank of universities in the world—an achievement unique in the history of higher education. Within the context of the present study, it is significant that President Harper not only encouraged Small and others to develop a science of sociology, but that he encouraged the advancement of pragmatism by Dewey, Mead, and other members of the philosophy department.

Harper expected research in every department and by every professor, and, along with colleagues in other fields, the sociologists responded. Thomas soon succeeded in raising the sum of $50,000 from a wealthy admirer of scholarship, an immense amount in those times. In a letter written many years later to Dorothy Swaine Thomas, he confessed that he obtained the money before he planned what research to undertake. The famous work, *The Polish Peasant in Europe and America,* on which Florian Znaniecki collaborated, eventually followed from that grant. Although the section titled "Methodological Note" reflected the Chicago urge to put research on a scientific basis, it represented more of a commitment to finding a method than the development of an effective method itself. Small and his early colleagues were determined to make progress, but they did not create a scientific sociology.

For the most part, it appears that Thomas did not seek his inspiration for a method from the American pragmatic philosophers, although Lewis and Smith discern some traces of their influence. The more important contributions of the pragmatists to sociology came later, by way of two Chicago scholars of the second generation—Robert E. Park and Ellsworth Faris, both of whom were philosophers by training. Park studied at Michigan under John Dewey and at Harvard, where he became thoroughly acquainted with the traditions represented by Royce, James, and others. Faris began his graduate studies in philosophy at Chicago and was influenced by Mead and the writings of Dewey before he made what seemed to him to be a minor change by taking his doctorate in psychology. Only in mid-career, at the age of forty-five, did he change to sociology.

The founders of sociology faced major problems, such as that of deciding whether groups, organizations, and societies are in any useful sense real, or are merely pluralistic collections of individual persons. If the latter were the case, the most that could be justified would be some sort of collective psychology or human biology, but not a useful sociology. It was on this point that American pragmatic philosophy could give comfort, and this may have been important in giving the early sociologists the courage to proceed, to find the right questions, and to discover the best operations for determining whether the answers they found had a reasonable probability of being true. There was, of course, the necessity of deciding what to mean by "true."

Such strength as these pioneers of Chicago sociology may have obtained from their philosophical nourishment apparently sufficed to provide them with the confidence and enthusiasm for the long and hard tasks that they faced, for soon they began prodigious labors which, around 1920, began to yield knowledge that seemed likely to become cumulative.

If there was one scholar more important than the others, a strong case could be made for Park as the man who took the crucial steps in the transition. From his varied background as newspaper reporter and journalist, as student of philosophy, as public relations secretary for Booker T. Washington, and as a student of big cities, he had learned to ask good questions that pointed the way to the kind of research that would bear fruit. While almost from the start of the Chicago department there had been some realization that the city of Chicago provided a rich opportunity for research, the celebrated tradition of urban studies, ecological and other, got its greatest impetus from an article by Park, published in 1916 in the *American Journal of Sociology*, asking hundreds of fruitful questions about the nature of big cities. With the cooperation of his younger colleague, Ernest W. Burgess, Park inspired and advised a long succession of graduate students to produce articles and books on urban studies. These became so conspicuous that the impression grew throughout the country that such studies were all that the sociologists did at Chicago.

The actual range of early Chicago sociology was broad. Apart from ecological studies there was research by faculty and graduate students on social movements, revolutions, sects, crowd and mass behavior, public opinion, race relations, occupations and professions, the family, social change, social psychology, various forms of social pathology, including crime and delinquency, and the theory and history of sociology.

In all this activity traces of influence from the philosophers can be perceived. The influences, however, are not all readily discernible, and they reflect the same metatheoretical inconsistencies which Lewis and Smith find in the pragmatists themselves. In the busy atmosphere of research, most attention was given to the immediate problems before the investigators. Sociology graduate students were urged to immerse themselves in their data, to attend to detail in the fashion of good newspaper reporters. There was neither time nor encouragement to step back and examine the philosophical foundations of the research process. Perhaps as a consequence, Lewis and Smith find divergences of social thought even within the writings of individual sociologists.

If the principal faculty members at Chicago were inconsistent within themselves, they were even more so among themselves. Park's background and interests were unique, and although the other members of the department respected him and learned from him, the amount of overlap in their views was not large, and in some respects there was disagreement on important matters. Park, for example, had had no training in statistical methods and openly expressed distrust of them. Faris, on the other hand, though himself lacking a statistical background, regarded the subject as important and encouraged students to get thorough statistical training. Burgess for a time followed Park on this issue, but toward the end of the 1920s he quietly attended the course in beginning statistics taught by Ogburn and eventually learned to make use of advanced statistical techniques in his studies of success in marriage. Similarly, Burgess and Ogburn were attracted to Freudian views in social psychology, while Faris, a good friend of both, regularly attacked the doctrine in his classes. Significantly, none of the differences were reflected in personal feelings.

Thus, as Lewis and Smith state, there was not a "Chicago School" of thought, although writers at other universities frequently referred to one. In the 1920s there was at Chicago no doctrine with a name ending in "ism"; rather there was a deliberate effort to avoid creating such a thing. Knowledge was being created, but was far from ready to be forced into a doctrine or to be given any short label.

The creation of social psychology at Chicago is an important topic in itself, and this justifies the lengthy and careful attention given to it in this volume. The debt to the tradition of American pragmatism is much greater in this field than it is in the rest of sociology. J. Mark Baldwin, William James, John Dewey, Charles H. Cooley, and, of course, George

Herbert Mead all took important parts in the early stages of this development. The systematic attention Chicago sociologists began to give social psychology at about the turn of the century is reflected in Charles A. Ellwood's doctoral dissertation entitled "Some Prolegomena of Social Psychology." Thus, sociology established an early claim to do research and teach in this field—activities which were for decades opposed, and sometimes obstructed, by academic psychologists.

It appears to have been Thomas who brought social psychology into the curriculum at Chicago. He developed a popular course with that name over the years of his teaching at Chicago, though, creative as he was, he put more emphasis on expressing seminal thoughts than on producing a systematic treatment of the subject. His thoughts progressed as he went along—in his early discussions of human motivation he spoke of food and sex as the prime movers of human beings, then later turned to a less physiological explanation in his famous set of "four wishes." In his later years he appeared no longer to consider these important. On the whole it may be that Thomas's most important achievements were to establish an influential course in the subject of social psychology and to establish its legitimate place within the field of sociology.

Lewis and Smith make a convincing case for holding that Mead did not play a highly visible role in the Chicago department as a whole; his contribution was limited to the field of social psychology. As a member of the Department of Philosophy, Mead did not take part in gatherings of sociologists and probably was never seen by the majority of graduate students. His classes met in a separate building and he was not easily available for conversations. He usually arrived at the campus on a bicycle, disappeared into an office, and arrived in his classroom only after the students were seated. Near the end of his lecture he moved toward the door, still talking, and vanished at the sound of the bell. He was a diffident man who limited his informal contacts to a few close friends, though with them he was warm and affectionate, and at ease in conversation.

Mead's classes did not usually draw large attendance. While the most motivated students listened eagerly and took careful notes, happy in the knowledge that they were privileged to be hearing the words of a rare thinker, there were others who found attendance in the courses close to drudgery. This was partly a result of Mead's manner of lecturing—he looked down at his desk, rotating a piece of chalk as he spoke in a low, unmodulated voice, repeating each day a considerable portion of what he had said on previous days. Unmotivated students became drowsy.

Mead's major contribution to social psychology was probably to supply a crucial link in the explanation of how man, a member of the animal kingdom, had become social. A series of attempts to provide an answer is found in philosophical literature from Aristotle to the present. To some theorists the answer lay in instinct, to others in a social contract, or in "consciousness of kind." By Mead's time communication, imagination, and interplay of images were believed to be involved, but it was Mead's contribution to show a process (which did not call for any mystical and unobservable principles of physiology) in which the mind and the self are not to be found in original nature at all, but are products of social experience. His argument was thought through to a far greater extent than had been those of previous theorists, and to some of Mead's admirers it constituted a breakthrough.

For whatever reasons, Park, Burgess, and Ogburn, though leading figures in the Chicago department in the 1920s, did not receive this knowledge, and social-psychological views reflected in their writing and remarks show a tendency to retain at least a degree of instinctivism and, thus, nominalism. Illustrative of this is the fact that Park had been heard to remark that racial differences naturally repel, that Burgess publicly stated that gambling was instinctive and should be made legal, and that Ogburn leaned toward Freudian theory and had been psychoanalyzed.

When Thomas left the University of Chicago, his position was filled by Ellsworth Faris. As Smith and Lewis make clear, it was Faris who brought Mead to the attention of the students of sociology. First as student, soon after as friend and admirer during the remainder of Mead's life, Faris was close to Mead. Mead's actions showed that the feelings were mutual.

Faris was an effective and often dramatic lecturer, and most of the sociology students, both undergraduate and graduate, enrolled in his courses, along with a considerable number of students from other departments, such as anthropology, psychology, and political science. Thus, he was able to reach and influence a large number of students and give them a rich acquaintance with the contribution of Mead. To the extent, then, that Mead's ideas reached into social psychology and sociology, Faris is responsible to an important degree, as the graduates of his department scattered to other universities and spread the knowledge throughout and even beyond the country.

Foremost among the graduate students influenced first by Faris, and then Mead, is Herbert Blumer, who came to Chicago in 1925 with an M.A. in sociology from the University of Missouri. At Chicago he enrolled in the courses and seminars in social psychology by Faris and also took Mead's course in advanced social psychology, auditing others. When

Mead was struck with his final illness part way through his course in 1931, he recommended that Blumer finish the quarter for him, and this was done. After Faris's retirement in 1939, Blumer largely inherited the responsibility for social psychology at Chicago, and from 1952 continued this at the University of California at Berkeley. During his unusually long career (he was still teaching at the age of 79) he trained large numbers of students, many of whom became productive through publication and by teaching still more graduate students. Central to the symbolic-interactionist social psychology Blumer advanced over these years is the recognition he has given the name and ideas of George Herbert Mead.

It is not possible to trace the full influence of Mead's ideas on sociology or any other field. Not all scholars can give a complete account of the sources of their knowledge, however well they try. It is a common experience to forget sources of knowledge and to assume that ideas learned in school are original in the thinker—a process which Göttingen mathematicians termed "unconscious nostrification." Thus, it is noteworthy that Lewis and Smith have not relied merely upon verbal assessments of Mead's influence offered by Chicago graduate students and contemporary scholars, but instead have provided a basis for interpreting these reports in light of such independent evidence as textual analysis, citations, course enrollments, and the like. Although the results of the present study are by no means conclusive, they should stimulate productive discussions and research regarding the contributions of the American pragmatists, and particularly Mead, to the development of American sociology.

ROBERT E. L. FARIS

Preface

This book is the product of our mutual interest in Mead and the history of the Chicago School of symbolic interactionism, an interest we developed as graduate students at the University of Illinois. Although each was generally aware of the other's concerns, we pursued our dissertation topics and research independently. It was only after the dissertations (Lewis, 1976b; Smith, 1977) were completed that we saw them as complementary and began plans to merge them into a single manuscript.

The focus of Part One of this book is primarily philosophical. The specific aim of chapters 2, 3, 4, and 5 is to build the argument that the pragmatic "tradition" in American philosophy existed only in a most general sense and that, in fact, one can discern two clearly separable forms of pragmatism: the philosophies of William James and John Dewey evince a nominalistic type of pragmatism, whereas those of Charles S. Peirce and George Herbert Mead reflect philosophical realism.

Not only does this analysis of the classic American pragmatists constitute a radical reinterpretation of the intellectual .affinities among the pragmatic philosophers, but it also carries some striking implications for a revised understanding of the intellectual antecedents of symbolic interactionism. Nearly all previous accounts of the genesis of symbolic interactionism (as first formulated by Herbert Blumer) have treated Mead as the key link between American pragmatism and symbolic interactionism. However, as one examines the theoretical orientations of Chicago sociologists during the 1892–1935 period, it is clear that most of their thought closely approximated the James/Dewey wing of American pragmatism and is inconsistent with the principles of Peirce and Mead (chapter 6). Although we made some attempts to support this reinterpretation by studying the biographical intersections among the pragmatists and Chicago sociologists, our principal methodology was the direct investigation of their essential writings.

Chapters 7, 8, and 9 corroborate our conclusion that Mead's work was peripheral to the mainstream of early Chicago sociology. In these chapters we present a detailed inquiry into Mead's recognition by Chicago sociologists. Stated briefly, we are able to show—through counts of Mead's citations in articles, dissertations, and books, through course enrollments, responses by early Chicago sociologists to a survey questionnaire, and other relevant data—that Mead was not a central figure in the Chicago sociology program. These statistics further call into question the assumption, taken for granted by the last two generations of American sociologists, that Mead was a progenitor of symbolic interactionism. We feel that a major strength of our argument is that two scholars—one working with philosophical methods and primary texts and the other employing historical methods and empirical data—independently reached substantially the same conclusions regarding the intellectual history of symbolic interactionism.

We doubt that many sociologists have the combination of sociological and philosophical interests that will render Parts One and Two equally engaging. Nevertheless, our guiding premise is that the intellectual impact upon Chicago sociology—by American pragmatism in general, and by Mead in particular—cannot be grasped and fully appreciated without first laying down the main directions of pragmatic philosophy itself. Moreover, we cannot begin to do justice to pragmatism's philosophical principles without delving into the technical terminologies and concepts peculiar to each of the classical pragmatists. Although Part One may be difficult for some sociologists to follow, we have made the philosophical discourse as straightforward as possible by using simple examples of all technical terms so that any sociologist with a moderate background in philosophy will be able to follow the argument.

Those who persevere will find the empirical data of Part Two more interpretable, and will thereby gain a more complete picture of the intersecting histories of American pragmatism and early American sociology.

Readers, however, will find that each part is self-contained and thus may be read independently.

We wish to gratefully acknowledge the encouragement, assistance, and information generously given us by several colleagues and friends during the years this research has proceeded. Among these, our greatest debt of thanks goes to our dissertation directors, Joan Huber and Clark McPhail, for their able guidance and enthusiastic support. We would also like to include four of our former teachers who provided much of the intellectual stimulation that encouraged us to pursue our respective interests in Mead and Chicago sociology—William H. Form, Robert A. Jones, Guenther Lueschen, and Robert L. Stewart.

There are many others who contributed substantially to this book by providing criticism and moral support. Among them we would like to mention Leonard S. Cottrell, Jr., Robert E. L. Faris, Roscoe Hinkle, Robert G. Pickens, Marilynn J. Smith, Paul Tibbetts, and Kurt H. Wolff.

Finally, there are persons who provided various types of assistance without which our research and this book could not have been completed: Paul J. Baker, James T. Carey, Lloyd and Helen Unger, Maxine Sullivan, Albert Tannler, and the University of Notre Dame, especially its steno pool.

Part One

1

A Synoptic Overview

C. Wright Mills, in the postscript of his pioneering work *Sociology and Pragmatism,* reflexively criticized his sociological account of pragmatism on several grounds. He charged that his study, and others in the sociology of knowledge, have not been sufficiently self-reflexive about their methodological approaches. He suggested that every substantive research project in the sociology of knowledge should be "accompanied by *explicit* self-awareness both of detailed procedure and of larger epistemological concerns" (Mills, 1964: 464–67). Regarding the more specific limitations of his presentation of the American pragmatists, Mills commented that he had endeavored to present the thought of each pragmatist individually, eschewing any attempt to "formulate the developmental phases of the movement as a whole and to state the commonalities and variations in foci, style, and result of respective pragmatists." He criticized his account of American pragmatism for failing to include George Herbert Mead, calling his omission of Mead "an unrepresentative act that is intellectually unwarranted."

Our book attempts to complement Mills's work precisely in those areas of his self-confessed limitation. First, chapter 1 describes our methodological procedure and discusses its epistemological rationale. Second, Part One systematically compares the pragmatists—

Charles Peirce, William James, John Dewey, and Mead—to show that there were two distinct types of American pragmatism. This divergence appears as we subject their theories to metatheoretical analysis and classification. Third, we give special attention to Mead's work in relation to that of the other pragmatists; and in Part Two we assess in detail the extent of his recognition among sociologists during his years at the University of Chicago.

Like all methodologically explicit approaches, ours will surely conceal more than it exposes. But the interests of science are better served by demonstrating one proposition clearly than by hinting obliquely at a multitude. As Peirce would remind us, scientific knowledge is incremental. Thus, for the scientific mind, the greatest sin is to block the continuance of inquiry. In this spirit, we are hopeful that others will reconsider the pragmatists through still other methodological lenses grounded firmly in the Meadian hypothesis that all knowledge is perspectively limited and incomplete. In the following sections, we present in greater detail our methodological orientation, its significance, and our major interpretive theses regarding the early American pragmatists and sociologists.

Historiographical Uses of Metatheory in Early American Social Theory

Above all other influences, American sociology of the late nineteenth century was inspired by British thought. Specifically, the evolutionary principles of Darwin, Malthus, and Spencer provided the foundation for the "evolutionary naturalism" (Hinkle, 1975) which all the founding fathers of American sociology endorsed. This doctrine, as applied to the field of sociology, conceives of social structures as the product of the interactions of individuals acting out of a desire to satisfy universal human needs of an organic or quasi-organic nature. Societies and individuals not socially organized in ways functionally compatible with these needs will eventually perish when forced to compete for resources with those more harmoniously adapted, thus providing the evolutionary thrust to human social history. Despite various internal disputes, the leading American sociologists of the 1880–1900 period adopted these fundamental principles of Social Darwinism (Hofstadter, 1945). Schwendinger and Schwendinger (1974:108) quote both Cooley and Ward to the effect that all American sociologists of the time closely followed Spencer in their general conception of the field. Marx, Weber, Durkheim, and other European sociologists were either criticized from afar or simply ignored. Spencer was also warmly embraced by Americans outside of academia as a champion of individualism, free competition, and, in short, the whole ideology of bourgeois capitalism.

Yet Spencer's philosophy of history was too materialistic to appeal unqualifiedly to American sociologists, many of whom had deep humanistic commitments stemming from earlier careers as ministers. They preferred a philosophy that preserved the naturalistic and individualistic overtones while nevertheless admitting the possibility of and, indeed, necessity for intelligently guided melioristic social reform.

Pragmatism, especially the pragmatism of James and Dewey, offered precisely this philosophical combination (Marcell, 1974:47 ff.). Pragmatic philosophy gained its first and strongest foothold in American sociology at the University of Chicago from 1894 to the 1930s. The pragmatic orientation was evident in the practical, empirical interests and methods of Park and Thomas, as well as in the humanistic and individualistic slant of much of the theory and social psychology of most Chicagoans. This loose tradition has since become retrospectively crystallized under the name "symbolic interactionism" (Blumer, 1937). With the advent of later varieties of symbolic interactionism, it has been renamed the "Chicago School of symbolic interactionism" (Meltzer and Petras, 1970). Herbert Blumer (1937, 1969), in many ways the father of symbolic interactionism, coined the name and has specified the basic assumptions and propositions of the theory. Symbolic interactionists credit James, Dewey, and especially Mead with laying down the basic philosophical principles (Blumer, 1969:78; Meltzer, Petras, and Reynolds, 1975:vii). The list of other early prominent contributors to symbolic interactionism includes J. M. Baldwin, C. H. Cooley, W. I. Thomas, R. E. Park, E. W. Burgess, F. Znaniecki, E. Faris, and J. M. Williams. Even the major texts in the history of American philosophy assert the existence of a unified "Chicago School" under Small, Dewey, Tufts, Mead, Thomas, Veblen, and others (Werkmeister, 1949:523; Schneider, 1963:345).

Over the past forty years, a historical account of the intellectual genesis and development of the symbolic interactionist "tradition" has become fully concretized within the discipline of sociology. This account cites Mead's social psychology as the major theoretical antecedent of symbolic interactionism—with supporting contributions being made by James and Dewey. Herbert Blumer and other sociologists then codified and articulated it into what is today known as symbolic interaction theory (see, for example, Manis and Meltzer, 1978:1–5; Ritzer, 1975:97–98; Young and

Freeman, 1966:564; Woodard, 1945:235–36; Faris, 1945:554; Warshay, 1971:28; Kando, 1977:104–29; Petras, 1966; Lindesmith, Strauss, and Denzin, 1977; Lauer and Handel, 1977:9 *ff.*). Not only is this account of the intellectual genesis of symbolic interactionism widely and unquestionably accepted by contemporary symbolic interactionists, but it has also been admitted into the folklore of American sociology through repetition in countless introductory sociology texts. The central feature of this account is the depiction of symbolic interactionism as a "tradition" or "school," thus minimizing internal differences among these scholars and fostering an impression of unilinear, cumulative theoretical development.

The history of American pragmatism basically follows the same pattern. Many philosophers commonly view pragmatism as a philosophical movement begun by C. S. Peirce, and further elaborated by James, Dewey, and Mead (e.g., Novack, 1975; Eames, 1977:xxvii; Moore, 1961:102–3; Morris, 1970; Thayer, 1968; Savery, 1971:485). Although some writers do not even differentiate the nominalism of James's pragmatism from the realism of Peirce's (e.g., Kuklick, 1977:329–30), their differences are more frequently recognized in the literature than are those between Dewey and Mead. Further, the differences between James and Dewey, while certainly extant, are sometimes exaggerated, whereas the fundamental parallels between the thought of Peirce and Mead have not been widely recognized (see Rosenthal, 1969; Lewis, 1972; Scheffler, 1974). But in general, continuities among the pragmatists are often emphasized at the expense of a detailed analysis of their significant points of difference. The intellectual histories of American pragmatism and symbolic interactionism have thus been painted with such broad, and sometimes faltering, brush strokes that they are of limited value in revealing and interpreting the easily discernible and fundamental intellectual bifurcations within both American pragmatism and early Chicago sociology.

Given the inherent limitations of this almost Gestalt approach to writing the history of American social theory, one must wonder why it is so popular. Hinkle (1975) has noted that one of the most common methodological approaches to historiography in sociology is to let oneself be guided by thé conception of the "great man" and his followers. Because this provides a facile device for ordering the history of the field, it is no accident that the bulk of the texts ostensibly dealing with the history of social theory are organized by the "great man" principle. A variation of this approach conceives of the great men ultimately converging toward the thought of a still greater man, but at this level the self-serving potentials of the device appear obvious.

To construct a history of sociological theory that amounts to more than a "Who's Who?" of the discipline, a methodology must be employed which permits one to classify and periodicize theories and theorists according to metatheoretical categories that are applicable transhistorically. This approach is used, for example, by Hinkle (1978, 1979), Rossides (1978), Wagner (1963), and Sorokin (1966). Such basic metatheoretical distinctions as holism / individualism, objectivism / subjectivism, materialism / idealism, and nominalism / realism suggest possible categories for this purpose. Hinkle (1975, 1980) has worked out an elaborate schema along these lines and has carefully applied it to several of the early American sociologists. His analysis demonstrates that this strategy is a far more systematic method for comparing theories than is the more usual procedure of scanning the texts for "definitive" statements while drawing whatever conclusions seem appropriate. The latter method can easily mislead the analyst, especially if one's interpretation of the texts is unduly influenced by known biographical intersections among the theorists under examination or by prior secondary accounts of their works. Conversely, the metatheoretical approach forces one to give equal attention to divergences and to convergences among the theories.

One aim of this book is to reassess, through the use of metatheoretical methodology, the development of American pragmatism, early Chicago sociological theory, and their interrelationship. We were unable to employ Hinkle's whole schema for this analysis: it was designed for classifying and periodicizing macrotheories in sociology, whereas—despite the important sociological implications of their thought—the pragmatists were primarily philosophers rather than sociological theorists. Additionally, some noted Chicago sociologists never formulated full-blown macrotheories—that is, theories that aim to integrate multiple levels of social structure ranging from social psychological phenomena to social phenomena on the institutional, societal, and historical planes.

Nevertheless, we need not fear that metatheoretical analysis is inapplicable to these texts. Although some sociologists adopt naïve scientism and profess to construct substantive theories that are metatheoretically neutral, one cannot theorize meaningfully about social reality on any level of abstraction without at least implicitly making metatheoretical presuppositions, any more than the logical positivists succeeded in their ambition to philosophize without metaphysics. They have only shown that the most crude metatheoretical position is the one *denied*, and therefore unanalyzed.

There are two generic metatheoretical problems for sociological theory. The first is social ontology. Whereas general ontology asks, "What is there?" with respect to the whole of existence, social ontology asks the same question but with specific reference to the social world. It asks, to borrow Cooley's phrase, what are the "solid facts" of sociology? Essentially, it is a question of whether social reality is to be reduced to properties of individuals and their interrelations (social nominalism), or alternatively, whether there are also characteristics of collective units not fully definable and explicable in terms of the properties of the individuals comprising them (social realism). Having made this general differentiation, further metatheoretical ontic distinctions such as idealism / materialism can be used to specify subtypes of social nominalism and social realism (e.g., radical sociobiology would be described as based upon materialist social nominalism, and Durkheim's sociology, as idealist social realism).

The second basic metatheoretical question is epistemological and methodological. Although the answer to the ontological question delimits the possible field of objects for social inquiry, the question remains as to the most appropriate method of inquiry into the character of these objects and their interrelations. Metamethodological distinctions—such as objective / subjective interpretation, or *Naturwissenschaft / Geistwissenschaft* and methodological holism / methodological individualism—are central to the formulation of possible orientations to the question, and these orientations are logically antecedent to the development of concretized research methods. Furthermore, the metatheoretical, ontological question logically occurs prior to the epistemological question, inasmuch as the subject of inquiry must be at least tentatively defined before methodological questions can even arise.

In view of the epistemic problem's logical dependency upon social ontology, it is understandable why the founding fathers of American sociology were far more preoccupied with the ontological than with the epistemic-methodological core problems of metatheory (Hinkle, 1979). Because the ontological issue is logically primary and was also primary in the thinking of the early sociologists, we shall concentrate on the ontological positions in our efforts to classify theorists by their metatheoretical commitments. We will appeal to their epistemic-methodological discussions only insofar as they illuminate the theorist's ontological assumptions.

Of the social ontological distinctions, we regard the social nominalism / social realism distinction as the most fundamental. Accordingly, throughout this book it is the analytical tool we apply most consistently to the texts of the pragmatists and Chicago sociologists. The issue lies at the heart of virtually all metatheoretical disputes in sociology for nearly the last two hundred years (see Lukes, 1973:110–22). Sorokin (1937:243–337) has presented a fascinating account of the history of the issue in both philosophy and sociology.

Peirce considered the choice between nominalism and realism as the single most pivotal decision. As we later show, he built a whole system of philosophy in defense of realism. Other pragmatists were also grappling with various nuances of the problem, but generally lacked Peirce's self-conscious awareness of the metaphysical implications of their respective pragmatisms. Thus, the issue cuts across the history of both sociology and philosophy in significant ways, thereby recommending itself as a category to which texts from both disciplines may be related for systematic comparative analysis.

Before outlining the results of that analysis presented in the following chapters, we will review the long history of the nominalism / realism problem in philosophy and indicate its ramifications vis-à-vis the American pragmatists and general philosophy of science. This review will show that the problem is most relevant to the interpretation of American pragmatism, and is an issue in itself worthy of attention. As a prelude to his own survey of the nominalism / realism issue, Sorokin (1937:243) stated: "The problem is not dead at all, but is living a full-blooded life. It makes one of the most basic principles of science and mentality." Regarding its specific relevance to sociology, Sorokin continued: "Many an actual problem of the social sciences, especially such as individualism-collectivism, society and the individual, universalism and singularism, are most clearly tied up with this problem and can hardly be studied fruitfully without its preliminary investigation." Because we fully agree with Sorokin's statement, we offer the following section as a preliminary and, indeed, very minimal investigation of the history and significance of the nominalism / realism problem.

Philosophical and Historical Background of the Nominalism/ Realism Distinction

It is not possible to understand fully the thrust of American pragmatism or any philosophical movement without first grasping the antecedent philosophical problems to which it is responding. One can evaluate its contribution to philosophy only through an awareness of prior formulations and solutions of its main problems.

Peirce coined the term "pragmatism," and James and Dewey each acknowledged the fact that Peirce provided the leading principles for the movement (Hartshorne and Weiss, 1931:iii). Although there were other influences—such as that of Hegel on Dewey, F. C. S. Schiller on James, and Wundt on Mead—the philosophies of these later pragmatists were in many respects either an expression or unintended distortion of ideas originated by Peirce. Thus, locating the philosophical context of American pragmatism requires that we outline the issues that gave impetus to Peirce's thought.

Peirce was one of the few modern philosophers whose roots were not primarily in modern philosophy. His philosophy can be described as an extreme form of scholastic realism influenced by Kant and Duns Scotus. The medieval metaphysical issue of nominalism versus realism forms the core of Peirce's system, in that much of his work in logic and philosophy of science can be seen as an attempt to articulate basic implications of the realist's answer to the ancient question (Feibleman, 1946:33). Consequently, pragmatism, insofar as it was inspired by Peirce, is not a direct outgrowth of the central problem of modern philosophy (rationalism versus empiricism) because, as Peirce (1.19) noted, "all modern philosophy of every sect has been nominalistic."[1] Before examining the nominalism / realism issue in detail, we present the following brief social history to explain how this issue evolved and why it was the central problem of scholastic philosophy.[2]

Historical Roots

The question of the metaphysical status of universals (i.e., general types, classes, or laws) was a key issue even in ancient Greek philosophy. Plato held that universals exist apart from mind and even apart from all of their particular instances. However, he never resolved the problem of explaining where these universal "forms" (as he called them) subsist or of explaining exactly what it means to say, for example, that an actual horse "participates" in the universal "horse," considered as a separate and distinct mode of being. Aristotle avoided his teacher's difficulties by realizing that universals are actualized only through their instances and have only potential being apart from those instances. With Aristotle, therefore, a naturalistic realism began to flower.

Following the decline of the Roman Empire, Western civilization entered a state of cultural decay. During such periods, it is not uncommon for skepticism—the most extreme form of nominalism—to dominate philosophy. Indeed, the second century A.D. gave to the world Sextus Empiricus, perhaps the most accomplished and thoroughgoing philosophical skeptic ever known. Epicureanism and Stoicism also gained strength, and, although radically opposed to each other, both were decidedly nominalistic. By the third century, the Aristotelian school was practically dead, and between the third and fifth centuries, Neo-Platonic theology and mysticism (e.g., Plotinus) were emerging as powerful influences. In the meantime, progressive philosophy was still viable in the Arab and Byzantine worlds. Especially noteworthy is the Aristotelian philosophy of Avicenna and Averroes. By the twelfth century, this Aristotelian philosophy drifted to Western Europe through Spain and Sicily.

Aristotle's ideas commanded fresh attention at a time when nominalism had begun to compete vigorously with Augustinean theology. Materialistic nominalism insists that physical particulars are the sole reality and, therefore, universals are not real. In the eleventh century, nominalism became prominent as a method of attacking theological dogmas, particularly the doctrine of transubstantiation of the Eucharist.[3] Nominalism's threat to Church theology was perfectly obvious. If, as nominalists argue, only physical particulars are real, then alleged spiritual or supernatural entities are mere figments of the mind along with universals. Nominalism thus undermined theology and thereby indirectly served to shake the political authority of the Church. The exchanges between nominalists and the Church were, in large measure, inspired politically as well as religiously. The appeal of realistic metaphysics to the Church and to science is that, unlike nominalism, realism proposes a conception of reality broad enough to include as "real," things that cannot be directly experienced (e.g., spirits and scientific laws).

These agitations of the status quo contributed to the philosophical revival that occurred in the thirteenth century. As DeWulf (1956) elucidated, the philosophy of the thirteenth century stands as a golden tower amid the philosophical rubbish produced during the rest of the scholastic period (from the ninth to the fourteenth century). The leading philosophers of that century were Thomas Aquinas and Duns Scotus. Both were strong defenders of realism, which was favored over nominalism in all the universities. Aquinas worked to correct Boethius's mistaken nominalistic interpretation of Aristotle and to use Aristotelian ideas to refute nominalism. Although Aquinas was an extraordinarily acute reasoner, he sometimes fell into dogmatic forms of argument. Duns Scotus, the most unabashed of the scholastic realists, might have said, in the vernacular of his day: "Redness is as real as your shoe. It is really *in* every red object. That the *word* 'redness' exists is an accident of convention, but the *property* which the word signifies is really and truly in the red things, and identical in them all."

The reign of realism was not long. The fourteenth century brought forth a tidal wave of nominalism led by William of Ockham. Peirce (1.29), in his own historical account of scholasticism, stated:

> William Ockham . . . was beyond question the greatest nominalist that ever lived; while Duns Scotus, another British name, it is equally certain is the subtlest advocate of the opposite opinion. These two men . . . are decidedly the greatest speculative minds of the middle ages, as well as two of the profoundest metaphysicians that ever lived.

Ockham was the first philosopher to give nominalism *prima facie* philosophical respectability. He attacked Scotus by arguing that every quality and object outside the mind is absolutely individual, unique, and particular. Thus, there is no evidence that universals exist in physical things. On the contrary, universals are mental fictions or names we attach to groups of particular things; there is no extramental identity shared by all members of each group. Ockham thus undermined the realists' assertion of the material identity between concepts and their corresponding external realities (anticipating Kant). The nominalism and realism issue again became clouded by political strife. Nominalists advanced their arguments as justification for their opposition to the power of the pope. As this opposition to the Church's political power intensified, nominalism became a popular philosophy, and, by the end of the fourteenth century, Scotism had virtually died out (Peirce, 1.17).

As a consequence, philosophy endured another period of utter decadence. Ockhamists advocated a philosophy in which reality is "dissolved into a chaos of individual entities with no stable causal structure open to our intelligence" (Wild, 1948:29). Thus, nominalists turned to formal logic and spurned philosophy of science. Wild (1948:29) concludes, "This inaugurated an era of verbalistic argument and logic-chopping which insidiously crept into all schools of thought and marked the final decay of medieval philosophy." DeWulf (1956:148) concurs: "The scholastic manuals and compilations of the later Middle Ages are no better than mere counterfeits of the masterly productions of the philosophic thought of the thirteenth century."

Since the fourteenth century, nominalism's victory over realism in philosophical circles has been almost complete. The history of modern philosophy, with a few exceptions such as Peirce and Whitehead, is the history of competing nominalist systems: skepticism, subjective idealism, materialism, empiricism, positivism, analytic philosophy, rationalism, existentialism, and numerous others. But science, as it must, has remained realistic. And, as Peirce constantly reminds his readers, the successes of science are the strongest witnesses in favor of realism.

Peirce's View of
Nominalism / Realism

Let us now analyze the heart of the controversy between nominalism and realism as Peirce saw it, inasmuch as our purpose in the following chapter is to show that Peirce's pragmatism was a consequence of his realism. Indeed, Peirce (5.503) once stated that the principle of pragmatism could occur only to a scholastic realist. We also show that important issues in the philosophy of science, namely the problem of induction and the problem of the ontological status of theoretical entities, involve the nominalism / realism question.

For Peirce (1.16), the nominalism / realism question was "whether *laws* and general *types* are figments of the mind or are real." Before considering the answers, let us examine the question. The realist wishes to distinguish universals (i.e., laws and general types) from particulars. Particulars are unique singular individuals usually identified in language by proper names such as John Smith or Washington Monument. By contrast, the distinguishing feature of a universal is that it can have instances, even an indefinite number of instances. In language, universals include all common nouns (e.g., "table" and "horse") and adjectives denoting sensible qualities (e.g., "red" and "hard"). Excluded are all syncategorematic logical connectives: prepositions, pronouns, articles, and conjunctions. Thus, for a realist, a sentence containing an "if-then" construction does not intend the existence of "ifs" and "thens" in the world corresponding to these words, but it does intend that the logical connection between subject and predicate applies to a situation in reality (Veatch, 1954:49–50). On the other hand, a universal such as "horse" does intend or signify a real class of animals in the world, *in rerum natura*. For the realist, there are natural kinds in the world as well as in language, and universal terms refer to these natural kinds.

Another way to explain the difference between universals and particulars is with the principle of extrapolatability. One learns the meaning of a universal by mentally separating and identifying the relevant characteristic from all of the nonessential attributes of instances of the universal. For example, if we wish to teach children the meaning of the word "red," we might begin by assembling a group of red objects. We would then try to cause the children to notice the common characteristic by instructing them to ignore shape, size, weight, and position. The scholastic realists devoted much attention to this process, which DeWulf (1956:131) describes as "stripping them of the individualizing features that characterize the objects of sense . . . our eyes see *this* oak, *this* colour; our intellect conceives oak, colour, tree, being in general." When children can conceive of the redness of the objects as something separate from all of the objects' other characteristics, we say that they have extrapolated the quality. As a result, if a new object is introduced, they can tell us at once whether it is red. Compare this to how we would teach the meaning of names of particulars such as "John Smith." In the case of particulars, there is no quality to be extrapolated. The child simply attaches the name to an individual person or object; consequently, if we introduce another man, the child cannot tell us whether or not he is a "John Smith." All red objects have an extrapolatable *quality* in common, but all John Smiths have only a *name* in common. Nominalists will accept the realists' definition of universals, but they deny that any generals are real. Only particulars are real to nominalists.

Nominalist and
Realist Conceptions
of the "Real"

In order to understand the nominalist position, we must clarify the realists' and nominalists' respective definitions of "real." The question at issue will then become clearer because it is their radically different conceptions of reality that lead realists and nominalists to pronounce differently on the reality of universals. Peirce (5.430) offers the following definition: "That is *real* which has such and such characters, whether anybody thinks it to have those characters or not." To cite one of Peirce's favorite examples, if we define the word "hard" as "would resist being scratched by a knife-edge," diamonds would be hard whether anyone thinks them so or not. Thus, hardness is a real property. Likewise, the laws of gravity are real because the general relationships the laws represent will continue to govern events in the world whether or whatever anyone thinks about them (Peirce, 1.26).

The nominalist has a much more restricted notion of reality, which became progressively articulated in modern philosophy by Descartes, Hume, and Kant. It approaches ontology through epistemology by reducing the question, "What is there?" to the question, "What can be known?" Modern philosophy has experienced no difficulty in demonstrating that the sensible qualities of external objects (e.g., redness, cold-ness, hardness, and extension) are all relative to the mind and therefore not truly "in" the object as the scholastic realists supposed. By saying that the qualities are "relative to the mind," we mean that their appear-ance in consciousness and the form of their appearance are at least partly dependent upon the structure of the sense organs and the cognitive fac-ulty. For example, the same object may appear to have different colors under varying perceptual conditions; consequently, the color charac-teristic is held to be in the mind of the perceiver and not in the object perceived. Qualities have no real being apart from the mind. The only entities which have being entirely independent of mind are the absolute material existents—Kant's "thing in itself," or the external correlate of Hume's "impressions." We can infer these external existents from the involuntary character of sense experiences, but can know nothing about their true nature. Reality is defined by the epistemological criterion on nonrelativity to the mind. Since anything that is perceived and described is *ipso facto* relative to the mind, it cannot be the reality. Reality itself must forever lie beyond the grasp of human knowledge. This is why modern empiricists hold that once a sense datum is classified or other-wise described, reality and epistemological incorrigibility (i.e., the quality of being known with absolute certainty) are lost in the process. Haserot (1950:474) expresses this consequence similarly:

> When universals are excluded from existent items, reason or ra-
> .tionality is removed from things; it is relegated to the mind. Once it is
> enclosed within that confine it is in an epistemological prison from
> which it can never escape. The world is made unknowable;
> metaphysics is reduced to futility, and man, whatever he may be, is
> and can be guided only by faith or practicality.

This result is evidenced by the nominalist's idea of the function of language. The nominalist contends that "horse" is just a word we have invented and that the only common feature of all horses is that the same general word is applicable to each of them. The nominalist flatly denies that any recurrence of qualities underlies the applicability of universals. As Butchvarov (1966) surmised, "For the interesting claim of the [nominalist] theory is that no genuine explanation of the applicability of general words can be given, that although a general word is applicable even to objects to which it has never been in fact applied, there is still nothing more that can be said about such objects than simply that the word is applicable to them."

The nominalist position regarding nouns such as "horse" is derived from its position on adjectives such as "red" or "hard." Perhaps this is why, in defending the realistic view, Peirce usually employed adjectives such as "hard" instead of nouns. From the nominalist argument for the unreality of sensible qualities, it follows—trivially—that there can be no real recurrence of qualities, for no qualities are real (Bergmann, 1958:475–78).

From the above discussion, it should be evident that the nominalism / realism question involves much more than an empty debate over words. One answer must be true and the other false, and that answer depends on the way the world is rather than the way Indo-European languages happen to be constituted (see Raphael, 1954:132). Either there is such a thing as the recurrence of qualities and general dispositions in the world or there is not. If there is, then some universals must be real, and if there is not, then no universals can ever signify anything real. Peirce (1.27) correctly identified conceptualism as merely a confused form of nominalism. One must be either a nominalist or a realist on the question. As Peirce (1.27 n.) reiterated the choice:

> Anybody may happen to opine that "the" is a real English word; but that will not constitute him a realist. But if he thinks that, whether the word "hard" itself be real or not, the property, the character, the predicate, *hardness,* is not invented by men, as the word is, but is really and truly in the hard things and is one in them all, as a description of habit, disposition or behavior, then he *is* a realist.

The position one takes on the question carries with it tremendous philosophical commitments. Nominalists cannot consistently hold the correspondence theory of truth because they must deny that general words correspond to a nonmental and nonlinguistic realm. However, realists can easily embrace the correspondence theory because they insist that real universals must refer to such a realm. In epistemology, as we have already indicated, the nominalists must endorse some form of subjectivism, either idealism or empiricism / materialism. There can be no belief that the mind can know objective reality through universal propositions grounded in the external world. Epistemologically, the nominalist ceases to postulate the reality of the external world (the idealist position) or the mind and its abstractions (the empiricist position). The realists admit the reality of *both* thought and existence. Moreover, they contend that thought apprehends classes of existents and nomological relations among them through universals.

Implications for the
Philosophy of Science

From epistemology to philosophy of science is not a long step. In some respects, philosophy of science is applied epistemology. It is not surprising, then, that the epistemological positions of realism and nominalism are directly expressed in their respective philosophies of science. In modern philosophy of science, a central issue has been the determination of the ontological status of theoretical entities—the so-called "realism-instrumentalism" controversy. As Morgenbesser (1969) convincingly argues, it is unfortunate that many people have assumed that instrumentalism and realism are entirely distinct and exhaustively alternative answers to the question. Upon careful examination, it appears evident that one can be an instrumentalist on one aspect of the question and a realist on another. Historically, nominalists and realists have often argued at cross-purposes because they have failed to formulate questions that pinpoint the issue. Therefore, for present interest, it will reduce confusion if we isolate the form of the question that sharply separates realists and nominalists.

For this purpose, one *wrong* way to formulate the question is to ask, "Do theoretical entities exist?"—when to "exist" means to be a material object such as a rock or table. Some scientific theories are intrinsically mathematical in the sense that mathematics can be eliminated only by circumlocution. The obvious examples are classical and quantum mechanics. No physicist would argue that the mathematical function which is part of a physical theory "exists" as just defined or is observable in the usual sense. The realist, along with the nominalist, would concur with that view. The realist and instrumentalist positions cannot therefore be distinguished on the basis of this question.

Another wrong question to ask is, "Are theoretical entities relative to the mind of the theorist?" This is, of course, the familiar nominalistic formulation. The question means to ask whether theoretical entities (protons, electrons, magnetic fields, etc.) have any recondite and timelessly antecedent being independent of the mind of the theorist. The answer is clearly "no," whether one is a nominalist or a realist (except perhaps an extreme Platonist who would answer that the scientist's conceptions participate in eternal Forms). There was no quantum theory until someone thought it, and the same is true of all theories and theoretical entities. Particles of matter were colliding long before any humans lived, but the *conception* of an "atomic particle" is clearly dependent upon the mind of a scientist. Nominalists and realists agree, but they differ in what they infer from this fact. The nominalist concludes that, because theoretical entities do not exist and come into consciousness through the conceptualizing activity of the mind, they are merely psychological phenomena—that is, unreal. This, as Peirce (1.21) noted, follows from the fact that nominalists restrict reality to physical particulars.

This finally brings us to the enlightening form of the question: specifically, "Are theoretical entities *real?*" For a thing to be "real" means that, as Peirce would say, it has its distinctive attributes regardless of what you, I, or any individual may think. The realist argues that red objects are really and truly red unless it is supposed that they lose their *capacity* to reflect light waves of a given frequency if put in a dark room. The red object retains that capacity regardless of how it may look to an observer. This is what the realist means by asserting that redness is a real property of the object. This contrasts to the characters of a hallucination where the qualities of the object hallucinated *are* dependent upon the psychological state of an individual. Unlike the hallucinatory object, the real object has characteristics *as* capacities which persist independently of any individual.

With the realists' criterion of reality now established, we can distinguish the realist and instrumentalist positions on the question of the reality of theoretical entities in scientific theories. The realist contends that, although such entities do not exist and are mind-relative, they are, nevertheless, real because the processes they signify are real in the sense explicated above, assuming that the theory is true. The instrumentalists predicate their argument on the fact that the scientist invents the theory. They observe that, for any class of physical phenomena, more than one theory can adequately explain observed relationships. For example, classical particle mechanics is as capable as quantum mechanics of explaining and predicting the behavior of objects that are large, at less than extreme temperatures, and not moving at close to the speed of light. The instrumentalist concludes that theories are "fictions" invented to solve some particular "puzzle" presented by observed phenomena (e.g., Kuhn, 1962). Alternatively, Dewey's form of instrumentalism casts theories as solutions to the scientists' "indeterminate situation" in a pseudo-naturalistic setting. *All* types of instrumentalists resist saying that any theory could be "true" in any unqualified sense. They prefer to call theories more or less "useful" or "workable," but always in the context of some problem at hand.

Thus, the instrumentalist view of scientific theories results from the nominalistic conception of reality. The instrumentalist follows the same line of reasoning in declaring theoretical entities unreal as the nominalist follows in judging all universals unreal. Hence, the instrumentalist presumes that once it is shown that theoretical entities are mind-relative, it is obvious that they are not real. But we must distinguish the symbol from the thing symbolized. Clearly, the words or the mathematical expressions are inventions of the scientist and, as such, are mind-relative. However, the physical relationships and processes they signify are not linguistic at all. They are objectively real because they continue to operate in the world whether or not any theory is ever constructed to describe and explain them. If the theory accurately models such classes of physical phenomena, the realist sees no reason why it should not be called "true" rather than merely "workable" or "useful." The realist asks what further condition a proposition must fulfill in order to be called "true."

The instrumentalist has another argument in favor of the nominalist view of theoretical entities. It proceeds similarly to Hume's refutation, in *Dialogues Concerning Natural Religion,* of the so-called "argument from design" for the existence of God. Briefly, the argument from design calls attention to the orderly features of the universe (i.e., physical constants, laws of planetary motion, etc.) and asks whether it is not outrageous to suppose that these could occur by chance. On the contrary, order appears to be the product of intelligent design, and a design presupposes a designer (i.e., God). Hume attacks the argument on several grounds, but his argument most relevant to our interests is based on the human capacity to conceive a nonrational arrangement in rational terms. For example, one could dump some wooden matches onto a table top and then observe that various patterns and relationships are created; but it would be a mistake to conclude that these patterns were created by a designer. There can be no such thing as an intrinsically orderly arrangement. The mind imposes order onto the configuration of matches rather than perceiving an intrinsic order. Furthermore, the number of orders is limited only by the creativity of the mind devising them.

Instrumentalists argue that scientific laws similarly create order rather than discover it. This instrumentalist argument is opposed only to one form of realism, which we shall call "naïve realism." Let us first distinguish naïve realism from the Peircean form of realism, which we shall call "critical realism" (not to be confused with the philosophical movement of the same name). The naïve realist holds a noncognitive theory of perception: that is, the perceptual object is not represented, inferred, or otherwise known through a mediating cognitive process; rather, it is apprehended directly and immediately. On the other hand, the critical realist believes that the perceptual object is, in part, the product of an inferential judgment based on past experience and present expectations. Thus, returning to the issue at hand, the critical realist and the instrumentalist agree that the scientist's mind imposes order onto the perceptual field; the naïve realist stands alone in holding that order is absolutely independent and directly grasped.

Naïve realists suppose that there is an intrinsic order in the universe which is captured by formulations of scientific laws. To the instrumentalist, the naïve realist errs in the same way as Hume's theist. The same physical phenomena can, in principle, be ordered by a multitude of theories, each of which exhibits an iconic relationship to some aspect(s) of those phenomena. On this point the instrumentalists are correct. Unfortunately, the instrumentalists proceed to reach the nominalistic conclusion regarding the reality of that which is represented by the scientific law. Like all nominalists, instrumentalists fail to appreciate the significance of the fact that events in the world will either conform to the scientist's formula or they will not; that the scientist's thinking has no effect on the conformity or lack of it because the actions and reactions of interacting physical entities are not influenced whatsoever by the scientist's thinking about them. It is true that the act of measurement sometimes alters the object operated upon, but in those cases, the scientist must either estimate and allow for these effects or else treat the measuring act as partially constitutive of the phenomenon itself. In any case, as long as the effects are general and replicable, they do not preclude formulation of nomological propositions. The Peircean realists' conclusion follows immediately, because what critical realists mean when they call scientific laws "real" is only that the relations signified by the laws would still have their being and character regardless of what any individual or finite group of individuals may think. There is no pretense that the law discovers any single intrinsic order.

Limited Generals
and the Induction
Problem: Choosing a
Framework

Expressed in these terms, the realists' case is plausible on the grounds of our common experience of the external world, but their assertion that there are real generals is not conclusively verifiable. In Hume's classic treatise, *An Enquiry Concerning Human Understanding,* he persuasively argued that we have no experience (sense perception) of casuality as a necessary connection between temporal events. The mind attributes the necessary connection to events by habit after continually experiencing their occurrence in a fixed sequence. Because there are no epistemological grounds to support the notion of a necessary connection between events (i.e., causality), we have no assurance that the future will be like the past. The conclusion is that the scientist (and everyone else) accepts on faith the principles of inductive logic.

Modern logicians have agonized over Hume's arguments, and various schemes have attempted to justify induction (Skyrms, 1966). Peirce advanced a pragmatic defense of induction which was later elaborated by Reichenbach and others. This defense notes that Hume's argument applies equally to all systems of inductive logic, not only scientific induction. Furthermore, it can be shown that if, in the long run, scientific induction will not allow us to reach true conclusions from true premises most of the time, then every other method would also fail. However, if there are any possible real generals, the scientific method would ultimately generate them.

Although this argument is sufficient to justify scientific induction as a matter of practice, it in no way guarantees that there are, in fact, any real generals. It is therefore worthless as a defense against the nominalists' charge that there are no real generals. This raises the question of what the realist means by a "general" relation. At one extreme, the notion of a scientific law with only an instantaneous duration leaves one to wonder whether it should really be called a "law," even though, for that instant, it governed the whole universe. If all scientific laws were of that type, scientific research would be physically impossible and without utility. Generality in scientific laws thus requires continuity as well as extension (if every small region of space had its own laws, there would be a similar problem). At the other extreme, do real generals entail an immutable universe controlled by eternal laws of limitless scope? If so, that would spell the death of realism because that conception of the universe is contradicted by experience.

Both common sense and modern physics support the belief that absolute chance is as real as general laws. Peirce (6.35 ff.), in his paper "The Doctrine of Necessity Examined," defended "tychism," his name for doctrine of absolute chance. Peirce held an evolutionary cosmology; for him, not only are animal species constantly evolving, but also the whole universe is evolving toward a more complex and orderly state of being. As the system evolves, its apparent constancies also change. Thus, Peirce advances a moderate conception of generality. Although general relations are ultimately spatiotemporally bounded, they are, nevertheless, real. They are general because they can have an indefinite number of instances over an indefinite, but extended, period of time; and they are real because they possess their characters independently.

The realist who maintains this tychistic notion of real generals can answer Hume's challenge to justify scientific induction. The answer is to admit that we cannot know that the future will be like the past; in fact, the presence of the evolutionary process indicates that what has generally been true in the past will eventually change. But this disturbs only proponents of the absolutist concept of generality. The successes of science testify to the reality of limited generals, as defined above. Nothing is more relative than time. Compared to eternity, a billion years is only an instant. But, in the context of human history, even if the universe becomes chaotic tomorrow, we would still say that the laws of physics held for a long time and that they were real and spatiotemporally general—in the limited sense. This view belongs to a realist of the Peircean stripe, because it combines the principles of chance (tychism) and continuity (synecism).

It can be charged that we have begged the question in favor of realism by assuming the realists' definitions of "real" and "universal." However, as we have seen, the nominalists' usual definitions of these terms will not lead to any disagreement on the question and, hence, do not raise questions that reach to the heart of the issue. Commenting on nominalists, O'Conner (1952:174) amusingly noted, "They adduce evidence which no one can controvert because everybody accepts it already." On the other hand, the realists' definitions have been accepted by philosophers from Plato to Peirce, and it is within the framework established by these definitions that nominalism and realism can be distinguished as clearly contrary positions. Moreover, we must assume *some* framework before we can meaningfully ask a question such as, "Are universals real?" Otherwise, we are making a pseudo-statement, in that no context has been established for interpreting the question. Carnap (1965) argues that many philosophical "problems" are really pseudo-problems because either such a framework has not been clearly established, or a question has been asked which transcends the framework. The "problem" of the existence of the external world is a classic example. "Is there a sheet of paper on this desk?" is a straightforward theoretical question when we presume the commonsense "thing language," as Carnap (1965:299) calls it. But the *general* question, "Do physical things exist?" is not a theoretical question within a framework which takes as axiomatic that physical things exist; it is a metaphysical or "external" question and, therefore, cannot be answered within the framework. For example, science can only answer scientific questions—that is, questions that presume acceptance of the physical thing language. It follows that no framework can meaningfully justify itself as a theoretical entity as, for instance, would be involved in asking science to justify itself scientifically.

We are, in principle, free to choose any sort of framework we want. Frameworks are arbitrary, and are accepted or not accepted according to their pragmatic utility relative to some higher ideal. But we cannot call them true or false. We cannot meaningfully ask if a framework is real, because the idea of "reality" itself must be interpreted within a framework. The best we can do is subject one ontology to the epistemic tests of another ontology; but this never leads any closer to "ultimate reality" or metaphysical truth. Realism, for the Peircean realist, is a choice rather than a metaphysical system (Smith, 1952). Taking the Aristotelian notion of "universal" as meaning that which is predictable of many, if we remove universals from our language, we are reduced to naming. The nominalist is free to opt for that linguistic form but, as Kant would insist, our mental dispositions are such that extrapolation may be psychologically unavoidable. This should prove disturbing to nominalists, who have barred themselves from speaking about universals even though, in their nonphilosophical moments, they are forced to acknowledge them. Insofar as, within a nominalistic language, abstract entities cannot be the subjects of propositions, nominalism renders science awkward if not impossible. The nominalist thus has a serious problem in justifying his choice of frameworks on practical grounds, if he admits that the practicality of science cannot be seriously questioned.

In summary, we have examined various meanings of the question, "Are universals real?", and have analyzed the realists' and nominalists' answers to each of those formulations. We have also traced the justification of induction debate and the instrumentalism / realism interpretations of scientific theories to their central issues which are rooted in the medieval nominalism / realism question.

Pragmatism and the Chicago School: Toward a Revisionist History

When the philosophical formulation of the nominalism / realism problem is translated into a question about social ontology, it asks whether there exists any social reality aside from concrete individuals and their particular features. Of course, most social nominalists do not deny that societies have institutions, laws, norms, and the like. They only wish to deny them their independent and determining effects upon the consciousness and behavior of individuals. The voluntaristic nominalist conceives of the individuals themselves as existentially free agents who accept, reject, modify, or otherwise "define" the community's norms, roles, beliefs, and so forth, according to their own personal interests and plans of the moment. This view thus undermines the generality of social structures, essentially leaving us only with situational and subjective phenomena. From a pragmatic standpoint, to deny the effects of any supposed object is to deny its reality.

Hinkle and Hinkle (1954:v) define voluntaristic nominalism as "the assumption that the structure of all social groups is the consequence of the aggregate of its separate, component individuals and that social phenomena ultimately derive from the motivation of these knowing, feeling, and willing individuals." As a statement of the opposing viewpoint—social realism—we offer Mead's (1934:223–24) discussion of the essential difference between social and individual theories of mind:

> And this entirely social theory or interpretation of mind—this contention that mind develops and has its being only in and by virtue of the social process of experience and activity, which it hence presupposes, and that in no other way can it develop and have its being—must be clearly distinguished from the partially (but only partially) social view of mind. On this view, though mind can get expression only within or in terms of the environment of an organized social group, yet it is nevertheless in some sense a native endowment—a congenital or hereditary biological attribute—of the individual organism, and could not otherwise exist or manifest itself in the social process at all; so that it is not itself essentially a social phenomenon, but rather is biological both in its nature and in its origin, and is social only in its characteristic manifestations or expressions.

For the social realist, individuals imternalize this social process in the form of cognitive and behavior dispositions. These dispositions are distributed generally across the whole community and are neither created nor controlled by the will of the individual. On the contrary, the language of the community is the very fabric of which individual minds are constituted and controlled, thus assuring that mind and self are fundamentally social products (see Ingram, 1976).

Social realism strongly asserts what voluntaristic nominalism emphatically denies. The individual and social theories of mind cannot be merged into a grand dialectical synthesis any more than the general positions of nominalism and realism can be dissolved into conceptualism. Just as it must be said that either there are real generals or there are not, it must also be said that—to borrow the Durkheimian term—either there are social facts or there are not. It is a clear "yes" or "no" question, notwithstanding the best efforts of social dialecticians to muddy every distinction. Only Hegelian logic permits one to escape the clarity of the distinction and the choice it offers.

Kurt Wolff (1959:580–82) observed that historically, American sociology has overwhelmingly endorsed the position of social nominalism and, more specifically, voluntaristic nominalism. Wolff adds that European sociology, on the other hand, has been equally supportive of social realism. We shall argue that both nominalism and realism are present in the early history of American pragmatism and early Chicago sociology. Contrary to the common understanding of American pragmatism as a more or less unified intellectual tradition, we contend in Part One of this book that the philosophies of Peirce, James, Dewey, and Mead diverged on the nominalism / realism question. Peirce and Mead proposed a social realist theory of mind, meaning, and conduct, whereas James and Dewey were mainly nominalistic with occasional lapses into realism stimulated by their close associations with Peirce and Mead. In chapters 2 through 5 we examine their writings with a specific focus on these differences.

The realization that there was a deep fissure within classic American pragmatism calls for a reevaluation of pragmatic philosophy's impact on early Chicago sociology in general, and on symbolic interactionism in particular. In chapter 6 we sketch an intellectual history of Chicago sociology from 1892–1935 (with Cooley included), specifically from the standpoint of identifying shifts in the tendencies of the major Chicagoans on the nominalism / realism dimension: Small, Thomas, Cooley, Ellwood, and Blumer were nominalists in the style of James and Dewey; Hayes, Faris, and Bodenhafer were realists, following the tenets of Peirce and Mead; Park, like Cooley, is very difficult to classify because of inconsistencies in his metatheoretical stance generated by his (necessarily) abortive efforts to wed elements of European realism (e.g., from Simmel and Durkheim) to the whole nominalist tradition of American social psychology. From this perspective, the Chicago sociologists did not constitute a unified tradition or intellectual community. Furthermore, although symbolic interactionists trace the roots of Blumerian symbolic interactionism to Mead, textual analysis shows that Blumer and Mead did not even belong to the same metatheoretical camp. Clearly, a radical reinterpretation of the intellectual history of the Chicago school is long overdue.

Unquestionably, Mead is the individual whose position is most dramatically changed in our revisionist history of Chicago sociology and American pragmatism. If, as we argue, Chicago sociology—like American sociology in general—were predominantly nominalist, and if Mead, conversely, were a staunch social realist, then one is led to question seriously the common supposition that Mead contributed substantially to the development of graduate education in sociology at Chicago as well as to the theoretical stance of the department overall. Our textual analysis of the pragmatists and Chicago sociologists suggests that social realism—and, therefore, Mead—was, at best, marginal to the development of American sociology at the University of Chicago.

Fortunately, the latter hypothesis is indirectly open to external empirical inquiry as well. In chapters 7, 8, and 9 we examine data on such indicators as patterns of sociology student enrollment in Mead's courses, citations of Mead in Chicago dissertations, citations of Mead in sociology journals, books, and so on, as well as the more qualitative evidence supplied by personal memoirs of former Chicago sociology students and faculty. All of these indicators point to the conclusion that, although Mead profoundly influenced a few Chicago sociologists, he was always marginal to the development of Chicago sociology both organizationally and intellectually. Lewis Coser (1977:345–46) has been one of the few to insist that:

> Something of a myth seems to have spread recently, namely that members of the Department of Sociology formed a unified Chicago school of social psychology around the person of Mead. . . . Mead never saw himself as head of a "school." And it might be noted that the term "symbolic interactionism" was never known at Chicago while Mead lived.

Our purpose in Part Two of the book is to put this myth to rest.

Our overall plan is as follows: In Part One we show that the classic American pragmatists actually developed two quite dissimilar types of pragmatism, as becomes apparent if one classifies them according to their stated or logically implied positions on the nominalism / realism question. When one similarly analyzes the works of the early Chicago sociologists for their metatheoretical underpinnings, the influence of the social nominalism of James and Dewey is far more evident than is the social realism of Peirce and Mead. In Part Two we present further evidence that Mead was peripheral to Chicago sociology, in stark contrast to what has been frequently assumed but never before systematically investigated. In the final chapter, we assess the implications of our theses, and suggest additional problems for future investigation.

2

Charles Peirce Logical Structures
of Sociological
Realism

The casual student of Peirce is tempted to proceed directly to his popular and lucid essays on pragmatism and to avoid the tedious study required to understand his logic and metaphysics. This approach makes impossible a full understanding of Peirce's philosophy or even of pragmatism itself. Conceived in the context of Peirce's logical system, the pragmatic maxim is a mere corollary of his theory of signs. Accordingly, compared to his voluminous papers on general logic, Peirce devoted relatively little writing to the exposition of pragmatism, and much of that was in defense of the maxim against James and other "pragmatists" who had violated its purpose. Again, it must be remembered that Peirce consciously approached every area of philosophy from the standpoint of realism. His fundamental purpose was to construct a system of logic and metaphysics consistent with realism and entirely free of nominalistic conceptions. Once the essential realism of Peirce's logic and metaphysics is understood, it is nearly impossible to misinterpret the intent of his pragmatic maxim. For this reason, we shall defer discussing Peirce's pragmatism until we supply the necessary foundation with an outline of the essential elements of his logic and metaphysics.

This is an extremely difficult task, in that Peirce's work in logic and metaphysics spans five volumes of the *Collected Papers*. Our first step, therefore, will be to define our purpose more modestly. Inasmuch as the general theme of this part of the present work is to trace realist and nominalist tendencies in American pragmatism, we may limit our presentation of Peirce's logic and metaphysics to some of those basic elements that most clearly reflect his realism. This approach allows us to exclude many of the subtle complexities of his logic without sacrificing its essential structure within which his pragmatism will appear intelligible.

Whether one should approach Peirce's logic through his metaphysics or vice versa is a difficult question. Peirce was never able to decide which was logically or philosophically prior to the other (Feibleman, 1970:86), but he argued that "a metaphysics not founded on the science of logic is of all branches of scientific inquiry the most shakey and insecure, and altogether unfit to support so important a subject as logic" (Peirce, 2.36). For this reason, Peirce was extremely critical of previous "metaphysics," calling it all "moonshine," "scrofulous," and "meaningless gibberish . . . or downright absurd" (1.7, 6.6, 5.423). Thus, he had no intention of producing the type of speculative ontology characteristic of the scholastic metaphysicians, and which has been correctly spurned by even the most sympathetic empiricists. Yet, although his basic ontology is entirely consistent with his logic, it is questionable whether he actually derived his metaphysical categories from the doctrine of signs—as he insisted ought to be done. In fact, as we shall see, Peirce's classifications of signs (e.g., icon, index, symbol) are direct analogues of his categories and are largely differentiated on that basis; moreover, it is difficult to imagine how one could possess a clear notion of the fundamental distinctions between the classifications of signs without first grasping the phenomenological categories. Notwithstanding his protestations to the contrary, Peirce was probably no exception.

Our general plan, therefore, is to present the categories through Peirce's phenomenology and then to show their embodiment in the logical classifications. Although this may reverse their ordering as perceived by Peirce, it may, nevertheless, be more coherent for explanatory purposes. Again, the primary purpose is to demonstrate that the metaphysical and logical foundation of Peirce's philosophy is realistic throughout; this approach will provide the basis for a realistic interpretation of Peirce's pragmatism.

Speaking very generally, we may define phenomenology as the description of the essential structure of *immediate* conscious experience, apart from any interpretation of its meaning or significance (Wolff, 1978:501). This requires establishing a certain state of mind in which one simply experiences states of consciousness (rather than objects), and only later attempts to formulate verbally the essence of the experience. Although phenomenologists would agree with this general description, they differ over some of the more specific aspects of the nature of their enterprise. It should be noted that Peirce's understanding of phenomenology is quite different from that of Hegel or Husserl. The latter emphasized the study of "phenomena" in the Kantian sense. Since Peirce rejected the phenomena / noumena distinction, he saw no need for Husserl's phenomenological reduction or "bracketing" of the natural attitude. No single individual can ever hope to establish the reality of anything; such determinations are solely within the province of the extended scientific community. For Peirce, what seems to be real under careful examination must be accepted *as* real until contradicted by future experience; this is all the assurance that an individual, per se, can ever have concerning the validity of a perceptual judgment. Consequently, Peirce's phenomenology was not involved in ontological predicaments. His only concern was to generate a taxonomy of everything that is ever present to consciousness. Accordingly, Peirce (1.284) labeled the unit of analysis of his phenomenology the *phaneron,* and defined it as 'the collective total of all that is in any way or in any sense present to the mind, quite regardless of whether it corresponds to any real thing or not." By inventing this new word, Peirce intended to avoid the connotations associated with words such as "phenomena" or "appearance," words he might have chosen instead of "phaneron." For the same reason, Peirce eventually called his study "phaneroscopy" instead of phenomenology. The purpose of the science of phaneroscopy is to develop exhaustive classifications of phanerons so that any possible phaneron can be identified as a member of one and only one of these classes. As with any science, the object of phaneroscopy is to reach the lowest number of classes that are still all-inclusive (1.287). When this is done, we have the universal categories of human experience. Peirce concluded that there are three and only three such categories. He was not consistent in what he called them. Sometimes they were *quality, existence,* and *law;* at other times they were *monad, dyad, triad.* But most often, they were simply *firstness, secondness,* and *thirdness.* Peirce preferred the latter terms because they are entirely free from misleading connotations. As shorthand definitions, firstness is any pure, unanalyzed *feeling,* secondness is the consciouness of *physical compulsion,* and thirdness is *thought.*

We shall now examine the categories in detail. The reader is reminded that great confusion will result from failing to remember that, in the context of phaneroscopy, the categories of firstness, secondness, and thirdness refer to the modes of phanerons—contents of mind, not modes of being. This is the distinction between phenomenology and ontology: "The difference between the phenomenology and the ontology is that the ontology determines what the formal principles of the categories themselves are, while the phenomenology discovers by an analysis of experience what the categorical characters of the categories are" (Freeman, 1934:29). We shall consider the categories of being in a subsequent section.

The Phenomenological Categories

One of the things Peirce retained from his long and dedicated study of Kant was a categorical approach to metaphysics. The central problem of all categoriology has been the question, "How can the categories be at the same time both universally valid and empirically objective?" (Freeman, 1934:4). This is the problem Kant faced in attempting to give a categoriological answer to his question of how synthetic a priori judgments are possible. Briefly, a synthetic proposition is one whose truth or falsity depends upon some fact about the world (e.g., "The cat is on the bed") rather than upon the logical structure of language (e.g., "All red roses are red"). An a priori judgment is one known independently of experience (e.g., a argument of symbolic logic). Kant agreed with Hume and the other empiricists that there can be no knowledge without experience, but he denied that all knowledge must flow directly from sense experience. He pointed to such synthetic a priori judgments as, "All external objects are extended in time and space," and noted that the truth of such propositions cannot be established simply on the basis of sense data, because we can neither see nor touch time and space. Yet only a fool would deny these judgments; hence, the epistemology of empiricism cannot adequately account for all of our knowledge. Kant was left with the problem of explaining how it is possible that we can have ideas of time, space, substance, causality, and so forth. He concluded that the intellect is active in the process of perception, and that it is through universal ideas or "categories" that the chaotic manifold of sense impressions are reduced to unity (i.e., perceptual objects). Given adequate experience, the mind (or brain?) has a disposition to generate the categories. As infants, peoples' senses are bombarded by the manifold of sensations. But once the categories emerge, the manifold is always ordered and interpreted through the categories so that what is given in consciousness is radically different from whatever is present in the manifold. This consideration led Kant to his distinction between phenomena (the constituted object) and noumena (the thing in itself).

In a brief autobiographical sketch, Peirce (1.4) revealed that in his youth he had studied Kant's *Critique of Pure Reason* "for more than three years, until I almost knew the whole book by heart, and had critically examined every section of it." It is thus not surprising that he also wrote, "My own list [of categories] grew out of the study of the table of Kant" (1.300). However, it would be a grievous mistake to label Peirce a neo-Kantian, for Peirce was quite critical of the transcendentalism contained in Kant's idea of the "noumenal" world (5.452). Kant's phenomena / noumena distinction is a nominalistic conception in that it undermines the objective reality of universals by postulating the ultimate, unknowable reality which is transmuted by being interpreted through the categories. Peirce's solution to this nominalist flaw in Kant's categoriology was to introduce a liberal dose of Scotistic realism into the categories. Peirce (5.525) noted that, once this is done, Kant appears as "nothing but a somewhat confused pragmatist." He further adds:

> The *Ding an sich* [thing in itself] can neither be indicated nor found. Consequently, no proposition can refer to it, and no thing true or false can be predicted of it. Therefore, all reference to it must be thrown out as meaningless surplusage. But when that is done, we see clearly that Kant regards Space, Time and his categories just as everybody else does, and never doubts or has doubted their objectivity.

Peirce's metaphysics preserves Kant's phenomenalism, but elevates phenomena to the level of reality and denies the existence of any unknowable substratum. With this general characterization, let us now consider Peirce's categories in detail.

Peirce identified *possibility, actuality,* and *destiny* as the three modes of being (i.e., the metaphysical categories). As Freeman (1934:5) notes, the phenomenological categories (firstness, secondness, and thirdness) can be viewed as an illustration of the empirical validity and applicability of the metaphysical categories. Peirce was anxious to empirically test the metaphysical categories through phenomenology (1.374). Clearly, then, the metaphysical categories are logically prior to the phenomenological categories. Yet, for explanatory purposes, it is better that we begin with an examination of the phenomenological categories, because they are more closely related to ordinary experience.

Firstness

Firstness is by far the most difficult category to explain. It is entirely singular and, therefore, cannot be *described*; it can only be *felt* in a noncognitive way. It is the leading concept of Kant's manifold of sense

(Peirce, 1.302). It is any quality of feeling experienced in total isolation. It is the pure feeling of some color, emotion, smell, taste, sound, poetry, music, or anything. Language is incapable of expressing any firstness, because any assertion immediately introduces a second element, and the firstness consequently evaporates under analysis: "The idea of the absolutely first must be entirely separated from all conception or reference to anything else.... Stop to think of it, and it has flown!" (1.357). The reason we have difficulty in apprehending the idea of firstness is that we never experience qualities apart from perceiving them as being instantiated in some existent object. One of the best ways to grasp the idea is to imagine someone with such an affliction that the only sensation he / she is ever capable of feeling is the drone of a single tone that never changes in any respect. That person would truly feel the firstness of that tone because the feeling would never be related to anything else.

This mental experiment illustrates an important characteristic of firstness: the quality of feeling cannot be decomposed into parts. Weiss (1965:133) has challenged this alleged characteristic by pointing out that any quality can exhibit endless nuances, variations, and intensities. He suggests, for example, "A patch of color varies in light and shadow throughout; it has swellings and depressions; here it rushes forward and there it retreats." Two replies are in order. Although all color experiences display these characteristics, Pierce (1.304) was emphatic that a quality of feeling is only a potential object of experience; thus, its characteristic as a firstness is in no way dependent upon its being actually present in some material object. The person in our experiment does not have the capacity of ascribing the sound to a source, but this does not preclude him from hearing the tone. Furthermore, even if that exact tone has never happened to occur in the world, it is still possible that it might occur in the future—and its being a firstness consists in this potentiality. In Peirce's words, "That mere *quality,* or suchness, is not in itself an occurrence, as seeing a red object is; it is a mere may-be. Its only being consists in the fact that there *might* be such a peculiar, positive suchness in a phaneron" (1.304). Even so, Peirce has another response to Weiss's attack: Any color experience, for example, can be analyzed in terms of hue, luminosity, and chroma. But, as Peirce (1.308) observed, these elements are not separate in the feeling, and are, therefore, not in the feeling at all; they only appear upon subsequent experimentation. The quality itself, as it is felt, has no component parts.

Secondness

Secondness is, in its essence, a simple idea. It is the dyadic relation of action to reaction, or of effort to resistance. Whereas firstness is a simple monistic feeling, secondness is essentially a dualistic type of consciousness. With secondness there exists the sensation of brute force, but force can only be manifest where there is some resistance to that force: "You get this kind of consciousness in some approach to purity when you put your shoulder against a door and try to force it open" (Peirce, 1.324).

Let us examine some of the important features of secondness. Its most distinguishing characteristic is that it is *brute*. There is no reason in it; or, more accurately, as it is present to consciousness, it offers us no reason for its being there. We are forced to admit the existence of an external world because we can run against it and be knocked down (Peirce, 1.431). Such is the character of secondness. Firstness "mildly hopes it won't be intruding" (1.434), but secondness boldly crowds its way into the world and insists on being recognized despite anything else. Connected with the bruteness of secondness, we have the idea of its being *accidental* (2.85). There is no reason why violet should be at one end of the spectrum rather than the other, or that the final score of a basketball game was "98 to 91" instead of some some other score. All individual facts are accidental taken in isolation; this includes permanent facts, in that they are contingent at each instant and from one moment to the next (if Peirce's tychism is taken seriously).

Another salient aspect of secondness is its relationship to firstness. A first—being mere possibility—is independent of any second, but a second must be absolutely determinate with respect to every quality: "Of it every quality whatever is either true or false" (Peirce, 1.436). Every material object is nothing apart from the qualities (firstness) it instantiates. This is one of the leading principles of Peirce's whole system because it foreshadows his ideas of truth, reality, and pragmatism:

> There can hardly be a doubt that the existence of a fact does consist
> in the existence of all its consequences. That is to say, if all the conse-
> quences of a supposed fact are real facts, that makes the supposed fact
> to be a real one. If, for example, something supposed to be a hard body
> acts in every respect like such a body, that constitutes the reality of
> that hard body; and if two seeming particles act in every respect as if
> they were attracting particles, that makes them really so. [1.432]

As with all elements of his system, Peirce analyzed secondness in minute detail and developed numerous divisions and subdivisions of the category (1.470). For our purposes, further discussion would be unnecessary and tiring. However, we should make explicit the two major divisions that are implicit in the foregoing account: (1) Feibleman (1970:160) observes that secondness can be regarded as the individual thing or as the entire field of individual things; (2) Peirce referred to the individual thing as *fact,* and the field of all individual things as *existence.*

The human mind craves order and rationality. We are not satisfied to wait for secondness to appear and then deal with it on its own terms. Secondness is the "teaching experience" (Peirce, 1. 358), but it can be a cruel teacher if the pupil is not ready for the lesson. Consequently, we seek to anticipate the appearance of secondness by discovering laws that govern facts. Such specification of a relationship between a firstness and a secondness is itself categorically different from firstness or secondness. This brings us to Peirce's final category.

Thirdness

The principal characteristic shared by firstness and secondness is that the feeling of a firstness or the shock of secondness are both direct experiences; therefore, they do not involve any cognitive activity. Thus, inference, perceptual judgments, and thoughts of all description must belong to a third category of phanerons, which Peirce called *thirdness.* Whether a complex inference or a simple perceptual judgment, all thought is characterized by *mediation.* In the case of a logical deduction, thirdness is that by which the premises are brought into relation to produce the conclusion. In perception, thought mediates between firstness and secondness to produce the conclusion such as, "This is red." Peirce (1.536) summarized the relations of his categories as follows:

> The first is a positive qualitative possibility, in itself nothing more. The second is an existent thing without any mode of being less than existence, but determined by that first. A *third* has a mode of being which consists in the Secondness that it determines, the mode of being a law, or concept. Do not confound this with the ideal being of a quality in itself. . . . A quality is how something may or might have been. A law is how an endless future must continue to be.

Some other ideas which connote thirdness are representation, combination, continuity, habit, and process. It is thirdness that gives meaning to our experiences of the qualities of existents. As a phenomenological category, thirdness is presented to the mind as a *sign.* Consequently, we shall defer further description of thirdness until we are ready to consider logic (the doctrine of signs) in a more systematic fashion.

One can ask why there is no fourth category. Peirce's answer is that

mathematics shows us that fours, fives, and all higher numbers are reducible to complexes of threes (1.363). A single point or two points are
not sufficient to determine any regularity, but three points can signify a
pattern, or thirdness, by being placed an equal distance from each other
as vortices of an equilateral triangle. By contrast, any number of dyads
cannot together form a triad. For example, placing any number of line
segments end to end will only determine two termini; hence, a genuine
triad cannot be reduced to two or more dyads. Similarly, dyads cannot be
reduced to monads. However, "analysis will show that every relation
which is *tetradic, pentadic,* or of any greater number of correlates is
nothing but a compound of triadic relations" (1.347). Peirce illustrates
this principle using graphs to show that figures with only two termini
cannot be combined to yield one with three, whereas the "three-tailed"
graphs can be joined to produce any number of termini (1.347).

Although Peirce's mathematical representations are interesting, they
do not conclusively support his categoriology because he has not proved
that what is true in mathematics must also be true of phaneroscopy. It is
not clear that such a proof is possible. Contrary to Peirce's classification
of sciences (1.245), it does not seem true that phaneroscopy is dependent
upon, or can be validated by, mathematics. The validity of the categories
can be ascertained only by the act of doing phaneroscopy. Whatever
appears to be a phaneron (a content of the mind), *ipso facto,* is one.
There can be no mistake in that regard. Consequently, we have only to
search thoroughly the contents of our minds to determine whether anything ever appears in consciousness that cannot be classified in one—and
only one—of the three categories. If there is any such phaneron, another
category must be admitted, but if there is not, this result would tend to
affirm the validity and universality of firstness, secondness, and thirdness.
Peirce was aware that his categories could be substantiated only by the
consensus of all those who seriously inquire into the matter: "The reader,
upon his side, must repeat the author's observations for himself, and
decide from his own observations whether the author's account of the
appearances is correct or not" (1.287).

We turn now to the metaphysical categories already foreshadowed in
this account of phaneroscopy.

The Metaphysical
Categories

The distinction between the metaphysical categories and the phenomenological categories was succinctly stated by James K. Feibleman

(1970:185): "The phenomenological categories are, as their name implies, modes of phanerons; the metaphysical categories are modes of being." Classical metaphysics is concerned with determining the irreducible forms of being, but phenomenology is concerned only with classifying the contents of consciousness as they actually appear. For example, a possibility, as such, is not a phaneron, but it has a distinct metaphysical status. The idea of "being," though central to metaphysics, has been conceived in countless ways throughout the history of philosophy. In simplistic metaphysical systems, there is only one mode of being; usually either mind, matter, or some kind of neutral "stuff." In Peirce's system there are, of course, three modes being; possibility, actuality, and destiny. If, in order to understand Peirce's meaning of "being," we begin by defining "nothingness" or "nonbeing," then positive "being" is the negation of that category. A pure "nothing" is the lowest possible ontological status. It not only does not exist, it could not even be conceived. Examples are "matter without qualities" and a "square circular shape." Of course, the number "two" cannot exist, but the difference between it and a "nothing" is that a nothing is not *thinkable* as anything that can be related to existence, as can the number "two." Certainly, we can put the words "square" and "circle" together, but this will not help us to imagine a square circle or a square circular shape. Before considering the metaphysical categories in detail, let us examine their connection with the phenomenological categories.

A cursory inspection reveals that firstness (or quality) is a species of possibility, and secondness makes firstness actual in existents (Feibleman, 1970:185; Peirce, 1.327–28). Thirdness (or law) is an integral part of what the infinite future will continue to be, but the principle of absolute chance is no less a part of that future ("destiny"). Thus, thirdness is only one component of the metaphysical category of destiny, and a corresponding relation holds for other pairs of phenomenological and metaphysical categories.

The nominalists will immediately charge that it is groundless to maintain that there is any correspondence between phenomena and being. They will point out that even a novice in philosophy knows that there is an unfathomable epistemological gap between these mere phenomena and external Being. Peirce, as we have seen, was very intolerant of this view. He argued that ordinary experience is sufficient to convince anyone not blinded by philosophical prejudice that we know many things about the external world, and this would be highly improbable unless the categories of our conscious experience closely correspond to the structure of external reality. Peirce (1.26) states this position as follows:

Five minutes of our waking life will hardly pass without our making
some kind of prediction; and in the majority of cases these predictions
are fulfilled in the event. . . . If the prediction has a tendency to conform to a general rule. . . . This mode of being which *consists,* mind my
word if you please, the mode of being which *consists* in the fact that
future facts of Secondness will take on a determinate general character, I call a Thirdness.

On the whole, the cognitive and perceptual powers of human beings
are extraordinarily well suited for achieving general knowledge about
the world. Those who deny this are, by consequence, denying their own
capacity to deal rationally with the external world (assuming they are
prepared to acknowledge its existence). Expressing a similar view, but
with considerable verbal truculence, Peirce (1.316) declared:

Every scientific explanation of a natural phenomena is a hypothesis
that there is something in nature to which the human reason is analogous; and that it really is so all the successes of science in its applications to human convenience are witnesses. . . . In the light of the successes of science to my mind there is a degree of baseness in denying
our birthright as children of God and in shame-facedly slinking away
from anthropomorphic conceptions of the universe.

The first grade of being is possibility. Qualities of feeling are possibilities because, even when they are not embodied in matter, there
remains the potential that they may be (Peirce, 1.422). This is a two-sided
possibility. The second possibility lies in the fact that an embodied quality retains the possibility of exhibiting its quality even when it is not
actually doing so. It was Berkeley's mistake to deny this possibility. For
example, if only one hard object existed, it could not display its
quality—nothing could test its hardness by resisting it; nevertheless, it
would still be hard because it retains its capacity to resist other hard
objects, should any appear.

Actuality is the realization of positive possibility. As Feibleman
(1970:185) states, "Actuality differs from secondness in that secondness
imparts actuality to the possibility of firstness (1.327–28) by introducing
a field of reaction and opposition." Although actuality is completely
determinate with respect to all qualities, it is characterized by generality:
the qualities it embodies are general in nature in that any quality is
capable of limitless actualization.

This brings us to Peirce's third, and highest, mode of being—destiny.
Recall that in chapter 1 we described limited generals or universals, and
concluded that the validity of scientific induction depends upon the reality of at least some general laws and propositions. The principle of

continuity (synechism) asserts that general relationships will continue to hold into the indefinite future. However, synechism is balanced by the principle of absolute chance (tychism), which asserts tht no law is necessarily immutable. Both principles are required if we are to have a conception of a universe that is neither wholly determinate nor wholly spontaneous and chaotic. Although the principles of synechism (continuity) and tychism (absolute chance) do not exist, their mode of being consists in the reality that they govern all that exists or will exist. For Peirce, synechism is the highest principle of philosophy; it is certainly far more central than pragmatism. Synechism is derived from the reality of thirdness. Morever, we must be careful in describing this reality if we are to avoid nominalism. Certainly, the laws of gravity never caused anything to fall. To assert this is to contend that thirdness (law) dynamically interacts with a material body, forcing it to earth. This is absurd. It is the earth's gravitational field that causes the object to fall. Insofar as it is a matter of force and compulsion, it is strictly an affair of secondness. But if falling bodies exhibit *regularities* in their manner and rate of descent, then these phenomena involve more than the brute pushing and shoving associated with secondness. All existent objects embody such regularities through their qualities. Tychism reminds us that the future is contingent; anything that is logically possible can happen. But we need not fear that all of the most improbable things will happen tomorrow. Thus, it is the interplay of these two leading ideas which creates destiny.

In summary, the modes of being can also be thought as modes of reality (i.e., as an answer to the question, "What sorts of entities can be real?"). Obviously, a positive possibility is real because it would remain a possibility even if everyone thought it impossible. Second, actuality is real insofar as its capacity to act is unaffected by what anyone thinks. Finally, destiny is real because, though the whole human race may embrace nominalism, events in the future will continue to conform to principles of law and probability. Hence, Peirce's metaphysical categories are not only consistent with his realism, they are a direct outgrowth of his realistic approach to every area of philosophy. Aided by this outline of Peirce's categories, we are now prepared to consider his logic, the theory of signs. As we proceed, it will become evident that the classifications of signs are built upon the categories and that the elements of Peirce's system are tightly interlocked. Finally, as shown on pages 48–58, once the general structure of Peirce's logic is understood, it becomes clear that the famous maxim is merely one brick in a large edifice.

Logic

In one of the few passages in which Peirce directly considers the relation of logic to the categories, he writes:

Now it may be that *logic* ought to be the science of Thirdness in general. But as I have studied it, it is simply the science of what must be and ought to be true representation, so far as representation can be known without any gathering of special facts beyond our ordinary daily life. It is, in short, the philosophy of representation. [1.539]

In this section, we consider the core of Peirce's doctrine of signs, or "the philosophy of representation." Because Peirce's logic papers are voluminous, multifaceted, and, in their totality, extremely complicated, it is necessary to severely limit our focus. Thus, we confine the analysis to three specific aims. First, we explain the relationships among the most general elements of any representation—namely, the sign, object, and interpretant. Second, we consider some of the principal classifications of signs, with particular emphasis on the icon, index, and symbol. Finally, we analyze Peirce's logic vis-à-vis his realism. Once the realistic implications of the theory of signs are understood, the relation of the pragmatic maxim to logic in general will become clear. This discussion will then provide a logical transition to the exploration of pragmatism.

The Sign, Object, and Interpretant

A *sign* is "something which stands to somebody for something in some respect or capacity" (Peirce, 2.288). The *object* of the sign is whatever it refers to. Anything can be represented by (i.e., be the object of) an endless number of different signs; thus, no sign stands for its object in every possible respect. Each sign stands for its object in some particular respect, which Peirce called *ground*. For example, the abstract quality "blackness" is the ground for an assertion that something is black (1.551). A sign, by definition, must succeed in causing someone to apprehend its object. It does this by engendering in that person's mind an equivalent sign, or sometimes a more developed sign, called its *interpretant*, which has the same object as the sign for which it is the interpretant. For example, one might say to a cook, "Your pie is burning." This statement is a sign, and its object is the condition of the pie. This sign may cause the cook to think, "Remove the pie," and this thought is the interpretant of the sign; accordingly, its object is also the pie. This thought may stimulate some further thought, such as "pick up the pot holder," which would be the interpretant of the interpretant (but which at this point is itself a sign). Thus, any interpretant can become a sign for a subsequent inter-pretant, and so on *ad infinitum*. In practice, the sign / interpretant series is terminated when its attendant line of conduct is completed (e.g., the pie is removed from the oven). Thomas A. Goudge (1950:139) adds, "The most generalized form of this infinite series is identical with the ongoing process of scientific thought." Indeed, it is quite possible that these three fundmental elements of signification occurred to Peirce while he was reflecting upon the process of scientific inquiry.

From this most general triad, Peirce's logic continues to break down into further sets and subsets of threes, or "trichotomies," as he called them. The sign-object-interpretant relation can be further analyzed into the sign-object, sign-interpretant, and object-interpretant relations, and each of these divisions, as we shall see, has its own triad. When con-templated in conjunction with the categories, these multitudes of triadic logical classifications are sufficient to cause nearly any reader of Peirce to suspect that he had some strange obsession with the number three. Peirce anticipated this suspicion and wrote a short response titled "Triadomany" (1.568–72), in which he pleads that it is false that he "attaches a superstitious or fanciful importance to the number three, and forces divisions to a Procrustean bed of trichotomy." With this disclaimer in mind, let us consider the basic triads of Peirce's logic so that readers may judge the case for themselves.

Trichotomies

The three elements of meaning—sign, object, interpretant—imply three broad divisions of logic. Peirce employed a variety of interchangeable names for each of these divisions, but we shall use the names *speculative grammar, critical logic,* and *speculative rhetoric* (2.93). Although we describe each of these divisions below, our primary interest is in specula-tive grammar. Critical logic and speculative rhetoric are defined in order to help us locate speculative grammar within Peirce's general logic. Fur-thermore, not all aspects of speculative grammar are treated in equal detail. Rather, we concentrate upon those elements that form the back-ground for our subsequent exposition of pragmatism; the more tangential divisions of signs will be described only briefly in order to fill out the general outlines of Peirce's theory of signs.

Speculative grammar is concerned with the general conditions necessary for signs to have their significant character, the conditions for the possibility of meaning. The previous section is an example of speculative

grammar. Critical logic encompasses all that is normally associated with
the term "logic." It is concerned with the conditions necessary for the
reference of signs to their objects. In less Peircean language, it is the
inquiry into the *truth* conditions of arguments. That Peirce thought of
critical logic in these terms is clear evidence that he defined truth as the
correspondence of a propositional sign and its object. Using this description, critical logic includes the study of all principles of valid deductive,
inductive, and hypothetical reasoning. Because critical logic leads directly
to the complexities of symbolic and mathematical logic, it lies beyond the
scope of our immediate interests. The third branch of logic, speculative
rhetoric, deals with the conditions of the reference of signs to their interpretants (2.93), and is sometimes called "methodeutic." It is not entirely
clear exactly what Peirce intended to include in this area of logic, and the
topic is not pursued in detail in any of the volumes of the *Collected
Papers*. He broadly defined it as the study of the methods that ought to be
pursued in the investigation, exposition, and application of truth (1.191).

Just as the triadic character of signs makes necessary the three general
branches of logic, it also leads to three divisions of signs. We can classify:
(1) the sign itself by its own mode of being irrespective of its object and
interpretant, (2) the sign in relation to its object according to its mode of
signifying its object, and (3) the sign in relation to its interpretant according to the mode of being the interpretant construes the sign as representing. The phenomenological categories assure that there are three and
only three possible classifications of signs within each of these divisions.
From the perspective of the first division, a sign is either a *qualisign,
sinsign,* or *legisign* (2.243–46).

A *qualisign* is a quality which is a sign: "It cannot actually act as a sign
until it is embodied; but the embodiment has nothing to do with its
character as a sign" (2.244). For example, the red color of a traffic light is
a qualisign.

A *sinsign* is an actual existent thing or event which is a sign. It can only
be a sign through its qualities, but none of its qualities are taken as signs
considered independently. A barricade is a sinsign. Of course, it must be
made of some material, have some color, dimensions, and so on, but none
of these qualities in their particularity are individually required to constitute the sign. In other words, a barricade must have qualities, but it is not
necessary that it be steel instead of wood or red instead of yellow. Thus, for
any sinsign, the existent thing itself acts as the sign, and no significance is
attached to its particular qualities; otherwise, we would have a qualisign.

A *legisign* is a law that is a sign (2.246). Words are the most common
legisigns. Words can be signs only because there is a conventional law

that whenever a sinsign—called its *replica*—is present, it compels the interpreter to think of the object of the legisign. The sinsign, however, would not have that capacity if it were not conventionally associated with the legisign. For example, the legisign "tree" can be spoken or written. The sound and the writing are replicas of the same legisign and have no meaning apart from convention.

If we consider the sign in relation to its interpretant, a second trichotomy of signs appears; the *rheme, dicisign,* and *argument* (2.250). The rheme is the most primitive sign-interpretant relation. The rheme is a sign interpreted as a qualitative possibility (i.e., firstness). Thus, it is not interpreted as providing any information about anything. A dicisign, in contrast, is a sign interpreted as affording some information. But "the readiest characteristic test showing whether a sign is a decisign or not is that a dicisign is either true or false, but does not directly furnish reasons for its being so" (2.310). The statement, "Lincoln died in 1865," is thus a dicisign. Finally, the argument is "a sign which, for its interpretant, is a sign of law" (2.252). All arguments contain three elements: premise, the conclusion, and some logical principle which is "the law that the passage from all such premises to such conclusions tends to the truth" (2.263). The argument is a "triple or rationally persuasive" sign (2.309). The three classes of arguments are deduction, induction, and abduction. Peirce expended much effort analyzing the forms of arguments, but here it must suffice to merely note the classifications.

The Icon, Index, and
Symbol

The relation of the sign to its object is the third trichotomy. Within this trichotomy, a sign is either an icon, index, or symbol (2.247). Peirce considered this the most fundamental division of signs (2.275), and it is the most important for the interpretation of the pragmatic maxim. For these reasons, this division is presented in greater detail than the others.[1]

Whether the signs are classified by their intrinsic character (i.e., qualisign, sinsign, legisign) or by their interpretation (i.e., rheme, dicisign, argument), it is clear that each element of the trichotomy corresponds to one of the phenomenological categories. And the fact that the categories provide an exhaustive base for broad divisions of signs affords support for their universality. This relation between classifications of signs and the phenomenological categories is preserved if we classify signs by a third trichotomy—namely, the relation of the sign to its object. The *icon* is related to its object by resembling it in at least one respect which constitutes its ground. The similarity between the icon and its object is the basis for the sign's capacity of reference to its object.

The icon is thus always related to its object by a firstness, because always "a quality that it has *qua* thing renders it fit to be a representamen" (2.276). Loosely speaking, its mode of being can be a qualisign, sinsign, or legisign. A portrait is an icon related to its object by an image, or qualisign, created in the mind of the interpreter which bears qualities similar to those of the person portrayed. A diagram is an icon which is a sinsign, in that it represents dyadic relations "of parts of one thing by analogous relations in their own parts" (2.227). Finally, a metaphor is an icon which is a legisign that signifies its object by exhibiting a parallelism between some common aspect of itself and its object. Because the metaphor is a legisign created by language, there is an element of convention involved, but it is by virtue of the iconic relation, not convention, that it is able to convey its object to the interpreter. This is why the metaphor must be classified as an icon rather than as a symbol.

As John J. Fitzgerald (1966:50) has noted, much confusion results if one fails to recognize the distinction between a potential sign and an actual sign. An actual sign has an object and interpretant; that is, a potential sign becomes an actual sign when it does in fact produce some interpretant. When we speak of the icon, index, and symbol as a division of signs, we are referring to potential signs and distinguishing them according to the categorical base (i.e., firstness, secondness, or thirdness) through which they have their capacity to refer to their objects. In the case of the icon, firstness is the categorical base of the sign because it is the *quality* of similarity which constitutes the basis of the sign's reference to its object. However, as a mere *potential* sign, an icon need not have an actual object. For example, the blueprint for some new type of car is an icon even though that car has not been produced or may have been destroyed. It is only the categorical nature of its *capacity* to refer to any potential object that makes the blueprint an icon. Thus, a thing need not have an object or an interpretant to be an icon; it need only be fit to be a sign, and that fitness is prior to its actual use as a sign.

It follows that an icon in itself does not tell us anything about what exists in the world. The painting of a landscape conveys no factual information because it may well have no actual object. Similarly, a diagrammatic floor plan for a building affords no information if it is merely a designer's dream. Consequently, an actual iconic sign requires that the relevant quality which constitutes the basis for some similarity actually be embodied in some existent things. Recalling our discussion of the phenomenological categories, a firstness is only a potentiality until it is embodied in some secondness; and then it is actual.

When we say that two things resemble each other, we mean that their qualities are similar; hence, the icon exists only in consciousness as an appearance of similarity. However, when speaking in less technical terms, we call the thing itself an icon, but it is the quality of the thing and not the thing *qua* secondness which acts as a sign. Peirce explains: "[The icon] is of the nature of an appearance, and as such, strictly speaking, exists only in consciousness, although for convenience in ordinary parlance . . . we extend the term icon to the outward objects which excite in consciousness the image itself"(4.447).

Unlike the icon, the *index* leaves no question about the existence of its object. In fact, the distinguishing feature of a genuine index is that it is causally connected with its object. A few examples will illustrate: A bullet hole (the index) signifies the passage of a bullet (its object). A weathervane (the index) signifies the direction of the wind (its object). A knock on the door (the index) signifies the presence of someone outside (its object). From these examples, it is evident that it is the dynamic existential relation of secondness (brute action and reaction) between the index and its object that compels the interpreter to apprehend the object of the index.

In addition to the genuine index just described, there are various types of "degenerate" indices. Peirce defined an index generally: "Anything which focuses attention is an index" (2.285). The genuine index focuses attention on its object, a singular existential fact, by being causally related to it. As a singular event, it is a pure relation of secondness. To the extent that an index requires some convention in order to denote its object, it is degenerate. For example, a pointing finger is a degenerate index; it certainly focuses attention on some existential situation, but a conventional element is involved in its interpretation.

Finally, some linguistic expressions act as indices although, strictly speaking, they are not indices: like all words, they have a general meaning and thus unlimited potential for applicability whereas a genuine index is a particular one-time occurrence (4.56). The grammatical subject of a proposition has an indexical quality. So do proper names and pronouns such as "this."/A third class of indexical symbols includes exclamations such as "Help!" or "Look out!" Peirce called all these indexical expressions "subindexes" or "hyposemes" to distinguish them from genuine indices (2.284).

This leads us to the third type of sign-object relation—the *symbol*. As we have seen, the icon is related to its object by firstness, and the index is related to its object by secondness. To complete the trichotomy the symbol is related to its object by thirdness: "A *symbol* is a sign which refers to the object that it denotes by virtue of a law, usually an association of general ideas, which operates to cause the symbol to be interpreted as referring to that object" (2.249). In itself, the symbol is a legisign and therefore cannot operate without a replica. To cite one of Peirce's examples, one can write the word "star" on paper, but that will not make him the creator of the word and, if it is erased, the word is not destroyed. The word itself lives on in the minds of those who use it.

The fact that the capacity of a symbol to designate its object depends upon the conventions of a language community, suggests that symbols are the class of genuine signs (i.e., all three elements of a sign are intrinsic to their foundation). In this sense, all icons and indices are degenerate signs. Inasmuch as firstness is the basis for the sign potential of icons, they can be described without reference to any object or interpretant. Similarly, because secondness constitutes the foundation of indices, their functioning as a sign requires an object, but can be described without reference to any interpretant. For example, "A piece of mould with a bullet-hole in it is a sign of a shot; for without the shot there would have been no hole; but there is a hole there, whether anybody has the sense to attribute it to a shot or not." By contrast, a symbol would lose its capacity to act as a sign if there were no interpretant (2.304). The symbol is fit to be a sign only because the language community has agreed upon the object to be represented whenever a replica of the symbol is invoked. Unlike the icon and index, the symbol is irreducibly triadic; the legisign, object, and interpretant are all essential to its character of being a sign.

The relation of symbols to thirdness is, as we shall see, fundamental to pragmatism. At this point, it will be useful to elaborate on that relation. We must first distinguish the genuine symbol from two kinds of degenerate symbols. Symbols are degenerate if their objects are some firstness or secondness instead of thirdness. The first of these, the "abstract symbol," refers only to some qualitative character apart from any instantiation, hence the name "abstract." For example, we are using "blue" as an abstract symbol if we are speaking of blue *qua* blue without reference to any particular blue thing. The second type of degenerate symbol, the "singular symbol," has as its object a singular individual and "signifies only such characters as that individual may realize" (2.293). Any proper name is an example of a singular symbol. A "genuine symbol" is a symbol which has a *general* meaning. Its generality consists in the fact that "something surely will be experienced if certain conditions are satisfied. Namely, it will influence the thought and conduct of its interpreter" (4.447). The genuine symbol acts as a sign by determining an interpreter to think of its object. It does this in two ways: it *denotes* some existent thing, and it *signifies* some character (2.293).

Peirce uses the symbol, "balloon," as an example. When the word is used in a sentence, it denotes an existent individual thing, but, unlike an index, it signifies the characteristics of the thing. It would be nonsense to maintain that someone knows the meaning of "balloon" but does not know any of the qualities of balloons. This is why Peirce characterized the symbol as a law or regularity of the indefinite future (2.293). Peirce defined "regularity" as "the future conditional occurence of facts not themselves that regularity" (4.464). In other words, we know that whenever we invoke the symbol "balloon," it will determine a mental icon of a balloon in the mind of the interpreter. This mental icon is the logical interpretant of the sign. The interpreter's idea of a balloon, which is the interpretant of "balloon," includes all of the counterfactual conditional proposition associated with the symbol. A counterfactual conditional proposition asserts that if a certain circumstance which is not, in fact, now actual (thus counterfactual) were to occur, then a certain consequence would follow (conditional). The following are examples of such propositions about balloons:

1. "If I blow into it, it will inflate."
2. "If I then slide a dry finger across its surface, it will squeak."
3. "If I insert a needle into it, it will burst."

An infinite number of conditional propositions are true of balloons, and one's knowledge of what a balloon really *is* can be equated with one's knowledge of the counterfactual conditionals which are true of it. This is the essence of the pragmatic maxim. It was inevitable that in explaining the operations of a symbol we would approach the pragmatic maxim, inasmuch as the maxim is a method for determining the meanings of words. Further discussion of the interpretation of symbols is thus deferred to the following section.

In summary, the thirdness of the symbol flows from two sources. There is a regularity in the sign's (conventionally linked) capacity to determine its interpretant. That is, the symbol "balloon" determines with great regularity that the interpreter will think of a balloon instead of a cat or professor. In addition to this convention-based regularity, there is the regularity of the conditional propositions which constitute the meaning of the symbol. If, for example, the three counterfactual conditional propositions we listed—and others like them which are true of balloons—did not hold with substantial regularity, there would be no general character signified by the expression "balloon." Hence, "balloon" could not be a symbol under those circumstances, because calling something a balloon would tell us nothing about it. The expression would be meaningless.

Realism and the
Theory of Signs

The essence of realism is so near the surface of Peirce's theory of signs that little effort is required to call attention to it. One could not accept Peirce's analysis of the functioning of symbols without also admitting the reality of thirdness. To a nominalist, all symbols act as indices; they simply *name* their objects and thereby focus the interpreter's attention on them. On the other hand, once it is held that symbols also *characterize* their objects, there must be some law or regularity that forms the basis for that characterization. As we have seen, there is a twofold regularity involved in signification: (1) the regularity of the sign determining a particular interpretant by convention, and (2) the regularity of the dispositional predicates which are true of the object of the symbol. Both of these regularities are *real generals:* they are *general* because they apply to an infinity of possible cases and circumstances in which the symbol could function, and they will hold in the future indefinitely; they are *real* because they will continue to govern existents regardless of what individuals may think about them. You or I may opine that "balloon" is not a real English word, but it will nonetheless continue to function as a symbol for millions of English-speaking people. Furthermore, one of us might decide to believe that balloons do not really possess those qualities previously described, but those qualities would still appear to any scientific mind.

Although we have thus far considered the icon, index, and symbol as separate elements, the actual sign process is an admixture of them all. Symbols are required to communicate information about some object or event. Indices or indexical symbols such as "this" or "his" are used to denote the particular existent to which the information is meant to apply. Finally, icons provide the vehicle by which the object of the symbol is represented in the mind of the interpreter.

Viewed in relation to the categories, the icon, index, and symbol are used to represent firstness, secondness, and thirdness, respectively. Realism requires such a developed theory of signs in order to explicate the mechanism by which minds are able to intersubjectively identify and characterize an external reality.

Pragmatism

Much of Peirce's work in logic was still unpublished at the time of his death and, with the exception of a few of his students (e.g., Josiah Royce), his logic was unknown to the philosophical community. The one momentous exception was the pragmatic maxim.

To explain the notoriety that pragmatism gained, it is necessary to recall some details of Peirce's biography. His cantankerous personality and his reputation as a reprobate, following the divorce of his first wife, created an insurmountable barrier to a professional academic career. In 1869, James predicted, "The poor cuss sees no chance of getting a professorship anywhere, and is likely to go into the Observatory for good" (Feibleman, 1970:16). Peirce became cynical about the Puritanical intellectual climate at Cambridge (1.650), and James's prediction was fulfilled when Peirce spent much of the remainder of his life working in virtual seclusion. During the last years of his life, Peirce suffered illness and poverty, and survived on the charity of James and other friends. Thus Peirce was never in a position to publicize his ideas extensively through students and books. The only reason that pragmatism became known was that James, who *was* in such a position (as a Harvard philosopher), adopted the name "pragmatism" for his own philosophy and credited Peirce as its founder.

We will analyze James's version of pragmatism in chapter 3, but we must note here his involvement because it was in response to the "pragmatism" of James and others that Peirce directed much of his writing and lecturing on pragmatism near the end of his life. It is well known to students of American pragmatism that by the time Peirce published his essay, "What Pragmatism Is," in 1905, he wished to disassociate himself from the "pragmatism" of that time because, in Peirce's words, the original meaning of the word had become "abused in the merciless way that words have to expect when they fall into literary clutches" (5.414). It was at this point that Peirce introduced the word "pragmaticism" to mean what "pragmatism" originally meant, and he hoped that this new word would be "ugly enough to be safe from kidnappers."

This conflict with later pragmatists prompted Peirce to emphasize that the reality of thirdness is entailed by the pragmatic maxim and, therefore, the maxim could not be the cornerstone of any nominalistic philosophy. The plan of this section, therefore, is to identify in substance and emphasis the transition that occurred between Peirce's early (1878) and later (post-1900) formulations of pragmatism. His later formulation appeals to his doctrine of the normative sciences to justify the pragmatic maxim.

Because that defense clearly illustrates Peirce's realization that the value
of pragmatism lies in its connection with synechism, or continuity
(5.415), it shows that the later formulation of pragmatism is far removed
from the positivism of the earlier version. This point is crucial because it
demonstrates that the essential thrust of Peirce's pragmatism is absolutely
foreign to that of James and Dewey.

The Early Pragmatism
(1878)

Peirce (5.11) declared that any completely new philosophical doctrine
would certainly prove to be completely false, but he hastened to add that
pragmatism can be traced to Socrates, Aristotle, Spinoza, and other principal characters in the history of philosophy. Although the pragmatic
maxim was used on occasion by each of these other philosophers, Peirce
was the first to name it and to advance it as a formal logical principle.

Peirce first developed the maxim during the meetings of the now-
famous "Metaphysical Club," which consisted of a number of young
Cambridge philosophers including Peirce, James, Chauncy Wright, and
Oliver W. Holmes, Jr.[2] Peirce recalled that he "drew up a little paper"
(5.13), as a souvenir of the proceedings of the club, which expressed the
fundamentals of pragmatism—the principle he had consistently defended
at the club meetings. The paper was expanded, and appeared in the
Popular Science Monthly in 1877 and 1878 as two essays, "The Fixation
of Belief" (5.358–87) and "How to Make Our Ideas Clear" (5.388–410).
Together these essays express what we have called the early pragmatism.

Let us examine their main theses. The early pragmatism is best perceived as the leading principle of Peirce's theory of scientific inquiry. In
1868, Peirce had published two essays which attacked the foundation of
Cartesian nominalism by defending his social theory of reality.[3] This
epistemological defense of scientific knowledge against the doubts of
Descartes is continued throughout the early pragmatism.

In his *Principles of Philosophy,* Descartes (1969:219) began by presenting the following rule of method: "It will even be useful to reject as
false all these things as to which we can imagine the least doubt to exist,
so that we may discover with greater clearness which are absolutely true,
and most easy to know." Descartes went to fantastic lengths to imagine
possible grounds for doubting even such simple assertions as "two plus
two equals four." For example, he supposed that there might exist
an "Evil Genius" who has limitless powers of deception and thus can
succeed in deceiving us into error at any time. Once the Evil Genius

hypothesis is countenanced, it is clear that no judgment can escape doubt. Having thus eliminated the possibility of ever removing doubt from any judgment about the external world, Descartes resolved to build up a stock of indubitable propositions about what is immediately present to consciousness. Thus, any conception he judged to be "clear and distinct" was admitted. He used this rule to establish his own existence by the famed *cogito* and the existence of God. Because God would not allow him to be deceived in his clear and distinct judgments about the external world, those propositions were also admitted. In the end, Descartes believed everything he had originally resolved to doubt.

In "The Fixation of Belief," Peirce argued that Descartes's entire method of philosophy was based on a misapprehension of the true nature of doubt, belief, and the thought process in general.[4] For Descartes, doubt is the product of mental concatenations. One reaches the state of philosophical doubt by imagining and postulating the possibility of circumstances which, if actual, would make false what is believed. Because these possibilities (e.g., I am dreaming what I now seem to see) cannot be epistemologically eliminated, they constitute grounds for doubt. Peirce countered this claim by arguing that real doubt of a proposition does not arise from contemplation of merely *conceivable* circumstances; there must be some *actual* experience which seems to conflict with what was believed prior to that experience. Before any doubt can be created, we must be surprised by some event which developed contrary to expectations. Thus, no kind of doubt, be it "practical" or "philosophical," can be established by speculations from the confines of one's armchair; pretended doubt is no species of doubt at all. The only way we may come to doubt any proposition is by having our expectations crushed by brute secondness. Peirce (5.370) notes that there is a difference with respect to firstness between the sensation of doubting and believing. Doubt and belief can be distinguished on the basis of thirdness and secondness (through thirdness): "The feeling of believing is more or less sure indication of there being established in our nature some habit which will determine our actions. Doubt never has such an effect" (5.371).

Peirce adds another distinction between doubt and belief which is wholly psychological: "Doubt is an uneasy and dissatisfied state from which we struggle to free ourselves and pass into the state of belief, while the latter is a calm and satisfactory state which we do not wish to avoid, or to change into a belief in anything else" (5.372). The "irritation" of doubt causes a struggle to establish belief, and Peirce (5.374) names this struggle *inquiry*.

If this notion of inquiry is taken out of the context of scientific problems and solutions (for which Peirce primarily intended it), it could be extended as a description of the whole process of human thought. It may be argued (though no Peircean scholars have) that Peirce allowed this extension by declaring that "the sole object of inquiry is the settlement of opinion" (5.375). It is entirely uncharacteristic of Peirce, as an extreme realist, to thus define the aim of inquiry in psychological terms. Viewed in relation to Peirce's system as a whole, he surely meant that the purpose of inquiry is to settle the opinion of the scientific community, not the individual inquirer, because no belief will prove stable where the "social impulse" is against it (5.378).[5] Inquiry ceases when doubt is replaced by belief; either the originally doubted belief is reaffirmed, or some contrary belief is established in its place: "When doubt ceases, mental action on the subject comes to an end; and, if it did go on, it would be without a purpose" (5.376).

After these preliminary remarks about the relations of doubt, belief, and inquiry, Peirce discusses four basic methods by which one may achieve the desired "fixation of belief." They are the methods tenacity, authority, a priori methods, and science. The method of tenacity requires that one stubbornly retain a belief in spite of all contradictory evidence, much like an ostrich burying its head in the sand. The method of authority establishes belief by placing confidence in a superior authority (e.g., the State or Church). The a priori method of Descartes and other rationalists aims to fix belief by "adopting whatever opinion there seems to be a natural inclination to adopt" (5.38n). All three methods will ultimately fail to fix belief because questions and disputes will inevitably arise, and there will be no means by which everyone can be brought into lasting agreement.

The fourth method, science, does have the potential to fix forever the opinions of the community, but not every opinion, due to the fact that omniscience would require infinite inquiry. However, the method of science could potentially fix belief on a great many questions. Science requires that everyone agree to allow belief to be determined by an "external permanency" which is unaffected by our thought, but which has the power to affect our thought. This nonhuman thing is the real. For Peirce (5.384), the fundamental hypothesis of science is this:

> There are Real things, whose characters are entirely independent of our opinions about them; those Reals affect our senses according to regular laws, and though our sensations are as different as are our relations to the objects, yet, by taking advantage of the laws of per-

ception, we can ascertain by reasoning how things really and truly are; and any man, if he have sufficient experience and he reason enough about it, will be led to the one True conclusion.

This passage explains Peirce's supreme reverence for science and his faith that we could all agree, if only scientific inquiry were pushed sufficiently far. The scientific method is stable, Peirce contends, because no experience will controvert it, every sane person accepts it and applies it, and science successfully settles opinions wherever it has been practiced with diligence and sincerity. He thus concluded, "It would be the merest babble for me to say more about it. If there be anybody with a living doubt upon the subject, let him consider it" (5.384).

The essay, "How to Make Our Ideas Clear" grew out of "The Fixation of Belief." It expressed the assumption that Peirce's readers were now enthusiastic supporters of science, and thus proceeded directly to the exposition of the details of scientific method. Because the method of science requires that inquiry proceed by subjecting hypotheses to the test of sense experience, the method can be applied only to hypotheses that, if true, clearly entail some experiential consequences. Thus the meaning of a scientific hypothesis consists in the sum total of the experiential predictions it makes; any hypothesis that does not allow such predictions must be discarded.

Scientists can avoid semantic confusion if they would only identify the experiential content of their conceptions. These considerations led Peirce to propose the pragmatic maxim for ascertaining the meaning of a scientific concept: "In order to ascertain the meaning of an intellectual conception one should consider what practical consequences might conceivably result by necessity from the truth of that conception; and the sum of these consequences will constitute the entire meaning of the conception" (5.9).

There are two important points to note about the remainder of the essay. They reveal possible sources of James's and Dewey's misunderstanding of Peirce's pragmatism, and will be useful in distinguishing Peirce's earlier and later accounts of pragmatism. First, in one example, Peirce misapplied the maxim by identifying meaning with what *will* happen in the future, not would *would* happen under various possible conditions. Peirce (5.403) declared that to ask whether a diamond that is forever encased in cotton is still hard is to ask a question that concerns "much more the arrangement of language than . . . the meaning of our ideas" (5.409). "There is absolutely no difference between a hard thing and a soft thing so long as they are not brought to the test"(5.403). Peirce lived to regret this statement probably more than any he ever wrote because it opened the way for James's nominalistic interpretation of pragmatism which identifies the meaning of a concept with particular future events that happen to occur. This identifies the meaning of a word with something *definite* (nominalism) instead of with something *general* (realism).

The second historically significant feature of this essay is that it approaches the concepts of "reality" and "truth" from the standpoint of their relation to inquiry: "The opinion which is fated to be ultimately agreed upon by all those who investigate, is what we mean by the truth, and the object represented in this opinion is the real" (5.407). This statement can be misinterpreted to mean that the real has no being antecedent to inquiry and thus becomes what it is as a consequence of inquiry. This subjectivistic conception of reality became the fundamental principle of Dewey's theory of inquiry. Later, Peirce generally defined truth in terms of the theory of signs, and although the above quoted statement remained true as a *consequence* of the nature of truth and reality, the *definitions* of these concepts were not framed in the language of inquiry. The following section examines some of these modifications.

The Later Pragmatism
(c. 1900)

Following the 1877–78 essays, Peirce wrote virtually nothing on pragmatism for over twenty years—although he continued to write extensively on multifarious topics.[6] There are two obvious reasons for Peirce's revived attention to pragmatism during the early 1900s. First, and most important, was the fact that the pragmatism of James, Dewey, Schiller, and others was beginning to flourish and, as we have already noted, Peirce was determined to disassociate his pragmatism from of the ideas of that movement. Second, the popularity of pragmatism offered an opportunity to earn some money through writing and lecturing on the subject—a consideration Peirce could not ignore, given his dire poverty at the time (Feibleman, 1970:28).

Reflecting in 1902 on his earlier pragmatism and James's extensions of it, Peirce (5.3) stated:

> In 1896 William James published his *Will to Believe,* and later his *Philosophical Conceptions and Practical Results* which pushed the method to such extremes as must tend to give us pause. The doctrine appears to assume that the end of man is action—a stoical axiom

which, to the present writer at the age of sixty, does not recommend itself so forcibly as it did at thirty.... Indeed, in the article of 1878, above referred to, the writer practiced better than he preached; for he applied the stoical maxim most unstoically, in such a sense as to insist upon the reality of the objects of general ideas in their generality.

It was about this time that Peirce began to link pragmatism systematically to the theory of signs. Signs do not *mean* their objects. They merely denote their objects, and their meaning lies in what they signify *about* their objects which is just another description of their interpretants (5.6). Consequently, the meaning of concepts can only be solved by studying interpretants (5.475).

At this point, one could quite reasonably object by asking for the meaning the word "the." What is its object? What does it signify about that object? These questions demonstrate that pragmatism is not intended to reveal the meanings of all concepts, but rather only what Peirce called "intellectual" concepts—those concepts upon which "arguments concerning objective fact may hinge" (5.8). Since no question of objective fact can hinge on the meaning of "the," it is not an intellectual concept. The meaning of many nonintellectual signs consists in a simple firstness—a quality of feeling. Music and poetry are, in most cases, examples of nonintellectual signs. Thus Peirce noted, "We must therefore conclude that the ultimate meaning of any sign consists either in an idea predominately of feeling or of acting and being acted on" (5.7). Only this second source of meaning is applicable to intellectual concepts and is thus contained in the pragmatic maxim. Hence, pragmatists hold that nonintellectual signs are meaningless insofar as pragmatism is concerned, but, unlike logical positivists, they insist that these signs may be meaningful in Peirce's first sense (i.e., instantiating a firstness as the only interpretant).

With the aid of James's sponsorship, Peirce delivered a series of guest lectures on pragmatism at Harvard in 1903. In his first lecture, he regretted that his earlier pragmatism had defended the maxim by defining truth "out of an impulse to act consistently, to have definite intention" (5.28). As a result, pragmatism was founded on the *psychological* principle that we seek to establish belief and remove doubt. Peirce added, "But in the first place, this was not very clearly made out, and in the second place, I do not think it satisfactory to reduce such fundamental things to facts of psychology" (5.28). The later pragmatism was therefore marked by an effort to explain and defend pragmatism in nonpsychological language.

The first step of that approach is to deny that the ultimate meaning of a concept consists in anything individual and particular. The nominalist holds to just such a psychological view by asserting that any concept means something singular and determinant. For nominalists, the word "tree" means just this or that material object that I am referring to when I utter the word, and has no general meaning whatsoever. To hold that the meaning of a concept consists in some *particular* action that *will* take place in the future, as did James, is the mark of a nominalistic pragmatist. On the other side, to hold that the meaning of a concept lies in its implications for what *general* events *would* take place under all conceivable circumstances, as did Peirce, marks one as a realistic pragmatist. The nominalist conceives meaning with respect to secondness while the realist lodges meaning in thirdness. No distinction is more crucial than this one to correctly understand the history of American pragmatism. Peirce (5.466–67) wrote that there appears to be "no slight theoretical divergence" between his pragmatism and James's, and summarized the core of his own pragmatism as follows:

> Intellectual concepts, . . . the only sign-burdens that are properly denominated "concepts"—essentially carry some implication concerning the general behaviour either of some conscious being or of some inanimate object, and so convey more, not merely than any feeling, but more, too, than any existential fact, namely, the "would-acts," "would-dos" of habitual behaviour; and no agglomeration of actual happenings can ever completely fill up the meaning of a "would-be."

To understand how Peirce came to this position we must further inquire into the nature of interpretants, because the meaning of an intellectual sign, as with other signs, is manifested in its interpretant. As with all other elements of his philosophy, Peirce approached the study of interpretants from the standpoint of the categories. He probably noticed that once a sign is interpreted within each of the categories, no further mode of interpretation is possible, although there appears to be no clear textual support for this assumption. In any case, Peirce distinguished four possible components of an interpretant: the emotional, energetic, logical, and ultimate logical interpretant. The first three correspond to the interpretation of the sign with respect to firstness, secondness, and thirdness, respectively. The fourth will be discussed presently.

The *emotional* interpretant is the quality of feeling the sign creates in the interpreter. Sometimes it is only a faint image or feeling of recognition (5.475). For some nonintellectual signs, such as a musical performance, the emotional interpretant may be the sole interpretant of the sign. However, any intellectual sign possesses all four elements to some degree.

The *energetic* interpretant, so named to connote secondness, is the physiological reaction the sign stimulates. For example, if a doctor says, "Roll up your sleeve," the emotional interpretant of that propositional sign is an uneasy feeling at the prospect of receiving a needle in the arm, and the energetic interpretant is the act of rolling up the sleeve. More commonly, the energetic interpretant is a mental effort rather than an outwardly physical effort. For instance, consider the tremendous mental energy expended during a chess game or a parliamentary debate.

The third possible effect that a sign can have on the interpreter, and hence be part of the interpretant, is the *logical* interpretant, so termed by Peirce to intimate thirdness. It is a thought or idea which verbally represents the signification of the sign. Since the function of an intellectual sign is to attach some general characterization to its object, the logical interpretant is the interpreter's conception of all of the experimental consequences of that signification. Without such a conception, the interpreter cannot be said to have apprehended the rational purport or the sign. It would, for example, make no sense to say that one knows the meaning of the word "hard," but has no conception of how hard things would react under various experimental conditions.[7]

Peirce clarified his position by noting that the pragmaticist does not make meaning consist in singular experiments, but rather in *experimental phenomena:* when the experimentalists refer to "Michelson's phenomenon," they do "not mean any particular event that did happen to somebody in the dead past, but what *surely will* happen to everybody in the living future who shall fulfill certain conditions" (5.425). In this regard, it is significant that in a 1905 article, Peirce corrected the assertion of the 1878 version of pragmatism that a diamond which is never tested need not necessarily be called "hard." Its being hard has nothing to do with whether it is ever actually tested; it is hard if it *would* resist being scratched (5.453). In other words, an untested diamond is hard only because there is a real possibility that *if* the diamond were brought into contact with other objects, it would resist being scratched. It is possible to perform this test at any time. Hence, real possibilities remain real even when they are not actualized, and this constitutes the essence of all general dispositions: "But the paper of 1878 evidently endeavors to avoid asking the reader to admit a real possibility . . . the distinct recognition of real possibility is certainly indispensable to pragmaticism" (5.527). To know perfectly the meaning of any intellectual concept, one would have to know what consequence would follow from every possible relation of secondness into which the object of the concept could enter. It is the purpose of science to bring us as near as possible to that goal.

This brings us to the *ultimate* logical interpretant. The logical interpretant, being a thought, is a word or combination of words. As such, they require an interpretant, and that interpretant will also require an interpretant; the series is endless (5.7). The meanings of words cannot therefore be ultimately grounded in other words without leading to an infinite regress. As Peirce (5.491) stated, "I do not deny that a concept, proposition, or argument may be a logical interpretant. I only insist that it cannot be the final logical interpretant, for the reason that it is itself a sign of that very kind that has itself a logical interpretant." Thus, the ultimate meaning must be something nonverbal. As we have seen, if we knew every real possibility that is true of the object of a concept, we would know exactly how it would act and react with other things under all conceivable conditions. This would be an infinitely complex verbal and mathematical formula. Moreover, it would instill in us an infinite set of expectations concerning the action of the object of the concept in all actual future situations; and these expectations would impel us to create habits of action toward that object as we anticipate its action under the presiding circumstances and adjust our action accordingly to produce some desired outcome. This is the epitome of rational conduct, and Peirce held it to be humanity's highest possible goal. Strictly speaking, the ultimate logical interpretant is not itself a sign, because it has no further interpretant. But Peirce calls it an interpretant, in a looser sense, meaning that it is the final effect the sign is calculated to produce in the interpreter. But this point is so fundamental that Peirce (5.491) should speak for himself:

> The interpreter will have formed the habit of acting in a given way whenever he may desire a given kind of result. The real and living logical conclusion *is* that habit; the verbal formulation merely expresses it. . . . The deliberately formed, self-analyzing habit—self-analyzing because formed by the aid of analysis of the exercises that nourished it—is the living definition, the veritable and final logical interpretant. Consequently, the most perfect account of a concept that words can convey will consist in a description of the habit which that concept is calculated to produce. But how otherwise can a habit be described than by a description of the kind of action to which it gives rise, with the specification of the conditions and of the motive?

From this passage, it is evident that Peirce clearly saw that logical principles, including pragmatism, are not ends in themselves. The ultimate use of language and logic is to help us acquire stable habits of action. Yet the modern existentialist will poignantly ask why rationality is more desirable than irrationality. Hence, even rational action cannot stand as a defensible ultimate aim. Such considerations led Peirce to advance his doctrine of the normative sciences as a justification of pragmatism (see Lewis, 1976b:90–101).

That Peirce linked the pragmatic maxim to the attainment of the more general aim of promoting rationality in the human community and, ultimately, the universe at large, shows that he sought to ground pragmatism in the most general principle of synechism he could imagine (see Mills, 1964:191–204). Peirce's conception of "evolutionary love" is totally opposed to the pragmatism of James, Schiller, and Dewey, which roots the pragmatic maxim in subjective, psychological dynamics roughly similar to the doubt-belief theory of inquiry underlying Peirce's early pragmatism. As we explore in the following chapters the nominalistic tendencies of James and Dewey, their radical departures from Peirce's realism will become increasingly apparent.

3

William James   Radical Empiricism
and Functional
Psychology

William James's philosophy was much ma-
ligned even during his own lifetime. Although
his flamboyant style of expression gave robust
life to his lectures and writings, it made him
vulnerable to criticism. It is easy to scan his
writings and single out some extravagant
statements to attack. For example, James
(1970a:145) stated, " 'The true,' to put it
briefly, is only the expedient in the way of our
thinking, just as 'the right' is only the expedient
in our way of behaving." Upon noting that
James equates truth with expediency, critics
quickly assumed that he meant that expediency
is the sole criterion of truth. If this one statement were all that James ever uttered on the
subject of truth, the critics' interpretation of his
position would be justiflable. But if the statement is placed in its proper context, it is clear
that James's analysis of truth is far more complex than this elliptical formulation indicates.
Critics also accused James of being a subjectivist because he held that the truth of an idea
consists in the "workings" of its practical consequences. They failed to recognize that these
workings involve uncontrollable sense experiences and, therefore, are not simply a function
of personal desires. These are only a few examples of critics' distortions of James's positions.
As Wild (1969:350–51) and other commentators have sympathetically observed, James's
philosophy was mercilessly caricatured in this
fashion.

To understand why this occurred, one must recall that in the later part of the nineteenth century, American philosophy was in a state of upheaval created by disputes between idealists and pragmatists, with James often in the center of the arena. When such radically different and opposing perspectives clash, misunderstandings and indignant reactions are virtually inevitable. In view of this perfervid philosophical milieu, one can appreciate James's frustration when he remarked during one of his Hibbert Lectures of 1909:

> Place yourself similarly at the center of a man's philosophic vision and you understand at once all the different things it makes him write or say. But keep outside, use your post-mortem method, try to build the philosophy up out of the single phrases, taking first one and then another and seeking to make them fit, and of course you fail. You crawl over the thing like a myopic ant over a building, tumbling into every microscopic crack or fissure, finding nothing but inconsistencies, and never suspecting that a center exists. I hope that some of the philosophers in this audience may occasionally have had something different from this intellectualist type of criticism applied to their own works!

If we are to avoid this myopic ant syndrome, we cannot afford to separate James's pragmatism from the rest of his philosophical thought, particularly his "radical empiricism"—the name he preferred to use to describe his general philosophy. John Wild (1969) and G. W. Allport (1943) have argued convincingly that James can be best interpreted as an existential phenomenologist. Thus, to view his *Principles of Psychology* as primarily an effort toward developing the science of psychology, fails to recognize that James's main interest in psychology was in the contributions empirical psychological research can make to the philosophy of mind and, in particular, to the ancient puzzle of mind-body interaction. James's radical empiricism was the cumulative product of his work and the core from which most of his other doctrines, including pragmatism, developed. As McDermott (1968:xxxvi) cautions, "One thing is obvious: to underplay the importance of radical empiricism in any understanding of James, is to risk missing him altogether." Therefore, this chapter will outline James's radical empiricism, beginning with its incipiency in his psychology and tracing its continued growth in his mature philosophy. In particular, we shall see that James's pragmatism is best understood as an extension of his doctrine of radical empiricism (pages 75–79). In the final section, we systematically contrast James's pragmatism to Peirce's pragmatism.

The Origin of James's
Radical Empiricism:
The Principles of
Psychology (1890)

James's treatise, *The Principles of Psychology*, the product of twelve years of sustained writing, must be regarded as a remarkable achievement even by his most vehement antagonists. Few philosophers have pursued any question as intensely as did James in his search to understand the nature of mind, experience, and their relation. James was caught in the throes of an endless inner struggle between commonsense metaphysical dualism and the neutral monism of his phenomenologically oriented radical empiricism. As Wild (1969:359–60) has noted, James hesitatingly and reluctantly accepted psychophysical dualism in the *Principles* but immediately began to move toward radical empiricism. This section will identify the seeds of radical empiricism contained in the *Principles*.

Before proceeding with the analysis, we should establish a makeshift meaning of "radical empiricism." Because the following section examines radical empiricism in detail, our sole need here is to provide a working familiarity with its central tenets so one can see how, in the *Principles*, James was approaching the position of radical empiricism. Flournoy (1917:69) summarized radical empiricism with the dictum, "All that is experienced is real, and all that is real is experienced." Notice that this is a more thoroughgoing or "radical" form of empiricism than traditional British empiricism. For example, even Hume unconsciously assumed an unexperienced faculty or ego which performs the associations of sense data. For James, everything real, including space, time, and all forms of relations, is known by direct experience. Nothing is known a priori. Radical empiricists therefore escape the need to postulate a Kantian transcendental ego in order to account for our knowledge of the Kantian categories. The categories are simply experienced directly in the same manner as other sensations (e.g., red, hard, heavy). Thus, James's brand of empiricism merits the appellation "radical," in that he pushed empiricism to extremes unimagined by his British predecessors. For the radical empiricist, philosophical analysis of any question begins and ends with sensations, and it is this pure phenomenalism that justifies classifying James as a phenomenologist. With this general notion of radical empiricism in mind, we will now trace those arguments in the *Principles* which signify the genesis of what James eventually and proudly introduced as "radical empiricism."

Early in the *Principles*, James (1950a:8, 11) draws attention to the fundamental differences between psychology's object of study and that of the physical sciences. Because inert matter does not plan its action, physical reactions can be explained adequately by the laws of physics. It would be silly to ask the physicist to explain the magnet's intentions in attracting particles of iron but not copper. By contrast, we regard it as a matter of common sense that human beings act purposefully. Therefore, if a man collects pieces of iron from a pile of scrap metal, we would not consider an explanation of his action as adequate unless it specified his intention. Although the man and the magnet performed essentially the same physical action (i.e., separating the iron from the other materials), we look for radically different types of explanations for these events. Further analysis reveals our belief that, unlike the magnet, the man has both a physical and a mental side and that his mental state (his motives and intentions) exerts a causative influence on his physical activities. It follows that any valid approach to psychology must consider both the physical and mental spheres and explain their interaction. Following a similar line of reasoning, James (1950a:11) concludes that the choice of ends and means should be taken as the criterion of mentality and, therefore, "No actions but such as are done for an end, and show a choice of means, can be called indubitable expressions of mind."

In metaphysical parlance, by this statement James endorsed *dualism*, the doctrine that there are only two distinct and irreducible orders of being—mind and matter—which are, nevertheless, causally interrelated. Dualism is opposed to all forms of monism such as materialism (everything is matter) and idealism (everything is mind). In another passage, James (1950a:218) explicitly approves of dualism as the psychologist's attitude toward cognition. But he was never really satisfied with dualism. His whole philosophy was a struggle to pull away from dualism toward his own peculiar brand of monism (i.e., radical empiricism).

Several problems led James to change his position on the monism / dualism issue. Although, as we have shown above, dualism certainly appeals more to common sense, the dualist finds it difficult to give an intelligible philosophical analysis of the meaning of "mind," "consciousness," or whatever term is used to designate the mental half of the dyad. The term cannot be equated with anything physical, such as the brain, for this would reduce the mental to the physical, violating dualism's basic tenet. On the other horn of the dilemma, if consciousness is not accepted as a physical entity, then, strictly speaking, it does not exist. But then what is it? Does not the admission of its nonexistence embarrass dualists into confessing that upon careful scrutiny, "consciousness" is just so much metaphysical entelechy?

James approached the problem by presenting and criticizing some of the prior theories of consciousness: the mind-stuff theory, the associationist theory, the soul theory, and the automaton theory. The *mind-stuff* theory, popularized by Spencer, is practically unintelligible. It holds that states of consciousness are produced by the summation of primordial atoms of consciousness. It is based on the observation that sensations are built up by the summation of millions of individual nervous impulses from the sense organs. According to the theory, different quantities of impulses from various centers of the body will produce different states of consciousness. For example, Spencer held that consciousness of different colors results from variations in the number of light waves hitting the retina. The theory was advanced by evolutionists in an attempt to explain how dead matter could evolve consciousness, and although it was a miserable failure, it is a valuable example of the futility of trying to reduce consciousness to atomistic units. The whole is qualitatively different from the sum of its parts in this case. The qualities of a conscious state bear no resemblance to those of nerve impulses; consequently, it is absurd simply to equate the two phenomena. James (1950a:161) therefore rejected the mind-stuff theory.

The *associationist* theory is similar to the mind-stuff theory in that it construes consciousness as the coalescence of separate elements. The theory, held by British empiricists, occupies an important place in the history of philosophy. All empiricists face the problem of bridging the chasm between concepts and bare sense data. As James described the predicament, the British empiricist has to explain how this bundle of disparate sensations becomes tied together to for a unitary state of consciousness. Kant saw the problem clearly and postulated the transcendental ego to account for the "transcendental unity of apperception," as he called it. Hume and other empiricists refused to directly adopt such a convenient solution because, to an empiricist, "mind" is an epistemologically inadmissable entity inasmuch as we have no sense impression of it. The empiricists resolved the problem by adopting associationism—a theory that, in effect, smuggles mind in through the back door. Concepts are produced by "associating" one sense datum with another. For example, although we have never seen a golden mountain, we have memory impressions of "gold" and "mountain," and can therefore produce the concept "golden mountain" by associating these impressions.

This theory suffers from the same confusion as the mind-stuff theory. The mere occurrence of two successive sensations is not sufficient to bring about their fusion into a unitary conception. One can think of gold and then quickly imagine a mountain, but this mere sequencing of the two images will not produce the composite conception. Hence, the association must involve some further process, but associationists never discussed how the association is performed. They probably recognized that further analysis would lead to the troublesome mentalistic notions the theory was designed to avoid. James (1950a:354) noticed this defect of the associationist theory, and remarked, "As a rule, associationist writers keep talking about 'the mind' and about what 'we' do; and so, smuggling in surreptitiously what they ought avowedly to have postulated in the form of a present 'judging thought,' they either trade upon their reader's lack of discernment or are undiscerning themselves." In his inimitable style, James (1950a:353) jolts his readers by declaring, "Hume is at bottom as much of a metaphysician as Thomas Aquinas."

Having disposed of the mind-stuff and associationist theory, James (1950a:180–82) briefly considers the *soul* theory. Spiritualists resolve the mind-body problem quite economically by blithely postulating an incorporeal soul to serve as the medium for combining sensations to produce conscious states. As James (1950a:181) stated, the advantage of the soul theory over the mind-stuff and associationist theories is that "we escape the absurdity of supposing feelings which exist separately and then 'fuse together' by themselves." Because the soul hypothesis is untestable, James concluded that scientific psychology must reject it, notwithstanding its logical simplicity.

All of these theories either explicitly or implicitly presuppose mind-body interaction, and take that causal interaction as the explanandum of their theory of consciousness. As James observed, even the associationists expose their implicit acceptance of the interaction premise when they speak of "we" as the agent performing the associations. Each of these theories encounters insuperable difficulties in attempting to provide a tenable account of the connection between conceptions and sensations.

One way to avoid this quandry is to deny outright the interaction premise. This is the approach of the "automaton theory." The theory posits two causally separate worlds: (1) our conscious world of thoughts and feelings, and (2) brain states and concomitant neurophysiological processes. The reality of the first world is acknowledged because its presence is as obvious as anything could ever be. However, the two worlds are totally separate and causally closed systems. Overt behavior is fully explained by the mechanics of brain processes. Likewise, thoughts and feelings are explained by other thoughts and feelings. Although events in the conscious world always occur temporally parallel to phsyiological events, there is no causal interdependence. This assumption of parallelism is, to say the least, no less perplexing than the mind-body interaction assumption. Intuitively, it seems extremely improbable. Commenting on the feasibility of the doctrine, James (1950a:136) states:

> For this "concomitance" in the midst of "absolute separateness" is an utterly irrational notion. It is to my mind quite inconceivable that consciousness should have *nothing to do* with a business which it so faithfully attends. And the question, "What has it to do?" is one which psychology has no right to "surmount," for it is her plain duty to consider it. The fact is that the whole question of interaction and influence between things is a metaphysical question, and cannot be discussed at all by those who are unwilling to go into matters thoroughly.

The rest of the *Principles* certainly remained faithful to that responsibility. James's extensive discourses cover every major aspect of consciousness—attention, conception, discrimination, memory, emotions, perceptions of time and space, sensation, imagination, and many others. Each topic is given a chapter-length study primarily *aimed toward describing its directly experienced characteristics.* It is in this sense that the *Principles* is a masterpiece of descriptive phenomenology.

This probing examination of the nature of consciousness led James to an awareness of the complete inadequacy of each of the theories of consciousness described above. He gradually, and perhaps unknowingly, began to discard metaphysical dualism in order to escape the paradoxes created by the supposition of dualism. But he also desired a theory that would preserve the undeniable efficaciousness of consciousness. In a famous chapter, "The Stream of Thought," James's theory of consciousness began to unfold. According to James, all prior theories mistakenly began the analysis with the supposition of bare sensations, and then attempted to explain the emergence of thought. James (1950a:224) points out that the notion of simple and unrelated sensations is difficult to grasp; he was referring to the same thing as Peirce's category of firstness. Yet, because thoughts are the currency of daily life, James reasoned that psychology is better advised to begin its study of consciousness with its most familiar and directly experienced data—namely, *whole thoughts:* "The first fact for us, then, as psychologists, is that thinking of some sort goes on." Notice that James is careful to avoid Descartes's mistake of saying, "*I* think." The Cartesian "I" is not given in experience; it is added after the fact. Only the thoughts themselves are given. Thus, to postulate an ego which exists separately on a nonphenomenal plane introduces an entity that Ockham's razor would shave clean. James (1950a:345) states: "[The] bald fact is that *when the brain acts,* a thought *occurs.* This spiritualistic formulation says that the brain-processes knock the thought, so to speak, out of a Soul which stands there to receive their influence. The simpler formulation says that the thought simply *comes*." When James says "I think," he actually means, "This brain is functioning and thought is occurring." But throughout the text he uses the more convenient terms "I" and "we" to keep readers from closing the book.

What we are left with, then, is a stream of thoughts which flows along in a continuous drift. For example in the thought, "The pack of cards is on the table," the individual words hang together to form a conscious unit. James (1950a:278–79) argues that the thought is not about the cards or the table. It is about nothing less than the *whole chunk*, "The-pack-of-cards-is-on-the-table." We do not have the individual ideas and then combine them into a thought as Hume, Kant, and all of the other reductionist psychologists presume: *"There is no manifold of coexisting ideas; the notion of such a thing is a chimera. Whatever things are thought in relation are thought from the outset in a unity, in a single pulse of subjectivity, a single psychosis, feeling, or state of mind"* (James, 1950a:278).

In the stream of consciousness, we never have an image of a perfectly definite thing. Rather, every image is "steeped and dyed in the free water that flows around it. With it goes the sense of its relations, near and remote, the dying echo of whence it came to us, the dawning sense of whither it is to lead" (James, 1950a:255). The significance of any conscious state is inextricably blended with other events in the stream of experience. Just as we can never step into a river twice at the same point, we can never have exactly the same idea twice because this would require that precisely the same brain-state recur. But this could never happen, because relations change as the stream of consciousness constantly marches on.

James used his stream-of-consciousness notion to provide the criterion by which truth and falsity are distinguished. A true idea fits in smoothly and permits the stream of experience to flow forward freely. A false idea blocks the stream by contradicting expectations. For example, I think that I have a dollar to pay for a purchase, but I find no money in my pocket. The idea is false because it is inconsistent with subsequent events in the stream of experience.[1]

In the chapter titled "The Perception of Reality," James (1950a:283–323) similarly employs the stream-of-consciousness idea to establish the criterion that distinguishes the real from the unreal. This marks an important episode in the history of James's thought, because the rudiments of his later full-blown radical empiricism and pragmatism are clearly discernible in this essay. James asks his readers to consider the difference between *believing* and *imagining*. We can imagine innumerable states of affairs which we do not believe actually exist; hence, belief is a sort of emotional consent that is added to the thought after it occurs (James, 1950b:283).

Consciousness is a brain function which classifies thoughts as they occur. The categories or "worlds," as James (1905b:292–94) called them, into which thoughts ultimately become classified could eventually be described in the language of brain neurology if experimental psychology ever becomes that advanced. James calls these "worlds" the worlds of sense, science, ideal relations, illusions and prejudices common to the human race, supernatural entities, individual opinion, and sheer madness. He adds, "Every object we think of gets as last referred to one world or another of this or of some similar list." Each person regards one of these worlds as the world of ultimate realities, and, for the vast majority, it is the world of sense. An idea may come to us from one of the other worlds, but it will not be admitted as a reality if it conflicts with the collective testimony of our sense organs.

On the other hand, once an idea is conceived, it will be believed as long as it does not contradict anything believed to be real (James, 1950b:289–90). The horse with wings was one of James's favorite examples: The dream-horse *does* have wings, and without once encountering any contradictions—we can imagine that horse flying to the moon and performing other miraculous feats, provided that the winged horse is confined to the dream-world. If, however, we conceive of the horse as part of the "world known otherwise" (i.e., as a *real* horse), then contradictions abound. For example, James (1950b:289) suggests, "That is my old mare Maggie, having grown a pair of wings where she stands in her stall." This proposition attributes a character to an object of our sense world, but it cannot be admitted to that world because it contradicts sense-world propositions already believed. The horse must be banished from the real world if our sense of reality is ultimately grounded in the sense world rather than some other world.

The real and the unreal are thus judged on the basis of how the conception "fits in" with our other conceptions in the stream of consciousness. For James, what is real (and what exists) is defined as a *judged relation* between elements of our stream-of-subjective experience. Reflecting on the nature of real objects, James (1950b:290n) states, "*Their* real existence, as we shall later see, resolves itself into their peculiar relation to *ourselves*. Existence is thus no substantive quality when we predicate it of any object; it is a relation, ultimately terminating in ourselves, and at the moment when it terminates, becoming a *practical* relation." From this account, it is clear that James was approaching a psychologistic theory of reality.

Besides the classificatory function, consciousness is also a *selecting* function of the brain. Depending upon our interests of the moment, we concentrate on some things in our experiential field and ignore other things. According to James, this selectivity constitutes another criterion by which grades of reality may be distinguished. For example, because I am concentrating on writing, the pen and paper are at this moment more real to me than is the clock on the wall. In the relative sense, "Reality means simply relation to our emotional and active life. . . . In this sense, whatever excites and stimulates our interest is real." But then James generalized the principle by declaring, "The *fons et origo* of all reality, whether from the absolute or the practical point of view, is thus subjective, is ourselves . . . . We reach thus the important conclusion that our own reality, that sense of our own life which we at every moment possess, is the ultimate for our belief" (1950b:295, 296–97). Following the above passage, James again asserts that sensations are the ultimate tribunal for separating the real world from the unreal world: "Sensible objects are thus either our realities or the tests of our realities. Conceived ideas must show sensible effects or else be disbelieved" (1950b:301).

The two criteria of reality, sensible effects and human interest, are finally synthesized as one principle: "That theory will be most generally believed which, besides offering us objects able to account satisfactorily for our sensible experience, also offers those which are most interesting, those which appeal most urgently to our aesthetic, emotional, and active needs" (1950b:312). Those who are familiar with James's "will to believe" doctrine will recognize his purpose in this formulation. He wanted to save religious propositions from falling into the "unreal" category, as they surely would if the showing of sensible effects were the sole criterion. The proposed principle would make propositions such as, "There is a rational purpose operative in the universe" express a reality for those who come to believe. At the end of the essay, James finally reveals the upshot of his double-barreled theory of reality: "We need only in cold blood ACT as if the thing in question were real, and keep acting as if it were real, and it will infallibly end by growing into such a connection with our life that it will become real" (1950b:321). Sociologists will readily note that this statement is a transposition of W. I. Thomas's idea that a situation defined as real is real in its consequences. James simply collapses the distinction between (1) being real and (2) being defined as real. We can *will* religious propositions into reality since they conflict with nothing in the sense world. Thus, the belief cannot be overturned by experience.

In summary, James's *Principles* is pervaded by a nagging and largely unresolved issue—namely, whether to reject metaphysical dualism. Although he gave dualism a tacit endorsement, he also showed that the theory is plagued by serious problems which all previous dualistic theories of consciousness had failed to surmount. He proposed the "stream-of-consciousness" theory as a partial remedy for those ills, and, we have seen, his theory of reality is a consequence of that theory of consciousness. In the end, James's realm of discourse was virtually reduced to the stream of particular sensations, emotions, desires, and their interrelations. This world furnished the elements of James's *ontology,* not just phenomenology. Consequently, it became increasingly difficult for James to refer to the extramental world of objects that exist independent of any individual's sensations and interests. For James, every real thing must be real *within the experience* of some individual. This is a consequence of James's definition of "real." As an adjective, "real" refers to a relation of congruence between the conception it modified and sensations or other ideas already believed. As a noun, "real" refers to a conception corroborated by the sense world or, if it is a religious proposition, by other religious propositions already believed. Within the framework of James's theories of consciousness and reality, it thus makes no sense to assert that reality is independent of individual experience. Individuals construct their own realities out of their own unique stream of experience. Different experiences lead to different constellations of realities believed in. There is my reality and your reality, but there is no reality in general.

Although this is the logical conclusion when James's theory is pushed to its ultimate implications, James never systematically pressed his position to that extreme in the *Principles*. He did admit that reality is subjective according to his theory (James, 1950b:296–97), but he failed to perceive that his view destroys the reference of concepts to nonphenomenal objects. Because the meaning of any event in the stream of consciousness is determined by its relation to other events in the stream, James can define knowledge, truth, reality, and existence in entirely psychological and subjective terms. Having gone this far, dualistic ontologies can only get in his way. It is far more convenient to unconditionally reduce all being to the stream-of-subjective experience. This is the position of James's mature radical empiricism to which we now turn.

Radical Empiricism

James's *Essays in Radical Empiricism* was postumously published in 1912, but most of the essays in it were written around 1905. *A Pluralistic Universe* was originally published in 1909.[2] The presentation and analysis of radical empiricism that follows is based on these volumes.

James never proposed a compact definition of radical empiricism. Any short definition would be incomplete because radical empiricism is not one answer to one problem; it is a general conceptual framework, or *Weltanschauung*, through which James interpreted every traditional problem of philosophy. To best understand radical empiricism, one must study how James applied it to concrete philosophical problems. We have already examined one result of the application of radical empiricism: the reduction of "consciousness" to the stream of subjective experience and the reduction of "reality" to relations between events in this stream of thought.[3] James made a tactical mistake in his book *Pragmatism* by not beginning with a thorough explication of radical empiricism. Although the philosophical community may not have received his pragmatism any more warmly, perhaps their criticism would have been less encompassing had they been forced to see his pragmatism as an outgrowth of radical empiricism.

In James's (1970b:xxxvi) general characterization of radical empiricism, he stated that the doctrine consists of a postulate, a statement of fact, and a conclusion. The postulate is that philosophers shall content themselves with debating questions formulated in terms drawn from experience. Transempirical entities, such as the Absolute, are not allowed into any philosophical discourse: "The statement of fact is that the relations between things conjunctive as well as disjunctive, are just as much matters of direct particular experience, neither more so nor less so, than the things themselves." Because the conclusion presupposes that the parts of experience are connected by relations which are themselves directly experienced, there is no need to postulate any transcendental ego or mind in order to explain the experienced continuous structure of conscious states. The remainder of this section traces the line of reasoning James followed to reach these general propositions.

James's well-known article, "Does 'Consciousness' Exist?" (1971:3–22), returns again to the core issue of the *Principles*. In this essay, James draws the ontological conclusions only implicit in the "stream-of-thought" doctrine in the *Principles*. He answers the question, "Does consciousness exist?", with an emphatic "No!" However, James (1971:4) is quick to add that in denying the existence of consciousness, he means "consciousness" as an *entity*—that is, as a distinct mode of being. He is thus rejecting the dualistic idea that mind and matter constitute two independent and irreducible types of being. But James is careful not to deny that "thoughts" actually occur. That thoughts occur must be accepted as an ultimate fact by any plausible theory of consciousness. James's problem, then, is to define and explain the occurrence of thoughts without appealing to any metaphysical (i.e., unexperienced) type of entity. The only solution is to hold that thoughts are part of *direct* experience just like the experiences of pleasure, pain, and other brute sensations. Moreover, thoughts about other thoughts are also held to be direct experience. The purpose of this doctrine is to eliminate the supposition that thoughts occur *because* of (i.e., by the activity of) some thinking agent which exists independent of the thought:

> To deny plumply that "consciousness" exists seems so absurd on the face of it—for undeniably "thoughts" do exist—that I fear some readers will follow me no farther. Let me then immediately explain that I mean only to deny that the word stands for an entity, but to insist most emphatically that it does stand for a function. There is, I mean, no aboriginal stuff or quality of being, contrasted with that of which material objects are made, out of which our thoughts of them are made; but there is a function in experience which thoughts perform; and for the performance of which this quality of being is invoked. [1971:4]

James contends that thoughts are not *made* by a supernal "mind"; they merely *happen*, just as the experience of pain happens if one's hand contacts fire. The function of the pain experience is to cause the person to pull the hand out of the fire. The function of a thought experience is to relate elements of the stream-of-conscious experience to each other, and, when the thought occurs, that relation is itself experienced. For example, if one thinks, "This is the same dog I saw yesterday," the two dog-experiences are related by a brain process, and a new experience occurs. This new experience is, of course, the thought itself, and James would argue that it is felt in the stream of consciousness just as surely as the two dog-experiences were felt. James (1971:25) explains:

> To be radical, an empiricism must neither admit into its constructions any element that is not directly experienced, nor exclude from them any element that is directly experienced. For such a philosophy, the relations that connect experiences must themselves be experienced relations, and any kind of relation experienced must be accounted as "real" as anything else in the system.

By constructing a vocabulary that accounts for thought processes without invoking "consciousness" as a separate entity, James eliminates the traditionally felt need to presuppose an absolute mind / body dualism, but he is left with the task of further articulating his ontological commitments. Dualism at least had the advantage of conforming to our commonsense notions by holding that thoughts comprise one mode of being, and material things comprise quite another. James recognized the difficulty in attempting to persuade many of his readers to disavow their natural, dualistic impulse. With his usual flair for incisive expression, he summed up the creed of dualism thusly: "Let no man join what God has put asunder." James replies that thoughts and things *are* joined, inasmuch as both are parts of the same stream of consciousness and are never known as anything but elements in that continuous stream: "Thoughts in the concrete are made of the same stuff as things are" (1971:21, 22).

What is the nature of this basic "stuff" of which thoughts and things alike are made? James has committed himself to some type of monism, but what type? The two classical forms of monism—idealism and materialism—are both incompatible with the tenets of radical empiricism. James cannot accept the idealist's "mind," because it is a transempirical entity; nor can he embrace materialism, because it neglects mentality completely or else fails to give a tenable account of thought processes. James's solution is to propose a third alternative. Because the thought / matter distinction ultimately dissolves when thoughts and material objects are perceived as *experiences* in the stream of consciousness, James concludes that the fundamental "stuff" of the universe is pure experience (1971:5). Pure experience should not be regarded as mental or physical; it is neither mind nor matter. On the contrary, mind/matter and subject / object are simply functional distinctions between different clusters of experiences. This ontology is commonly called neutral monism.[4] Because it holds that mind and matter are merely different aspects of the *one* fundamental mode of being, it is "neutral" between idealism and materialism.

To illustrate this point, James (1971:9–10, 14–15) uses the example of the perception of a room. To speak of "perceiving a room" implies the dualistic subject (perceiver) and object (external room) separation. We can avoid this misleading connotation by employing, with James, the neutral term "room-experience" to refer to the instantaneous happening of the room-event as an element within the stream of consciousness. At the instant it occurs, it is simply present and only later becomes classified as a physical room, a dream-room, or something else depending upon how it is experienced in relation to other happenings in the continuing stream of events. In the language of James and other phenomenologists, the room-datum is a *that* before it is a *what*. This locution conveys the idea that the conscious state first occurs as a pure awareness or present-ness before its relation to other experiences is itself experienced, whereby the simple, unidentified *that* becomes known as some particular *what* complete with its experienced relations. James (1971:15) explains:

> The instant field of the present is at all times what I call the "pure" experience. It is only virtually or potentially either object or subject as yet. For the time being, it is plain, unqualified actuality, or existence, a simple that. In this *naif* immediacy, it is of course *valid;* it is *there,* we *act* upon it; and the doubling of it in retrospection into a state of mind and a reality intended thereby, is just one of the acts.

The room-experience can be analyzed as either a subject or as an object: "Its subjectivity and objectivity are functional attributes solely, realized only when experience is 'taken,' i.e., talked of twice, considered along with its two differing contexts respectively, by a new retrospective experience, of which that whole past complication now forms the fresh content" (James, 1971:15). As part of my subjective experience, the room-experience is totally controllable. I can make it disappear and re-appear by blinking my eyes, or I can change its content by turning my head. I can imagine it changing in innumerable ways (e.g., burning, changing colors, becoming larger), and all of these characteristics are real attributes of the room-experience *taken in its subjective context.* How-ever, if the room is taken in its objective context (i.e., as a real physical room), then the case is altered. As an objective, real room, it will not burn unless one starts a real fire, and it will not change colors unless it is covered with real paint. It cannot be destroyed unless real and physical action is brought against it. In short, the room-experience *qua* real room coheres with other taken-as-real experiences and, if it did not cohere with them, it would be banished from the real world to some other world. The objective room "maintains a definite foothold, to which, if we try to loosen it, it tends to return, and to reassert itself with force" (1971:14). This idea of the brute resistance of real things recalls Peirce's category of secondness. However, it should not be concluded that James fell back into dualism by describing the objective context of experience in this way. He offered no explanation of *why* some experiences exhibit stable relations which cannot be destroyed by simple acts of will, whereas other experiences are totally malleable. Perhaps James would not have re-garded this as a meaningful question. In any case, he was content to point out that this distinction is a fact of direct experience and constitutes the criterion by which any pure experiences are taken as subjective or objec-tive (1971:65–66).

James (1971:113) endorses a *practical* dualism, but not an *essential* dualism. Thoughts and physical realities are made of the same essential "stuff": pure experience. But radically different consequences accrue from physical realities than from mere mental images. For example, if we stand in the path of a charging bull, it is a matter of utmost practical importance whether the bull-experience is taken in its subjective or objective context. In general, experiences get classified not only according to subsequent sensations but also according to our immediate purposes (1971:74). The bull-experience *may* be a hallucination, but we do not stop to consider that possibility at the moment of that experience. Our purpose—staying alive—demands that it be classified as a *real* bull.

If we desire real-world results, we must use real-world means, but in the dream-world we can obtain results by any means we choose. This practical saliency of the process of connecting the subjective / objective context of experience to their corresponding imaginary / real ends and means led to James's definition of "consciousness." Consciousness, then, is the brain *function* by which pure experiences are assigned to their proper "worlds" and are experienced in relation to other objects. If consciousness does not operate efficaciously, others will regard the individual as insane.

James similarly defined "knowledge" as a functional relation between experiences. He distinguished two types of knowledge: knowledge by "direct acquaintance" and "knowledge about." Knowledge by direct acquaintance requires that we have a sense contact with the object of knowledge. It is by direct acquaintance that we "know" the taste of cinnamon and the smell of cooked cabbage. There are, however, many things that cannot be experienced directly but that we "know about" by experiencing their effects. For example, Jones knows by acquaintance that he is angry, but we cannot know directly Jones's anger. Nevertheless, we know that Jones is angry when we see that he is red-faced, screaming, and breaking furniture (James, 1971:40). Thus, the conception that "there is cinnamon in that bottle" is not a case of "knowing" unless we have (or can have) a series of experiences with respect to the bottle (e.g., removing the cap, pouring out some of its contents), which *terminates* in the taste of cinnamon. Similarly, we do not know that Jones is angry unless we can experience some of the effects. James (1971:32) remarked, "In this continuing and corroborating, taken in no transcendental sense but denoting definitely felt transitions, *lies all that the knowing of a percept by an idea can possibly contain or signify.*"

This statement brings us to the brink of James's pragmatic theory of meaning and truth. Assisted by the foregoing account of James's psychology and radical empiricism, we are now prepared to examine his pragmatism as a further elaboration of radical empiricism.

Pragmatism

The core of James's pragmatism is contained in the two volumes *Pragmatism* (1970a) [1907] and its sequel *The Meaning of Truth* (1970b) [1909].[5] Our analysis of James's pragmatism is based upon these writings. James (1970a:53) stated that the scope of pragmatism deals with two principal concerns: (1) like Peirce, James regarded pragmatism as a method of clarifying the meanings of words; and (2) unlike Peirce, James considered pragmatism as a theory of what is meant by truth.

Let us first consider pragmatism as a general theory of meaning. James was notoriously inconsistent in stating, on the one hand, that the meaning of a word consists in its *particular* consequences which *will* happen, and on the other hand, in stating the maxim with reference to the *general* and long-term consequences which would happen under all possible circumstances. Consider these examples in which James requires definite and particular consequences:

1. "The whole function of philosophy ought to be to find out what definite difference it will make to you and me, at definite instants of our life, if this world-formula or that world-formula be the true one" (1970a:45).
2. "[Pragmatism] agrees with nominalism for instance, in always appealing to particulars; with utilitarianism in emphasizing practical aspects; with positivism in its disdain for verbal solutions" (1970a:47).
3. "Pragmatism . . . asks its usual question. 'Grant an idea or belief to be true,' it says, 'what concrete difference will its being true make in any one's actual life?' " (1970:133).

Perhaps Peirce's constant badgering of James on this point caused James to occasionally emphasize long-term, general consequences. Thus, the statement immediately prior to quotation (1), above, declared: "There can be no difference anywhere that doesn't make a difference elsewhere—no difference in abstract truth that doesn't express itself in a difference in concrete fact and in conduct consequent upon that fact, imposed on somebody, somehow, somewhere, and somewhen." Also, James (1970a:43), paraphrasing Peirce, wrote, "Our conception of these effects, *whether immediate or remote,* is then for us the whole of our conception of the object so far as that conception has any significance at all" (italics added). James continued by noting that he (James) had applied

Peirce's formulation to religion (1970a:193). Throughout James's pragmatic writings, similar generalized formulations of the maxim are inter-
spersed with the more common particularistic formulations.

Because the effect (if any) that the truth or falsity of an idea *will* have
on one's actual life is in no way identical to all the consequences it *would*
have under all conceivable circumstances, it is clear that these two formulations of the pragmatic theory of meaning are far from equivalent.
Which formulation, then, did James actually accept? When his writings
are reviewed in their entirety, one can say fairly that James most energeti-
cally asserted and defended the particularistic pragmatism, and that he
retreated into the Peircean generalistic pragmatism only when critics accused him of subjectivism or when he became dissatisfied with some of
the implications of his own doctrine. But, in the end, he always came
back to the particularistic maxim. For this reason, we shall ignore
James's periodic inconsistencies and focus on the relation of the particularistic version of pragmatism to radical empiricism.

Recalling James's functional theory of consciousness and knowledge, it
is evident that his theory of meaning (pragmatism) must conform to the
same outlines. The first and foremost requirement of pragmatism, therefore, is that it must intimately link the meaning of concepts to other
things in the stream of pure experience. Otherwise, ideas and beliefs
would have no function and, as this supposition would deny the efficaciousness of mentality, it contradicts the self-evident ends-means activity
which is continuously experienced.

One must further admit that all conceptions are pieces of pure experience, and as such, must occur within one and only one stream of consciousness. That is, there are *my* conceptions and *your* conceptions but
there are no isolated conceptions existing apart from *some* particular
stream of thought. Hence, a conception can be experienced only in relation to other experiences of the same stream of consciousness in which it
occurs; therefore, if it is to have any purpose at all, that purpose must be
to lead to some other experience inside of that same stream.

Finally, the same conception can arise in an infinite number of different
situations, and its purpose will vary according to the context of each
occasion:

> Each reality verifies and validates its own idea exclusively; and in
> each case the verification consists in the satisfactorily-ending conse-
> quences, mental or physical, which the idea was able to set up. These
> "workings" differ in every single instance, they never transcend ex-
> perience, they consist of particulars, mental or sensible, and they admit
> of concrete description in every individual case. [James, 1970b:237]

These considerations led James to a personalized theory of meaning. He was interested only in analyzing concepts *in use.* He often attacked the "vicious intellectualism" of scientists and idealists for stripping concepts of their particular situation-bound relations from which their meanings operate in actual instances (James, 1970a:123; 1970b:99). A concept *means* the experience to which it aims to lead. The purpose of the pragmatic method is "to determine the meaning of all differences of opinion by making the discussion hinge as soon as possible upon some practical or particular issue" (1971:83). Because the meaning of a conception is inextricably bound to that unique stream of experiences in which it occurs, concepts have no abstract, decontextualized meaning or significance.

It is thus not surprising that James distrusted even the fundamental principles of symbolic logic (James, 1971:222–37). He nevertheless did hold that abstractions, even though comparatively "empty," can be useful if they fit into some actual and ongoing sequence of experiences (1970b:202–3): "The full reality of a truth for [a pragmatist] is always some process of verification, in which the abstract property or connecting ideas with objects is workingly embodied." This, briefly, is James's pragmatic theory of meaning.

We now turn to the pragmatic theory of truth, which is merely an extension of the account of pragmatic meaning. James's critics misunderstood his definition of truth as thoroughly as they criticized it. It was often claimed, for example, that James accepted as true any idea that affords emotional satisfaction. James (1970a:151) once retorted:

> A favorite formula for describing Mr. Schiller's doctrines and mine is that we are persons who think that by saying whatever you find it pleasant to say and calling it truth you fulfill every pragmatistic requirement. I leave it to you to judge whether this be not an impudent slander. Pent in, as the pragmatist more than any one else sees himself to be, between the whole body of funded truths squeezed from the past and the coercions of the world of sense about him, who so well as he feels the immense pressure of objective control under which our minds perform their operations?

According to James, a conception is true if its meaning (i.e., the experience toward which it aims to lead) is fulfilled by the subsequent flow of experience: "The truth of an idea is not a stagnant property inherent in it. Truth *happens* to an idea. It *becomes* true, is *made* true by events" (1970a:133). To cite another of his examples, the front of a building is experienced and leads to the idea, "I can get a glass of beer there." Then, a series of experiences follow (approaching the building, turning a doorknob, entering the building, ordering a beer, etc.). This is what James calls the "ambulatory" phase of the stream. Each experience aims toward the ultimate terminus of the original idea, in this case, the taste of beer. If one can ambulate smoothly through the intervening experiences without being led *away* from the intended terminus (the building is closed, they do not sell beer, etc.), and if the terminus of the idea is finally reached, then the idea is true. It has worked satisfactorily.

This example can be used to refute two common objections to James's pragmatism. First, the mere feeling of satisfaction at the *prospect* of some idea is not sufficient to qualify the idea as truth. One might be extremely thirsty and thus crave a glass of beer, but that desire is itself no guarantee that its intended terminus will be realized. Without the pragmatic *workings,* no satisfaction and, therefore, no truth, results. Those who accused James of holding that anything we would like to believe is thereby true, neglected James's further requirement that the conception must cohere with other truths and future experiences.

This brings us to the second misconception of James's position. He was often charged with denying that a true idea must correspond to some independent reality. This contention is also groundless. In the example cited, the pragmatic workings of the idea involve experiences clearly beyond one's control. There are numerous circumstances under which the terminus (i.e., beer-experience) cannot be reached. James (1970:160) similarly states:

> *Reality is in general what truths have to take account of;* and the *first* part of reality from this point of view is the flux of our sensations. Sensations are forced upon us, coming we know not whence. Over their nature, order and quantity we have as good as no control. *They* are neither true nor false; they simply are.

In the restricted sense of "realist"—as meaning one who regards sensations as the immediate, uncontrollable, and ontologically unquestionable object of conceptions—James was certainly a realist, and continually called himself one (James, 1970b:100n, 158, 195, 217–18, 269).

If "truth" meant only conceptions that, when followed through, lead to the expected particular sensation, then James's "will to believe" doctrine would be left without intellectual credibility. Religious sentiments would be worse than unverified, they would be *meaningless* if strictly tested by the pragmatic maxim. For example, whether or not God exists and the universe is destined to be governed by rational principles, such an issue cannot be reduced to the question of whether or not some particular sensation will occur in any individual's actual life. Consequently, James

had to "broaden" the pragmatic maxim beyond Peirce's restricted scientific formula in order to allow generalized religious beliefs to be
counted as pragmatically meaningful and true.

His solution was to argue that a true idea is one that "works best in the
way of leading us, what fits every part of life best and combines with
the collectivity of experience's demands, nothing being omitted" (James,
1970a:61). According to this general definition, religious beliefs are true
to anyone to whom they bring solace. They do not incidentally clash with
logic or sensations and, therefore, will not cause any contradictions in the
believer's stream of experience. On the contrary, their practical consequence is the experience of peace and contentment they engender for the
believer: "If theological ideas should do this, if the notion of God, in
particular, should prove to do it, how could pragmatism possible deny
God's existence? She could see no meaning in treating as 'not true' a
notion that was pragmatically so successful" (1970a:61–62).

Based on this account, truth is *personal* insofar as a religious belief
which comforts one person may grieve another and clash with other
beliefs. In general, for James, truth was always a dynamic relation between ideas and events in some individual's life. Truths come into existence in the process of knowing, and, as we have seen, knowledge is itself
a living relationship between experiences in some stream of consciousness. Of course, James did not deny that dusty library books contain
much truth and knowledge, but such truths live on the "credit system,"
on the assumption that *someone* verified them in experience and others
could likewise verify them in the future. But it is actual truth being
verified in *present* experiences that is most real for us and contributes to
the satisfactory workings of daily life (James, 1970b:240–43).

James and Peirce

We have already made a few scattered comparisons between the
philosophies of James and Peirce, and the reader may have drawn others.
In this section, we contrast their philosophies more systematically,
drawing freely from Peirce's reviews of James's writings and from the
correspondence between them. We restrict discussion to their
metaphysics, phenomenologies, and pragmatisms. Much of this material
and its analysis is taken from Ralph Barton Perry's masterful work, *The
Thought and Character of William James* (1935).[6]

Peirce (8.296) once wrote to James, "Your mind and mine are as little
adapted to understanding one another as two minds could be, and
therefore I feel that I have more to learn from you than from anybody. At

the same time, it gives great weight in my mind to our numerous agreements of opinion." Perry (1935a:538–39) offered a penetrating description of their personal and intellectual differences, which is worth quoting at length:

> James was adapted to social intercourse . . . was a man of the world. . . . Peirce was ill at ease, of uncertain temper . . . with his fellow men. . . . Peirce, both by aptitude and by training, was an exponent of exact science, where a man might be sure of his ground, and where inaccuracy was the deadliest of sins; whereas James was at home in literature, psychology, and metaphysics, where accuracy is likely to be pretentious or pedantic, and where sympathy insight, fertility, and delicacy of feeling may richly compensate for its absence. . . . James was comparatively defective in that formal or symbolic mode of statement which Peirce, as a trained mathematician and logician, regarded as the acme of clearness.

Perry's characterization sheds some light on Peirce's statement that he and James were poorly adapted to understanding each other.

Let us examine one example of Peirce's insistence on precise terminology and James's equally strong tendency toward loose expression. Peirce (8.279) was troubled by James's statement that James's psychology developed in opposition to the theory that consciousness is an *entity* rather than a functional relation between parts of experience. Peirce asked James to clarify what his opponents meant by "entity"—one of the most vague words in the English language—and added, "This word . . . has never conveyed to my mind any idea except that it is a sign the writer is setting up some man of straw whom he imagines to entertain opinions too absurd for definite statement." To this James replied: "As for what entity may mean in general I know not except it be some imperceptible kind of being. In my article it meant a *constituent principle* of all experience, as contrasted with a certain *function or relation* between particular parts of experience. The distinction seems to me plain enough" (8.285n).

In response to this letter, Peirce (8.301) again chastised James's terminology: "What you call 'pure experience' is not experience at all and certainly ought to have a name. It is downright bad morals so to misuse words, for it prevents philosophy from becoming a science." Recall that, for Peirce, any experience—even a percept—requires a cognitive act. In perception, some quality of feeling (firstness) is felt, then compared to some general concepts, and finally classified as something. A *judgment* always mediates between the firstness (which is only *felt*) and the percept (which is a virtual cognition). In the notes to his book review of James's *Principles,* Peirce (8.65) explained, "In perception, the conclusion has the peculiarity of not being abstractly thought, but actually seen, so that it is not exactly a judgment, though it is tantamount to one."

James collapses sensations, perceptions, and thoughts into one category—pure experience. Peirce, as we have seen, recognized three distinct and irreducible types of consciousness. James's theory of consciousness, in effect, attempts to reduce secondness, and thirdness, to pure experience. Pure experience is like firstness in being absolutely singular, but it also has the seemingly impossible characteristic of, in some instances, being dyadic (sensation) and triadic (thought). James called this the problem of how one can also be many. He admitted that his doctrine is logically impossible according to the canons of formal logic, and decided to give up logic rather than give up radical emiricism. In James's words, the question is: "How can many consciousnesses be at the same time one consciousness? . . . Well, what must we do in this tragic predicament? For my own part, I have finally found myself compelled to *give up the logic,* fairly, squarely, and irrevocably" (1971:220, 222).

Peirce, of course, held a different view. Formal logic applies to experience as assuredly as it applies to abstract symbols. The difficulty lies rather within James's own phenomenology. Feelings are not the starting point of cognitions. It is the *reactions* (secondness) of ourselves with things and between things that reveal their characteristics. As Peirce (8.80) correctly noted, James's confusions originated in large part from his refusal to admit the radical distinction between thoughts and simple feeling-qualities. It is true that every cognition involves a firstness (Peirce's emotional interpretant), but to hold, as did James, that a thought consists of nothing more than its direct sensual impact (e.g., the feeling of pleasure or pain), is simply inconsistent with the phenomenological evidence.

For example, let us examine the thought, "This is the same dog I saw yesterday." If, for the moment, we grant James that the perceptual qualities of the dog are directly (noninferentially) experienced, the mere perception of the dog is not sufficient to lead to the thought that it is the same dog. Between the perception and the thought must be the *memory* of yesterday's dog and a *comparison* of the qualities of this dog to that dog. These processes can occur so rapidly that it may seem that the thought is monadic. But the mediate processes are evident in cases where we are *not* quickly sure of ourselves. We stop to ask ourselves questions: "Did that dog have this type of collar?" And then, "But wait, I remember this brown spot on his ear." And finally, "Yes, this must be the same dog I saw yesterday." Thus, a thought is not a simple and indecomposable phenomenon such as the feeling of pain; on the contrary, it is irreducibly triadic.

Peirce also objected to two theses of James's "stream-of-consciousness" doctrine. First, he attacked James's (1950a:225) claim that every thought is *owned* by some personal self. If Peirce had turned his efforts to sociology, he would be known today as the most extreme Durkheimian social realist that ever lived. He flatly denied the reality of individual "selves" or personalities (see Singer, 1980); he once wrote that individuals are "mere cells" of the social organism. In response to James's idea of the personal "self," Peirce (8.82) wrote:

> Everybody will admit a personal self exists in the same sense in which a snark exists; that is, there is a phenomenon to which that name is given. It is an illusory phenomenon; but still it is a phenomenon. It is not quite *purely* illusory, but only *mainly* so. It is true, for instance, that men are *selfish*, that is, they are really deluded into supposing themselves to have some isolated existence; and in so far, they *have* it. To deny the reality of personality is not anti-spiritualistic; it is only anti-nominalistic.

Peirce labeled belief in personal selves "nominalistic," because that belief, which is the essence of nominalism, implies the denial of the reality of thirdness. There are no private languages; words are given their signification by the community, not by individuals. Thus, the general sign-bearing function of words is entirely independent of any individual opinions about them. Since there are no private languages, there can be no perfectly private thoughts.[7] This social relativity of thought is, of course, the central thesis of the sociology of knowledge. Approaching the matter from the other side, if thoughts were somehow totally private and subjective, communication of thoughts would be impossible—there would be no conventional link between any sign and any potential object. We would be limited to rudimentary forms of communication of affective states (fear, anger, approval, etc.) through facial gestures and primitive sounds. Yet communication of complex thoughts does occur, and this is proof that thought is social and objective, not private and subjective. Of course, society does not think; only individuals think. But the *possibility* of thought and the *meanings* of thought are both grounded in the society's language, not in the individual thinker.

For this reason, Peirce regarded as utter nonsense James's claim that no thought ever occurs twice. Words do not take their meaning from the context in which they are used. It is a corollary of James's "stream-of-consciousness" doctrine that the meaning of a thought depends upon the thoughts that temporally surround it. Because no extended thought sequence is ever perfectly duplicated, no thought ever recurs exactly. Peirce (8.88) remarked, "This seems perfectly absurd. The essence of thought lies in the law of relationship that it implies." The "law" (convention) that determines the meaning of a thought extends to every possible occurrence of that thought, and is identical for every instance. Consequently, two persons can have exactly the same thought, and one person can have the same thought at different times. James's denial of these facts stems from his belief that thoughts acquire their meanings from the unique conscious state within which they occur. This view, in turn, follows from his belief that thoughts are subjectively owned by a personal self.

These fundamental differences between James's and Peirce's phenomenological outlooks are clearly reflected in their respective views on pragmatism. For Peirce, the pragmatic maxim's dependency on the normative sciences (5.35) was proof that the import of any conception lies in bringing our actions under the control of general laws. For James also, the meaning of a concept is related to the future. But James was more interested in the *immediate* future, specifically, its function in relation to other events in the actual stream of experience into which it enters. As Perry (1935b:410–11) lucidly explained:

> In short, for Peirce a conception has meaning only in so far as it expresses and promotes the idea of a well-ordered life. It is a habit reflecting the stability and uniformity of things; and its formulation is at once an adaptation to this stability and uniformity, and a participation in its growth. With James, on the other hand, the significance of a conception lies in its leading into the field of particulars and adapting the agent to the exigencies that arise therein. It is not merely that Peirce is more explicit in linking pragmatism to an ethical ideal, but also that there is an important difference *in* that ideal. For Peirce the good lies in coherence, order, coalescence, unity; for James in the individuality, variety, and the satisfaction of concrete interests.

This stark contrast between Peirce's concern for the long-run consequences and James's interest in the immediate "cash value" of the idea is apparent in their theories of truth. Truth, for Peirce, means the set of beliefs the ultimate scientific community would hold after *infinite* scientific inquiry. According to Peirce, truth is thus a regulative principle: although it is never completely realized, it is the ideal toward which all inquiry aims. A corollary of Peirce's conception of truth is that any scientific question is capable of final resolution if inquiry is pushed far enough by the extended scientific community, and thereafter all scientific minds would remain in catholic agreement on the matter. James's critics rarely recognized that he actually had *two* theories of truth. His definition of absolute truth was adopted from Peirce: "Truth absolute, [the pragmatist] says, means an ideal set of formulations towards which all opinions may in the long run of experience be expected to converge" (James, 1970b:226–27). But James also had a "relativized" kind of truth, which is anything that works satisfactorily for present purposes. Absolute truth is fine as an ultimate goal, but "we have to live today by what truth we can get today, and be ready tomorrow to call it falsehood" (1950a:145). By this theory, the same proposition can be (relatively) true within one individual's experience, but false within another's. This "humanistic" conception of truth, which James developed jointly with British pragmatist F. C. S. Schiller, was relentlessly attacked by numerous critics, including Peirce. In a 1904 letter to James, Peirce (8.258) wrote: "You and Schiller carry pragmatism too far for me. I don't want to exaggerate it but keep it within the bounds to which the evidences of it are limited. The most important consequence of it . . . is that under that conception of reality we must abandon nominalism." It was this individualistic, psychological and, hence, nominalistic tendency of James's pragmatism which most alarmed Peirce—who, as we know, considered nominalism / realism *the* basic philosophical question.

That this implicit nominalism in James's philosophy was the basic cause of Peirce's distress is especially evident in another of his letters to James. James's book, *A Pluralistic Universe*, inspired by his study of Bergson, is unquestionably James's most blatantly nominalistic work. He argued that logical and mathematical principles do not apply to concrete, real-world situations. In the "pure" world of abstractions, if A caused B, and B caused C, then it is true that A caused C. But, James would say, when we attempt to trace any actual real-world causal chain we become entangled in the multifarious contextual relativities of the succeeding events and are inevitably led away in various directions, losing track of our original intention to trace the straight line causal sequence (James, 1971:281). The abstract model cannot therefore be applied to the concrete situation. This doctrine attacks Peirce's synechism at its core. Thus James's (1971:283) statement that this "pluralism" is consistent with Peirce's ideas demonstrates that James had absolutely no understanding of Peirce's cosmology. In Peirce's system, *synechism*, not tychism, is most central. The most wondrous thing about the universe is the reality of continuity, generality, and law. Tychism, the principle of absolute chance, is a necessary ingredient in Peirce's approach to probability theory. But in his overall system, novelty is controlled by the applicability of statistical probabilities to chance occurrences. James seized Peirce's label "tychism," much as he had "pragmatism," and fashioned it to suit his own religious and moral interests (Perry, 1935b:411). In James's hands, tychism is the fundamental principle of the universe (hence, the "pluralistic" universe), and a minute degree of synechism is postulated to escape the conception of a *totally* chaotic and disjoined universe. Inasmuch as James's view of the world suppresses the reality of general laws and relations, it is nominalistic in its implications. Peirce perceived this increasingly nominalistic drift in James's thinking and desperately attempted to influence him to reconsider his position:

> I thought your *Will to Believe* was a very exaggerated utterance, such as injures a serious man very much, but to say what you now do is far more suicidal. I have lain awake several nights in succession in grief that you should be so careless of what you say. The only thing I have ever striven to do in philosophy has been to analyze sundry concepts with exactitude; and to do this it is necessary to use terms with strict scientific precision . . . it is not very grateful to my feelings to be classed along with a Bergson who seems to be doing his prettiest to muddle all distinctions. [Perry, 1935b:438]

James (1971:131) wrote that "a man's vision is the greatest fact him." If this is true, James completely missed the most salient fact about Peirce and his philosophy. As Peirce's above statement indicates, he and Bergson could hardly be farther apart philosophically. Yet James (1971:283) called their philosophies "altogether congruous." In a letter to one of his correspondents, James referred to a book written by Bergson, and said, "This book . . . is destined to rate with the greatest works of all time. . . . By all means send it to Charles Peirce" (James, 1920:294).

Perry (1935a:542) offers an interesting theory to explain James's lack of comprehension of the essence of Peirce's system. James's conception of Peirce's philosophy was mainly derived from his interpretation of what we have called Peirce's "early pragmatism" (see above, chap. 2). Recall that the early pragmatism is psychological in that its theory of the meaning of words is predicated upon the doubt-belief process, rather than upon strictly logical considerations. As we have seen, Peirce later noticed and corrected this defect in his pragmatism. Perry (1935b:409) suggests, and we agree, that Peirce's early pragmatism was sufficiently "flexible" to allow James's individualistic and particularistic interpretation of it, and Peirce's later pragmatism was sharpened to preclude that interpretation.

Despite Peirce's public and private attempts to dissassociate his philosophy from some of the key principles of the "pragmatic movement" initiated by James, Schiller, and Dewey, it seems that James never recognized the deep-seated differences between his thought and Peirce's. In particular, he never grasped Peirce's categories or the logical relation of pragmatism to those categories. Consequently, he failed to see that pragmatism is a mere corollary of Peirce's categories and the essential realism imbued therein. Indeed, Peirce (8.263) wrote James that it seems "entirely inscrutable" why the categories are "so luminous to me without my being given the power to make them understood by . . . my fellow-pragmatists. . . . you must have a blind spot . . . not to see . . . what pragmatism ought to make so much plainer." Considered from the standpoint of the categories, pragmatism is the view that the rational purpose of thought (thirdness) is to represent the possible qualities (firstness) of existents (secondness). If James had ever understood Peirce's pragmatism in the context of Peirce's wider system, it is doubtful that he would have ever called his philosophy "pragmatism"—a choice both he and Peirce eventually regretted.

John Dewey

Inquiry and Genetic Logic

For several reasons, it is impossible to give a short, yet reasonably comprehensive, synopsis of John Dewey's thought. First, he was an incredibly prolific writer whose work covered every substantive area of philosophy. Second, his work spans nearly seventy years and, naturally, his views underwent some transitions during that long period. Third, and perhaps an even more knotty problem, is Dewey's style of exposition. The positive characteristics of his philosophy are embedded in his criticisms of "absolutist" or "dualistic" philosophies; and his attacks were thoroughly diffuse in that virtually every major philosopher from Plato to Kant became Dewey's target at some time during the course of his writings. It is often easier to discern what Dewey regarded as the objectionable features of the position he opposed than it is to understand Dewey's *own* view of the matter. Despite his attempts to use technically precise terminology, Dewey was sometimes vague at critical points in his writings. Consequently, any succinct statement of his philosophy risks distortion; one must proceed cautiously, examining alternative interpretations of the texts. Finally, the difficulty of a synopsis is compounded by the fact that Dewey's philosophy cannot be pigeonholed into any traditional school of philosophy. In that respect, he is unlike Peirce and James who can be identified as descendents of scholastic realism and British empiricism, respectively.

Dewey's ideas were superhybrids, in the sense that his thought was influenced by several contrasting philosophies. In addition to his fellow "pragmatists" (Peirce, James, and Mead), Dewey was strongly influenced by Hegel and Darwin. During the last two decades of his life, his voluminous philosophical correspondence with Arthur Bentley appears to have been an important influence in forcing Dewey to develop and clarify his ideas (see Dewey and Bentley, 1949, 1964).[1] Richard J. Bernstein (1960) suggests that there were three broad and overlapping stages of Dewey's philosophical development. The first period (from 1882 to the 1903 publication of *Studies in Logical Theory*) marks the Hegelian influence. Although Dewey later rejected overtly Hegelian modes of thought, he retained a monistic ontology by attacking all dualistic distinctions such as mind-body, subject-object, thought-existence, and the like. Hegel's conception of Being as a unified whole of functionally interrelated components remained a leading principle in Dewey's lifelong crusade against all philosophies that proposed an ontological or epistemological bifurcation between the experiencing organism and its environment.

Dewey's antidualism made him entirely receptive to the incipient radical empiricism in James's *Principles* and, even more clearly, in James's article, "Does Consciousness Exist?" During this second period (from 1903 to the major work, *Experience and Nature*, in 1925), James's influence on Dewey operated in conjunction with Darwinism. Commentators on Dewey's life and philosophy invariably note that he was born in 1859, the same year as the publication of Darwin's *Origin of Species*. During the latter half of the nineteenth century, Darwinian ideas dominated American intellectual life in psychology, sociology, and philosophy. There was a tendency to generalize Darwin's theory into a general principle of the universe, especially in the natural and social sciences. Dewey accepted Darwin's idea of adaptation between organism and environment and, through his theory of inquiry, molded and expanded it into a completed philosophical account of thought, meaning, knowledge, truth, and science. His so-called "naturalism" was simply the wholesale extension of the biology of adaptation to every problem of philosophy (see Mills, 1964:360–61, 374). The culmination of the influence of James and Darwin is best captured in Dewey's *Logic: The Theory of Inquiry* (1938).

Bernstein identifies as the third stage of Dewey's development the period from 1925 until his death in 1952. During this period, according the Bernstein (1960:xix), Dewey "re-examines" and "critically analyzes" his position. Bernstein concludes that the common belief is not true that during his later years Dewey only said in a more elaborate way what he had been saying all along. If Bernstein means to say that Dewey made substantial alterations in his views, we must disagree. The core of Dewey's philosophy remained the biocentric theory of inquiry. Although Dewey's contact with Mead and his "re-discovery" of Peirce caused him at least to acknowledge the social context of thought and inquiry, this recognition was awkwardly tacked on to the old edifice rather than causing a restructuring of the whole system. Unlike Mead and Peirce, Dewey never viewed the social embeddedness of thought as more fundamental than the bioadaptive aspect. Therefore, the third stage of Dewey's philosophical career should be understood as depicted here rather than as a period in which he reexamined and modified his basic philosophy.

In summary, Dewey's philosophy is a collage. The theory of inquiry is the core from which the bulk of his philosophy emanates, but it is loosely conjoined with ideas taken from Peirce and Mead which, if pursued rigorously, would surely have overturned the whole Darwinian and Jamesian slant of his epistemology and philosophy of science.

Given the foregoing considerations, it would lie well beyond the scope of this chapter to present a critical examination of all of Dewey's major works. That task has never been attempted, and would surely require several lengthy volumes.[2] Accordingly, we confine our discussion of Dewey to two limited concerns. First, we show that there is a high degree of continuity between Dewey's theory of inquiry and James's radical empiricism, with the result that, with some modifications, Dewey's account of thought, knowledge, and truth is quite similar to James's. This analysis, in consequence, draws attention to the fundamental differences between Dewey and Mead. This is a radical thesis—argued more explicitly in chapter 5—in that all previous commentators on American pragmatism have minimized these differences. Our second purpose is to evaluate Dewey's philosophy, with special focus on its essentail nominalism. This, of course, is a continuation of our overall plan to trace realistic and nominalistic strains in the whole pragmatic movement—in philosophic and social thought—from Peirce to the Chicago School.

The Genesis and
Development of
Dewey's Theory of
Inquiry

The Hegelian period of Dewey's philosophical development lasted only about seven years and, as Ratner (1963:13) notes, the more general qualities of Hegel's philosophy which attracted Dewey's admiration were more salient in his subsequent development than were any specific elements he may have retained. The most important of these qualities was Hegel's idea that all Being is a unified whole. In an autobiographical skech, Dewey speculated that this desire for a holistic conception of the universe was probably prompted by his undergraduate study of Huxley (see Ratner, 1963:10). His study of physiology instilled in Dewey a fascination with the organic integration and unity of the human body, and he sought a philosophy in which all modes of Being are interrelated in a single whole containing no absolutely distinct ontological realms. Hegel's philosophy admirably satisfied this need. Hegel relentlessly attacked the traditional dualisms of mind / matter, mental / physical, subject / object, and every other distinction that challenged the absolute ontological unity of all Being. This ardent antidualism remained central to Dewey's philosophy throughout his life.

Dewey became disenchanted with Hegel, primarily because Hegelian modes of thought are not closely aligned with the method of the natural sciences. Dewey's desire to base logic and epistemology on the methodology of scientific inquiry (as he conceived it) was stimulated by his devotion to Darwinism. Dewey's imagination was so captured by the successes of Darwinian principles in biology that he came to believe that these principles were applicable to many processes including logic, knowledge, science, and thought in general. Dewey's 1910 essay, "The Influence of Darwin on Philosophy," reveals the impact of Darwin on Dewey's thought. Dewey contends that Darwin's work brought forth a "new kind" of logic to replace Aristotelian logic. The new "genetic" logic shifts emphasis from "wholesale essences" to "concrete purposes" (Dewey, 1973:38–39). The Greek world relied upon fixed categories and stable rules for logical deduction. By contrast, the Darwinian world is characterized by ever-evolving new forms and relations and, according to Dewey, therefore cannot be governed by permanent logical rules. What is required is a "logic" constructed from a study of the actual method we use to deliberately modify hostile elements of the environment.

These considerations go far toward explaining Dewey's excitement over James's *Principles of Psychology*. In a biography of Dewey's life (prepared from materials supplied by Dewey himself), his daughter Jane wrote, "William James' *Principles of Psychology* was much the greatest single influence in changing the direction of Dewey's philosophical thinking" (Mills, 1964:297). As we have seen, James's psychology satisfies two of Dewey's crucial demands. First, James's analysis of thought is essentially biological, in that thoughts are regarded as experi-

ences which function to "lead" toward other experiences which the organism intends. Second, James was moving away from dualism in asserting that thoughts and things are different functional aspects of the
same basic "stuff" (pure experience), rather than absolutely distinct
metaphysical orders.

Dewey, however, discarded some of James's attempted corollaries,
particularly the "will to believe" doctrine. In that respect, Dewey is closer
to Peirce's hard-nosed pragmatism. Esthetic satisfactions count nothing
toward validating a hypothesis; only the intended experimental consequences have any significance in rendering "truth" (Dewey, 1908:95).
Dewey also rejected James's category of knowledge by "acquaintance."
For Dewey, all knowleddge is generated by inquiry (Dewey, 1910:79).
Another point of discontent was that in the *Principles,* James never totally repudiated dualism—traces of the "ego" still remained, whereas in
"The Ego as Cause," Dewey (1894) criticized these lasting remnants of
dualism. In general, Dewey adopted James's radical empiricism, criticized
it where it faltered in its radicalism, and ignored or rejected the appended
religiously motivated modifications.

It is more difficult to assess Peirce's influence on Dewey. While Dewey
was a graduate student at Johns Hopkins in the early 1880s, he took
courses in logic from Peirce. However, he was still a doctrinaire Hegelian
at the time and, by his own admission, Peirce's lectures were of no great
influence. In a letter written in 1949, Dewey observed, "The influence of
Peirce upon me *was* late and was through James and his references to
Peirce" (Fain, 1949:app.). Obviously, the main Peircean contribution
was the doubt-belief theory of Peirce's early pragmatism. Possibly indirectly, it gave Dewey support his own all-embracing theory of inquiry.
But, as we shall show, Dewey's theory was designed more in accordance
with James's particularistic pragmatism than with Peirce's principles. It
was not until 1938 and thereafter that Dewey tried to link his philosophy
to Peirce's. Peirce's *Collected Papers* were not published until the 1930s
(about twenty years after his death). He became a fashionable topic in
philosophic circles, and Dewey himself was prompted to study the papers
of his old logic professor. Dewey was probably trying to anchor his
theory of inquiry to something or someone in the mainstream of philosophical thought. Peirce's early pragmatism, especially as presented in the
article "The Fixation of Belief," was the obvious candidate. This is particularly apropos, for, as we have seen, Peirce's early pragmatism at times
lapsed into the particularistic pragmatism.

The influence of Mead must be noted as well. Aside from Dewey's
(probable) desire to locate some clear historical antecedent for his theory

of inquiry, he was probably driven to a fresh study and appreciation of Peirce by the constant influence of Mead. Like Peirce, Mead emphasized the social foundation of thought and science. Although Jamesian radical empiricism remained the core of Dewey's theory, Dewey clearly admits to the presence of the social aspects of inquiry (as opposed to its purely biological function). This admission is evident in parts of *Nature and Experience* (1925) and *Logic: Theory of Inquiry* (1938), and attests to the influence of Peirce and Mead. It created conflicting tensions in Dewey's later writings which we analyze in a subsequent section.

In summary, Dewey's mature philosophy as presented, for example, in *Logic* (1938) reflects the various influences of Hegel, Darwin, James, Mead, and Peirce. Dewey never succeeded in integrating these diverse elements in his theory of inquiry. It is not that he did not have sufficient time or intellectual capacity; on the contrary, he had an abundance of both. Rather, the problem was a deep-rooted incommensurability between the James-Darwin biologistic philosophy (which is irremediably nominalistic) and the social realism of Peirce and Mead. Perhaps it was due to his Hegelian heritage that Dewey had a tolerance for asserting essentially incompatible ideas.

In the following section, we dissect Dewey's theory of inquiry into its component parts and propose a general assessment of the whole theory.[3]

The Structure of Dewey's Theory of Inquiry

It would be a mistake to say that the theory of inquiry is merely the core of Dewey's philosophy, because taken broadly, the theory of inquiry *is* Dewey's philosophy. His analysis of thought, meaning, knowledge, truth, and science are all derived from the theory of inquiry and would be virtually unintelligible if detached from the terms of the theory.

The theory of inquiry first blossomed in 1903 with the publication of *Studies in Logical Theory,* but the psychological foundation upon which the theory rests was developed in Dewey's famous 1896 article, "The Reflex Arc Concept in Psychology." The article clearly signifies Dewey's break with Hegel and his budding attachment to James. Indeed, as McDermott (1973:136) has indicated, James's *Principles* (1890) was the decisive factor in enabling Dewey to rid his thinking of the German tradition in psychology.

The central theme of the article is decidedly Jamesian. Dewey argues that the error of the "reflex arc" concept is that it erects a barrier between the "stimulus," which is regarded as wholly external, and the "response," which is considered to be wholly internal. Following James, Dewey contends that this is a fallacious distinction which came into psychology by the assumption of the mind-body dualism. The stimulus and response are not distinct; they are part of one coordinated whole. We do not passively and reflexively react to sensations that have a fixed and predetermined meaning: "What the sensation will be in particular at a given time, therefore, will depend entirely upon the way in which an activity is being used. It has no fixed quality of its own" (Dewey, 1973:146). How one constitutes any given stimulus will depend upon the immediately previous sequence of experiences insofar as they contribute to the interpretation given to present sensation. This interpretation makes the experience a stimulus, i.e., an object toward which one is prepared to act. Thus Dewey suggests that the stimulus-response relation is an organic circuit of functionally interrelated parts, not a reflex arc between two otherwise unrelated occurrences. Notice that Dewey's "circuit" is similar to James's "stream of consciousness," and that all dualistic distinctions are collapsed by the notion that those characteristics which common sense would attribute to independent and external realities are actually dependent upon the particular experiential context in which the stimulus is constituted. Hence, it makes no difference whether we prefer James's label of "pure experience," or follow Dewey's terminology by calling it the "organic circuit." The essential point is that Dewey's psychology, like James's, requires only one metaphysical category. The mental category (i.e., the "ego" of the idealists) is effectively eliminated, but Dewey is left with the same ontological predicament we found in James—namely, how is one to construe the remaining category? Does Dewey's psychology entail materialism? If not, how can it be avoided without falling back into some form of dualism?

To understand Dewey's answer to these questions, we must recognize that his psychology is not based on any philosophical, historical, or social principles. It is thoroughly biological. Piatt (1971:107) states, "Much of the difficulty in understanding Dewey would be obviated if more attention were paid to his naturalism and less to his empiricism." Given Dewey's enthusiasm for Darwinian "genetic" logic, probably, for Dewey, the most appealing aspect of James's psychology was the argument that thoughts are simply brain functions and therefore not substantially different from sensations and other "experiences."

For Dewey, the one metaphysical category is "nature."[4] Both mind and matter, the traditional metaphysical modes of being, are defined as parts of nature. Thus, "nature" was Deweys monistic, all-inclusive category of being, just as "pure experience" was the sole category of James's metaphysics. Hence, "nature" has the same function in Dewey's philosophy as "pure experience" has in James's—both concepts serve as monistic metaphysical categories. It must be recalled that Dewey uses the Darwinian biologistic conception of reality as a means to refute all dualistic metaphysical systems. Human beings are part of the natural world; therefore all human activity, including the use of intelligence, is also part of nature. For Dewey, "thought" is a process that occurs within nature rather than an inexplicable and transcendental mode of Being which somehow subsists independently. Naturalistic metaphysics views reflective intelligence as a biological function by which organisms adapt to environmental hazards. As threats arise, either the organism's biological structure must change to meet environmental demands, or the organism must change the environment to suit its requirements. The latter adaptive response requires the application of intelligent reflection in order to successfully modify the environment in accord with some end-in-view. The whole history of human technology is a record of human efforts to further modify the environment to satisfy human desires. Dewey's point is that when humans are faced with a problematic environmental situation, they employ reflective intelligence in order to hit upon a hypothesis which, if applicable, will lead to an environmental modification which solves the problem. Dewey's whole "logic" (theory of inquiry) is merely an elaborate specification of the stages of this adaptive process. What Dewey calls the "biological and evolutionary attitude" consists in "looking at mind as fundmentally an instrument of adaptation" (1963:310).

Let us now present Dewey's theory of inquiry in somewhat more detail. Dewey (1938:104–5) defines "inquiry" as "the controlled or directed transformation of an indeterminate situation into one that is so determinate in its constituent distinctions and relations as to convert the elements of the original situation into a unified whole." Our first task must be to clarify the terms of the definition. Dewey (1938:66) tells us that a "situation" is a "contextual whole"; a situation exists when there is at least enough coherence among one's surrounding experiences that they can be grasped as a singular environmental field of interrelated elements. Hence, there is no "situation" if one is in a totally delirious state because, under that condition, the sequence of experiences is completely disjointed and thus does not constitute an integrated experiential field. In short, we are not in touch with a situation unless, to some minimal degree, we have command of our experiential "bearings." This is fairly commonsensical.

The meaning of "indeterminate situation" is more problematic. The situation is indeterminate if its constituent existential elements do not "hang together" (Dewey, 1938:105); the situation is "disturbed, troubled, ambiguous, confused, full of conflicting tendencies, obscure, etc." Dewey emphatically insists that it is the situation *itself* that has these qualities: "*We* are doubtful because the situation is inherently doubtful" (1938:105–6). MacKay (1942:142) understandably questions the sense in which psychological states (confusion, doubt, etc.) can be attributed to existential conditions. Existential realities cannot help but "hang together" spatiotemporally. The only possible sense in calling any of them inherently indeterminate is with respect to their future relations. Imagine an egg precariously teetering on a narrow ledge. Existentially, the situation is as determinate as any other existential situation. *It simply is what it is.* The only thing about it that, by any stretch of ordinary language, might be called "indeterminate" is whether it will remain on the ledge at the next instant and, if not, in which direction it will fall. If we accept Peirce's thesis that chance is an operative force in the universe, something may be gained by calling such existential situations inherently indeterminate in the sense explained. But Dewey's theory requires a different type of indeterminacy. For him, the situation necessarily agitates the organism into seeking some definite resolution of the matter, because the indterminate situation involves a disturbing "inbalance in organic-environmental interactions." Dewey's favorite example of an indeterminate situation (because it comes closest to meeting the specified condition) is the state of hunger. Hunger is an objective existential organic-evironmental relation. The problem exists in the environment-organism relation and waits for the organism to identify and define it. A problem is not a task to be performed that people put upon themselves or that is placed upon them by others—like a so-called arithmetical "problem" in school work (Dewey, 1938:108).

Dewey fails to see that no situation, even imminent death, is intrinsically problematic to anyone. To take Dewey's example of hunger, there is nothing problematic about hunger if one is fasting or dieting. The only problem is that of keeping the situation "indeterminate." Problems exist only when there is some concern over the outcome of events; otherwise, no matter how uncertain the situation, it will be regarded with total indifference, and no effort will be made to anticipate or control the possible outcomes. Moreover, concern over outcomes exists only where some value is involved; that is, where one outcome is valued over others. Unless one adopts animism, one will admit that the brute physical elements have (1) no values, thus (2) no concerns, and therefore (3) cannot embody any self-contained problems. Dewey is wrong when he says that people do not place problems upon themselves. Of course, there is a distinction between the "problem" of a paranoiac who merely thinks someone is chasing him with an ax and the problem of a person really in that situation. Dewey denies that the first situation is indeterminate because, as described above, the indeterminacy must be *in* the organic-environmental situation but, in this case, the existential environment is entirely determinate. There can be no genuine problem.

The second case seems to be one of the strongest possible examples favoring Dewey's thesis. Yet, upon careful examination, it is evident that the situation is not inherently indeterminate. For instance, consider the case in which the person being chased is leading the ax murderer into a predetermined trap. The plans were carefully designed in every detail, and the execution is as determinate as brushing one's teeth. There is nothing doubtful or confused about the situation. A situation cannot be confused and doubtful, only people can. And a problem is always someone's problem; there are no problems inherently planted in any situation. Finally, people do place problems on themselves, in that no existential situation poses a problem unless it is related to someone's desires. This fact is illustrated by the above examples. Dewey would not have made this mistake if he had read James's *Principles* more carefully. James (1950a:311) wrote:

> Everything added to the Self is a burden as well as a pride. A certain man who lost every penny during our civil war went and actually rolled in the dust, saying he had not felt so free and happy since he was born. . . . Neither threats nor pleadings can move a man unless they touch some one of his potential or actual selves.

Dewey adopted Peirce's doubt-belief matrix, but elected to locate doubt in the situation itself rather than in the mind of a doubter. We have revealed the fallacy of this movement. But it will clarify our later discussion of the theory if we digress from explicating the terms of Dewey's definition of inquiry, and examine Dewey's reason for taking this ostensibly bizarre position.

Dewey actually adhered more faithfully to James's "radical empiricism" than did James himself (cf. Geiger, 1958:160). For James, the idea of "self" is an experience that appears in the stream of thought just as do other experiences. But Dewey was anxious to avoid any hint of what he saw as "subjectivism" in the admission of self-awareness. Intellectual activity is a biological adaptive function—nothing more. From the purely Darwinian attitude, the only difference between a human being and a protozoan is that the human has a far more sophisticated coping mechanism. But, according to Dewey's logic, the difference can be explained in totally biological terms without requiring recourse to the "self," "ego," or any other mentalistic notion. To allow such concepts in one's theory can only lead to the metaphysical puzzles of traditional dualistic ontologies. But once the "self" (or some equivalent term) is denied, Dewey cannot intelligibly ascribe psychological states (doubt, uncertainty, confusion, etc.) to the organism if only a self-conscious life-form is capable of experiencing such states. As a result, the only way Dewey could retain any semblance of the Peircean doubt-belief theory of inquiry, and still avoid the mentalistic (for Dewey, "subjectivistic") implications of holding that the *organism* is in a state of doubt, was to contend that the existential situation is itself inherently doubtful and confused. It is our position, stated in later sections, that Dewey's erroneous conception of the indeterminate situation set up a condition for "truth" and "knowledge" that is thoroughly nominalistic.

Besides the "indeterminate situation," other key terms in Dewey's definition of inquiry should be explained further. The obverse of the indeterminate situation is, of course, the determinate situation or "unified whole." It is an organism-environmental situation in which the organism is "in tune" with its environment. That is, the organism is proceeding with a course of behavior which is not being blocked, threatened, or otherwise disrupted by its environment. For example, consider a cow routinely grazing in its pasture. Nothing unusual is happening and, so far as the cow is concerned, it is just a typical day. The contented cow and its environment are in the state of balanced equilibrium Dewey calls a "determinate" situation.

Having defined "determinate" and "indeterminate," we must now examine what Dewey means by a "controlled transformation." First, let us consider the term "transformation." Note that it is the *situation* that inquiry transforms and not the emotive or psychological state of the organism. This observation is consistent with the definition of "indeterminate," in that, if the source of indeterminacy lies in the existential situation, the indeterminacy cannot be removed unless the situation is transformed. Relieving the organism's anxiety by drugs or other methods only masks the problem and therefore does not produce a determinate situation. This again reveals Dewey's determination to have a nonsubjectivist theory of inquiry. The mental state of a subject is neither the source of doubt and indeterminacy nor the locus of the transformation from indeterminacy to determinacy.

But not all transformations qualify as inquiry. It must be a controlled transformation. By this, Dewey means that the situation is transformed by action predicated on some hypothesis which intelligent reflection suggests as a plausible means of resolving the indeterminacy. Thus, a perfectly random trial-and-error solution, because it is not controlled, does not qualify as inquiry even though the requisite transformation is achieved.

To repeat the definition, inquiry is the controlled transformation of an indeterminate situation to a determinate situation. Now that we understand the terms of the definition, let us consider the basic stages or components of the transformation. The first stage is the identification of the situation as "problematic." There is no chance of controlled transformation unless the indeterminate situation is recognized as such. This initial stage might be followed by some intermediate stages in which the problem is brought into sharper focus. For example, if one has an upset stomach, it is clearly important that the problem be accurately clarified (i.e., identified as indigestion, flu, etc.), because different problems require different solutions. Once the problem is delineated, one formulates possible alternatives for meeting the problem and logically deduces their experimental implications. One then selects the hypothesis that, on the balance of the evidence, seems most plausible. Then, the hypothesis is tested experimentally and, if verified, the transformation of the situation is completed.

This description is sufficiently general so that every type of intelligent behavior—ranging from the solution of everyday problems to experimental physics—is an instance of "inquiry." If Dewey's functional / biological theory of mind is to enjoy *prima facie* validity, it must apply to every instance of thought. Although Dewey's theory appears to meet this condition, it does so with considerable strain and with violence to our basic assumptions of logic, knowledge, and truth. These conceptions are subsidiary consequences of James's functional psychology, which Dewey adopted as the basis of his theory of inquiry. Therefore, in criticizing these arguments, we are only indirectly evaluating Dewey's core theory. The core theory is itself amenable to direct refutation, but we shall not dwell on its weaknesses here because it was Dewey's corollary position on the nature of knowledge and truth that became most popularized and influential. Suffice it here to note that Dewey's psychological presuppositions are entirely too unidimensional. Biological adaptation is only one of many incentives to thought, and not all thought is adaptive (e.g., daydreaming during an examination). Similarly, most people want a certain degree of indeterminacy in the environment. A long-lasting determinate situation is a sure road to boredom. This again takes us back to the important point that people do create their own problems, and thrive on them. Dewey's logic lacks an adequate theory of motivation—something it desperately needs; otherwise, there are no grounds to explain why some indeterminacies are defined as "problematic" whereas others are not, or why one solution is deliberately preferred over another even though they are equally effective in rendering the situation determinate. There is a plethora of such objections pointing to the serious defects of this Darwinian approach to psychology (see Nissen, 1966). For our purposes, however, the logical and epistemological consequences of Dewey's theory of inquiry are more crucial than the insufficiencies of the theory's psychological base; therefore, we shall examine those matters without further delay.

Dewey's Critique of Aristotelian Logic

To most people, including philosophers, the word "logic" denotes the study of criteria of validity in inferences and demonstrations. In other words, it is the study of the general rules by which one may validly pass from premises to conclusions in a formal argument. Following Peirce (2.589), we might call these general rules of inference the "leading principles" of the argument. Peirce notes that two persons might reach the same conclusion from the same premises, while using different leading principles. Thus, in an isolated case, one may reach a true conclusion from true premises by a leading principle which, if applied to all possible cases, would lead to false conclusions more often than not. We cannot confidently judge the validity of a logical rule on the basis of the outcome of a single application. For Peirce, a valid leading principle of inference would—in the long run—usually lead to reaching true conclusions from true premises. One's reasoning is good only if the leading principle is valid; thus, valid reasoning is, for Peirce, a matter of *method,* not the particular outcome of a specific instance.

Unless we are trained logicians, we usually are not aware of the leading principles which underlie most of our inferences. One can ferret out the leading principle of a species of valid inferences by a process of abstraction. This involves removing the specific content from the premises and conclusion, and replacing it with symbolic expressions. This allows us to see the basic form common to all such inferences, and we can thereby formulate the general leading principle of the inference. Aristotelian logic is essentially concerned with deriving these universal rules of inference.

The value of knowing leading principles rather than merely using them unknowingly and inconsistently is that, given a set of premises, a skilled logician can more systematically and accurately determine what conclusions are (and are not) warranted. This, then, is briefly the general nature and purpose of Aristotelian logic.

Dewey seems to take an extremely radical sociology of knowledge standpoint in his criticism of Aristotelian logic. His position is that Aristotelian logic was admirably suited to Greek culture, in that the Greek cosmology pictures the universe as fixed formal relations: "As a *historic* document it deserves the admiration it has received. . . . What has been said is a criticism of the effort to maintain that logic . . . as adequate or even relevant to the science of today" (Dewey, 1838:94). The science of "today" is, of course, Darwinism applied to every scientific field. Accordingly, everything is viewed as process and change. From Dewey's perspective, fixed and formal logical principles have no force in a Darwinian world-view; what is needed is the "new" logic which has no permanent laws.

To understand the "genetic" logic, one must, to borrow a Jamesian quip, "dissolve one's intellect into a kind of mush." No proposition is simply true or false in isolation. That would be too Aristotelian. The proposition is true or false relative to the outcome of its application to particular problems in specific situations, and nothing can be said of its truth-status in general (cf. Geiger, 1958:99). Dewey's contextualized "logic" infuriated Peirce, who was a pioneer in formal mathematical logic. In a letter to Dewey, Peirce (8.241) remarked, "I find the whole volume [*Studies in Logical Theory*] penetrated with this spirit of intellectual licentiousness, that does not see that anything is so very false."

Let us consider what lies at the heart of Dewey's criticism of traditional logic.[5] Charitably, let us grant that Dewey did not seriously mean that Aristotelian logic is *merely* an historical document expressing no transhistorical truth. The laws of identity, excluded middle, bifurcation, *modus ponens,* and the like, are as valid today as they were in 400 B.C. We will therefore assume that Dewey's position is not based upon some type of incredibly misguided radical historicism. We also do not take seriously Dewey's assertion that logic is irrelevant to modern science. There is, nevertheless, a kernel of truth in the claim that modern science rests on a different cosmological base than did Greek science. Whereas Greek science presupposed absolute determinism, modern physics does assume tychism (chance), but still deals with constancies, some of which are statistically based. The point is that quantum mechanics and genetics have not forced modern science to discard fundamental logical principles. It is still true that if A entails B, and A is given, then B may be inferred even if A and B are both probability functions theoretically applicable to some class of phenomena. Thus, indeterminacy can be a property of a system without destroying basic logic's applicability to that system. This is true in physics, genetics, sociology, and all modern sciences that admit the reality of genuine indeterminacy in their subject matter. There is absolutely no force in the argument that modern science is so radically different from Greek science that it requires a new set of rules of logical procedure.

But our view is that the sociology of knowledge and the demands of modern science actually are not central to Dewey's position. Instead, his arguments against logic are rooted in his functional psychology. If one adopts the axiom that all thought (a word Dewey scrupulously avoided) is to subserve in transforming an indeterminate situation into a determinate situation, then any reflective activity which does not aim to transform a situation is, by this axiom, intellectualist babble. Now it is clear that the study of symbolic logic is divorced from concrete temporal situations. A man sitting in a chair attempting to resolve some problem of symbolic logic is not in an indeterminate situation because there is nothing "doubtful" about his existential environment. By Dewey's definitions, he has no genuine problem because he has placed the "problem" on himself rather than constituting the problem out of an indeterminate environment. Moreover, when he "solves" his problem, there will be no transformation of the situation (excepting internal changes which Dewey discounts as solutions). No problems exist in the mind; they all exist in the relationship of the organism to its environment. It follows that no one ever solves a problem by thinking about it. Thought can suggest hypotheses, but physical action is required to transform a situation, and no real problem is resolved unless some physical situation is transformed (Dewey, 1938:117–18).

Dewey's philosophy is an action philosophy. He concurred with the Marxian attitude that the purpose of philosophy, and all thought for that matter, is to transform the world, not to interpret it. For example, the following passage is typical of Dewey's formulations in *Logic* concerning the role of universal principles in inquiry: "No amount of reasoning can do more than develop a universal proposition; it cannot, of itself, determine matters-of-fact. Only operational application can effect the latter determination." For our purposes, the key part of the passage is the assertion that no amount of reasoning can determine matters of fact. There are at least two possible meanings of "determine" in this context.

First, one can determine what the facts *are;* that is, learn what is the case. Second, one can determine facts by altering the physical environment; for example, make it a fact that a book is on the table. It is true that reasoning cannot determine facts in this second sense; this is evidently what Dewey meant, because he speaks of *operations* determining facts. This shows that, for Dewey, the ultimate aim of inquiry is not to discover what the facts are, but rather, to transform the world to produce a new set of more "determinate" facts.[6]

Insofar as the study of formal logic has no existential content, Dewey had no use for it. The universal propositions which have force for Deweyan inquiry are replete with confirmed existential content, and thus suggest means of transforming the environment. Every inquiry generates its own rules, and they are tailored to the situation at hand. The validity of the principles is judged according to whether actions based upon them produce the required transformation of the situation. Dewey's "logic" is not abstracted from all specific contents; on the contrary, it emerges and is confirmed within the borders of particular inquiries. We are not the first to call attention to this characteristic. For example, Kaufmann (1959:834) wrote: "Dewey states that the rules of inquiry originate within inquiry and that their retention depends upon their success. But here again we must bear in mind that the logician is not concerned with the process of inquiry *qua* temporal, but only with its formal structure; that is, with different types of methodological terms and canons and their interrelations." Feibleman (1946:87) similarly noted that once it is held that "there is no logic operative in the world apart from the intentions and actions of human beings," it follows that "there can be no guide to inquiry in the sense of a valid principle lying outside of inquiry."

It is precisely Feibleman's point that most sharply distinguishes Dewey's "genetic" logic from Peirce's studies. Dewey repeatedly claimed to be following Peirce,[7] and some recent commentators on American pragmatism (e.g., Morris, 1970) also seem to perceive no basic difference between Dewey and Peirce. Yet Peirce (8.243) once wrote to Dewey, "Your *Studies in Logical Theory* certainly forbids all such researchers as those which I have been absorbed in for the last eighteen years." Morris (1970:58) claims that Peirce's complaints against Dewey are "groundless." Morris argues that because Dewey's "inquiry" employs logical inference at some stage of the process, this confirms that Dewey approved of formal logic (Peirce's "critical logic") as a legitimate and productive enterprise. Dewey's polemic against Aristotelian logic testifies otherwise, to say nothing of the fatuity of Morris's own logic in this case.

In summary, one could accurately say that Dewey took Peirce's "Fixa-

tion of Belief" and transformed it into the "Fixation of the Situation."
Even further, Dewey judged the fixation of the situation to be the whole
purpose of all reasoning and scientific investigation. As we have argued
throughout this section, Dewey's single-minded emphasis on reducing all
logic to his conception of "inquiry" is a consequence of his biologistic
functional psychology derived from James and Darwin. Notwithstanding
Dewey's disclaimers to the contrary, all purely intellectual values drop
from sight if his theory is pressed to its ultimate conclusions. This is no
clearer than in the case of knowledge. Dewey's theory precludes one from
responding, "Because I just want to know" to the question, "Why are
you doing this investigation?" That answer would not be sufficiently
genetic. Yet this is precisely the answer he would receive from most
scientists engaged in basic research if he kept asking them why they are
studying one phenomenon rather than another. Dewey had no conception of knowledge except as a hypothesis that successfully transforms an
indeterminate situation in some particular instance. Thus, it is our contention in the following section that Dewey's theory of knowledge, like
logic, is a derivative of his psychological premises.

Dewey's View of
Knowledge and Truth

Dewey's essay, "The Experimental Theory of Knowledge," succinctly
expresses his basic epistemology. As the title indicates, Dewey regarded
all knowledge as produced within an experimental setting. He thus
shared James's opposition to the so-called "transendentalist" theory of
knowledge. The distinguishing feature of the experimentalist epistemology is that "knowledge" is construed as a relationship between an "organic anticipation" (Geiger, 1958:67) and some actual experience.

The traditional conception of knowledge is much broader. It generally
defines knowledge as "justified true belief," and conforms closely to
ordinary usage. Each of these three factors—justification, truth, and
belief—are part of our commonsense understanding of the meaning of
the term "knowledge." First, in ordinary language, it would be senseless
to say that one knows something but yet does not believe it to be truth.
Second, one cannot know that which is not true. Finally, although true
belief is a necessary condition of knowledge, common usage of the term
suggests that it is not quite a sufficient condition. The belief must be
substantiated—justified by adequate evidence. For example, if one has a
strong hunch that the die will turn up six and it does, we would refuse to
say that he *knew* it would be a six. Since he had no good reasons for the

prediction, we say that he was simply guessing and hence did not really *know* before the fact. Historically, epistemologists have generally agreed that knowledge is justified true belief, and most of the dissension has centered around the degree of justification required.

A new epistemological vocabulary entered with James and Dewey. For Dewey, knowledge is not a propositional formula; it is a relation between experiences in the Jamesian stream. Indeed, there is no essential difference between Dewey's conception of knowledge and James's notion of "knowledge about." Consider, for example, Dewey's (1910:90) general definition of knowledge:

> An experience is a knowledge, if in its quale there is an experienced distinction and connection of two elements of the following sort; one means or intends the presence of the other in the same fashion in which itself is already present, while the other is that which, while not present in the same fashion must become so present if the meaning or intention of its companion or yoke-fellow is to be fulfilled through the operation it sets up.

This definition embodies James's idea of one experience in the stream of thought "leading up to" another experience it organically anticipates. As an example, Dewey cites the relation between a rose and its smell. The smell of rose intends or anticipates the occurrence of other rose qualities (the sight of the plant, the feel of its petals, etc.). The smell knows the rose if the anticipated experiences eventuate. As Dewey (1910:106) states, "The function of knowing is always expressed in connections between a given experience and a specific possible wanted experience."

This is a purely nominalistic epistemology. Knowledge is never more than a connection between some given experience and some other specific experience. There is no element of generality in Dewey's formula, a consequence of Dewey's idea that knowledge is experiential, not propositional. According to Dewey, the aim of inquiry is *not* to know the truth or falsity of any proposition (see Thayer, 1968:197–98). If such were its purpose, it would have a very broad objective, insofar as all propositions embody universals. But such a generalized interest would lead our concern well beyond the specific issue of the indeterminate situation at hand. This result would be inconsistent with Dewey's theory of inquiry. From the biologistic-adaptive standpoint (which is always Dewey's), what is required is a solution to this immediate situation; consequently, the aim of inquiry and criterion of knowledge is the successful transformation of the indeterminate situation. In the example of the rose, the smell functions as a hypothesis which suggests the presence of a rose, and the validity of the "hypothesis" depends upon the consequences of acting upon it. The necessary condition for validity is that "these consequences are operationally instituted and are such as to resolve the *specific* problem evoking the operation" (emphasis added) (Dewey, 1938:iv). This is why the confirmation of propositions is not the goal of inquiry. The verbal formula is only an instrumental guide to the situational transformation. What is known is the experiential connection, and *not* propositional representations. Dewey (1941:176) stated:

> Upon my view "propositions are *not* that about which we are inquiring," and that as far as we do find it necessary or advisable to inquire about them (as is almost bound to happen in the course of an inquiry), it is not their truth and falsity about which we inquire, but the relevancy and efficacy of their subject matter with respect to the problem at hand.

Once this is recognized, one can understand why Dewey held that knowing alters what is known:

> Speaking from this point of view, the decisive consideration as between instrumentalism and analytic realism is whether the operation of experimentation is or is not necessary to knowledge. The instrumental theory holds that it is; analytic realism holds that even though it were essential in *getting* knowledge (or in learning), it has nothing to do with the known object; that is makes a change only in the knower, not in what is to be known. [Dewey, 1903:32]

Geiger (1958:82), a disciple of Dewey, asserted that if the claim is made that what was discovered was there all the time and that nothing has really changed except the mind and knowledge of the observer, then the fact has been forgotten that the object of knowledge is the result of inquiry. Hook (1939:97), another Dewey follower, similarly declared, "An experiment always involves a modification or reordering, of a literally physical kind, of the elements which allows the termination of inquiry when that which it intends is experimentally verified."

Critics of Dewey's epistemology have rightfully attacked his contention that what is known is changed by the inquiry by which it is known, but most have done so for the wrong reason. For example, Murphy (1971:203) observes that "knowledge" is ordinarily understood to mean true belief "based on adequate evidence or arrived at by a method which leads reliably to true conclusions," and he notes that there is no equivalent of this conception of knowledge anywhere in Dewey's theory of inquiry. This fact is not at all surprising given that Dewey's theory has no interest in propositional knowledge. As Dewey stated, "That which satisfactorily terminates inquiry is, by definition, knowledge." We know that only a physical transformation of an indeterminate situation into a determinate situation can satisfactorily conclude inquiry. Now, a mere proposition cannot transform a situation; therefore, knowledge does not consist of propositions. Thus, if Dewey's theory is to be criticized, that criticism should deal with the theory on its conceptual level rather than beg the question by pointing out that the theory precludes a conception of knowledge which, in fact, it was designed to preclude.

Let us consider a simple example. Our favorite clock is broken. We "inquire" into this indeterminate situation by disassembling the clock and inspecting the mechanism. We find that a gear has slipped out of position and, when we put it in place, the clock functions normally. If the purpose of the inquiry were simply to discover the cause of the malfunction, the inquiry would stop when we found the misplace gear and saw that the other parts were in proper order. On the other hand, if our purpose is to fix the clock, then inquiry is terminated when the necessary repairs are effected. In the first case, inquiry is terminated by an intellectual apprehension (and is therefore propositional), but in the second case, inquiry is terminated by the situational transformation (and is therefore a physical action).

From this example, it is clear why Dewey asserted that the object of knowledge (i.e., the transformation) is created by inquiry, rather than existing antecedent to inquiry. This thesis is also argued at considerable length in *The Quest for Certainty*. In a typical passage, Dewey (1929:205) states:

> If we persist in the traditional conception, according to which the thing to be known is something which exists prior to and wholly apart from the act of knowing, then discovery of the fact that the act of observation, necessary in existential knowing, modified that pre-existent something, is proof that the act of knowing is a form of doing and is to be judged like other modes by its eventual issue, this tragic conclusion is not forced upon us.

From such statements, one might infer that Dewey believed nothing exists prior to inquiry. This is the conclusion drawn by Feibleman (1946:88), Murphy (1971:203), and other critics of Dewey. Although this interpretation is invited by some of Dewey's statements taken in isolation, it is not warranted by the theory as a whole. Certainly the indeterminate situation exists prior to inquiry, and it has real existential being. We must distinguish between what Dewey called the "subject matter" of knowledge and the "object of knowledge" (Dewey,

1938:105 *ff.*). The subject-matter is the original indeterminate situation on which inquiry operates. The object of knowledge is the final remodeling of the situation. In the clock example, the subject-matter was the broken clock and the object of knowledge was the activity that fixed the clock. In this context it may be intelligibly said that the subject-matter of knowledge is changed by inquiry and that the object of knowledge is the product of inquiry.

Dewey's theory of truth is closely allied to his theory of knowledge. For Dewey, an idea is true if and only if it *is* verified. By "idea," Dewey meant a plan for action—a hypothesis to be tested (Hook, 1939:75). The idea, or plan, must be actually verified in order to be true; it is not sufficient that it be verifiable in principle. Dewey (1910:140–41) employed the following example: One hears a noise in the street, and the noise suggests as its meaning a streetcar. The suggestion might be verbalized, "That was the sound of a streetcar passing by." In order to verify the idea, the person goes to the window to intently look and listen. Dewey explains:

> I hear a noise in the street. It suggests as its meaning a street-car. To
> test this idea I go to the window and through listening and looking
> intently. . . . an idea is made true; that which was a proposal or
> hypothesis is no longer merely a propounding or a guess. If I had not
> reacted in a way appropriate to the idea it would have remained a
> mere idea, at most a candidate for truth that, unless acted upon upon
> the spot, would always have remained a theory.

Dewey equates knowledge and truth (see Lorenz, 1961:22). If an idea is "known" (by the Deweyan conception of knowledge discussed above), it is by definition true, and vice versa. There is little chance of misinterpretation on this point because, on other occasions, Dewey explicitly equates knowledge and truth (see, for example, Dewey, 1938:7). In *Logic*, Dewey used the expression "warranted assertability" as a double-duty surrogate for both terms (Dewey, 1938:9*f*, 546). In a separate essay, Dewey (1910:107) stated, "The operation either gives or fails to give the object meant. Hence the truth or falsity of the original cognitional object."

From the above statements, it is apparent that truth is bound to the outcome of some specific operations on some specific occasion. Hook (1939:79) saw this consequence, and justified it thusly: "Actually, however, all the consequences of an idea do not have to be verified before we can call the idea 'true.' If we take into account the problematic context in which the idea arises, then we can see that only those consequences are relevant which bear upon the resolution of the difficulty." Dewey

(1910:150) made essentially the same claim: "The aim of the predicate is not to bunch all possible meaning and refer it in one final act indiscriminately to all existence, but to state the standpoint and method through which the difficulty of the particular situation may most effectively be dealt with."

Like James before him, Dewey did not consistently hold to this particularistic pragmatism. As mentioned earlier, Dewey's *Logic* attempted to link his theory to Peirce's philosophy. For example, Dewey stated, "All special conclusions of special inquiries are parts of an enterprise that is continually renewed, or is a going concern." And, "The best definition of *truth* from the logical standpoint which is known to me is that of Peirce. . . . 'Truth is that concordance of an abstract statement with the ideal limit towards which endless investigation would tend to bring scientific belief'" (Dewey, 1938:345n). It scarcely needs to be argued that Peirce's definition of truth is inconsistent with the idea that truth is any hypothesis "verified" by transforming a specific problematic situation into a determinate situation when the operations indicated by the hypothesis are experimentally implemented. Yet this latter conception of truth and knowledge is the very core of Dewey's theory, and it is the position he urged almost constantly. Hence, the fact that on a few occasions he made Peircean statements and paid tribute to Peirce should not lead us to believe that Dewey's theory of inquiry is essentially in harmony with Peirce's.

We have already shown that Peirce had no sympathy for Dewey's logic. He was equally scornful of Dewey's epistemology and theory of truth. About 1906 (three years after the publication of Dewey's *Studies in Logical Theory*), Peirce (5.555) sarcastically wrote, "It appears that there are certain mummified pedants who have never waked to the truth that the act of knowing a real object alters it. They are curious specimens of humanity, and as I am one of them, it may be amusing to see how I think." It is interesting that in the same article from which Dewey quoted Peirce's definition of truth, Peirce (5.569) also wrote, "To say that a proposition is true is to say that every interpretation of it is true." This is a consequence of Peirce's theory of signs, for the logical interpretant of a propositional sign is the infinite set of counterfactual propositions it predicts. Accordingly, its meaning is not confirmed unless all of its practical consequences are verifiable. Consequently, "A true proposition is a proposition belief which would *never* lead to such disappointment [i.e., contrary perceptual judgment] so long as the proposition is not understood otherwise than it was intended" (emphasis added). From this, it is clear that Peirce would never equate truth or knowledge with the solutions of specific indeterminate situations, because a hypothesis which might happen to "work" in one situation might fail on all similar future occasions, and vice versa.

It is easy to imagine concrete examples of such conditions. For instance, suppose that Jones is searching for his friend Smith. He sees a coat that looks exactly like Smith's hanging outside a door. He naturally thinks, "That's Smith's coat." This idea leads him to look inside that room for Smith and, indeed, Smith happens to be there. The idea, according to Dewey, has been made true by satisfactorily leading to Smith. Let us further suppose that someone who has a coat exactly like Smith's in all apparent respects had accidentally taken Smith's coat, leaving his own behind (which Jones saw and mistakenly identified as Smith's). When Smith leaves the building with Jones, he naturally thinks that the coat is his, and the error is not discovered.

In this example, what should be said about Jones's idea, "That's Smith's coat"? First, it should be observed that the fact that it is not Smith's coat does not, in Dewey's view, make false the idea that it is his coat. The truth or falsity of the idea depends solely upon whether the experimental consequences intended by the idea in relation to the specific "problem at hand" are actually verified in experience. It was this thoroughly particularistic aspect of Dewey's notion of truth and inquiry that prompted Bertrand Russell, one of Dewey's most fervent antagonists on the question of truth, to comment, "The only essential result of successful inquiry [in Dewey] is successful action" (Dewey, 1941:181). As a result, Dewey's definition of truth is a "power perspective," in that, if short-term consequences are the criteria of the truth or satisfactoriness of an idea, then a person or persons with some vested interest in promoting an idea can, if they command sufficient sociopolitical power, engineer an environment in which that idea is true, i.e., its intended consequences are actualized (cf. Huber, 1973; Thayer, 1968:202).

Possibly the clearest indication of the fundamental difference between the purpose and direction of Dewey's theory of inquiry, truth, and knowledge in contrast to Peirce's was Dewey's usual emphasis on immediate problem-at-hand consequences as opposed to Peirce's concern with the indefinitely extended, long-range scientific results. This reflects the focus of Dewey's theory of inquiry on bioadaptive control of contextually specific problematic situations in contrast to Peirce's stress on inquiry as a means of inexorably leading the scientific community closer and closer to scientifically incontrovertible beliefs. Notwithstanding Russell's (1971:144–45) uninformed objections to Peirce's definition of truth,[8] it is decidedly not a power perspective. On the contrary, Peirce was keenly aware that a future-oriented theory of truth could fall into subjectivism if it rests upon short-run consequences. This concern is illustrated in the following passage in which Peirce (5.565) specifically mentions the possibility of political manipulation of conditions and beliefs:

> The truth of the proposition that Caesar crossed the Rubicon consists in the fact that the further we push our archaeological and other studies, the more strongly will that conclusion force itself on our minds forever—or would do so, if study were to go on forever. An idealist metaphysician may hold that therein also lies the whole *reality* behind the proposition, for though men may for a time persuade themselves that Caesar did *not* cross the Rubicon, and may contrive to render this belief universal for any number of generations, yet ultimately research—if it be persisted in—must bring back the contrary belief.

Thus far, we have concentrated upon differences between the Deweyan and Peircean conception of inquiry, but the above passage also accentuates their different assumed inquirers. For Peirce, the inquirer is the scientific community—not merely the present scientific community, but the scientific community extended indefinitely into the future. But for Dewey, the inquirer is an individual. This difference is a consequence of Peirce's social theory of mind in contrast to Dewey's Jamesian biologistic psychology, or radical empiricism. Dewey's essential individualism is further clarified in the following section.

Dewey's Social Philosophy

Describing Dewey's *Logic,* Felix Kaufman (1967:230) wrote, "It is like a witch's mirror in which every man may see his sweetheart—or the devil." It might be added that it is even possible to see one's sweetheart on one page, only to find the devil waiting on the next! It is truly a book that can both delight and disgust nearly any philosophical temperament. Taken *in toto,* Dewey's works have the same effect; hence, in that respect, *Logic* is quite representative.

We have analyzed the psychological and biological core of Dewey's theory of inquiry. But no assessment of the theory is entirely adequate without also considering what Dewey regarded as the cultural context of inquiry. And this is where the witch's mirror enters. In the previous sections, we have argued that the theory of inquiry is based upon the functional psychology which, in turn, is based upon James's radical empiricism—with its reduction of thought to biology. James's psychology evinces precious little interest in social realities. He did include a discussion of the "social self," but he was no social theorist. Although James's psychology formed the foundation for Dewey's philosophy, the influence of Mead and, later, Peirce should not be ignored. Particularly in the period after 1920, there is obvious evidence of Dewey's desire to more deliberately incorporate the sociocultural aspects of the environment into the theory of inquiry. This is especially apparent in two of his major works of the 1920s—*Human Nature and Conduct* (1922) and *Experience and Nature* (1925). His concern with the "cultural matrix" of inquiry is continued in his later works, including *Logic,* and he wrote numerous nontechnical articles dealing with the pressing social and political issues of his times.

But educational reform was undoubtedly Dewey's most constant social concern because he saw the educational institution as a salient factor in enhancing the development of intellectual potential. He desired an educational institution that would maximize democracy and individual freedom, thus allowing free exploration of alternative solutions to social and scientific problems. Only in such an intellectual environment could individual talents and resources be fully released: "Freedom for an individual means growth. . . . It signifies an active process, that of release of capacity from whatever hems it in" (Dewey, 1957:207–8). Hence, in Dewey's view, the ideal function of an educational system would be to liberate individuals from socially instilled patterns of inquiry which limit their capacity to devise new and creative ideas.

Dewey's philosophy of education is an illuminating indicator of his outlook on social psychology. His educational theory commits him to the position that social institutions psychologically affect individuals; otherwise, institutional reform (including educational reform) would have no effect upon individuals. On the other hand, Dewey could not accept the social determinism of Durkheim because it precludes uniquely individual expressions. As Allport (1971:283) observed, "What Dewey wants is a psychology compatible with democracy and he rejects any mental science having contrary implications. His opposition to . . . Durkheim's school of collective mind can be understood on this ground. . . ." Dewey had to have an intermediate fence-straddling social psychology in order to admit the force of social institutions in conditioning individuals while still insisting upon individual freedom.

These opposing strains are recurrent in nearly all of Dewey's writings on social psychology. A good example is chapter six of *Experience and Nature* (1958) [1925], entitled "Nature, Mind, and the Subject." Dewey

(1958:215) sets up a dichotomy, and ultimately rejects both poles. First he describes the Greek and "French school" conception of the individual vis-à-vis society which pictures individuals as "something complete, perfect, finished, an organized whole of parts united by the impress of a comprehensive form. The other extreme, the "modern" conception of the imdividual, sees the individual as "something moving, changing, discrete, and above all *initiating* instead of final" (emphasis added). If these conceptions must be taken as mutually exclusive, Dewey (1958:217) declines to adopt either: "An adherent of empirical denotative method can hardly accept either the view which regards subjective mind as an aberration or that which makes it an independent creative source. Empirically, it is an agency of novel reconstruction of a pre-existing order."

The last statement is the key to understanding Dewey's viewpoint. Even in these discussions, there are definite signs that Dewey's thought is directed by his general theory of inquiry. Dewey's social psychology always emphasizes the individual as an agent for transforming the social situation. In Dewey's *Human Nature and Conduct* (1922), the principal operative terms of his social psychological theory are "habit" and "impulse." Dewey attempts to formulate a theory of social change based on the interplay of habit and impulse, and the whole process occurs within the context of his general theory of inquiry. Among one's habits (predispositions to action) are certain methods and principles of thought and action that are socially prescribed. They are the customs of the society where "customs" is intended in the broadest sense. The impetus for social change emerges when people become dissatisfied with the customs. Obviously, only chaos would result if all prior habits were questioned simultaneously. The inquiry must focus upon the conflict of some particular habits against a background of taken-for-granted physical and social constancies. From this point, inquiry is guided by impulse: "Impulse defines the peering, the search, the inquiry" (Dewey, 1922:180). To be truly creative requires that one surmount old habits and surrender to impulse, for there is no sure conceptual bridge between the old custom and the new one being instituted. To cite Dewey's metaphor, the type of transition he had in mind was like the change from covered wagons to steam locomotives, in the sense that the new form cannot be produced simply by improving or reordering the parts of the old one. A whole new principle is required: "Imagination which terminates in a modification of the objective order, in the institution of a new object is other than a merely added occurrence. It involves a dissolution of old objects and a forming of new ones in a medium which, since it is beyond the old object and not yet in a new one, can properly be termed subjective" (1958:220).

It is this subjective stage of the transition from the old to the yet-to-be that marks the presence of "consciousness" (Dewey, 1958:221) and the application of intelligence.[9] Subjectivity, or individuality, is characterized by "initiative, inventiveness, varied resourcefulness, and assumption of responsibility in choice of belief and conduct" (Dewey, 1957:194). But these characteristics are not innate properties of individual personalities; they are achieved within a social environment. That environment can either facilitate or inhibit their development; thus it is of utmost importance that social institutions (e.g., education) be structured so as to promote individuality.

Dewey was preoccupied with the prospect of piecemeal reform of social conditions by means of individual ingenuity. The ideal society, for Dewey, would be one in which social control is minimized, institutions are debureaucratized, and, most of all, no person or institution infringes upon anyone's capacity to release creativity. The aim of social reform is to produce institutions that foster the exercise of freedom and democracy.

Although Dewey's social psychology is framed in vague and general terms, he saw no need for general theories of society, or even for general theories of particular institutions and social processes (Ratner, 1971:63). This attitude is consistent with Dewey's epistemology. General social theories are of little use in directing modifications of very specific problems. For example, Parsonian structural-functionalism or Marxian theory are of little help in plotting ways to overturn a policy of the local school board. As Dewey (1957:198) noted, "What is needed is specific inquiries into a multitude of specific structures and interactions." Presumably, Dewey's idea was that a long sequence of such specific inquiries and attendant changes would eventually add up to fundamental institutional reform: "In the question of methods concerned with reconstruction of special situations rather than in any refinements in the general concepts of institution, individuality, state, freedom, law, order, progress, etc. lies the true impact of philosophical reconstruction" (Dewey, 1957:193). It is for this reason that Dewey regarded social theory as an "idle luxury." For Dewey's purposes, it is necessary to understand the particular patterns of interaction between actors in the specific social network under study. His theory is consistent with the methodological position of Blumerian symbolic interactionism:

Society is one word, but infinitely many things. It covers all the ways in which by associating together men share their experiences, and build up common interests and aims; street gangs, schools for burglary, clans, social cliques, trade unions, joint stock corporations, villages and international alliances. The new method takes effect in substituting inquiry into these specific, changing and relative facts (relative to problems and purposes, not metaphysically relative) for solemn manipulation of general notions. [1957:200]

In summary, Dewey's social philosophy is another illustration of the fact that meaning, knowledge, truth, social reality, and indeed *every* philosophical conception is defined as part of inquiry or some subspecies of inquiry. It can be said that Peirce built his philosophy upon the number three, but for Dewey the number was one—and the one was inquiry.

Dewey's Nominalism

Dewey was a nominalist. But, like James, he was not particularly interested in the nominalism-realism question. Inasmuch as it is a question that is abstract from all special circumstances, Dewey probably regarded it as a typically vague and pointless issue of transcendentalist metaphysics. Yet the very fact that he refused to treat universals as realities and analyze them on their own level of generality is a significant indication of his nominalistic bias. Howard (1919:4–5) made the same observation:

But in spite of Dewey's lack of explicitness, it is evident that he tends to view his "objects of philosophical inquiry" as so many concrete particular existences or things. The idea that they can be empirically marked out and investigated seems to imply this. But subject, object, individual, and universal are certainly not reducible to particular sensations, even though it must be admitted that they have a reference to particulars. These abstract concepts have been a source of difficulty to empiricists, because they had not been able to reduce them to particular impressions, and Dewey's proposed method appears to involve the same difficulty.

Howard's point that Dewey's theory is incapable of conceiving of universals as anything but particular existents merits further discussion. Because universals are not physical entities, they cannot be inquired into. This consequence of Dewey's theory of inquiry not only undercuts exact logic, as has been shown, but it also precludes modern science. Although laboratory experiments do transform the physical constituents of the experimental material, the transformation is not the ultimate aim of the activity. The experimental operations are performed as *means*— not merely as a means to transforming a situation, but as a means to acquire scientific knowledge. Moreover, scientific knowledge is not a

transformation of a situation: it is *propositional*, and the terms of the
propositions are universals, not names of specific elements of some physical "situation." For Dewey, to know the world is not to understand it; it
is to transform it. Although we sometimes must transform things in order
to understand their structure and operation, it is the understanding rather
than the transformation which constitutes knowledge. Yet in Dewey's
theory of inquiry, there is no place for knowledge as understanding. As
Howard (1919:130) concludes his analysis of Dewey's logical theory,
"Dewey expressly denies, indeed, that the purpose of knowing is to give
an account of things. . . . Knowing is designed to transform experience,
not to bring it within the survey of consciousness." Dewey and his supporters believed that his philosophy was derived from scientific method;
yet, the correspondence is only superficial. At heart, the aim of Dewey's
theory of inquiry is very far removed from that of science. Science is
concerned with understanding relations among universals, whereas
Dewey's theory was concerned with transforming particulars.

If we survey Dewey's writings for an explicit position on the realism/
nominalism issue, a somewhat less than consistent picture emerges.
In the essay, "The Pragmatism of Peirce," Dewey (1916:710–11)
displays at least a basic understanding of the nominalism/realism
issue *as formulated by the scholastics and Peirce*. He contrasts the
generality of Peirce's pragmatism to the particularity of James's,
and concludes that Peirce was less a nominalist than James. But
later in the essay, Dewey changes the criterion by which nominalism and
realism are distinguished. Accepting the reality of universals is no longer
defined as the critical issue. By the new criterion, a realist is one who
makes "the assumption of real things which really have effects and consequences" (Dewey, 1916:715). Clearly, one can believe that an explod-
ing bomb has real consequences without being a *scholastic* realist. Dewey
was quite correct in stating that, by this second criterion, both Peirce and
James were "realists." Indeed, James sometimes used the same criterion
to establish himself as a "realist." Like James, Dewey usually adopted the
second criterion because he too wanted to call himself a realist.[10] ·

The most interesting consequence of Dewey's definition is that realism
then contrasts with subjective idealism rather than with nominalism
(classically defined). To be a realist, one has only to admit that there is
some type of brute physical existence which subsists independent of all
mind. Obviously, only an idealist would deny such an assertion, and it
was in this sense that Dewey called himself a realist. For example, in his
introduction to *Essays in Experimental Logic*, Dewey (1903:35) wrote,
"The position taken in the essays is frankly realistic in acknowledging

that certain brute existences, detected or laid bare by thinking but in no way constituted out of thought or any mental process, set every problem for reflection and hence serve to test its otherwise merely speculative results." But by scholastic definitions, the key issue separating nominalism and realism was not the reality of brute existence; the question was whether there is any reality *except* brute existence. Feibleman (1946:91) correctly notes, "[Dewey] seems to think that there is only one kind of nominalism, that of mentalism, yet the ancient definition of nominalism relies upon another kind: the belief in the sole reality of physical particulars." Dewey's theory of inquiry is so permeated with the biologistic functional psychology that it is unable to give priority to the *social* constitution of mind and scientific procedure over bioadaptive transformations of individualistic situations.

Turning next to the philosophy of George Mead, we shall see that Mead, like Dewey, keenly recognized the biological aspect of the human condition. But for Mead, the *social* nature of thought, meaning, and science was the very heart of his behaviorism. Although Dewey sometimes wrote as if he totally shared Mead's perspective (e.g., Dewey, 1958:166–207), such writings were never more than an ill-fitting adjunct to his theory of inquiry which itself always remained particularistic, individualistic, and therefore nominalistic.

5

George
Herbert
Mead

Philosophical
Bearings of Social
Behaviorism

Historians of American pragmatism often assert that no important differences separate the philosophies of Mead and Dewey (e.g., Thayer, 1968:232; Morris, 1934:x; Miller, 1973:xx–xxi; Rucker, 1969:19). This common view is seriously mistaken and probably has diminished the opportunity for Mead's ideas to be received and evaluated by the philosophical community apart from his association with Dewey.

Yet, like most common misunderstandings, the idea that Mead's and Dewey's philosophies are complementary has some factual base in at least three obvious areas. First, both Dewey and Mead rejected the subjectivism of Hume's and Locke's empiricism as well as the subjectivism of Descartes and the other seventeenth-century rationalists. Kantian philosophy and the simplistic realism of some of Dewey's and Mead's American contemporaries are among the several other philosophical systems which could also be added to that list. However, it should be noted that Peirce and James would also reject any philosophy that does not locate meaning and knowledge squarely within the process of human conduct. In a broad sense, all four were "pragmatists." But, as we have seen from the discussion of Peirce, James, and Dewey, there still remains considerable room for fundamental differences.

A second ostensible source of support for the idea that no important discontinuities exist between the philosophies of Dewey and Mead is the fact that Mead adopted the broad outlines of Dewey's theory of inquiry in his own philosophy of science. We can see the concept of adjustment operating in Mead's view of science through the sequential appearance of the blocked activity, hypothesis formation, experimentation, and subsequent reconstruction of the perspective. On a superficial level, it appears that Mead exactly followed Dewey. However, a close examination of Mead's position reveals that his philosophy of science closely resembles Peirce's in stressing the central importance of community and universals. Because Dewey's theory of inquiry is more biologistic than social, it places primary emphasis on individuals and particulars. This basic difference is often obscured by the fact that Dewey sometimes asserted Mead's ideas almost verbatim even though Mead's social theory of mind was poorly suited to Dewey's theory of inquiry. Referring to Mead, Dewey said, "I dislike to think what my own thinking might have been were it not for the seminal ideas I derived from him" (Dykuizen, 1973:271). Similarly, Mead sometimes slipped into asserting Deweyisms. This is understandable given that Dewey and Mead were close personal friends for many years and regularly exchanged ideas. Indeed, it would be surprising if there were no evidence of their intellectual contact in their writings. Undoubtedly, they wanted to be saying the same thing, and both tried without much success to integrate the other's ideas into his own philosophy. Consequently, one may, by selective quotation, build a strong *prima facie* case to support the alleged convergence between Dewey's and Mead's philosophies.

The third area of support for the argument also results from Dewey's and Mead's close friendship. David L. Miller (1973) and Darnell Rucker (1969) cite the same incident in Mead's biography as evidence for the supposed total continuity between the views of Dewey and Mead. According to the report, when Mead was once asked whether he believed Dewey's arguments in *Quest for Certainty,* he replied, "Every word!" (Rucker, 1969:19). For Miller and Rucker, this incident conclusively settles the issue. However, we should recall Felix Kaufmann's caution that Dewey is sometimes like a witch's mirror. Mead saw in Dewey what he had developed by himself; and, if one is seeking that conclusion, there is certainly enough textual material in *Experience and Nature* and elsewhere in Dewey's writings to substantiate a Meadian interpretation of much of Dewey's philosophy. The situation is not unlike James urging someone to send Bergson's new book to Peirce, expecting Peirce to be equally excited about it although, in reality, Peirce held Bergson's philosophy in deepest contempt. James felt tremendous personal and professional respect for Peirce and, therefore, treasured the idea that he and Peirce were working basically within the same framework. Even faced with Peirce's robust criticism, James managed to believe that they were separated more by misunderstanding than by anything substantive. Like James, Mead may have been unaware of the salient differences between his own philosophy and that of his much admired friend and philosophical comrade. In any event, contemporary scholars should not substitute Mead's personal testimony for a thorough and objective evaluation of the writings of Dewey and Mead. Only the latter approach can resolve the question of their degree of agreement.

This chapter calls then for a radical reinterpretation of Mead's place in the pragmatic tradition. Employing the distinction between nominalism and realism discussed in chapter 1, we shall argue that Mead was a realist insofar as his core philosophy is concerned. In chapter 4 we discussed the implicit nominalism embodied in Dewey's theory of inquiry. If we can substantiate our claim that Mead was a realist, we will have shown that there are important differences between Dewey and Mead. Such a result would require us to reconsider the purely philosophical—as opposed to biographical—connections among Peirce, James, Dewey, and Mead. When classified according to their explicit or implicit positions on the nominalism / realism question (scholastically defined), we see that Peirce and Mead were realists, and James and Dewey were basically nominalists. Notwithstanding Mead's various affinities with Dewey, the *direction* of Mead's philosophy was thus far more aligned with Peirce's system. We defend this contention by analyzing the basic structure of Mead's philosophy of perception and knowledge. This analysis will provide the basis for understanding Mead's social behaviorism (see pages 138–39), and will also demonstrate the strong realistic foundation of Mead's philosophy.

Given Mead's interests in philosophical questions about the nature of meaning, science, and knowledge, as well as complementary questions about the foundations of social psychology, it may be said that his work stands at the intersection between general philosophical realism and sociological realism. Indeed, we will argue that Mead's realistic social psychology was tightly interwoven with his broader realist philosophy of science and philosophy of mind.

This integration of philosophical and social realism is by no means logically necessary. One may, for example, hold to the (philosophical) realist claim that some universals are real, and yet accept the (social) nominalist position that none of these happen to be social. According to this view, there are real generals in the physical world but not in the social world. Consequently, sociological propositions about social universals (groups, institutions, organizations, societies, etc.) and relations among their collective properties can, and should, be understood as a shorthand, fictional way of talking about what is *really* real—individuals and their particular characteristics. By arguing that mind, self, and society constitute a prior, independent, and irreducible mode of social being in relation to individuals, Mead clearly rejected social nominalism. As we will show, he did so for reasons stemming directly from his general Whiteheadian philosophy of perspectives and his related social behaviorism.

Our interpretation of Mead's theory of perception is based primarily upon the two principal sources of Mead's writings. The first is Mead's *Selected Writings,* a posthumous compilation of his major journal articles, edited by Andrew Reck and published in 1964. Materials from this volume will hereafter be cited as "Mead: 1964." The second source is Mead's *Philosophy of the Act,* a compilation of Mead's unpublished manuscripts published posthumously in 1938. The other major sources of Mead's thought are mostly the lecture notes of Mead's students.

The most important single reference for the following discussion is Mead's 1927 essay, "The Objective Reality of Perspectives." This article deserves much more attention than it has hitherto received. It brings together virtually every basic concept of Mead's philosophy and shows clearly how, near the end of his life, Mead worked hard to bring social behaviorism into harmony with Whitehead's philosophy of relativity. The essay will be supplemented by frequent references to *Philosophy of the Act,* which was also inspired by Whitehead more than anyone else.

The Murphy Question

Before we get into the difficult business of explaining what Whitehead and Mead meant by "perspective," it is necessary to clarify some historical details[1] which would otherwise appear confusing. Arthur Murphy[1] (1927) identified Whitehead's philosophy as "objective relativism,"[2] and argued that Whitehead and Dewey converged in approaching objective relativism from different points of philosophical origin. If Murphy's contention is valid, then Whitehead, Mead, and Dewey were all in basic agreement, and we would be wrong to suggest that Dewey was, unlike Mead, a nominalist. Whatever else may be said of objective relativism, as developed by Mead and Whitehead, it is a thoroughly realistic philosophy. For this reason, we now pause to consider the merits of Murphy's case.

Early in his paper, "Objective Relativism in Dewey and Whitehead" (1927), Murphy admits that the alleged convergence between Dewey and Whitehead has been a "devious and difficult affair" (122). He warns that readers will not be able to see this convergence unless they stop reading Dewey in terms of James. Yet Murphy does very little to help the reader do this. He reminds us, for example, that Dewey held that all reality is experience (1927:124)—a supposition at the very heart of James's radical empiricism. Murphy (1927:128) continues by quoting the following passage from Dewey: "To see the organism in nature, the nervous system in the organism, the brain in the nervous system, the cortex in the brain is the answer to the problems that haunt philosophy." To anyone familiar with James's psychology, this statement can hardly fail to suggest that Dewey's philosophy is primarily an outgrowth of James's radical empiricism and biocentric functionalist psychology. Even where Murphy attempts to draw attention away from the relation of Dewey's philosophy to James's, such statements defeat his purpose.

Murphy (1927:122) also concedes that Dewey's objective relativism appears clearly only in *Experience and Nature*. There are approximately a dozen references to Dewey's writings in the article, and most are to *Experience and Nature*. We have already noted that large sections of this book seem taken directly from Mead and do not appear in Dewey's other books, including his *Logic*. It would appear, then, that in parts of *Experience and Nature*, Mead's ideas are being expressed rather than those of the Dewey who wrote *Logic*. It would be unfair and unwarranted to accuse Dewey of conscious plagiary, but this distinction between parts of *Experience and Nature* and the rest of Dewey's writings does suggest that Dewey may have been a victim of what Merton (1973:402–12) calls "cryptomnesia"—unconsciously asserting as one's own the ideas gained from another person. Merton demonstrates that cryptomnesia is not an uncommon phenomenon in the history of science. It is surely a far more common occurrence than is outright plagiary.

Dewey's apparent cryptomnesia is especially evident in chapter five of *Experience and Nature*, in which Mead practically jumps off the pages. In passage after passage Dewey asserts the details of Mead's theory of meaning and the origin of language. Dewey (1958:176), for example, discusses the process by which animal "organic gestures" are transformed in "things with significance" as language emerged in human communities. He also discusses Mead's notion of taking the attitude of the other, only in slightly different terms: "The latter puts himself at the standpoint of a situation in which the two parties share. This is the essential peculiarity of language, or signs. . . . The characteristic thing about B's understanding of A's movement and sounds is that he responds to the thing from the standpoint of A" (1958:178). Dewey also asserts Mead's (and Peirce's) triadic theory of symbols: "Thus every meaning is generic or universal. It is something common between speaker, hearer and the thing to which speech refers" (1958:187). We could cite such examples indefinitely, but these illustrate the point. Here we see Dewey discussing topics of no particular concern to this theory of inquiry—his nearly lifelong philosophical passion. Moreover, we find him taking positions on these questions which are detailed reproductions of Mead's. On the other hand, questions concerning the origin of language, the operation of significant symbols, and the like were of keen and continuing interest to Mead. Yet Dewey never referred to Mead in *Experience and Nature*. Interestingly, as Miller (1973:xxxvn) notes, neither did Murphy (1927) refer to Mead. Hence, one is led to suspect that whatever traces of Whiteheadian objective relativism do exist in *Experience and Nature* are due largely to Dewey's cryptomnesia, of which Murphy was not aware. It is significant that in building his case, Murphy relies very heavily on *Experience and Nature,* and makes very sparse reference to Dewey's *Essay in Experimental Logic*—although the latter work is unquestionably closer to the mainstream of Dewey's thought which culminated in his *Logic,* his *magnum opus* (if Dewey can be said to have one). Moreover, if one searches through Dewey's *Logic,* convergences with James abound; but it would require masterful interpretive gyrations to view Dewey's theory of inquiry as converging with Whitehead's philosophy.

In fact, near the end of his essay Murphy (1927:142f) considers Dewey's wider philosophy (e.g., beyond the contents of *Experience and Nature*), and virtually concedes that Dewey's pragmatism is incompatible with Whitehead's philosophy: "When pragmatism tries to reduce this context [the range of possible Whiteheadian contexts] to that of human use and to judge the reality of electrons by the way in which they function as human tools, it is precisely taking one context as privileged, as a standard by which to measure everything else. It is the essence of nonempirical method." If Murphy had recognized the full significance of this disclaimer, he would have been immediately forced to surrender completely his "convergence" thesis. Murphy was correct to point out that, for Dewey, there is only one context: the Darwinian perspective of the human animal faced with an indeterminate situation. From this perspective, the meaning and reality of an object matter only insofar as the object *functions* in producing the necessary transformation or "inquiry" which holds Dewey's perspective together. It, and it alone, defines the conditions for meaning, reality, and truth.

Dewey's theory does not require any principle of sociality or inter-subjectivity. One need only postulate an organism, its physical environment, and the organism's capacity for controlled transformation of the environment. Whatever Meadian principles are stated in *Experience and Nature,* they are not necessary to Dewey's perspective. If Dewey had taken Mead's ideas more seriously, rather than simply pitchforking them into the book alongside his own, he would have seen that his own perspective was restricted. When the basic components of Dewey's theory of inquiry are analyzed, his theory can be seen to have James's humanistic focus which denies reality to relations among entities subsisting in the world of Peircean secondness. This is what Murphy meant in saying that Dewey's pragmatism is "the essence of non-empirical method."

There *is* an element of relativity in Dewey's theory. But, in Dewey the meaning of the object is relative to the indeterminate *situation,* whereas for Whitehead it is relative to the *perspective.* A perspective is much broader than a situation in that a situation is always defined within a perspective. For Whitehead, there are a plurality of possible perspectives from which any event may be understood. For Dewey, there is only one perspective—that of his theory of inquiry. Dewey lodges relativity in the organism-environment situation, but Whitehead assigns relativity to the perspective without rejecting the independent reality of the content of the situation apart from all perspectives, including Dewey's. Inasmuch as Dewey allows only his own perspective, he cannot meaningfully make this admission. Feibleman (1970:481) notes the same nominalistic consequence of Dewey's theory:

> The emphasis of Dewey's logic upon controlled inquiry leaves no doubt as to its pervasive nominalistic cast. In the notion that being is exhausted by conscious activity, as in the conception of a controlled inquiry which either constitutes or causally originates objects and their interrelations, we have one variety of subjective nominalism, a reduction of ontology to epistemology which has divided the world between subject and object and, while requiring both, somehow assigned the primary reality to the subject.

Dewey's frequent assertions that inquiry takes place completely within the ubiquitous category he calls "nature" does not attenuate the essentially subjectivistic and nominalistic tenor of his philosophy.

To summarize, Murphy's thesis is defensible if based solely upon the Meadian portions of *Experience and Nature,* but those passages appear as an aberration when viewed in conjunction with Dewey's theory of inquiry. When the latter is taken as Dewey's core philosophy, as it should be, Murphy practically admits that his arguments collapses. We therefore conclude that whatever "convergence" Murphy perceived between Dewey and Whitehead, as revealed in *Experience and Nature,* was due to Dewey's importation of Mead into that book rather than to any genuine convergence between the general philosophies of Dewey and Whitehead.

The Nature of Perspectives

Perhaps the most effective way to explain what Mead meant by "perspectives" is to cite one of his favorite examples. To city dwellers, grass is just something that has to be fertilized and mowed occasionally. It enters into their experience infrequently and almost never appears as a salient object. But to a cow, grass is a food and, as such, is an object that enters into its experience on a regular and important basis. Grass thus enters into the conduct of a cow in very different ways than it does for the city dweller.

For the cow, grass is a different object than it is for the city dweller. We are using the term "object" in its technical sense as used by Mead. That is, an object is an experience which has a definite and recurrent relationship to the organism's past experience and future expectations. The object is a determinate part of the organism's ongoing conduct, in that the object has certain definitive qualities [for the organism] which allow the organism to integrate the object with other objects in the course of its normal activities. The whole set of such interrelated objects constitutes a *perspective.* In the perspective of the cow, grass is a food-object because it has the quality of being food by satisfying the cow's hunger. In the perspective of the city dweller, grass is mainly a social object. A neat yard has a symbolic significance vis-à-vis the other members of the community, and an unmowed, weed-infested yard has the obverse social significance. The quality of the grass in the city dweller's perspective is its potential to arouse the admiration or ire of the neighbors—the objects to which it is related within the perspective.

If the perspective were to change—as would happen should the community, for example, change its norms regarding the maintenance of grass—then grass would become a different object to the organism. From this we see that, as Mead so often insisted, the qualities of the object are equally dependent upon the environment and the structure of the organism (Mead, 1938:248). Kant was the first modern philosopher to see this clearly. The appearance of the color quality "blue" in the experience of an organism can occur only if that organism has a physiological constitution that allows it to discriminate blue. However, it is equally true that the experience of blue would never occur if there were never things in the environment with the capacity to reflect light waves in the blue region of the spectrum. Uniform interactions among particles of dead matter is a prerequisite for the appearance of perceptual qualities in the experience of the organism. Mead (1938:15) stated:

> It is certainly true that what is the precondition of an experience cannot be the experience itself. Thus the hardness of a stone may be said to be the precondition of John Smith's experiencing that hardness. The hardness that John Smith experiences is in some measure different from that which is experienced by James Brown. In this sense the color of the book as its exists before it comes to the eyes of John Smith, or before the eyes of anyone, is a precondition of its being experienced.

Mead's position on this matter is identical to Peirce's: Mead is asserting the reality of Peirce's category of firstness. Before there ever existed an organism with sufficient physiological complexity to be able to experience blue, the sky was blue in the sense that it would have appeared blue to any animal having the appropriate physical structure. But before such animals existed, blue was only a qualitative *possibility* (firstness). Nevertheless, that was a real possibility because certain objects really had the capacity to reflect light waves of the frequency we call blue. Without such objects, the appearance of blue would have always remained only a possibility. In Peircean terms, a firstness can become actual only if it is instantiated in some secondness. However, one should never forget that it is the uniformities in nature apart from the constitution of any and all sentient beings that provide the *possibility* of the appearance of qualities in the experience of the organism. This is what Mead meant in saying that the hardness of a stone is a precondition for John Smith or anyone else to experience its hardness. The hardness is not in Smith's mind. It is truly in the hard thing itself, as a capacity. Mead's philosophy of perception is, like Peirce's, predicated upon the objective reality of universals (Mead, 1938:292). "The identical characters of objects in the different situations are the basis for intelligent conduct, which involves different situations" (Mead, 1938:215). We have, then, a network of dependencies. The situation arises only within a perspective. As previously noted, it was Dewey's mistake to postulate that a situation can have some objective character (e.g., indeterminacy) apart from any perspective. The perspective is itself constituted by a set of interrelated objects and events. These objects and events are identified within the perspective according to their perceptual qualities. Finally, the appearance of these qualities ultimately depends upon the presence of universal relationships among inanimate atomic particles and an organism that, in one manner or another, is physiologically structured so that it can experience recurrent qualities made possible by these relationships.

By "universal," Mead (1938:388) meant "that the language symbol as a stimulus can be indifferently addressed to any one of the members of the social group and calls out a response which is adequate to the carrying-out of the social act." But the stability of the response is possible only because there is a relatively persistent and predictable causal relation between certain actions and the effects that constitute the response. In other words, the universal has the capacity to call out the same response in all members of the social group because each person can anticipate the probable outcome of various alternative actions and therefore knows how to effect the required response. This anticipation would not be possible unless there are relatively timeless relationships among the constituent elements of the external world, which Mead (1938:257, 260) simply called "the world that is there."

Mead was, however, insistent that the possibility of universals does not require a universe of absolutely fixed and permanent relations. It is only necessary that, within the bounds of the prespective, there is sufficient continuity of nomological relationships (Peirce's principle of synechism) to allow the members of the social group to act and communicate intelligently. Thus, relative to the perspective, the universe *is* timeless (Mead, 1938:113–15). Mead wished to defend the reality of what we have called limited generals or universals (see chapter 1).

From this, one can readily see that not only was Mead a realist of the Peircean type, but also that his whole analysis of universals, objects, and perspectives is so deeply rooted in the postulates of realism that it is virtually unintelligible if one attempts to interpret it otherwise. For example, if we try to read Mead in terms of Dewey, we have great difficulty. It is not justifiable to reduce Mead's discussions in *The Philosophy of the Act* to Dewey's model of the organism faced with the problem of transforming a hostile indeterminate situation in an essentially biological, functional, and (therefore) Darwinian situation. Mead was concerned with interpreting and understanding the world through the universal symbols of perspectives, especially the scientific perspective. Dewey, as we have seen, was concerned only with transforming the physical environment to suit our biological and social needs, and universals were to be admitted only insofar as they are necessary in planning the transformation of the specific environmental situation. Consequently, for

Dewey, whatever idea leads to the successful transformation is thereby considered truth and knowledge. We have already analyzed the weaknesses of this subjectivistic and nominalistic doctrine, but we must now point out that it is the very *antithesis* of Mead's interest in discerning the conditions that make possible universal symbols and perspectives. This calls attention to a second incongruity between Mead's philosophy and Dewey's theory of inquiry. From the standpoint of Dewey's logic, the situation is basically the relation of an organism to its environment. Following the Darwinian "genetic" logic, it is an individualistic, one-to-one encounter. The "cultural matrix" of society is, like everything else, only relevant to the extent that it will support or oppose the organism's idea for transforming the environment. Thus, it is the individual organism which is the agent of the transformation, and the society is the element of the environment.[3] As we have shown, the situation for Mead is quite different. Every situation develops within a perspective and, because every human perspective is grounded in universal symbols, even the most seemingly individualistic situation is rooted in social conduct which is irrelevant to the particular characteristics of the individual organism: "This situation arises . . . when the individual through the development of social conduct has reached the point of indicating to himself the results of past action present in tendencies to response" (Mead, 1938:282–83).

Mead's discussion of the nature of perspectives suggests that his philosophy of perception basically agrees with Peirce's social and realistic focus, and only broadly relates to the bioadaptive psychology of James and Dewey. Moreover, Mead explicitly rejected the nominalistic conception of thought and meaning which is central to the pragmatism of James and Dewey. This will become even clearer as we now turn to Mead's analysis of the objectivity of perspectives.

The Objectivity of Perspectives

In the transition from nineteenth to the twentieth century, relativity replaced evolution as the watchword of science and philosophy. This transition occurred as philosophers debated the philosophical implications of new advances in physics, particularly relativity theory. The realization that the object is relative to the perspective has forced philosophers of science to redefine the basis of the objectivity of scientific knowledge. The positivist's equation of the scientific object with sense data was no longer tenable once it was understood that, because the scientific object is constituted within a perspective, it can be defined only in terms of its relations to other objects within that perspective. Because many of these relationships are not immediately observable, logical positivism collapsed due to its inability to reduce to sense data the meanings of the objects of modern physics. We must place ourselves within the perspective in order to experience its objects. For example, the physicist observes the readings of an instrument and "sees" that an electron has been emitted. Meanwhile, a layman may be standing alongside the physicist and have a qualitatively similar retinal image (sense datum) without seeing that the electron has been emitted, because the two persons are observing within different perspectives. The *same* sense data became constituent elements of *different* objects in the experience of two observers. Thus, mere sense data cannot serve as the basis for establishing intersubjective agreement concerning the object observed. Each person saw a different object even though they had qualitatively similar sense impressions: "One can see only that which he is looking for, and what else comes within the field of vision must be seen in terms of this" (Mead, 1964:33).

In recent decades, much work in epistemology and philosophy of science has sought to determine the implications of perceptual relativity. A major theme of *The Philosophy of the Act* is that, although the object is relative to the perspective, it does not follow that the experienced object is a subjective phenomenon. Mead, Peirce, and Whitehead shifted the focus of objectivity from sense data to the perspective. The mistake of the positivists and British empiricists was in thinking that sense data are the objects of conscious experience. As Kant realized, perception requires a cognitive judgment by which the raw sensory impulses are organized and interpreted as a perceptual object such as "tree" or "house" (see Mead, 1936:44–45). The percept is an inferential judgment, not the passive receipt of nervous stimuli: "What Hume did not recognize is that the something that is there is an entire passage. It is not just a series of instantaneous impressions on the mind. That is the causal future in it, a something going on" (Mead, 1938:650).

Since Hume's impressions are not given in experience, they cannot be the reference of the symbols by which a group of individuals can achieve communication and intersubjective agreement concerning the character of their experiences (Mead, 1938:17). Two individuals cannot have identical sense impressions without sharing the same nervous system and, even if they could, they would not be aware of the fact. What they *can* consciously share is a common perspective and, through the perspective, common objects. Mead (1938:258) used this insight as the foundation of his theory of objectivity:

> A number of individuals may belong to a consentient set. The same objects will be at rest and in motion for all who belong to that set. The same object is food for all animals with a certain digestive apparatus. In other words, this relativity is in no sense solipsistic. It represents a certain relation between the field and individuals. In so far as this relationship is identical, objects may be identical. A solipsistic relativity arises out of a doctrine of consciousness which identifies the object with states of experience of an individual.

No object can be more objective than a Durkheimian collective representation or object within a Meadian perspective. The search for a higher grade of objectivity than what occurs relative to what Whitehead and Mead called the consentient set has led philosophers to postulate unknowable realities involving unanswerable and unnecessary metaphysical perplexities. Peirce once said that there is no greater reality than the object of a true cognition. This is the response of the scientific mind to those empiricists who wish to challenge the reality of secondary qualities. Mead (1938:359) similarly commented, "What I wish to point out is that the theory of mind found itself obliged to make a place for contents which, for immediate experience, belong as definitely to the outer object as those characters which science conceives to be the nature of the things that are entirely independent of mind."

Having defined objectivity as an attribute of a perspective, and having justified that definition, Mead devoted much of his later thought to the problem of explaining how it is possible for a group of individuals to have a common perspective. To summarize his conclusions, there are two preconditions for the emergence and persistence of a communal perspective: first, the group must have a language consisting of the significant symbols by which they designate the objects that constitute their perspective; second, there must be what Mead calls the "world that is simply there." It corresponds exactly to Peirce's category of secondness. The world of action and reaction, of brute material existence, is always there independently of all perspectives (Mead, 1938:67, 205, 250). Like Peirce before him, Mead (1938:286) realized that resistence is the essential property of all existence. By changing the lighting by taking drugs, we can make a brick wall appear to change color, change shape, or even disappear. Nevertheless, it will stand there always resisting our efforts to move through it. Only brute physical attack against the wall itself can destroy its property of resistance. If more subtle methods worked, cannon balls might have never been invented.

This unfailing quality of resistance which all existents possess led Mead to declare that the ultimate reality of any object depends upon the possibility of our having tactile sensation of it in what he called the "contact experience." We may seem to see something at a distance but, if the visual experience is the only testimony to its existence, it must remain a hypothetical existence. It is only when we can approach this hypothetical distant object, touch it with our hands, and feel its resistance to our tensed muscles that we *know* that something is there.[4] Whether consciously or unconsciously, we base our conduct upon this simple, but extremely fundamental principle.

This principle is reflected in the structure of language—it is the basis for the reference of signs to their objects: "The ultimate experience of contact is . . . that into which every perspective can be translated" (Mead, 1938:281). Without something overt and brute to which our symbols refer, they could not be significant. The only way a symbol can call out the same response in two organisms is by causing them to each anticipate the same contact experiences with reference to the object of the symbol. Ultimately, the meaning of a significant symbol must be grounded in the nonhuman world of pure resistance. We previously discussed the same point in connection with Peirce's theory of signs. The ultimate meanings of concepts must be located in some nonmental and nonlinguistic reality if we are to escape the infinite regress of verbal definitions of definitions of definitions, *ad infinitum*. Mead thus observed that "the ultimate touchstone of reality is a piece of experience found in an unanalyzed world." Mental objects must be referred to worlds that are not mental (Mead, 1938:32, 70).

The functioning of significant symbols ultimately rests upon the possibility of different individuals having qualitatively similar sense experiences. These experiences allow the organisms to respond identically to the gesture. This potentiality depends upon two related forms of continuity. First, there is the physiological continuity of the members of the community. If the physiological constitution of the organisms is qualitatively similar, they will have the same sensations if placed in the same sensory environment. But again, this is not to say that they will necessarily experience the same objects. That depends upon the congruity of their perspectives. We only mean, as Mead (1964:274) stated, "While we assume that the color of the object perceived, even if it vary from eye to eye, is in some respects identical for all eyes insofar as the organs are alike, it is not assumed that the image which one has is there for other eyes, or imaginations." In addition to this physiological continuity of the species, the effective operation of symbols requires the continuity of physical laws and relations which allow the symbol to have the same reference over time. For example, in the case of colors, if objects constantly changed colors in a random fashion, there would be little use in specifying color symbols. Likewise, if hard objects became soft and soft objects became hard in rapid and unpredictable successions, there would be small value in having the concepts "hard" and "soft." The same is true of other similar types of symbols. The utility of symbols lies in the fact that we can, for example, base our future activities on the assumption that a hard red object will continue to be hard and red unless something happens to change those characters. Moreover, because we know what types of events are necessary to change those qualities of the object, we can estimate the short-run probability that such changes will occur. Intelligent action (i.e., an act that involves significant symbols) requires that the qualities of the objects implicated in the act possess a stable or predictable character throughout the duration of the act (Mead, 1964:307). Within the act, time and change are irrelevant (Mead, 1938:115). In short, we are emphasizing again that the efficacy and utility of symbols requires the reality of what we have called "limited generals" (see chapter 1).

In Meadian terms, reflective action must take place against a background consisting of the world that is there; the act is irrelevant to passage because the object is "in a system in which the law of action and reaction holds" (Mead, 1938:205): "the intelligibility of the world is found in this structure of relations which are there in experience, and in the possibility of following them on beyond the specious present into a future in so far as this future is determined" (Mead, 1932:97). Although there must be at least this much continuity in the relations among external existents in order for communication and rational conduct to be possible, Mead's position does not entail the conception of a universe governed by perfect and eternal laws. Indeed, Mead frequently denied such a conception. Like the other pragmatists, he acknowledged the reality of genuine contingency.

Mead (1964:318) summarized the nature of objectivity and the conditions for its attainment as follows:

It is then such a coincidence of the perspective of the individual organism with the pattern of the whole act in which it is so involved that the organism can act within it, that constitutes the objectivity of the perspective. The pattern of the whole social act can lie in the individual organism because it is carried out through implemental things to which *any* [emphasis added] organism can react, and because indications of these reactions to others and the organism itself can be made by significant symbols.

It must be stressed that objectivity is an attribute of perspectives. To state that an object is objective is only a truncated way of saying that the object functions within the perspective of a community or "consentient set" in such a way as to permit its members to anticipate and communicate the experiential content associated with it and the other objects to which it is related within the perspective. There are, of course, many possible perspectives, but the perspective in which Mead was most interested is the scientific perspective. In the following section, we show that Mead's defense of the objectivity of the scientific perspective is grounded in the criteria of objectivity presented thus far.

The Perspective of Scientific Method

The Functions of Particulars in Science

One permanent fact about science is that the scientific community's theories and objects change over time. By analyzing how scientific theories rise and fall, we can gain a better understanding of the method by which the perspectives of scientific communities change. Whatever else may be said of these changes, a careful study of the history of science reveals that they come slowly. Even Kuhnian "revolutions" have their own histories. Scientific communities, like other human communities, are reluctant to give up their perspectives, and they typically do so only after exhausting every scientifically acceptable alternative.

Mead's account of the process by which scientific perspectives change is similar to Kuhn's (1962), in that the seeds of change are seen in the anomalous experience of an investigator. The perspective has to break down at some crucial point before there will be any impetus to change it; otherwise, the scientific community will doggedly persist in following the established perspective.[5] As Peirce noted, we continue to hold beliefs until contrary experience shocks us into a state of hesitancy and doubt.

Let us consider the nature of the "emergent" event which breaks down the perspective. Mead (1938:634) criticized the Hegelian approach to science for failing to recognize that, if only holistic conceptions are allowed into one's perspective, then a *particular* can never arise within that perspective. Furthermore, because the *appearance* of the particular

gives rise to the problem, the Hegelian standpoint could never generate
any genuine scientific problems (Mead, 1936:143).

Mead (1938:635) went on to point out that "we observe particulars
only in the case of exceptions." In the context of Mead's philosophy of
perspectives, this is an extremely meaningful statement. Recall that what
we ordinarily observe are objects constituted within perspectives. As
such, they are identified as instances of a general class of experiences.
They do not stand alone as unique and unanalyzed events. If they were
individual in that sense, they would not be objects at all (Mead,
1938:71). To repeat Mead, we are capable of seeing particulars only
when the perspective breaks down, and the particulars can then be
understood only as exceptions. But exceptions to what? Particulars
cannot be exceptions to other particulars; they can only be exceptions to
some general law (Mead, 1936:135). Thus, for Mead, a scientific
problem consists of an exception to some generalization which links
together the objects within the perspective. The objects of a scientific
perspective are necessarily very abstract and general: "The method of
exact measurement of the physical sciences has made use of
approximations to situations of ideal simplicity in order to discover the
laws of change in nature" (Mead, 1938:516). The scientist is interested in
particulars, but only insofar as they emerge as exceptions to universals.
Once the problem is solved, "the particular instances are gone; they are
sunk in the universality of the law" (Mead, 1938:634).

On many occasions, Mead asserted that science must postulate the
uniformity of nature. It need not postulate any single, eternal, and
absolute uniformity. However, science must assume the possibility of
devising theories that have explanatory and predictive power with
reference to the world of brute facts which they govern. Nevertheless, the
scientist does not exclude the possibility of other perspectives and
theories of the phenomena under study (Mead, 1938:30). The point is
that Mead's philosophy of science is frankly realistic in acknowledging
the role of universals in the process of the development and modifications
of scientific perspectives.

We are now in a position to contrast Mead's notion of the emergence
of the particular in the course of scientific activity with Dewey's concept
of the indeterminate situation. As we have seen, the Deweyan indeterminate situation is a specific condition capable of specific solution.
The Meadian emergent particular is defined in the context of a general
law which appears to have failed. The difference between these two
notions is as important as it is obvious. Dewey's problem is solved by
whatever hypothesis—when actually tested in the situation at

hand—proves to transform the situation into something determinate. It need not work tomorrow. It need not work for other organisms. It need work only here and now for the organism in the indeterminate situation. Dewey's only interest was in the successful conduct of inquiry (i.e., the transformation), and the solution has no social or temporal requirements. For Mead, the problem is not that some biologically unpleasant event (Dewey's usual model) has appeared in the experience of the individual. The significance of the sensory datum lies solely in its relation to an object and the relation of that object to other objects within the perspective. Consequently, from the Meadian standpoint, nothing less than a reconsideration of the whole perspective is required to solve the problem created by the emergent event, and this may well require new objects and new general laws relating those objects—in other words, a new perspective. Since the problem arises as an exception to a general law, it is the general law which may be the object of reconstruction. Therefore, the solution must be a *general* solution because the reconstructed perspective, like all perspectives, consists of objects and connecting universals. Dewey's theory of inquiry never adequately provided for the salient place of universals and laws in the conduct of science because his philosophy was, to a significant degree, always grounded in James's radical empiricism.

From the foregoing discussion we see that, in Mead's theory of scientific method, general laws are involved both in the appearance of the emergent event and also in the reconstruction of the perspective. We turn now to the collateral condition for the objective reality of the perspective—namely, the process of sociality.

The Necessity of
Sociality in Science

In the previous subsection, we examined the conditions for the appearance of the emergent event which initiates scientific inquiry. The objectivity of the perspective breaks down when, in the experience of an individual scientist, the general propositions which relate contact experiences to objects seem to have been violated. In this section, we describe the procedure by which scientists resolve the problem created by the emergent event. We emphasize the consequences of the fact that, in the process of reconstructing the perspective, scientists assume the role of the scientific community to which they belong.

The emergent event which occurs in the experience of an individual scientist cannot be assimilated within the perspective. It is thus not an object inside the scientist's working perspective. Nevertheless, it is still meaningful within a broader perspective (Mead, 1964:19). For example, suppose we perform a chemical experiment in which it is hypothesized that the precipitate will be green but, in fact, it turns out to be red. A green precipitate would have been pregnant with meaning, for it would have been an object that adds support to the perspective. Although the red precipitate does not occupy that place, it is still meaningful in that we can at least agree that it is *red*: "It is true that the barest facts do not lack meaning, though a meaning which has been theirs in the past is lost" (Mead, 1964:173). But even the barest facts are sufficient to serve as the point of departure for reconstructing the perspective. The red precipitate is both "the debris of the old" theory and "the building material of the new." The emergent event in the old perspective eventually becomes an object as the reconstructed perspective develops. It is this common explanandum which makes possible both theory reduction and, hence, the cumulative advance of scientific knowledge (Mead, 1964:204).

Once the emergent event has occurred, the next stage of scientific method is formulating the explanatory hypothesis to account for the emergent event. From a cursory inspection, Mead's (1938:82–83) proposed stages of scientific method appear to be quite similar to Dewey's theory of inquiry, but a closer look shows some critical differences. First, the locus of the problem for Dewey was always one of action—the physical transformation of an environmental situation. But for Mead (1938:82), the locus of the inhibition may be in action, thought, or feeling.[6] Thus, Mead's viewpoint encounters no difficulty or inconsistency in admitting that a problem in mathematical logic is a genuine problem even though no Deweyan inquiry may be required for its solution. That is, the problem may be solved by thinking about it without taking any physical action beyond the mental energy consumed by thought.

Similarly, even though Mead was not a logician of Peirce's caliber, he demonstrated an awareness of the central importance of abductive and deductive logic in the intermediary stages. Dewey, at best, only grudgingly tolerated the application of rules of general logic which, as we have seen, he tended to regard as intellectualist chicanery. There is no sure logical bridge by which the scientist can pass from the emergent event to a hypothesis which might explain it. If there were, there would be no need for imagination and creativity in science. An element of subjectivity is involved in imagining a theory that, if true, would explain the anomalous event. The scientist draws from the community's stock of prior knowledge in formulating the idea, but still must provide the spark of insight necessary to transport the event back into the old perspective or into a new one (Mead, 1964:52).

Intelligent scientists do not immediately prepare to observationally test the first hypothesis their abductive reasoning suggests. The hypothesis must first pass what Mead called the "mental" test. The scientist deduces as many consequences of the hypothesis as possible and, by mental experiments in imagination, checks their plausibility. There is no place for this type of mental testing in Dewey's theory of inquiry. If we take seriously Dewey's experimentalist theory of knowledge, the only way to *know* whether the elephant will fit into the telephone booth is by conducting the physical experiment because for Dewey knowledge is an actual experimental datum, not a propositional formula. Mead, however, would eliminate that hypothesis at the stage of mental testing: "Indeed all formulations of problems are deductive whether we undertake their solution or not" (Mead, 1938:83).

By a series of such logical deductions and mental experiments, the scientist builds a world consisting of the hypothesis and the logical network of its implications. As Mead (1964:198) stated:

> In discovery, invention, and research the escape from the exceptional, from the data of early stages of observation, is by way of an hypothesis; and every hypothesis so far as it is tenable and workable in its form is universal. No one would waste his time with a hypothesis which confessedly was not applicable to all instances of the problem. A hypothesis may be again and again abandoned, it may prove to be faulty and contradictory, but insofar as it is an instrument of research it is assumed to be universal and to perfect a system which has broken down at the point indicated by the problem. Implication and more elaborated instances flow from the structure of this hypothesis.

As a classic example of this process, Mead (1964:198) cited Galileo's hypothesis that the rate of the velocity of a falling body is proportionate to the time elapsed during the fall. Galileo then determined the implication of the hypothesis by adapting the hypothesis to the accepted perspective, or mathematical model, of the physical world. From this, he was able to derive a specific experimental implication, which "would be actually secured and which would be so characteristic an instance of a falling body that it would answer to every other instance as he had defined them." The other implications of the theory still hold as implicit meanings presented by "symbols which generalize innumerable instances." They may become problematic at a later time. Galileo's method of dealing with the problem is an exemplar of what Hempel and other modern philosophers of science have called the "deductive-nomological model of scientific explanation."

The scientist always tries to link the hypothesis to general laws: "We want to have our statement of the universe as uniform as it is possible" (Mead, 1938:318). Science must postulate and seek uniform laws; otherwise, the *exception* could never occur and Mead's theory of scientific advance would be untenable (Mead, 1936:170–71). To be scientific, these generalized propositions must be of a special type. Mead's most common criticism of Hegel was that the Hegelian perspective set up a dialectic between universals rather than between universals and particulars (Mead, 1936:132). Consequently, it is impossible to observationally test the empirical validity of any universal from the standpoint of the Hegelian perspective. Unlike the Reality of Hegelian metaphysics, the scientists' general propositions are formulated to allow one to derive experimental implications.

Ultimately, the experimental test signals the reconstruction of the perspective. The particular event in the experience of an individual scientist has been incorporated into a (perhaps new) object of the perspective:

> Research defines its problem by isolating certain facts which appear for the time being not as the sense-data of a solipsistic mind, but as experiences of an individual in a highly organized society, facts which, because they are in conflict with accepted doctrines, must be described so that they can be experienced by others under like conditions. The ground for the analysis which leads to such facts is found in the conflict between the accepted theory and the experience of the individual scientist. [Mead, 1964:196]

Thus, the observation of scientific objects is as Mead said, impersonal. That is, anyone who shares the perspective can follow the prescribed experimental procedures and experience the object (Mead, 1938:40, 61, 196). As Mead and Peirce so many times reiterated, the objectivity of the perspective consists in the fact that its objects are defined to lead all members of the community to the same brute sensations: "In other words, those individuals who corroborate the facts are made, in spite of themselves, experiencers of the same facts" (Mead, 1964:196).

The realism of Mead's philosophy of science may be summarized by three logically interconnected propositions:

1. Objectivity depends upon communality.
2. Communality depends upon the replicability of experimental phenomena.
3. Replicability depends upon the reality of limited general (as a bare minimum).

Thus, Mead's philosophy of science is rooted in his theory of the objectivity of perspectives which is itself predicated upon the assumption that universals are real. The principles of realism (as we have defined the term) consequently enter into Mead's philosophy at every stage and, at each of those stages, Mead's view may be contrasted with the individualistic and particularistic pragmatism of James and Dewey.

The Methodology of
Social Behaviorism

Many debates in the philosophy of social science center around the issue of whether the methodological approach of the social sciences should differ from that of the natural sciences. Some argue that the intentional nature of human action necessitates an introspective technique which supposedly reaches those key data (i.e., the actor's intentions) not open to direct observation. Other theorists have argued that empirical observations are the core of scientific method and must remain so regardless of the subject matter under study. According to this view, scientists *qua* scientists cannot allow their introspective "insights" to substitute for direct empirical observation of external phenomena. Mead (1964:61) took the latter position: "There is certainly no fundamental distinction between the researches of the historian, the philologist, the social statistician and those of the biologist, the geologist or even the physicist and chemist, in point of method. . . . For their solution hypotheses must be constructed and tested by means of experiments or observation."

Mead's social behaviorism recognizes the presence of subjective or "psychical" elements in individual experience, but insists that psychical events can, and should, become objects of scientific study only insofar as they "correspond to definite conditions of objective experience" (Mead, 1964:34). Just as science in general is concerned with particulars only as exceptions, the social psychologist deals with the content of subjectivity only as it *relates* to an objective phase of experience (Mead, 1934:33). As Mead (1964:45) stated:

> I should add that the experimental psychologist is apt to trouble himself comparatively little about this or any other content of subjectivity. He assumes its existence answering to the physical situation, and confines himself to determining these physical situations with reference to the conditions under which this subjectivity is supposed to appear.

Mead (1934:5–6) criticized Watsonian behaviorism for passing over the subjectivity aspect of consciousness (see Cook, 1977). Watson's mechanistic behaviorism denies the reality of *self*-conscious social action. Mead's argument with Watsonian behaviorism was that Watson failed to recognize that the overt, observable phase of the act is but one temporal event in a whole process originating in the inner experience of the individual in the form of a neurophysiological state or "attitude" (as Mead generally called it). The act is a process which can be traced backward into the attitude of the organism and forward into the organism's response to its own gesture. Thus, overt behavior is part of an ongoing act which neither begins nor ends with overt activity. Manis and Meltzer (1972:1) correctly assert that Watson's exclusion of the covert phase of the act reduces his psychology to a mechanistic level which cannot allow for the social character of human action.

Manis and Meltzer (1972:2) are, however, mistaken in their claim that Mead favored intuitive, *verstehende* method over the scientific method. On the contrary, one of Mead's primary aims in his lectures on social psychology was to show that the sociological theses of his social behaviorism do not necessitate the methodology of introspective psychology. For Mead, the principle commendable feature of behavioristic psychology was that it shifts the interest of psychology from psychical states to external conduct. Any psychical content that is assumed to subsist apart from the conduct of some act is a scientifically inadmissable assumption (Mead, 1964:267, 48).

On many occasions during his lectures, Mead stated with great clarity that if the psychical is regarded as the attitude constituting the earlier stages of the act,[7] it is possible to account for and deal with it "in behavioristic terms which are precisely similar to those which Watson employs in dealing with non-mental psychological phenomena" (Mead, 1934:10). This type of study would require that the experimental methods of physiological psychology monitor physiological changes occurring during the act: "We can, therefore, in principle, state behavioristically what we mean by an idea" (Mead, 1934:13). Analysis of all phases of the act must be lodged in the study of observable reactions, whether overt or physiological (Mead, 1934:105). Nowhere in any of Mead's writings does he call for what Manis and Meltzer (1972:2) term "'subjective' or non-communicable techniques of study." From our analysis of perspectives, it should be obvious that such an admission would violate every postulate of Mead's philosophy of science. According to our understanding of Mead's position, his behavioristic methodology assumes an entirely unyielding stance toward all forms of noncommunicable, subjectivist techniques.

The Subject Matter of
Social Behaviorism

Having discussed the "behaviorism" aspect of Mead's social behaviorism, we now consider the "social" dimension which distinguishes his social psychology from the naive stimulus-response behaviorism of Watson and more modern behaviorists. In this section, we examine how some of the basic concepts of Mead's social psychology (e.g., self, other, significant symbol) helped to delineate the distinctively *social* quality of the subject matter of social behaviorism.

Let us begin by citing a few of Mead's more programmatic statements regarding the proper subject matter of social psychology and social science. Note Mead's emphasis on the point that social psychology restricts itself to those behaviors that occur as significant gestures because the individuals are acting from the perspective of the social group:

> Thus, in the study of the experience and behavior of the individual organism or self in its dependence upon the social group to which it belongs, we find a definition of the field of social psychology [Mead, 1934:1]

> And the fact that the nature of meaning is thus found to be implicit in the structure of the social provides additional emphasis upon the necessity, in social psychology, of starting off with the initial assumption of an ongoing social process of experience and behavior in which any given group of human individuals is involved, and upon which the existence and development of their minds, selves, and self-consciousess depend. [Mead, 1934:81–82]

> In the second place, it is only insofar as the individual acts not only in his own perspective but also in the perspective of others, especially in the common perspective of a group, that a society arises and its affairs become the object of scientific inquiry. . . . In the field of any social science the objective data are those experiences of the individuals in which they take the attitude of the community, i.e., in which they enter into the perspectives of the other members of the community. [Mead, 1964:310]

These statements clearly define the line of demarcation between social psychology and general psychology. The social psychologist is not concerned with individual behavior or experience that is merely subjective or psychical. That is the domain of the clinical psychologist. Thus, any social psychologist who claims an interest in subjective experiences per se is exceeding the proper field of social psychology. As Mead stated, the social psychologist assumes that individuals act from the perspective of the social group to which they belong, and he describes and explains the conduct from that standpoint: "Action takes place in a common world into which inference and interpretation has transmuted all that belonged to the individual subjectively considered" (Mead 1964:26).

An individual's unique personality characteristics are totally irrelevant to the understanding of the meaning of that subset of his or her behavior with which social psychology is properly concerned. This irrelevancy becomes obvious once it is recognized that such social conduct is an expression of the objective meaning structure of the social group with reference to which it occurs. The conduct has the same meaning regardless of which member of the social group acts or responds (see Scheffler, 1974:154, 159). "The significant symbol is then the gesture, the sign, the word which is addressed to the self when it is addressed to another individual, and is addressed to another, in form to all other individuals, when it is addressed to the self" (Mead, 1964:246). The behavioral data of Mead's social psychology are significant gestures, and because of the universality of significant symbols, these data are completely objective.

Mead's theory of meaning had the same triadic structure as Peirce's sign-object-interpretant. Mead (1964:246) noted that signification has a double reference, one to the thing indicated (i.e., Peirce's "object") and the second to the response (i.e., Peirce's "interpretant"). Thus, if one says, "Close the door," the object or thing indicated by that gesture is the physical door, but the interpretant or response to that gesture is the *act* of closing the door. To know a language is to have a complex set of behavioral dispositions, each of which will be released by the appropriate complex of significant symbols (Mead, 1964:128–29). This, of course, does not mean that B will close the door as A demands, but it does mean that both A and B will respond to A's gesture by taking the same (physiological) attitude toward it. This "door-closing" attitude is the preparatory phase of the act and, from a strictly logical standpoint, constitutes the whole meaning of the gesture. It is not necessary that either A or B *fully* carry out the indicated act for both to grasp the meaning of the gesture (see Cottrell, 1980).

The "self," as a concept of Mead's social behaviorism, can be understood as a system of habituated responses to an indefinitely large set of potential significant gestures, which may be made within the perspective of the social group to which the individual possessing such a "self" belongs. The responses occur whenever the significant gestures are made either by the individual himself or by some other person or agent (newspaper, radio, etc.). It follows that individuals have a different self for each distinct social group to which they belong: "We divide ourselves up in all sorts of different selves with reference to our acquaintances" (Mead, 1934:142).

Mead repeatedly insisted that the self is not antecedent to the social process. It arises simultaneously with the organism's ability to take the role of the other toward himself or herself. Mead (1934:155) characterized this process as follows: "Only in so far as he takes the attitude of the organized social group to which he belongs toward the organized, cooperative social activity or set of such activities in which that group as such is engaged, does he develop a complete self or possess the sort of complete self he has developed." The individual owes every content of the self to the social structure of the community. The structure of society determines the structure of individual selves, not vice versa: "What goes to make up the organized self is the organization of the attitudes which are common to the group. A person is a personality because he belongs to a community, because he takes over the institutions of that community into his own conduct" (Mead, 1934:162). A social institution is objectively real only because its members base their conduct upon the attitude of the generalized other and, as a result, "the structure of the self expresses or reflects the general behavior pattern of this social group" (Mead, 1934:164).

Mead's theory of the self denies the reality of the individual personalities supposedly maintained in isolation from the social process. Mind is not located in the individual at all. Mental processes are inextricably bound to the social reality out of which they arise (Mead, 1938:372, 616–17; 1934:222). It was the error of Descartes and other rationalists (including phenomenologists) to attempt to tear down and analyze the content of consciousness apart from the social process within which mind emerges and operates. This error leads to subjectivism and its various attendant forms of nominalism, including the biofunctional psychology of James and Dewey.

For James and Dewey, mind is essentially a biological function by which an organism adjusts and controls events in its stream of experience. For Mead and Peirce (5.128), mind is essentially a *social* function by which different individuals coordinate their activities and relationships to each other. As such, the locus of mind is not in the individual—it is in the social *process* which binds together the activities of members of the community. In Mead's terms: "If mind is socially constituted, then the field or locus of any given individual mind must extend as far as the social activity or apparatus of social relations which constitutes it extends; and hence that field cannot be bounded by the skin of the individual organism to which it belongs" (1934:223n).

In the midst of expounding his extremely sociologistic theory of self and mind, Mead (1934:255) apparently paused during his lectures (published as *Mind, Self, and Society*) to answer disgruntled romantic individualists:

Hence social control, so far from tending to crush out the human individual or to obliterate his self-conscious individuality, is, on the contrary, actually constitutive of and inextricably associated with that individuality; for the individual is what he is, as a conscious and individual personality, just in as far as he is a member of society, involved in the social process of experience and activity, and thereby socially controlled in his conduct.

If the process of socialization is understood in the terms indicated by the above passage, then an "oversocialized conception of man" (Wrong, 1961) is as impossible to attain as the idea of a square triangle. In fact, according to Mead's theory, an individual who is socialized into many social groups has a greater capacity for innovative thought and expression than an individual who is a member of only one group and, therefore, can experience the world from only perspective. Mead (1934:262) added that there is no necessary reason for institutions to be repressive and inflexible. Indeed, sociologists should know that most norms must be somewhat general, especially in the area of specifying means of compliance. As Mead (1934:262) stated:

There is no necessary or inevitable reason why social institutions should be oppressive or rigidly conservative, or why they should not rather be, as many are, flexible and progressive, fostering individuality rather than discouraging it. In any case, without social institutions of some sort, without the organized social attitudes and activities by which social institutions are constituted, there could be no fully mature individual selves or personalities at all; for the individuals involved in the general social life-process of which social institutions are organized manifestations can develop and possess fully mature selves or personalities only in so far as each one of them reflects or prehends in his individual experience these organized social attitudes and activities which social institutions embody or represent.

The mistaken belief that social realism commits one to the view that institutions straitjacket individuals into social robots is probably the main reason it has been summarily dismissed by most American sociologists. For example, the sociologies of Durkheim and Parsons are frequently caricatured as representing such an extreme position. In the passage quoted above, Mead proposes a social behaviorist definition of social institutions as "organized social attitudes and activities," and explicitly states that, although by this definition a mature self is one that internalizes the social process, these social attitudes may (and, for Mead, should) promote rational, progressive, and democratic forms of social organization.

This liberal social philosophy was endorsed by all the pragmatists, but with different points of emphasis. James and Dewey were mainly concerned with its implications for the welfare of individuals, while Peirce was more interested in its function in promoting further "concrete reasonableness" in the community-at-large. Mead's orientation was more evenly divided between the individual and societal consequences of pragmatic liberalism.

In summary, the proper subject matter of a truly *sociological* social psychology—such as Mead's—is the activity of individuals insofar as they are acting as self-conscious members of a social group. Because such acts necessarily involve significant symbols (and, therefore, selves), their meaning is objective. Only such objectively meaningful data are admitted by social behaviorism. The *covert* phase of the act (i.e., taking attitudes) is a subject of physiological psychology to which social psychology, as the study of the *overt* phase of the act, is its counterpart (see Mead, 1964:94–104). Given organized social activity and the development of the nervous system which enables the organism to take the attitude of others, Mead (1934:366) concluded that "one does not have to come back to certain conscious fields lodged inside the individual." For Mead, the appeal of social behaviorism lies in the fact that its subject matter consists of entirely objective data. Although social behaviorism postulates the reality of subjectivity (the feelings of the individual *qua* individual), it defines the study of such subjective sensations as lying outside the field of social psychology (Mead, 1964:310).

Our analysis of Mead's philosophy and social psychology concludes by returning to the problem with which we began: the question of compatibility between the philosophies of Dewey and Mead. By delineating the social realist undergirdings of Mead's thought in contrast to the social nominalist foundations of Dewey's philosophy (see chapter 4), we clarified and supported our thesis that their philosophies diverge at the core. Yet it would be misleading not to reiterate that there remained tangents of Mead's pragmatism which were seemingly nourished, if not inspired, by his relationship with Dewey. We are referring, for example, to Mead's rather naïve and idealistic political philosophy which reflects a Deweyan preoccupation with democracy, individualism, and rationality.

We will not continue to systematically identify such Deweyan lacunae in Mead's philosophy. Instead it will be more productive to display—against the backdrop of Mead's more Peircean social realist core—the James / Dewey nominalist fringe of Mead's pragmatism. This will be done with a detailed examination of its manifestation in one illustrative case. Mead's view of the nature of "truth" is especially appropriate here, for as we have seen previously, this issue sharply divided the other pragmatists.

It is a curious fact that, although truth is a key philosophical concept, Mead wrote very little about it. This may be explained partly by Mead's constant insistence upon the need to separate science from epistemology (see Natanson, 1956:87). For the epistemologist, the meaning of truth is an important and extremely difficult problem. But for science, truth is not a critical issue. Scientists ask only whether the object will operate within the perspective—they have no need to define or demonstrate truth in any absolute sense. Mead's preoccupation with the study of scientific methodology never forced him to consider truth from the epistemological standpoint. The word "truth" does not appear in the index of *The Philosophy of the Act*.

Mead's only lengthy comment on the nature of truth was his 1929 paper entitled "A Pragmatic Theory of Truth." Even in this paper, Mead's interest is in scientific truth, and he rejects all epistemological pretenses of "Truth at Large" (Mead, 1964:324). Much of the article is concerned with describing the scientific method of attaining truth, and "truth" is usually defined as the product of the application of that method:

1. For science, truth is the accord of its hypothetical construction with the world within which the problem has appeared [1964:324]

2. The test of truth which I have presented is the ongoing of conduct which has been stopped by a conflict of meanings. [1964:328]

3. Truth is then synonymous with the solution of the problem. [1964:328]

4. Many so-called truths are insignificant and trivial, but this overlooks the character of the judgment, which is one of reconstruction and does not attain truth until experience can proceed where it was inhibited. [1964:338]

5. The truth is not the *achievement* of the solution. [1964:328]

The above statements reflect what Mead regarded as the nature of truth. According to (1), truth is the "accord" of the reconstruction with the world of the perspective. The verb "accord" suggests some type of congruence or correspondence. The reconstruction asserts that certain relationships will hold between the hypothetical object and objects in "the world that is there." If these relationships can, if fact, obtain, then the reconstruction is in "accord" with the world—it is true.

However, ambiguities arise when we consider statements (2) and (3) together. According to (2), the ongoing of conduct is not truth—it is only the *test* of truth. Truth itself must be defined in some other way, such as in (1). Yet (3) *equates* truth with the solution of the problem. If we also equate the solution of the problem with the ongoing of conduct, then (3) is a flat contradiction of (2), insofar as truth is not the test of truth. If we assume that Mead's statements are logically consistent with each other, in order for (2) and (3) to be consistent, we must deny that the problem's solution is logically interchangeable with the ongoing of conduct. To give an alternative interpretation of (3), we must ask what constitutes the solution of a problem.

Statements (1), (2), and (3) are logically consistent with each other if we take Mead's position to be that the problem is solved when the reconstruction makes it *possible* for conduct to proceed within the perspective. The ongoing of conduct (the test) merely confirms the reality of the possibility (the truth). This would represent a clean break with Dewey, because for Dewey, it is the activity itself and not the possibility of such activity which constitutes truth. Not only does this interpretation of Mead render (1), (2), and (3) consistent, it is also supported by (4) and (5). Notice that in (4), Mead says that the reconstruction is true if experience can proceed (but not necessarily *does* proceed). This distinction is more explicitly stated in (5), where Mead emphatically states that truth is not the *achievement* of the solution. If we may return to our example of the broken clock (pp. 106–10), truth was at hand at the moment we hit upon the right hypothesis. The actual achievement of the repairs simply tests and confirms the truth of the hypothesis—it does not constitute its truth. The truth of a hypothesis is antecedent to its working because truth consists in its real *capacity* to work and not in its *actual* working on any specific occasion.

On this point, Mead's theory of truth more closely approximates Peirce's than James's and Dewey's. Like Peirce, Mead expressed faith in the self-correcting method of science. Although he never explicitly defined truth as the beliefs the scientific community would reach if inquiry were continued indefinitely, he appears, at least in the following passage, to have moved in that direction:

Our problem is the attainment of an intelligible universe, and we advance toward it by processes of scientific hypothesis, which are never out of the range of possible attack and which are generally but provisionally adopted; and this advance toward a goal at infinity, so far as our minute endeavors are concerned, takes place by continual reconstructions in many fields that confessedly implicate one another. The goal of experience lies indefinitely beyond experience, and the method of approach is by a thought constructed which can have no criterion but the growing coherency of their objectives and their partial attainments. [Mead, 1964:332]

Yet on the whole, we cannot unqualifyingly identify Mead's theory with that of any of the other American pragmatists. We have already noted disparities between Mead's statements and the James / Dewey theory of truth—although, to be sure, there are many points of agreement on a more general level. Regarding Peirce, Mead's thought was definitely oriented toward the continued growth of the scientific perspective by peicemeal increments directed at a goal we can barely see over the horizon. There was, however, a profound difference in the intensity of this futuristic orientation. At the time Mead's article was written (1929), he was only beginning to hint at a conception of truth and science that Peirce had warmly embraced for decades. Furthermore, it is not clear that Mead would deny truth to a proposition that had "worked" for a time but that later became problematic and was discarded. For example, consider the statement, "The earth is flat." For centuries, navigators plotted their courses according to that hypothesis and sailed from point A to point B without difficulty. It was only with the advent of long-distance voyages that the hypothesis failed. Can we say that the hypothesis was true then but false today? Dewey, of course, said "yes" to that question. Peirce, equally assuredly, would have answered "no." If Mead remained true to the principles of his philosophy of science, he would answer "no," because according to his theory of scientific method, all genuine solutions to scientific problems must be *general* solutions. If the earth is flat, then every experimental implication of that fact must be true or else the perspective is destined to collapse. This points toward Peirce's conception of a perspective that never collapses as the ideal limit toward which scientific belief is slowly converging and which serves as a regulatory principle in terms of which truth is defined. On the other hand, Mead never specifies any temporal requirements for the problem solution. Is it a sufficient condition for the definition of truth that a hypothesis "work" one time? We have already discussed the weaknesses of that theory in analyzing Dewey's philosophy. At times, Mead seems to be taking the Deweyan extreme contextualist approach to truth due to an unreasonable fear of embracing some grandiose metaphysical truth spelled with a capital "T." But his theory of scientific perspectives dictates a more Peircean approach. Mead oscillated between the extreme particularism of the James / Dewey theory and the extreme universalism of the Peircean theory, finally settling with a theory not entirely like either.

Mead's theory of truth vividly illustrates the relationship of his philosophy to that of the other pragmatists. The dominant direction of his thought was decidedly contrary to the subjectivism of the James / Dewey psychology and epistemology, and yet he felt a certain sympathy for both of them, especially Dewey. Whatever nominalist undertones persisted in Mead's philosophy—such as exemplified in his article on truth—should be attributed to the lingering influence of James and Dewey (see Coser, 1978:309–11). However, this should not prevent us from recognizing that, inconsistencies notwithstanding, Mead's core position is essentially opposed to the pragmatism of James and Dewey for the same reasons we found to prevail in Peirce's philosophy.

Part Two

Toward an Intellectual History of Chicago Sociology

Consider the following quotations from James and Peirce:

> And I for my part cannot but consider the talk of the contemporary sociological school about averages and general laws and pre-determined tendencies, with its obligatory undervaluing of the importance of individual differences, as the most pernicious and immoral of fatalisms. [James, 1956:261–62]

> Now you and I—what are we? Mere cells of the social organism. Our deepest sentiment pronounces the verdict of our own insignificance. Psychological analysis shows that there is nothing which distinguishes my personal identity except my faults and my limitations—or if you please, my blind will, which it is my highest endeavor to annihilate. [Peirce, 1.673]

The above quotations starkly contrast the nominalistic and realistic forms of pragmatism. Nominalistic pragmatism defines reality, thought, truth, science, and knowledge by reference to that which is particular, biocentric, and individual. Realistic pragmatism finds the meanings of these concepts in that which is universal, social, and general. Peirce's philosophy is undoubtedly a purified example of realistic pragmatism, and James's radical empiricism is an equally pristine example of nominalistic pragmatism.

Dewey was in the unfortunate position of becoming the third member of this pragmatic "tradition." Much of the intellectual strabismus of Dewey's later philosophy was created by his futile attempt to synthesize the insoluble foci of James, Peirce, and his other influence—Mead. But in the end, one cannot remain true to two masters who were so much at odds even over fundamental matters as were James and Peirce. Ultimately, Dewey's theory of inquiry remained faithful to James's psychology and forsook Peirce's principles. Although Dewey tried to retrieve Peirce in his *Logic* by claiming Peirce's theory of truth as his own and crediting Peirce as the precursor of the Deweyan theory of inquiry, the thrust of Dewey's philosophy is decidedly toward nominalistic pragmatism. The same must be said of his attempts in *Experience and Nature* and elsewhere to incorporate Mead's social theory of meaning and self into the biological framework of Jamesian functional psychology.

Petras (1968a) and other sociologists have praised Dewey's "reflex arc" article as a landmark in social psychology. As we have shown, however, the basis of that article is firmly rooted in the "stream-of-experience" concept of James's functional psychology, by which "consciousness" is reduced to the selecting function of neural circuits in the brain. This selecting function of the brain allows the organism to constitute stimuli and coordinate experiences in the "stream." There is absolutely nothing social about the theory. One need postulate only a brain, nervous system, and a sensible environment. It is this biologistic psychology that underlies Dewey's theory of inquiry and leads to his nominalistic, individualistic concepts of meaning, knowledge, and truth which are virtually identical to James's.

Viewed in the context established by Peirce, James, and Mead, Dewey's work at different times responded to all of them. But the voice his mind heard most clearly and consistently was James's. We, however, do not wish to make any grandiose claims of finality in our interpretation of Dewey. Our only firm contention is that, if Dewey's philosophy is classified according to the nominalism / realism criterion, he belongs on the nominalistic side with James, and essentially for the same reasons. On other grounds, all the pragmatists were in harmony. Consequently, Dewey can be viewed from standpoints other than ours, some of which would present Peirce, James, Dewey, and Mead as comprising a unified tradition which might be called classical American pragmatism. We have no quarrel with such characterizations, provided they are submitted as broad generalities. In constructing a collective taxonomy of philosophical systems, this type of sweeping overview is required. But our analysis demands scrutiny of the deeper structure of these various philosophies from the particular point of view of the nominalism / realism issue. Unquestionably, this focus has caused us to emphasize those points that distinguish Peirce from James and Dewey, and to understate points of agreement among them.

It is particularly important to keep this disclaimer in mind in Mead's case. We have purposely drawn attention to the realistic underpinnings of Mead's philosophy in order to highlight some essential differences between Mead and Dewey. On the basis of the nominalism / realism issue, a wedge can be driven between Dewey and Mead. But, from the perspectives of nearly all commentators on the history of pragmatism, the philosophies of Dewey of Mead seem practically indistinguishable. As far as we have been able to determine, James Feibleman (1946, 1970:464–83) is the only eminent historian of American pragmatism to have undertaken the systematic study of Peirce, James, and Dewey explicitly from the standpoint of the nominalism / realism question. He proposed a radical split between the realistic pragmatism of Peirce and the nominalistic pragmatism of James and Dewey. We have argued that, from this particular perspective, Mead must be classified as basically a realistic pragmatist with occasional inconsistencies in the direction of Dewey.

In this chapter, we outline some of the pragmatists' major lines of influence on the intellectual history of Chicago sociology from 1892 to 1935. Given the sharply contrasting views of the nature of meaning and individual consciousness represented in the social realism of Peirce and Mead, as compared to the social nominalism of the functional psychology of James and Dewey, one might suspect that these two branches of American pragmatism had equally dissimilar and contrasting effects upon the Chicago sociologists. By applying a schema for classifying the metatheoretical orientations of the Chicago sociologists, we show that this is substantially the case. Blumerian symbolic interactionism will be shown to be theoretically continuous with the social nominalist branch of Chicago sociology rather than the social realist thrust of Mead. This result calls for a reexamination of the intellectual antecedents of Blumerian symbolic interactionism as well as a reassessment of Mead's relation to the Chicago sociologists.

Introduction: The "Chicago School"

Reflecting upon the sociologists comprising the "Chicago School," Morris Janowitz (1966:x–xi) lamented, "They have all disappeared without

having caused an adequate intellectual and social history to be written."
With the 1970 appearance of R. E. L. Faris's admirable effort, Janowitz,
in the foreword to the book, added that "with the passage of time such an
effort became increasingly difficult and it is now perhaps impossible."
    We are inclined to agree with Janowitz's observation. However, this
does not imply that a *specific* question about the social or intellectual
history of the Chicago School cannot be studied adequately with existing
resources. The first and most obvious such question is in what sense did
there ever exist a Chicago "school"? To this query, Janowitz (1966:vii)
argued that "it is a disputable question whether there was a distinct or
unified Chicago approach to sociology. . . . the Chicago school contained
theoretical viewpoints and substantive interests which were extremely
variegated." Nevertheless, a mountain of sociology textbooks refer to the
Chicago "tradition" of Dewey, Mead, Thomas, Blumer, Faris, and
others, while giving comparatively little attention to the notable *differences* between these theorists. As a result, an over-simplified portrayal
of Chicago thought is presented.
    Our purpose in Part Two of this book is to begin to correct this
conception of Chicago sociology. Extending the approach used in Part
One, the aim of this chapter is to assess the extent to which the
nominalistic and realistic branches of American pragmatism were per-
petuated in corresponding enclaves of the Chicago sociology department.
Thus, our specific interest in the intellectual history is confined to identifying currents of social nominalism and social realism among Chicago
sociologists and their associates. For this reason, we have selected for
discussion sociologists who were most instrumental in shaping the
theoretical orientations of early Chicago sociology and who, by virtue of
their contact with Dewey and Mead, best exemplify these contrasting
perspectives. Inasmuch as we have included a sufficient number and variety of theorists for this purpose, the addition of other Chicagoans, such
as E. S. Bogardus, L. L. Bernard, or members of the ecological group,
would lengthen our presentation without contributing to the refinement
of our schema. We must leave it to future studies to supply these details.
We argue that a social nominalistic metatheoretical orientation predominated during the early years (1892 until roughly 1916), and that
social realism emerged from certain corners of Chicago sociology from
1920 onward. This general movement is unmistakable, but there remain
a number of smaller questions concerning classifications of particular
sociologists and the identification of subcategories or substantive approaches.
    Given our special interest in the history of symbolic interactionism, a
primary concern is to locate George Herbert Mead and Herbert Blumer

within their respective intellectual niches. To achieve this, it is necessary to distinguish two groups of theorists prevalent during the nominalist period: the "social forces" group and the "interactionist" group. We will then show that Blumer's theory follows the interactionist orientation, whereas Mead, as we have already seen, was continuous with the social realists. Although the nominalist / realist split between Blumer and Mead is as clear as the same split between some members of the Chicago sociology faculty itself, our particular classifications of the other theorists into categories and subgroups is a tentative proposal offered merely to provide a rough framework for situating Blumer and Mead within the intellectual history of Chicago scholarship. In particular, it must be stressed that we are not proposing to investigate the institutionalization of sociology or social psychology at the University of Chicago. If such an inquiry were even possible, it would greatly detour us from tracing the intellectual impact of pragmatic philosophy in general, and of Mead in particular, upon the Chicago sociologists. Therefore, this chapter is designed to serve a limited purpose.

The Early School: "Social Forces"

The Chicago Department of Sociology originated in the nineteenth century, 1892 to be exact, and intellectually, it remained there for over two decades. To be sure, there were changes and developments, but all were variations of old themes. As the chairman and central figure in the department, Albion Small contributed the most toward articulating and maintaining a distinct theoretical orientation (see Dibble, 1975). Charles R. Henderson and George Vincent, other members of the department, shared Small's desire to make academic sociology responsive to social and moral issues, but they were much less involved in developing abstract theoretical perspectives; consequently, Small dominates our attention.[1]

Small's most significant work was *General Sociology,* a textbook published in 1905. The sociology of Small's era is best described as an effort to determine the scope of the implications and applications of Darwin's theory (which was at the height of its prestige in scientific circles) to the newly formed and still ill-defined field of sociology. Small and other sociologists sensed the danger that sociology would be coopted by the more mature science of biology, and the complexity of social reality thereby would be reduced to its biological substructure.

For Small, this danger was clearly evident in Herbert Spencer's sociology, and Small expended considerable energy debunking it. He was particularly critical of Spencer's practice of accumulating masses of factual data grouped under static classifications without adequately explaining their mechanism of origin (Small, 1905:113). Small (1905:142) similarly rejected Spencer's biological homologies: "These individuals do not grow together into a great animal. They adjust themselves to each other in a society."

The latter statement reveals Small's conception of the proper object of sociology, reiterating his belief that "the subject matter of sociology is the process of human association." The individualistic thrust of Small's social thought is further emphasized by his declaration that sociology must abandon the "fantastical interpretations of society, in which individuals figure as so much material in the course of cosmic evolution, or so many cogs in a social machinery, or so many cells in living social tissues." Small could not accept any form of social holism, asserting his reductionist principle in simple language: "All social facts are combinations of individual facts" (Small, 1905:3, 50, 185).

If the goal of sociology is to explain the actual social processes of human association instead of subsuming and concealing them under the rubric of some grandiose organicist or mechanistic metaphor, what theoretical alternative should be adopted? As much as Small saw the need to transcend organic sociology, he never entirely escaped from that framework. His position was that sociology must tolerate the organic analogy as the best available formulation until something better appears (Small, 1905:75–76). Biological notions were not expressions to be embraced; they survive only as a hypothesis (Small, 1900:58). Nonetheless, this shift constituted a significant advance over Spencer in the evolution of social thought, though it may seem a small achievement to some modern sociologists. The general format of Small's substantive theory follows the "social forces" tradition of Edward Ross and, even more, Lester Ward's *Dynamic Sociology* (1883). Ward challenged Spencer by contending that, in addition to the purely biological survival instincts, there also exist within each person inner *social* compulsions. These "social forces' impel humans to associate in order to satisfy these forces, just as the food instinct impels us to eat.

Small (1905:196–97) called his own list of six primordial social forces "interests": health, wealth, sociability, knowledge, beauty, and rightness.[2] Presumably, any social act could be traced to one or more of these interests; or, as Small succinctly put its, "In the beginning were interests."[3] His position was imbued with Social Darwinist overtones. The universal process of association is characterized by the "antithesis of individuals" who stimulate each other "through the medium of conflicting wants," resulting in "self-assertion" by the individuals and the establishment of a "system of dominance" (1905:11). The parallel with the process of social organization in animal societies is indeed striking.

That Small viewed social institutions as simply a means to satisfy individual wants is further reflected in his invocation of the old contract theory of the State (Small, 1905:242–322). The social process consists in dynamic interaction between conjunction of interests and conflict of interests (1905:203), and, as the process continues, there is a gradual shift from a preliminary conflictual mode of association toward a primarily conjunctive mode (1905:205, 279): "Natural life is conflict, but it is conflict converging toward minimum conflict and maximum co-operation and sociability" (1905:371).[4]

Turning to the early work of W. I. Thomas, one sees another example of "social forces" theory. As a graduate student, he studied under Small and Henderson, but instead of Small's six interests, Thomas proposed four "wishes": new experience, mastery, recognition, and security. Still, Thomas remained within the social forces paradigm, and his books *Sex and Society* (1907) and *The Unadjusted Girl* (1923) most clearly employ biologistic notions and psychological reductionist assumptions. However, Thomas was less philosophical about theorizing than were Small and the other early sociologists. He managed with a few simple concepts (e.g., wish, attitude, value, crisis, situation), devoting most of his energy to research—his famous book (written with Znaniecki) *The Polish Peasant in Europe and America* being the prime example.

Although Thomas is remembered for this work, one forgets that he began his career as a purely biologistic sociologist. He opened his dissertation with the declaration, "It is increasingly apparent that all sociological manifestations proceed from physiological conditions" (Thomas, 1897:31). His efforts to demonstrate this proposition led to some amusingly ludicrous statements. Fortunately, Thomas eventually broadened his conceptual horizons—although traces of his four wishes and other social forces trappings remained in his later work—and he drifted toward a more psychical interactionist model. It is this orientation we now consider.

The Early School: The Psychical Interactionists

Even before the last vestiges of the social forces formulations disappeared, a competing theoretical orientation was on the scene. We call it the "interactionionist" theory, because it draws attention away from the

biological givens and centers upon the actual field of interpersonal interaction as the primary source of social organization. The psychical interactionists were more aware that the biological universals can be accom-
modated through a wide variety of social structures. It is, therefore,
impossible to explain the diverse array of concrete forms of social organization by pointing to a list of universal "instincts" or "forces." Rather,
each form must be interpreted through the specific interpersonal and
historical processes that conditioned its occurrence.

Methodologically, the interactionist approach forces the sociologist
out of the armchair; no theory can be based upon universal principles of
human nature derived from a philosophy of history. All concrete and
social facts must be comprehended as manifesting the drama of human
interactions in a particular historical setting. Because the actor's personal
motives and intentions are central to understanding the social action, the
method of "sympathetic introspection" becomes an indispensable tool
for the sociologist.

The interactionist theory constituted a far more radical departure from
the social forces theory than did the latter from the biological sociology
of Spencer. The interactionists did not simply modify and weaken the
organic analogy as did social forces theorists; rather, they pushed it into
the background. Their theories were essentially psychical in that, by
deemphasizing genetic-organic conceptualizations, the social process was
rendered more "open" to manipulation by self-conscious individuals—
each of whom was capable of voluntarily cooperating or competing with
others, depending upon which strategy appeared more conducive to
achieving his / her social or biological ends. The individual is not a passive organism driven by blind, inner social compulsions; on the contrary,
the organism is consciously interpreting the environment and scheming
with and against others in pursuit of personal goals which are mostly
nonorganic. The interactionist theory is still Social Darwinist in its general view of society, but it is a psychically based Social Darwinism rather
than the more organically based Darwinism of the instinct or social forces
theory.

This movement toward psychological sociology, while still nominalistic, marked a monumental advance in American social theory. The social
forces school died and was buried unceremoniously along with its proponents. Today the names of Ward, Ross, Giddings, and Small are little
more than historical footnotes. By contrast, not only has the interactionist school survived, but new strains also have appeared under such
names as "existential" sociology, "phenomenological" sociology,
"humanistic" sociology, and "dramaturgical" sociology. Moreover,
some early proponents, such as Cooley and Blumer, are still widely read.

As John W. Petras (1970) has shown, the development of the thought
of W. I. Thomas exemplifies the shift from the organic to the interactionist framework. Edmund H. Volkart (1951:16–18) noted that
Thomas found the four wishes increasingly unworkable. They could not
be proven to exist, nor could their connection with behavior be demonstrated. For this reason, Thomas eventually adopted the "situational"
approach, wherein the individual's definition of the social situation is the
critical unit in explaining social action, and universal human impulses
reduce to background assumptions. Thomas's *The Child in America*
(1928) is a good example of the use of the situational approach:

> Focusing on "instincts," "consciousness," "original nature," [the
> traditional interpretations] attempted to explain why the organism
> behaves in given ways in view of its internal nature and structure,
> and the attempt has led to a great deal of controversy and much
> confusion. On the contrary, we find that all the programs which we
> outlined in the preceding chapter are behavioristic. They ignore
> largely questions of the organic causation of behavior, the *"why"* of
> behavior reactions, and limit themselves to the observation, mea-
> surement and comparison of behavior manifestations—*how* the indi-
> vidual behaves in specific situations. [Thomas and Thomas,
> 1928:557–58]

The situation encompasses three elements (Thomas, 1951:57). First,
there is the set of social objects, or "values," which in some respect bear
upon the consciousness of the actor. They arise from all institutionalized
sectors of society and are relatively objective. Second, we have the actor's
preexisting attitudes with respect to these relevant social objects. The
"attitudes" are essentially subjective, arising uniquely from the actor's
prior experiences. Third, the actor's "definition" of the situation must be
counted as part of the total situation. The definition of the situation is the
actor's understanding of the values, attitudes, and environmental conditions.[5] Because the actor always acts "as if" the situation is as he
subjectively defines it, the definition is the most reliable predictor of the
actor's behavior. The objective reality of the situation is of secondary
concern: "If men define situations as real, they are real in their consequences" (Thomas and Thomas, 1928:572).

The situational approach commits the researcher to the following
interpretive principle: "The cause of a social or individual phenomenon is
never another social or individual phenomenon alone, but always a combination of a social and individual phenomenon" (Thomas, 1951:55).
The individual acts toward an object according to the meanings that
object has acquired through both personal contact and prior socialization
as a "consciousness member of a social group" (1951:156). But can we

say which of these meanings will take precedence in the individual's definition of the situation, either in general or in particular cases? Thomas (1951:164) saw a persistent tension between the individual and society over which meanings will dominate:

> There is, of course, no pre-existing harmony whatever between the individual and the social factors of personal evolution, and the fundamental tendencies of the individual are always in some disaccordance with the fundamental tendencies of social control. Personal evolution is always a struggle between the individual and society—a struggle for self-expression on the part of the individual, for his subjection on the part of society—and it is in the total course of this struggle that the personality—not as a static "essence" but as a dynamic, continually evolving set of activities—manifests and constructs itself.

Out of this struggle, Thomas (1951:159) saw the emergence of three basic personality types: the thoroughly socialized "Philistine," the unstable and unsystematized "Bohemian" personality, and the self-evolving reflective "creative individual."[6] Thomas conceived of the individual as a superconscious organism, always deliberately reflecting upon every situation and defining it anew on every occasion (Thomas, 1951:158). Apparently, he was seeking to minimize the biological view of the individual as fundamentally a passive agent. His position can be contrasted with Mead's who saw *most* acts as habituated responses proceeding without self-conscious reflection. Thomas deemed individual personality dynamics the crucial force in the social process and, indeed, defined social psychology as "an extension of individual psychology to the phenomenon of collective life" (Barnes, 1948b:797). Even allowing Thomas's shift in emphasis from organic to psychical conceptions, he remained a social nominalist and always retained the individualistic, goal-oriented image of humans (see Hinkle, 1952:481–83). Barnes's (1948b:795) observation that Thomas was "cordial to John Dewey's instrumentalist philosophy" is quite correct and very telling. Thomas himself was not sure of his respective intellectual debts to Dewey and Mead (see Baker, 1973).

Berenice Fisher and Anselm Strauss (1978b:460) argue convincingly that Thomas and Mead belonged to two distinctly different types of interactionist psychology. They argue further that Thomas and Park established a theoretical approach significantly inspired by the James-Dewey psychology and a style of empirical research which became the dominant scholarly orientation of Chicago sociology. Thomas's *Polish Peasant* was an exemplar for the Chicago style of empirical research, and it stimulated a strong monograph tradition at Chicago. Fisher and

Strauss (1978b:485) note that, although "both critics and interactionists tend to take Blumer's version of Mead and of symbolic interactionism," it is ironic that, in his substantive works, even Blumer himself has followed the Thomas-Park mainstream.

From a superficial reading, the interactionist theory may appear to be a variant of social realism, in that it admits the reality of social structures and the limitations they place upon individual action (while also maintaining reciprocal influences). Yet one characteristic of the interactionist theory, especially evident in Thomas and Blumer, clearly distinguishes it from social realism: the interactionist theory perceives the individual as cognitively free from social control. This is accomplished by externalizing social roles, belief systems, and all other forms of social structure. As a result, they restrain the individual only in that they entail positive and negative sanctions; the individual coldbloodedly calculates such sanctions in the course of struggling to plot a strategy to achieve personal goals, whether socially approved or not. Social conventions and constraints are placed outside the individual—never inside. The individuals totally objectify and externalize their own cultural system; thus, in a sense, they are only half-socialized. The individual learns the system for the purpose of better manipulating it to fulfill personal demands:

> In order to become a social personality in any domain the individual must therefore not only realize the existence of the social meanings which objects possess in the domain, but also learn how to adapt himself to the demands which society puts upon him from the standpoint of these meanings and how to control these meanings for his personal purposes; and since meanings imply conscious thought, he must do this by conscious reflexes. In order to satisfy the social demands put upon his personality he must reflectively organize his attitudes; in order to obtain the satisfaction of his own demands, he must develop intellectual methods for control of social reality in place of the instinctive ways which are sufficient to control natural reality. [Thomas, 1951:156–57]

Thomas was well aware of the methodological implications of his Social Darwinian interactionist theory. Since the theory accords explanatory primacy to internal psychical processes, no social act is adequately explained and verified until the sociologist has produced sympathetic introspective interpretations of the actor's innermost motives and definitions. Clues must be sought in letters, diaries, and other "backstage" personal documents or expressions. The observation of overt behavior can only supply hypotheses; confirmation awaits introspective data interpretations.

Shifting our attention to C. H. Cooley, although he was never on the

Chicago faculty, the early Chicago sociologists were keenly aware of his work. Cooley (1964:123) would remind us that, sociologically speaking, his psychical presence was far more significant than his corporeal absence. It is, however, difficult to place Cooley within any of the three metatheoretical orientations under discussion. Hinkle (1966:xii) has, with good reason, called Cooley a "romantic idealist." Cooley continually insisted upon the organic unity of the individual and society: "Self and society go together, as phases of a common whole" (Cooley, 1962:8–9). Unlike Small, Cooley was not close to the debates which raged between the other early sociologists; he was more attuned to the literary thought of Emerson and Goethe, and this holistic quality of Cooley's sociology may be traced to Spinoza's philosophy through Goethe, but without Spinoza's pantheism (Cooley, 1964:154).

If we again ignore the religious element, Cooley's organistic idealism is remarkably similar to the philosophy of Josiah Royce, a contemporary of Cooley's and, for a time, a central figure in American philosophy. Yet Cooley made no reference to Royce. Yet there is adequate reason to hypothesize that Cooley developed his position independently, even though both were connected to the American pragmatists—Royce to the realistic branch through Peirce, and Cooley to the nominalistic branch mainly through James. These connections had predictable consequences for the different theories of self-development and language acquisition proposed by Cooley and Royce. Briefly, Royce developed his theory of self-emergence out of Peirce's theory of signs which, as we have shown, involves a highly sociologistic philosophy of mind, whereas Cooley's account of self-formulation ultimately falls back on Jamesian psychologistic principles and presuppositions.

Interestingly, Mead (who, it may be recalled, studied under Royce) detected the psychologistic underpinnings in the self-theory of both James and Cooley. Of Cooley, Mead (1930:701) wrote: "I think that Cooley was Emersonian in finding the individual self in an overself, but he does not depend upon such a doctrine for his sociology. He comes back to what he calls 'ordinary psychology' for his interpretation of what goes on in the mind." And later: "In conduct [self] is a precipitate about a fundamental impulse or instinct of appropriation and power, while the primary content appears as a feeling or sentiment, the self-feeling which defies further analysis. Here Cooley follows James very closely" (Mead, 1930:696). Mead continued by remarking that Cooley reduces the self to inner, psychical experience rather than conceiving of self as a genuinely *intersubjective* phenomenon occurring within, as Mead (1964:xxxv) put it, "an objective phase of experience which we set off against a psychical phase." Cooley inherited this nominalistic error from James, about whom Mead (1964:386) similarly observed, "For all his analysis of the self, James's individual remained a soul."

Mead perceptively noticed the fissure in Cooley's thought. In reading Cooley, one hardly gains the impression that he was a rigorous, systematic theorist (Gutman, 1958:253). Mead (1930:702) commented that part of *Human Nature and the Social Order* is an unscientific "ethical treatise." In fact, the bulk of Cooley's writing is more accurately described as social commentary than social theory in any strict sense. From this standpoint, it is understandable how Cooley could be oblivious to the fact that his Emersonian idealistic organicism on the macrolevel is negated by a Jamesian social psychology on the microlevel. It is this radical cleavage, even more than his undisciplined, editorializing style of discourse,[7] which makes it impossible to neatly categorize Cooley's theory. It is fair to join Hinkle in calling Cooley a romantic idealist but, approaching his thought from another direction, it is equally defensible to label him a Jamesian radical empricist. Thus, the contradiction is only apparent in Mead's assertions that Cooley's theory of self is an advance over James's and, at the same time, Cooley's view of self-genesis is subject to the same objections as James's from the perspective of a social realist.

Let us begin to document these claims. As Hinkle (1963:708) stated, Cooley held to a subjective, organic idealism. It is essential to distinguish this idealistic organicism from the biologic organicism of many of Cooley's contemporaries. Cooley (1964:37) regarded the words "society" and "individuals" as "simply collective and distributive aspects of the same thing." And in only slightly different language "Society and the mind are aspects of the same whole" (Cooley, 1964:181). These statements lead one to question Cooley's social ontology; in other words, exactly what is the "whole" of which the society and individual are aspects? Like Dewey, Cooley committed himself to a monistic ontology, but, whereas Dewey consistently referred to his single metaphysical category as "nature," Cooley was less concerned with specifying even a name. When he did identify the common whole, he called it "human life" (Cooley, 1966:26) or, more reverently, "Human Life" (Cooley, 1962:36).

What is the character of this entity called human life? A materialist might suggest that human life is confined to the mass of physical organisms which, although they may be *conceived* collectively or distributively, are real only in their individual manifestation—the conception of the collectivity being a mere fiction. An idealist solution, on the other hand, would regard the whole as the only reality, making illusory the notion of an independent individual. Second, the idealist formulation conceives of the whole as a psychical unity rather than a material unity. That Cooley adopted the idealistic view is abundantly clear throughout *Social Organization* and *Human Nature and Social Order*. Concerning the independent individual, Cooley (1962:5) remarked, "Self and society are twin-born, we know one as immediately as we know the other, and the notion of a separate and independent ego is an illusion." Similarly, "In so far as one identifies himself with a whole, loyalty to that whole is loyalty to himself; it is self-realization, something in which one cannot fail without losing self-respect" (Cooley, 1962:38). Cooley's idealism destroys all traces of individualism or individual "personality" in a way very reminiscent of Peirce (1.673). The individual is devoted to his own particular work and primary groups but "feels himself and that work as part of a large and joyous whole." This sentiment is tantamount to Peirce's doctrine of "evolutionary love." Cooley's idealism is almost Platonic and merges with Durkheim's group mind orientation in the assertion that "the individual mind is not a separate growth, but rather a differentiation within the general mind" (Cooley, 1962:71; 1964:134). It follows that group conditions are the source of personal character (Cooley, 1962:48).

When one looks to the internal structure of Cooley's theory to gain a glimpse of the generic social processes by which this "whole" is created and maintained, the aforementioned disjunctive quality of his thought surfaces. It is from this vantage point that one can understand Hinkle's claim that Cooley's idealism is subjective, as well as Mead's criticism that Cooley relied on psychology to provide a theory of the genesis of the social self. The key at this interpretive juncture lies in recognizing Cooley's reliance upon James's psychology, a debt Cooley (1964:125n, 170, 175; 1930:4) made clear.

Recall that James's radical empiricism holds that consciousness is a brain function by which feeling impulses in the stream of experience are selected and related. Cooley drew his conception of "self" directly from James's psychology, imagining one's self to be a peculiar type of "excitement" or "emotion" (to use James's terms) which is aroused by everything that can be called one's own (Cooley, 1964:170). Cooley called this emotion "self-feeling."[8] This feeling is instinctive, but exists only in a vague form at birth. With experience, this emotional mass of energy partially breaks up into separate "self-sentiments." Through contacts with other humans, primitive emotions (e.g., fear and anger) become somewhat socialized into sentiments (Cooley, 1964:86, 126, 138). Cooley followed James further by making no sharp distinction between thought and feeling (Cooley, 1962:177); he joined James in virtually reducing all types of consciousness to modes of feeling. This reduction of self to a type of feeling, or Peircean firstness, guarantees a concept which Mead charged "defies further analysis." This is an even greater error than supposing that the individual is born with self-feelings, because it assures that Cooley, like James, would be unable to produce an adequate account of thought and symbolic communication.

This result is manifested in Cooley's analysis of the social process by which feelings are socially shaped into sentiments. He treated symbols simply as events which become associated with certain feelings (Cooley, 1964:100). Cooley's theory is a tight paraphrase of James's: "In our minds the comparatively simple ideas which are called suggestions are by no means single and primary, but each one is itself a living, shifting, multifarious bit of life, a portion of the fluid 'stream of thought' formed by some sort of selection and synthesis out of simpler elements" (Cooley, 1964:53).

Notice that in the above statement and elsewhere (e.g., Cooley 1964:114–15), Cooley freely introduces the word "mind" most innocently. Had Cooley maintained that the associations take place by simple physiologically conditioned stimuli and responses, he would have been a pure behaviorist. In fact, his position is not in the least behaviorist because he smuggles a "mind" into the picture. As we have seen, James struggled vigorously, albeit not always successfully, to rid his functional psychology of the lurking "ego" behind the scenes. Cooley glibly adopted James's psychology, but remained impervious to its inherent dilemmas. This is yet another indication of Cooley's insensitivity to deeper theoretical issues.

What, then, does the "mind" do in Cooley's theory? Mainly, it conjures up *imaginations*. Through imaginations, symbols are associated with feeling states and social sentiments are created. These socialized sentiments (love, respect, honor, mortification, generosity, emulation, etc.) constitute the cornerstone of Cooley's theory of social organization and social control. Above all, the most critical imaginations are ego's imaginations of how he or she is imagined by others: "Directly or indirectly the imagination of how we appear to others is a controlling force in all normal minds" (Cooley, 1964:203). The imaginations, even when inaccurate, lose none of their force (Cooley, 1964:95). Thomas may have derived his notion of the situational "definition" from Cooley's "imaginations"; in any case both serve similar purposes and render both Thomas's and Cooley's theories of social interaction subjective and psychological. Moreover, Cooley made "imaginations of imaginations" as central to his sociology as Thomas made "definition of the situation." Cooley (1964:121) forcefully summarized, "I conclude, therefore, that the imaginations which people have of one another are the *solid facts* of society, and that to observe these must be a chief aim of sociology."

Methodologically, Cooley must embrace sympathetic introspection just as other psychical interactionists. It follows from Cooley's theory that the object of study for sociology is "primarily an imaginative idea or group of ideas in the mind, that we have to imagine imaginations." Accordingly, "In other words, we want to get at motives, and *motives spring from personal ideas*" [emphasis added] (Cooley, 1964:122). The imaginations of imaginations is complicated for Cooley by the fact that "self-respecting" persons may reject and deny what appears in the famous looking-glass as well as fake certain presentations of self (1964:236, 352).

Cooley (1930:289–309) endorsed several methodological principles shared with Thomas. He argued that we must distinguish between material knowledge and social knowledge, for although sensation and measurement are adequate means for knowing the material world, they fail to capture the essentially dramatic character of the social world. Nevertheless, Cooley and Thomas proposed that human knowledge is both behavioristic and sympathetic. Cooley admitted, "I am a behaviorist as far as I think I can be without being a fanatic." Similarly, Cooley tolerated statistical methods, but only as "complementary" to introspection into imaginations.

To summarize, Cooley's romantic, idealistic cosmology is disconnected from his theory of human interaction, communicative processes, and the self. While the former tended toward social realism, the latter being rooted in Jamesian psychology, is nominalistic and subjectivistic. In both theory and method, Cooley's social psychology follows the interactionist orientation.

Charles A. Ellwood, like Thomas, entered graduate school in the Chicago department at a time when instinct theory and social forces doctrines were dominant. He came to professional maturity when interactionism had more or less successfully challenged social forces theory. Not surprisingly, then, Ellwood's thought reflects both the organic and psychical approach to sociology—a trait that prompted Faris (1926b:306) to complain of Ellwood: "The middle-of-the-road scholar, like the middle-of-the-road politician, is safe, never far wrong but sometimes not a little tame." Despite his sympathy for instinct theory, Ellwood developed a psychological sociology not unlike that of Thomas and Cooley.

Ellwood is of special interest for two reasons. First, he was the only Chicago sociologist who was a true disciple of Dewey, and his early thought was dedicated to making Dewey's instrumentalism the basis of sociological theory. Other Chicagoans borrowed sporadically from Dewey, but none nearly so much as Ellwood. Consequently, any assessment of the impact of pragmatism upon Chicago sociology must give careful attention to Ellwood. The second source of interest in Ellwood lies in his relationship to Blumerian symbolic interactionism. It is somewhat odd that Blumer (1977) has denied any intellectual debt to Ellwood, in light of their personal association and the similarity of their thought (Lewis, 1977). Not only was Blumer Ellwood's student, but Ellwood directed Blumer's master's thesis. If the similarity of their social thought is simply a case of coincidences, then the roots of Blumer's theory must be sought in other interactionists, especially Thomas and Cooley, or in Blumer's perception of Mead. The problem is probably impossible to resolve, but any serious attempt to trace the intellectual history of symbolic interactionism must, in our view, deal with Ellwood.

Ellwood's doctoral thesis, *Some Prolegomena to Social Psychology,* is an example of the pitfalls of any attempt to apply Dewey's functional psychology to social psychology. One simply cannot explain social facts in terms of psychological theories without distorting one or both of them in the process. In the present case, the nature of social reality or society is distorted in order to fit Dewey's psychology to its processes. Ellwood (1901:13) managed to remain true to the Darwinian biofunctional theory of mind proposed by James and Dewey:

> The coordination is, therefore, the fundamental and central fact of the psychical life. All other psychical facts are functional expressions of the coordination, or of the relation of one coordination to another within the life-process. Thus the psychical life presents itself as a system of means and ends, whose unity finds expression in the general end of control over the means of existence, that is, over the conditions of survival. Summarizing, then, we may say that Professor Dewey's psychological point of view is that of a life process or life-activity, functioning to secure control over its own life-conditions, and thereby its own development.

Functional psychology is an individual rather than a social psychology. Individual behavior is the unit of analysis, and the constitution of the organism is taken as the basis of explanation. But from a sociological perspective, it is group processes (not individual) which constitute the proper object of inquiry for social psychology, and the explanatory base must be found in group dynamics, not in the psychological attributes of its particular members (Lewis, 1976a). Hence, there is a deep chasm between the aims and methods of functional psychology and those of a social psychology based upon sociological principles instead of concepts taken from biology and individual psychology.

Ellwood attempted to solve this problem by treating society as a superindividual: "Social psychology, then, in regarding social groups as functional unities, necessarily regards them as individualities or individuals" (Ellwood, 1901:35). However, this should not be taken as a metaphysical reification of society. Ellwood only claimed that, on wholly metaphorical grounds, the social psychologist must view social groups *as if* they were individuals. With this assumption, one can describe group processes as the coordinating activity of an individual organism toward its environment. But, for Ellwood, only in a metaphorical or fictional sense can it be said that the social group coordinates, adjusts, and so on. According to Ellwood (1901:36), it is only through the psychical interactions of individual members that group processes occur.

Ellwood's analogy of the society to the individual organism involves a functional parallelism without any corresponding structural parallelism. That is, although the social group makes the functional adjustment and coordination of its environment just as if it were an individual organism, that coordination is made possible *not* by the social structure of the group—which acquires a *sui generis* social force apart from its individual elements—but by psychical interactions among group members. The group per se has no unified structure—there is no such reality as Durkheim's collective conscience: "In all the higher reaches of organic life individual organisms usually present a unified consciousness. . . . They are, structurally, then, of a much lower type than their individual elements" (Ellwood, 1901:35–36).

In the final analysis, Ellwood left the gulf between functional psychology and sociology as wide as ever. That outcome was inevitable from the onset, but Ellwood must be recognized in the history of sociology as the sociologist who, far more than any other, attempted the wholesale application of Dewey's psychology to sociology. That the experiment failed so miserably by the standards of contemporary sociological theory challenges the popular notion held by Faris (1970), Petras (1968a), and many others that Dewey's psychology is an important contribution to sociology. If anything, as our earlier discussion of Dewey suggests and Ellwood's dissertation plainly illustrates, Dewey's psychology was an intellectual impediment to the development of realistic sociology at Chicago.

Ellwood gradually moved away from purified Deweyism, although the

Deweyan influence is contained in three quite redundant books: *Sociology in Its Psychological Aspects* (1912), *An Introduction to Social Psychology* (1917), and *The Psychology of Human Society* (1927). Ellwood (1927:7) defined society as "collective or group life carried on by means of conscious relations between its members or, concretely, as any group of individuals who carry on common activities or a common life by means of mental interstimulation and response." For Ellwood, the correct image presents society as a group of individuals who are "coadapting" to each other (Ellwood, 1912:180); for example, one individual stimulates another by suggesting something, and the second person then responds to that suggestion in some way. This response then serves as a stimulation for the first person, and the process continues. Ellwood called this the process of "interstimulation and response," and this principle forms the core of his sociology.

Although Ellwood conceded the importance of institutions as established and habitual patterns of mental interaction, his position was characteristically interactionist in holding that the institutions are externalized. Society (i.e., other individuals) conditions the individual mind by being a part of the individual's environment to which he or she must adapt. The individual approaches this social environment from an independent, autonomous position: "Human society is not a simple mass, but is made up of relatively independent, autonomous individuals" (Ellwood, 1917:75). And again, "The external mark of the 'social' is the interdependence in activity or behavior of a group of relatively independent individuals" (1927:8). Finally, "Here we wish only to emphasize that the individual must be conceived of as a self-active and relatively independent unit, more or less capable of determining his own behavior among the conditions and forces surrounding him" (1927:77).

Ellwood was well aware of the methodological position logically entailed by the interactionist theory of society. If the social process is "a process of reciprocal adaptation of individuals to one another in the carrying on of some phase of group life" (Ellwood, 1927:82), it follows that "the individual mind is the basis of group behavior." Consequently, all sociological explanations of social processes must be based upon laws of individual psychology: "The scientific analysis of society leads back to the psychic individual" (1927:464). Ellwood's theory of society methodologically entails psychological / biological reductionism, a position he did not hesitate to assert (1912:58–59).

Against methodological objectivism, which Ellwood mostly identified with behaviorism, he argued that it is based upon a false analogy between the social sciences and the physical sciences. Since the causative force underlying all social life is the psychical life of autonomous, coadapting individuals, sociology requires a method that will uncover the subjective content of individual minds. Obviously, all objective methods are inadequate for this purpose. Ellwood (1933:57–59) concluded, therefore, that sociology must rely upon introspection into one's own subjective states or those of others: "After deduction from ascertained laws and principles of psychology, sympathetic introspection is probably our chief instrument at the present time for the psychological analysis of existing social life" (1917:15). By "introspection," Ellwood simply meant that the "social observer puts himself in imagination in the situation of the person or class of persons who he wishes to understand" (1921:90).

Herbert Blumer is the last psychical interactionist we shall consider. Like Ellwood, Blumer has proposed a psychological sociology which views "interpretive interaction" (Blumer, 1964:170–71) as the source of social organization. Because Blumer professes to base his symbolic interactionism on Mead's theory, we must organize our discussion of Blumer around a comparative analysis in order to show that Blumer follows the psychical interactionist position of James, Dewey, Thomas, Cooley, and Ellwood, rather than the social realism of Peirce and Mead (see Cottrell, 1980).

Blumer's 1928 doctoral dissertation was directed by Ellsworth Faris. The dissertation is an historically useful document because it records the influence of Faris and Mead on Blumer's early thought, as well as the roots of certain tensions thereby created, tensions he has since overcome by moving toward a more purified psychical interactionism. We suspect, for example, that contemporary symbolic interactionists would be surprised to learn that the young Blumer (1928:22) asserted that "experimentation should always accompany the framing of hypotheses" or that "public accessibility" of instrumental relationships between phenomena is a necessary condition for the possibility of a science, and "there is nothing in human behavior which prevents the application of the natural scientific method to human behavior" (Blumer, 1928:31–32). Clearly, these statements—as well as Blumer's (1928:341) attack on the methodological validity of sympathetic introspection—mark, at this early stage of his career, Blumer's acceptance of Mead's claim that the social sciences and natural sciences are methodologically continuous. That Blumer (1969a) has since totally reversed himself on this question barely requires statement.

Blumer was able to see how Mead's social psychology opposed Watsonian behaviorism, but he failed to appreciate the radical differences between the psychical interactionism of Thomas and Cooley as opposed to

the social realism of Mead and Faris. Blumer (1928:266) merely groups
all these theorists together as opponents of psychological behaviorism.
Although correct, this unfortunately does not make further important
distinctions. Hence, they were eventually to be defined by Blumer as the
symbolic interactionist "tradition."

In discussing Cooley's theory, Blumer (1928:336) seemed aware of
Cooley's subjectivistic and nominalistic leanings: "To conceive, as does
Cooley, of social objects as existing in one's mind, lays one open to a
dangerous and difficult logical position and makes him easy game for the
realist." Yet Blumer was not fully prepared to accept Mead's attack on
Cooley, for he continued, "Fortunately, Cooley's own writings show that
this formulation has not led him into difficulty."

Blumer (1928:66), in fact, regarded Cooley as "an eminent social psychologist" (a high compliment coming, as it does, from one who has spent
a career playing critic). And, in his interpretation of Mead, Blumer attempted to recast Mead's theory of meaning and consciousness along the
lines of Cooley's social psychology. For instance, "Mead's views [sic]
that the interaction is primarily through the interpretation of gestures
would not secure assent on the part of those who seek explanation in
physical causation." This is the first step toward transforming Mead into
a psychical interactionist. The second step is to undercut Mead's social
theory of meaning by making meanings dependent upon subjective,
Cooleyian "imaginations" rather than on the objective, communal
character of significant symbols: "This indication, or meaning, of the
activity or gesture, is secured by the individual filling out *in his imagination* the act represented by the gesture" (Blumer, 1928:182). The theory
of meaning is thus supplied by Cooley's mentalism rather than by Mead's
social behaviorism.

We can determine a possible source of Blumer's misunderstanding of
Mead by returning to Mead's theory of meaning, and noting how Blumer
proposes to explicate its key principle. Recall that, for Mead, the meaning of a significant symbol consists in the common attitude the interactants take toward the gesture; furthermore, this taking of the attitude
of the other toward one's own gesture is, for Mead, a covert, physiological, habitual response. It is thus *not* a mentalistic or conscious process.
Blumer's first step in rejecting this conception was to substitute the term
"role" for "attitude." While the Meadian "attitude" has a strict physiological referent, the term "role" implies a more nebulous and dramaturgical meaning and is therefore conducive to a psychical interactionist
formulation. One can then explain the organisms' common attitude toward the significant symbol as being a *result* of the psychical process of

each interactant taking the "role" of the other. If the common attitude toward the gesture is to occur, all this cognitive activity on the part of each interactant must first transpire.

But did Blumer really believe that this accurately represents Mead's theory of meaning? Blumer (1928:217) appeared content in his dissertation to claim that Mead's position is unclear between psychical interactionism and social behaviorism. "It is not clear whether this similarity of inner response is to be identified with the taking of the role of the other or is a result of such activity." Blumer generally opted for the latter interpretation, although on at least one occasion he went so far as to assert the Meadian view that "meanings are in behavior; not in the mind" (Blumer, 1928:337).

To summarize, Blumer's dissertation is torn between the social behaviorism of Mead and the psychical interactionism of Cooley, Thomas, and others, even though he did not consistently admit their differences or his own ambiguous stance respecting those differences (e.g., his tendency to accept Cooley's theory but Mead's methodology). To the extent that Blumer did attempt to resolve his ambivalences, he did so by interpreting Mead in such a way that Mead's theory of human interaction became virtually equivalent to Cooley's.

By the time Blumer wrote the 1937 essay announcing "symbolic interactionism" to the world, he had come even closer to the psychology of Thomas, Ellwood, and Cooley. Blumer (1937:164, 192) postulated primordial "impulses" which become channeled by social definitions into culturally accepted goals. The parallel to Thomas's relations between wishes, values, attitudes, and definitions of situation is obvious. Blumer's formulation is also reminiscent of Cooley's notion of the progressive refinement of social sentiments. Blumer (1937:171–72) moved completely toward psychical interactionism: "A acts; B perceives this action and seeks to ascertain its meaning, that is, to ascertain A's intention; B responds to what meaning or interpretation he has attached to A's act." Unlike the Meadian social behaviorist, the psychical interactionist holds that the meanings of symbols are not universal and objective; rather, meanings are individual and subjective in that they are "attached" to the symbols by the receiver according to however he or she chooses to "interpret" them.[9] The 1937 essay also begins to more closely align Blumer's methodological position with his theoretical commitments. The emphasis is now away from the Meadian prescription for an objective, experimental approach, and more toward the qualitative, interpretive methodology of Thomas, Cooley, and Ellwood (see Blumer, 1937:194).

Moving to Blumer's (1969a) more recent statements of symbolic interactionism, the only significant change since the 1937 essay has been a gradual departure from the organicist model of the earlier theorists in favor of a more purely phenomenological orientation. References to interaction between organic and psychical phenomena have virtually disappeared. Nevertheless, Blumer's voluntaristic nominalism has remained intact and is, if anything, stronger than ever.

Blumer (1969a:7) has stated that "society consists of individuals interacting with one another." This statement invites several questions: Must this interaction have some particular form? Persons engaged in open warfare are interacting with one another; do they therefore constitute a society? How are these "individuals" to be conceived? Are they biological organisms, free-willed agents, or, as Peirce said, mere cells of the social organism?

We shall consider the last question first, in that it provides the key to understanding Blumer's conception of interaction. Blumer (1969a:7, 19) repudiates any view which conceives of individuals as mere passive responders whose thoughts and actions are determined by biological or sociological forces outside their control. For this reason, he rejects both stimulus-response behaviorism and structural sociology. He correctly observes that symbolic interactionism implies a humanistic philosophy.[10]

Blumer does not accept the reality of socialization in the usual sense—as a process by which individuals' actions are guided by internalizing the norms and values of the social groups to which they belong. Rather, social organization simply "sets conditions" for the individual's actions (Blumer, 1969a:87–88). The social structure of one's society merely exists as a tool to be used or as an obstacle to be avoided in the process of constructing one's actions (Blumer, 1969a:75). The individuals take social organization "into account" and make the necessary adjustments in order to successfully carry out the line of action they are "mapping" (Blumer, 1969a:15).

A temporary social order is negotiated by the interactants on each occasion of their interaction and must by renegotiated on every subsequent occasion. Blumer (1969a:75) grants that in "highly ritualized relations" the content of the actions can be explained by roles: but even these actions are formed anew each time by the same psychical process as less routinized types of interaction (Blumer, 1969a:18). Consequently, Blumer finds the locus of *every* social act in the individual (Blumer, 1969a:84). The individual never merges his or her identity with the social group as, for example, Mead and Durkheim said occurs in religious experiences. Blumer's individual remains absolutely sacrosanct and detached from any degree of social determination.

When these disaffected individuals are brought together to interact, that interaction can be understood only in terms of a Social Darwinain model of society such as that implied by Ellwood's notions of "cooperation" and "coadaptation." There is no place in Blumer's theory for Mead's generalized other—only flesh-and-blood others figure in calculating one's actions. Blumer could not admit the generalized other without also admitting the relatively stable social structure that concept logically entails. But for Mead, the generalized other is involved in every thought and, therefore, every act.

This consideration underscores the fact that Blumer's conception of interaction and the locus of meaning is diametrically opposed to Mead's, as evidenced by Blumer's (1969a:2) very first premise: "Human beings act toward things on the basis of the meanings that the things have for them." Mead's followers would subscribe to this premise only if "for them" were deleted, a phrase that makes meanings individual rather than universal. Once Mead's social theory of mind is taken seriously, even one's most private thoughts are perceived as extensions of the social process of communicating with a generalized other through significant symbols. To think without invoking significant symbols is impossible; therefore, any meaning an object can have is grounded in the universal symbolism of the thinker's community. For Mead, Peirce, Durkheim, and all realists, there is no such thing as meaning *for me;* there is only meaning *for us.* The phrase "subjective meaning," commonly used by nominalistic thinkers, is a contradiction of terms. Sensations are subjective, but meanings are not. Only by confusing the two is one led to entertain the notion of "subjective meaning."

From his nominalistic first premise, the only direction in which Blumer could move was deeper and deeper into subjectivism. The name "symbolic interactionism" is a misnomer for Blumer's theory. Indeed, Blumer (1969a) very rarely uses the word "symbol" and never uses the term "significant symbol." Whereas the significant symbol is the key concept of Mead's theory of meaning, the essence of Blumer's theory of meaning rejects symbols as "significant" in the Meadian sense. The term most central to Blumer's theory of meaning, and to symbolic interactionism in general, is "interpretation." One person exhibits some behavior, and a second person "interprets" it, first by attempting to ascertain what that person intends to do and then by determining what implications that action would have for his or her own contemplated action. This interpretation takes place through a process Blumer (1969a:14–15) calls "self-indication," by which the individuals take into account their interpretations of each other's acts and relate those interpretations to their own intended action. The outcome of all this thinking is the "meaning" for the individual, which his "interpretation" has "given" to the other's behavior (Blumer, 1969a:14, 18).

Mead, on the contrary, lodges meaning in significant symbols, not in the "interpretive" activity of individuals (see Lewis, 1977:292). According to Mead, the individual does not have to *give* meaning to significant symbols because they already *have* meanings, and the same meanings for *every* member of the community. To the extent that any intellectual communication takes place at all, it must take place through significant symbols. The reason Blumer does not make significant symbols the center of his own theory of meaning is that, as Mead said, the response (attitude taken) to a significant symbol is given in advance. This conception precludes both Blumer's self-activating individuals and their "interpretations" from contributing anything to its meaning.

If Blumer understood Peirce's and Mead's triadic theory of meaning, he would see that the meanings of symbols are universal and therefore grounded in the collective intelligence of the community, not in the subjective experience of individuals engaged in their own actions. Blumer (1969a:9) asserts that, according to the triadic theory, "the meaning of the gesture flows out along three lines. . . . It signifies what the person to whom it is directed is to do; it signifies what the person who is making the gesture plans to do; and it signifies the joint action that is to arise by the articulation of the acts of both." Blumer's joint action framework is far too narrow to render an intelligible account of the full range of meaningful activities. But, more to the point at hand, it seriously distorts the triadic theory of Peirce and Mead, destroying its realistic foundations. To use Mead's terminology, the three elements of the triad are the gesture, object or thing signified, and the response. The main principle of the theory is that the conventions of the community assure that the significant gesture will cause both persons to take the same attitude toward the object of the symbol. The speaker responds to his / her own gesture by taking the attitude of the other toward it. But, as we have seen, Mead views this as an automatic conditioned physiological reaction, and thus does not require Blumer's "interpretative" process of taking account of goals and intentions. Consequently, the significant symbol has the same meaning (i.e., causes the same response) when addressed to any member of the community by any other member; it is universal. The particular personalities of the individuals (including their anticipated actions) are irrelevant to the meaning the symbol carries. The operation of symbols thus does not depend upon any individualistic factors.

This impersonality of meaning implied by the triadic theory runs contrary to Blumer's voluntaristic nominalism; it places the meaning structure on which significant symbols depend *antecedent* to the use of such symbols rather than construing it as being created *after* the gesture through an individual's particular "interpretation" of the act. The particular individual, in the triadic theory, becomes precisely what Blumer (1969a:7) seeks to avoid by his own theory—namely, the conception of social interaction as a "forum" through which "sociological determinants" bring about "given forms of human behavior." According to Mead, if symbols did not determine responses, they would, indeed, not be symbols at all—they would be utterly meaningless, and thought would be impossible.

Another grave distortion of Mead's theory is Blumer's (1969a:14, 15, 73) concept of "self-indication." According to Blumer, Mead's theory imposes this process between "initiating factors" and "the action that may follow in their wake." It is through "self-indication" that the alleged "interpretation" finally "gives meaning" to the behavior of others. It is difficult to locate the sources of Blumer's misinterpretations of Mead because Blumer does not use Mead's terminology to portray Mead's theory and, to further complicate matters, he never quotes from or makes citations or explicit references to any of Mead's writings. In light of this difficulty, we can suggest only two possible referents to Mead's writings for Blumer's term "self-indication," and both misrepresent Mead's intentions.

First, individuals respond to their own significant symbol by assuming the attitude of those to whom it is directed. Vaguely speaking, this might be called "self-indication." But, because this process of attitude-taking does not require or produce any Blumerian "interpretations," it sharply contrasts with Blumer's understanding of self-indication.

The second possible referent of "self-indication" in Mead's theory is the interplay between the "I" and the "me." Yet this would be another misinterpretation if taken in Blumer's sense. In the first place, as Mead repeatedly stated, the evaluation of the "I" (response) from the standpoint of the "me" must necessarily take place *after* the reponse that occurred; therefore, this process cannot be understood as a *prelude* to the act it concerns (see Lewis, 1979). Furthermore, there is no "me" in Blumer's theory; indeed, Blumer (1969a:14) denies that human beings act from attitudes as "imported societal organization incorporated from the social structure of one's group." Blumer must reject Mead's "me" and "generalized other" as guiding influences upon human behavior because they contradict Blumer's conception of the individual as a spontaneous actor whose dispositions to act are not subject to social control. In contrast to this position, Mead (1934:78) stated:

The "me" represents a definite organization of the community there
in our own attitudes, and calling for a response, but the response that
takes place is something that just happens. There is no certainty in
regard to it. There is a moral necessity but no mechanical necessity
for the act. When it does take place then we find what has been done.
The above gives us, I think, the relative position of the "I" and "me"
in the situation, and the grounds for the separation of the two in
behavior.

The individual is always responding to a "me" but humans are not
infallible in executing responses; thus, the response may be different from
what was expected. At the instant the response occurs, it is not consciously controllable. It just takes place. Mead's term, "moral necessity,"
refers to the fact that the individual necessarily acts from the attitude of
some "me" and is therefore acting as a member of some community
which, for Mead, is a necessary condition for moral conduct. Because
human beings are not perfect machines, the actual response or "I" is
uncertain and thus occurs without "mechanical necessity." After the response occurs, the individual morally evaluates the "I" from the attitude
of the "me." Blumer's concept of "interpretation" has no place in Mead's
philosophy of the act at any of its stages.
    Yet a careful examination of Blumer's theory will show that the
explanatory term in the theory is "interpretation." He does, of course,
posit that actors have certain intended actions they hope to carry out,
although he does not explain how they came to have these intentions. In
any case, as Blumer constantly insists, the act does not follow directly
from having a certain intention. The act follows only after the completion
of the whole procedure of "self-indication" during which the original
intention to act may have become modified or discarded. Thus, to explain
an act, one must discover the "interpretation" on which it is predicated
because it is the interpretation that ultimately structures the act. Inasmuch as the "interpretation" is a psychical, not a social, phenomenon,
to explain any incident of collective behavior one must regard every
individual act as an independent event which grew from each individual's
unique concatenation of "interpretations" in concert with those of other
individuals. There is no collective conscience or generalized other; there
exist only so many individual consciences coadapting to each other from
autonomous positions. Therefore, a sociological explanation of an interpretative process is clearly out of the question. Because Blumer
(1969a:83) does not allow sociological explanations of behavior, neither
would he permit sociological explanations of interpretations, for that

would only result in adding one intermediate link to the social determination of behavior rather than totally eliminating it.

For the same reason, Blumer (1969a:83) also rejects all traditional psychological explanations of behavior (e.g., by reference to such factors as drives, motives, attitudes, internalized social factors), and would not permit such explanations of interpretations as well. The question then becomes, How are interpretations to be explained? That is, how does one explain why an individual interpreted something one way instead of another? Blumer has already implied that he does not accept biological, psychological, or sociological explanations. From a logical point of view, the only way Blumer can escape the conclusion that individual behavior is ultimately determined by factors that produce the interpretations, is to hold that *the interpretations are absolutely inexplicable.* Although Blumer never directly asserts this conclusion, he gives no hint of how interpretations are to be explained, either abstractly or in concrete cases. Indeed, he has attempted to close every avenue of explaining behavior beyond "interpretations."

Under the scrutiny of logical analysis, it is thus clear that, in Blumer's theory, interpretations "explain" every act but are themselves left unexplained, and must be left unexplained, in order to preserve Blumer's voluntarism. Practically speaking, all explanations have to stop at some point, but from a scientific standpoint, "interpretations" are an extremely undesirable terminus for the explanation of human behavior (see Stryker, 1977:150 n. 8). They are undesirable because there are no *laws* of interpretation—i.e., general propositions of the form, "under conditions 'c,' individuals of group 'y' (signifying types of interpreters if more than one type exists) will interpret an 'a' as 'b.'" This would at least approach "interpretation" as a scientific concept even though we have not reduced such laws to some more general theory. But without such laws of interpretation, we can never say that interpretation 'a' was a necessary or sufficient condition for the appearance of act 'b.' Consequently, to say that a person did 'b' because she / he had made interpretation 'a' is always unjustified and fails to explain the behavior scientifically.[11] Nonetheless, this outcome accords with the interest of Blumer's theory in keeping the action of individuals indeterministic. Blumer has certainly achieved that purpose by introducing "interpretations."

Because there are no observable indicators of any interpretations, Blumer rejects all objectivistic and behavioristic methodologies. Blumer's (1969a:174–82) attacks on objectivism in social psychology match Ellwood's in vigor if not in thoroughness. Mead's social behaviorism easily falls within the scope of his sword (see McPhail and Rexroat, 1979). The first premise of Mead's social behaviorism is that the proper subject matter of social psychology is the behavior of individuals only insofar as they are acting as members of social groups. Such actions are significant—their meaning is given in their performance rather than being dependent upon someone's "interpretation" of them. Mead did not encounter Blumer's methodological problems because he defined all purely idiosyncratic behavior as lying outside the scope of social psychology. But for Blumer, *all* behavior is idiosyncratic in that it originates from the actor's private "interpretations" which are free of social control: "One has to get inside of the defining process of the actor in order to understand his action" (Blumer, 1969a:16). This statement clearly reveals Blumer's psychical interactionism by placing the locus of social action within the subjective thought processes of individuals rather than in the context of a symbolically organized communal enterprise.

To summarize the interactionist theory, two points should be emphasized. First, Thomas, Cooley, Ellwood, and Blumer in no way comprised as strong an interpersonal network as did Peirce, James, Dewey, and Mead. If there was a "leader" in the group who influenced the others it was Cooley. But the more correct interpretation is that each drew more from *outside* this group than inside. This shows that psychological sociology was "in the air," and multiple avenues of cross-fertilization were utilized by interactionists even though no self-conscious "school" of interactionism crystallized at that time. Second, the separation between social forces theory and interactionism should be made but not exaggerated. Both orientations were simultaneously present in the first ten to fifteen years of Chicago sociology and, although the interactionists stressed psychical interactions over organic analogies and forces, each retained some rudiments of the instinct approach. Many of the major early American sociologists accepted Lamarckian principles which preclude any rigorous separation between human organic-genetic and psychic constitution. Nevertheless, they differ considerably over which of these structural dimensions receives primary theoretical attention, and this difference in emphasis forms the basis for distinguishing social forces theory from psychical interactionism. The psychical interactionists leaned more toward idealism, whereas the social forces theorists tended more strongly toward organicism-materialism. Although neither approach is perfectly univocal on the idealism-materialism question, both perspectives are reductionistic and, therefore, nominalistic, which ultimately makes them more alike than different. Because both were grounded in subjectivism, the only dispute that could arise between them was over the question of whether explanatory primacy should be granted to quasi-organic "forces" or to social realities negotiated through psychical contact. It remained for the social realists to elevate social psychology beyond nominalism and individualism.

The Intrusion of
Social Realism

For over twenty years, Albion Small's commentaries in the *American Journal of Sociology* were a serviceable barometer of the intellectual climate of American sociology. This was partly due to his advantageous position as editor of the only major sociology journal. But it also stands as a testimony to his intellectual flexibility which allowed him to grow with the discipline (Carey, 1975:103–4). By his own admission, Small always had a lively interest in the historical roots of sociology (Goodspeed, 1926:248).

By 1924, Small had long since ceased to write streams of book reviews for the journal, and so it may well have been with some purpose in mind that in that year he chose to "review" Durkheim's *Education et Sociologie*. We use the word "review" loosely because Small's intent seems to have been more concerned with going on record with a reconsideration of Durkheim than with offering a review of the particular book in question:

> Signs are not lacking that Americans may some time reconsider their estimate of Durkheim. All the American sociologists of the passing generation have read him, at least in snatches. They have punctuated their lectures and writings with references to him, more or less critical. It is doubtful if one among them feels that his appraisal is final. [Small, 1924:608]

Small's remarks, of course, were not running ahead of the community; rather, they were a reflection of the general consensus. By the mid-1920s, social realism's challenge to social nominalism was well under way in Chicago thought. One is tempted to credit Park's and Burgess's monumental text as the principal stimulus to realism. We do not wish to depreciate the value of the book or its impact upon American sociology; its reputation is well deserved. But a careful study of the intellectual history of the period suggests that Park and Burgess must share with some lesser appreciated sociologists the responsibility for bringing sociological realism to the surface.

One such individual was Edward Hayes. As the eleventh president of the American Sociological Association, he was hardly unknown and un-appreciated among his contemporaries. But somehow his role in the history of American sociology has become obscured, at least in comparison to Cooley, Thomas, Park, and others of his generation. His most influential single article probably was "The 'Social Forces' Error" which appeared in the *AJS* in 1911. The paper was a sustained attack upon the social forces paradigm, and surely hastened its demise. Roughly following Durkheim's reasoning, though possibly not knowingly, Hayes argued that it is hopeless to try to explain the variations in patterned social activity by appealing to the attributes of individuals or universal "forces." Rather, forms of social organization must be explained by referring to other structural variables and environmental / biological restraints. Indeed, Hayes's model was more inclusive than Durkheim's.[12] From the following passage, it can be seen that Hayes anticipated some of the directions of modern sociological theory:

> At any rate we must say that reference of social activities to the social forces does not constitute a proper idea of sociological explanation and that sociology abandoning quasi-explanation by reference to so-called forces must adopt the method of other sciences and account for its realities in terms of conditioning phenomena and relations between phenomena. If its explanations should become complete enough to justify prophecy, its forecast would be framed like this: give a population whose psychophysical organisms have such and such recognized tendencies, set in the midst of such and such a *material* environment, supplied in part by nature and in part by the labor of man, and in such and such a social environment, consisting of already prevalent activities, then such and such further activities will on the whole thereafter prevail, and if given modifications are now introduced into their physical and social environment such and such changes in the prevalent activities will ensure. [Hayes, 1911:625]

Hayes was aiming toward a macrotheory which integrates genetic, ecological, and social structural conditions as interacting factors that account for any given form of social organization and its processes of transformation. Changes in social structure (i.e., "prevalent activities") forced by ecological or technological changes will have consequences for other structured activities. Hayes's social realism shifts the focus of sociological theory and explanation away from atomistic individualism toward relationships between structural units. According to this account, explanation of behavior in terms of social forces or psychical interactions is superficial at best. The social forces theorists reacted strongly to this attack. For instance, Ross (1911:641) replied:

When a phenomenon such as falling off in births and increase in suicides, a growth in solidarity of labor, an increase in the number of elopements, or a shrinkage in crimes against the person is followed back link by link along the causal chain until we arrive at some impulse, appetite, propensity, passion, desire, or purpose of human beings in a specific situation, then, and not until then, is it *explained* from the point of view of the sociologist.

To this response, Hayes (1911:642) rejoined, "It seems to me on the contrary, that motive, instead of being explanation sought, is the thing to be explained." This head-to-head encounter between social nominalism and social realism, each defended by a skillful proponent, could hardly have failed to stimulate American sociologists' awareness of their metatheoretical commitments.

A similar exchange, also worth recounting, occurred between Hayes and Ellwood. Hayes (1910:613) commented:

My criticism of Professor Ellwood's paper is upon the matter of emphasis assigned to *activities* and *relations* . . . dependent on "psychic activities"; I should reverse that and say that society is a plexus of psychic activities dependent upon their interactions. This is not a *mere* matter of emphasis. There is no more fundamental methodological question than: What is to be explained, and what kind of causal relations furnish this explanation? The interwoven *ac--tivities* are the realities to be explained; the relations between them are the *main* factors in the explanation. There is no third reality to be called *inter*actions.

Ellwood (1910:617) clearly perceived the fundamental nature of their disagreement, retorting that Hayes "seems to me to lean toward a social realism which I cannot endorse."

The impact of Hayes upon his fellow sociologists was vividly registered, and thereby doubtlessly enhanced in Small's extensive chronicle, "Fifty Years of Sociology in the United States," written for the *AJS* in 1916. Small begins by reviewing Ward's challenge to Spencerian sociology, and then cites Hayes as initiating the next development: "In brief, Hayes charges Ward with falling into interpretations of 'social forces' which virtually nullify his other attempts to set them apart from mechanical forces" (Small, 1916:758). Small (1916:790) confessed his own role in advancing the social forces theory: "We were all more or less consciously and avowedly devoted to search for or to assertion of some single, central genetic principle, or force, or method of human society in all times and places." Reflecting back, he lamented, "The emptiness of this sort of work now almost makes my teeth chatter" (Small, 1916:773).

Without specifically naming Hayes, Small (1916:804) was obviously referring to him when he wrote that "the 1892–1901 group was challenged
by those for whom the primary interest was *interrelations between
human activities.*" Stressing the group concept, Small (1916:825) pointed
to the new horizon (new to most American sociologists, that is) introduced by Hayes: "Sociology is that variety of study of the common
subject-matter of social science which trains attention primarily upon the
forms and processes of groups."

Following Hayes's 1911 paper, there appeared two articles by John
Boodin in 1913 and 1918. Both are mainly of historical worth in that
they evidence further growth of the social realist seed planted by Hayes.
Boodin's (1913:28) article, "The Existence of Social Minds," gives no
notice to Durkheim but is frankly antinominalistic in declaring, "Whatever reality can be accorded to the abstract particular mind can be accorded to the social mind." In his follow-up article entitled "Social Systems," Boodin did grapple with Durkheim and justifiably criticized him
(and Hegel) for their overly idealistic "juristic formalism." but, more
significantly for our purposes, he was also highly critical of previous
American sociology, noting that "American sociologists in particular have
been infected with the old germ of solipsism" (Boodin, 1918:705–9).

Although there was a realistic trend, as exemplified by Boodin's articles, the only true landmark work in that tradition—coming from the
Chicago sociologists between Hayes's early essays and the Park / Burgess
text—was the dissertation of Walter Bodenhafer (also published in in-
stallments in the *AJS*). Although not a trailblazer in extending social
theory, the essay served a vital function for American sociologists at a
transitional point in the growth of the discipline by accurately depicting
in historical perspective the social forces, interactionist, and then-
budding social realist theories.

Bodenhafer (1921:441–42) observed that "there has been going on a
swing to the social interpretation of the origin of the mind both
phylogenetically and ontogenetically," which he called "the most
significant shift in the social sciences" and described it as "essentially the
shift to the group as the center of thought and investigation." He echoed
Hayes's criticisms of Ross, noting that Ross made only partial use of the
group concept: "His thinking is essentially individualistic" (Bodenhafer,
1921:443). Furthermore, it is especially noteworthy that Bodenhafer
(1921:443) quoted Mead's criticism of Ross: "Sociality is for Professor
Ross no fundamental feature of human consciousness, no determining
form of its structure."[13]

Bodenhafer's critique of Ellwood was most insightful in appreciating that, although Ellwood did not bridge the gap from interactionism to realism, the interactionist perspective constituted a significant advance over the earlier social forces tradition: "[Ellwood] has gone a long distance in attempting to bring sociology the results and methods of a newer type of psychology.... The chief criticism that might be made is that he did not go far enough" (Bodenhafer, 1921:454).

It would be a serious overstatement to say that the work of Hayes, Boodin, Bodenhafer, and others in the 1910–20 decade swept away social nominalism, but it is fair to say that they cleared enough room for social realism to gain a tenuous foothold. In other words, a mild drift toward social realism slightly preceded and continued concurrently with the Park / Burgess text. In this connection, it is notable that when Small (1921:231) listed the names of key individuals influencing the evolution of American social thought, the last names mentioned were Hayes and Bodenhafer.[14]

Thus, while the Park and Burgess text was in preparation, American sociological theory was in an unsettled condition. Most of the earlier social forces theorists were moving toward interactionism and were being challenged by the social realists for "not going far enough." This division can be detected even within the the the Chicago faculty, students, and associates, with Small, Thomas, Cooley, Blumer, Dewey, and Ellwood on the interactionist side, and Faris, Bodenhafer, Mead, and Hayes on the realist side. Reflecting upon the criticisms (cited thus far) which the realists directed toward the interactionists, it is clear that the social nominalism / social realism controversy lay at the heart of most of the disputes.

Park[15] was thus in a position—with respect to the other members of the Chicago extended family—in many ways parallel to Dewey's relationship to James and Peirce. As we shall see, the results were similar in both cases. Both men became part of an epistemic community divided to the core over the nominalism / realism problem. We have already shown the tension in Dewey's thought generated by his attempt to integrate elements of Peirce, James, and Mead into a single philosophy. Park faced a very similar situation.[16] Reading the Park / Burgess text, one is struck by the impression that, figuratively speaking, the authors are trying to pray at the altars of many gods. When these various threads are disentangled, two main strands emerge. First, Park, like the other Chicago sociologists, was immersed in the thought of the earlier American theorists, especially Cooley, Dewey, and Thomas. Second, and no less vital to Park's development, was his direct contact with German sociology—especially Windelband and Simmel—and his study of Durkheim (see Raushenbush, 1979). These latter influences account for the European style of Park's social psychology (see Coser, 1977:374–75). Together, these two divergent intellectual stimuli may explain some of the paradoxical shifts within the Park / Burgess text.

Park studied philosophy under James, Dewey, and Royce, but acknowledged in his dissertation that "the final development of my philosophical ideas owes most to the influence of Wilhelm Windelband" (Park, 1972:4). The 1904 dissertation, "The Crowd and the Public" was written under Windelband while Park studied in Europe. During this period, he developed principles that served as the basis for his later work in collective behavior, and that provided the theoretical overview of the Park / Burgess text.

Park's dissertation is substantively concerned with the explanation of crowd behavior, an interest that led him to confront the issue of whether to adopt a psychological or sociological theory of social organization. After reviewing the alternative conceptions, Park opted for the sociological approach in the second chapter, "The Sociological Process": "Only when the group itself is viewed as a subject, as one which takes positions and acts as an entity, can it become the object of a social psychological explanation" (Park, 1972:58). It was here that Park worked out his notions of the collective psychology versus individual psychology—what came to be called in the Park / Burgess text "corporate action." The significance of Park's dissertation work was summed up by Everett C. Hughes: "The results of Park's work in those four years of study in Germany are diffused throughout American and even world sociology, even unto today" (quoted by Elsner, 1972:vii).

Hughes, of course, was intimating that those results were carried over into Park's subsequent work, most notably the Park / Burgess text.[17] Interpretation of the Park / Burgess text does, however, present formidable difficulties. Although the dominant position of the text seems to reflect Park's European social realism, he made a deliberate effort to include Dewey, Cooley, Thomas, and, in short, the whole social nominalist tradition of American sociology. The following discussion of the book displays both of these qualities.

Park and Burgess (1970:40–42) explicitly distinguished social nominalism from social realism, and declared that the position of their text would be a realistic one. They rejected the conception that society consists of a group of independent individuals who create social organization through psychical interactions. They pointed out that American social psychology from Baldwin to Ellwood has been preoccupied with "the effects upon the individual of his contacts with other individuals," which can be contrasted and opposed to the study of collective behavior from the social realist perspective. Sociology, then, is regarded as the science of collective behavior made possible by the social control of the individual by groups (1970:189). According to Park and Burgess (1970:43), the nominalists follow in the manner of Spencer, whereas realists maintain the tradition of Comte; the same could have been said, in general, about American and European sociology, respectively. Park and Burgess (1970:33) also emphasized the nominalist / realist opposition by contrasting Tarde to Durkheim on the constitution of individual consciousness. They perceived that the intense dispute between Tarde and Durkheim revolved around the essential difference between interactionism and social realism: "Conscience . . . is a manifestation, *in* the individual consciousness, of the collective mind and the group will." They stressed the word "in" to call attention to the social character of consciousness in the realist theory.

This social realist theme was continued likewise in Park's 1927 article, "Human Nature and Collective Behavior," in which he wrote, "The same forces which co-operate to create the characteristic social organization and the accepted moral order of a given society or social group determine at the same time, to a greater or lesser extent, the character of the individuals who compose that society." Citing Durkheim, he further noted that society is possible through social control, or by "the fact of speech and by the existence of a fund of common symbols and meanings" (Park, 1927:737). He concludes that the individual lives a public existence wherein "all his acts are anticipated, checked, inhibited, or modified by the gestures and intentions of his fellows." Not only do we play social roles or, as Park put it, wear "masks," but the masks also become our "truer self" and "an integral part of our personality" (see also Park and Burgess, 1970:342). As a consequence, "We come into the world as individuals, achieve character, and become persons" (Park, 1927:739). The self is based upon the person's social roles in society (Park and Burgess, 1970:55), rather than existing as some sort of autonomous agent.

Examining the Park / Burgess text from the other side, however, reveals ample traces of social nominalism. It can be argued that the text suffers from the same ailment we have seen in Cooley's sociology. There are, in effect, two planes of discourse running through the book. On the macrolevel question of the relationship between consciousness and social organization, Park was, as shown above, a self-professed realist. Yet when required to provide an account of the process through which social consciousness is formed, Park relied upon the American tradition of

Dewey, Cooley, and Thomas. The structural component of Park's thought was definitely realistic, but his processual analysis remained essentially nominalistic. The absence in the text of any substantial recognition of Mead is as conspicuous as the prominence of Dewey.[18]

Janowitz (1970) has remarked that the text at points is subjectivistic and phenomenological. This tendency is particularly evident in the constant references to Cooley. Also, the claim that race prejudice is instinctive (Park and Burgess, 1970:285) is telling of the older tradition in American sociology. Indeed, the inclusion of a whole chapter of the text on the social forces following, as it did, the efforts of Faris, Hayes, Bodenhafer, and others to discredit the social forces doctrine, must be regarded as a nearly total anachronism. Schwendinger and Schwendinger (1974:408–9) charge that Parks' and Burgess's appeal to appetites, desires, and wishes as motives that underlie collective behavior "was obviously identical to the idea advanced by Ward at the very beginning of the formative years." Turner (1967) offered somewhat of an apology for Park's decadence in this area: "Park's reference to the social forces can perhaps be dismissed as a concession to completeness which he never followed up in his own work." Since the book was intended as a text, one might accept Turner's suggestion. Janowitz (1970:xvi) was much less sympathetic. Regardless, the fact remains that the Park / Burgess text, despite its metatheoretical realism, never worked out a complementary sociological psychology. Ironically, not only was a sociological social psychology available to Park, it was easily accessible in the person of Mead.

It appears that Faris was the only Chicago faculty member of the 1920s to fully avail himself of Mead. His article, "The Concept of Imitation," was a major step in breaking ties with an earlier sociological tradition. Following Mead, Faris (1926:373) stated, "The key seems to lie in the normal human tendency to converse with one's self, that is to stimulate one's self, and to answer one's own stimulation, in which process one takes the role of the other, and new attitudes of the other enter the repertory of the person." Faris thus argued that behaviors which the early sociologists attributed to imitation were actually the product of habit, attitude-taking, and conscious choice. Consequently, Faris (1926:377) wrote, "It is the conclusion of this discussion that imitation is hardly a justifiable psychological category."

Faris (1937a:99) likened social groups to the waves of an ocean. We cannot comprehend the effect of the wave by studying properties of the individual drops of water which form it. Analogously, the group acquires characteristics not present in its individuals. The group is therefore as real

as the individuals because any given group structure entails certain consequences which occur independently of the interests and intentions of
particular individuals: "Thus, the whole is greater than the parts and
precedes the parts. The whole even creates the parts, as the cultural unit
encourages those aspects which are consistent with it and attempts to
eliminate what seems to be undesirable." Hence, "The institutions and
groups in our modern life are not alone altering personality; they are
creating personality" (Faris, 1937a:35, 98).

Hinkle (1963:715) distinguished Faris from Ward, Ross, Giddings,
Small, Cooley, Thomas, and Park, designating all the others
"nominalists." If Hinkle's classification is correct, and we regard Park as
the only seriously disputable case, Faris's realistic psychology may have
pushed him to the social periphery of the Chicago school; there is no
doubt that this is true of his intellectual position. This would account for
the failure of the other Chicago faculty to cite Faris, even where his work
was of obvious relevance. Faris's work is also ignored by contemporary
symbolic interactionists.

Faris (1937a:133) was the only Chicago sociologist to criticize Thomas
for never achieving the social realist perspective, protesting against
Thomas's retention of the "instinctive equipment" and an "arresting
quartet of wishes." In another paper, Faris (1937:185) commented, "The
attempt to make wishes the atoms or elements of personality results
either in a rough classification of them or in a list of instinctive wishes
which present all the logical difficulties of any instinct doctrine." He also
analyzed the weaknesses of Thomas's attitude-value model, showing that
the social attitude is always directed toward a social object. Accordingly,
the attitude cannot be specified apart from its object, as Thomas attempted to do (Faris, 1937a:138–39). Lacking European contacts and
surrounded by nominalists, it is doubtful that he could have maintained
his position without Mead, a debt Faris (1937a:165) fully acknowledged.

Perhaps motivated by personal feelings, Faris was never quite content
to leave Thomas's core theory in the state of ruin entailed by this critique.
Besides his occasional flattering comments about Thomas's contributions
to sociology (see, for example, Faris, 1937a:71, 143), Faris was intent
upon nominally salvaging the "wishes" term. He did so by radically
redefining "wish" as a specific "incomplete act" (reminiscent of Mead's
concept of "distant object"), and then speculated that Thomas's wishes
were meant to signify stable behavioral tendencies which Faris termed
"attitudes" (Faris, 1937a:130–31, 151). Although Faris thus preserved
Thomas's terminology, he reformulated these concepts in Meadian fashion.

Faris was uncritical of Cooley, and appears to have been completely incognizant of the psychical interactionist base of Cooleys' social psychology. Like so many after him, Faris viewed the theories of Cooley and Mead as wholly compatible and complementary. In explicating Mead's theory of self-genesis, Faris (1937b:400) even went so far as to assert that Mead saw the self as built up through "imaginations."[19] As we have seen, Mead himself totally rejected the subjectivism of Cooley's theory of self, but he seems to have been unable to convince many sociologists, including Faris, of the essential differences between his theory and Cooley's.

In retrospect, what were the contributions of the pragmatists to the development of Chicago sociology? Peirce was probably unknown to nearly all of them, and James exerted influence indirectly, mostly through Cooley and Dewey. Cooley was the only sociologist to have derived a major portion of his theory directly from James, although it is likely that most of the Chicagoans read *Principles* with some mild effect. Faris was the only Chicago faculty member profoundly influenced by Mead, and there is little evidence that other Chicago faculty were more than dimly aware of Mead for many years. If they were, it is certainly not reflected in the formulation of their thought. Nor were Bodenhafer and Faris successful in bringing Mead to their attention in a meaningful way. Our examination of the major works of Small, Cooley, Thomas, Ellwood, and Park consistently points to the conclusion that Mead was a marginal figure in the intellectual history of Chicago sociology, having influenced Faris and perhaps a handful of graduate students but never the basic character of the department (which was always shaped by Small, Thomas, and Park). Ellwood was Dewey's only true disciple, but the other Chicagoans (especially Park) referred to him with some regularity—probably due more to his stature and the fact that he had something to say about nearly everything than to any deep commitment to his philosophy. Overall, the pragmatists exerted some direct and indirect effect upon Chicago sociology but were not the dominant force implied by many writers such as Carey (1976:163) in his sweeping generalization, "The framework for the sociological enterprise was provided by the Chicago pragmatists, represented by John Dewey and George Herbert Mead." With the exceptions noted above, most of the Chicago sociologists were reacting to other sociologists, and only secondarily to the pragmatists.

There remains the question of Mead's historical relationship to Chicago sociologists and the wider sociological community. We have developed the premise that intellectual divergence largely characterizes the metatheoretical position of Mead vis-à-vis most Chicago sociologists.

Even those sociologists who developed positions compatible with Mead's seem to have been minimally influenced by his social thought. Consistent with this analysis, one would predict that Mead maintained only limited organizational ties to sociology. In the next three chapters we systematically address this historical question. As we shall establish, the historical record is consistent with our metatheoretical analysis.

7

Quantitative
Indicators of
Mead's Role in the
Development of
Chicago Sociology

Graduate Student
Enrollment and
Social Recognition

We earlier noted Coser's observation (1977: 345–46) that something of a myth has spread regarding Mead's role in the development of Chicago sociology. The heart of this myth rests on Mead's nearly forty years of teaching:

> Any serious student of symbolic inter-actionism becomes convinced that George Herbert Mead must have been a superb lec-turer. Beginning in 1894, he taught for nearly forty years in the University of Chicago's philosophy department. One of his courses was in advanced social psychol-ogy, and it was *taken by most sociology graduate students.* He published no books during his career, yet his *influence on American sociology through his Chicago graduate students* alone has been enormous. [Mullins, 1973: 76; emphasis added]

As this statement suggests, it is commonly ac-cepted that most sociology graduate students enrolled in one or more of Mead's courses, es-pecially his course in social psychology. It is further assumed that Mead's "enormous" influence on American sociology was largely the consequence of these widespread student con-tacts. Fortunately, the extent of Mead's popu-larity among sociology graduate students and their recognition of him as a scholar is open to historical analysis and interpretation.

In this chapter we explore two related fea-tures of the premise that Mead exercised widespread influence over American sociology through his contacts with numerous Chicago graduate students. First, we examine the enrollment of graduate students in Mead's courses, bringing the enrollment of sociology graduate students into perspective with the enrollment of all graduate students. Second, we construct an index of Mead's "influence" by examining the extent of social recognition extended him in the doctoral dissertations of graduate students. In chapter 8, we consider the extent of Mead's recognition outside the University of Chicago, and whether this recognition was largely from his sociology graduate students.

Graduate Student Enrollment

General Composition of Audience

Mead was in almost continuous residence at the University of Chicago between 1894 and 1931, the year of his death. During his nearly four decades of teaching, graduate students from a wide range of disciplines enrolled in his courses. Table 1 shows the departmental affiliations of the students enrolled in Mead's courses. As the evidence in this table and others will establish, only from a comparative perspective does the proportion of sociology students enrolled in Mead's courses appear distinctive.

An inspection of the five-year intervals establishes that Mead had a substantial student audience.[1] However, it is especially apparent that

Table 1   Composition of Mead's Graduate Student Audience by Departmental Affiliation 1894–95 to 1930–31

Academic Year	Sociology	
	%	N
1894–1899	10.6	12
1899–1904	5.6	10
1904–1909	7.1	9
1909–1914	14.8	36
1914–1919	16.9	48
1919–1924	12.8	27
1924–1929	12.4	31
1929–1931	28.0	23
Total	13.2	196

Mead's graduate students were not drawn equally from all departments
of the university.[2] The largest proportion of his graduate student audience consisted of philosophy students (37.2%), followed by graduate
students from the Divinity School (18.2%). Ranking third were graduate
students from the Department of Sociology, who constituted 13.2% of
the graduate students Mead taught over a forty-year period. Psychology
graduate students added 8.1% to the total, and education graduate students contributed 4.4%. Although not identified by specific departmental
affiliation, 18.9% of Mead's graduate students were from departments
other than those designated in Table 1.[3] These graduate students were
affiliated with the departments of English, French, German, Latin, History, Economics, Political Science, Social Science Administration, Com-
merce and Administration, Law, Zoology, Physics, Medicine, and Mathematics.

Of central interest is the enrollment of sociology graduate students.
With the exception of the 1899–1904 and 1904–09 periods, when they
constituted only 5.6% and 7.1% of his audience, sociology graduate
students were always a significant proportion of Mead's graduate audience. Indeed, sociology graduate students provided Mead with 28.0% of
his graduate audience during the 1929–31 academic years. However, this
enrollment deviation, rather than suggesting an increase in Mead's
popularity, is related to: the reduced number of courses Mead taught due
to a year-long sabbatical; his death prior to the end of the 1930–31
academic year; and, as we shall shortly establish, the fact that one of the
courses he did teach during this period was Advanced Social Psychology.
Most of Mead's sociology graduate students concentrated their enrollment in his social psychology courses.[4]

Philosophy		Psychology		Education		Divinity		Other		Total	
%	N	%	N	%	N	%	N	%	N	%	N
46.0	52	3.5	4	6.2	7	13.3	15	20.4	23	100.0	113
48.6	86	4.0	7	8.5	15	12.4	22	20.9	37	100.0	177
25.4	32	24.6	31	7.1	9	12.7	16	23.1	29	100.0	126
26.7	65	11.9	29	3.3	8	28.0	68	15.3	37	100.0	243
28.2	80	6.7	19	4.9	14	25.4	72	17.9	51	100.0	284
37.9	80	3.8	8	1.9	4	21.3	45	22.3	47	100.0	211
47.8	120	8.7	22	2.4	6	10.4	26	18.3	46	100.0	251
46.3	38	1.2	1	2.4	2	7.4	6	14.7	12	100.0	82
37.2	553	8.1	121	4.4	65	18.2	270	18.9	282	100.0	1487

The Popularity of
Courses

The graduate enrollment data cited above shows the disciplinary origins of Mead's graduate students, but do not measure Mead's popularity among graduate students. What we call "popularity" can only be ascertained by examining the proportion of all registered students from each discipline who were enrolled.[5] The relevant data, presented in Table 2, are limited to registered graduate students from sociology, philosophy, pyschology, and education from the time Mead began teaching in 1894 through the 1918–19 academic year.

The proportion of student enrollment during this period may be used as an index of Mead's popularity among students in these disciplinary areas. That is, the percentages do not indicate what proportion of graduate students who entered these departments eventually enrolled in one or more courses by Mead. Rather they represent the number of graduate students who enrolled in on one or more of Mead's courses during any academic year as a proportion of registered graduate students for that year. Given the restricted time period covered by these data, it is notable that the rank ordering of the departments is similar to that of the composition of Mead's graduate audience. Mead was most popular among philosophy graduate students, followed by psychology, sociology, and education, in that order.[6]

Table 2   Number and Proportion of Registered Graduate Students in Sociology, Philosophy, Psychology, and Education Enrolled in Mead's Courses, 1894–95 to 1918–19*

Academic Year	Sociology		Philosophy		Psychology		Education	
	%	N	%	N	%	N	%	N
1894–1899	9.0	12/133	28.3	52/184	21.0	4/19	8.9	7/79
1899–1904	7.3	10/137	32.8	86/262		7/0	9.3	15/161
1904–1909	5.3	9/171	17.4	32/184	28.4	31/109	9.3	9/97
1909–1914	12.0	36/299	36.5	65/178	15.5	29/187	1.3	8/632
1914–1919	15.1	48/318	39.8	80/201	13.5	19/141	0.8	14/1844
Total	10.9	115/1058	31.2	315/1009	19.7	90/456	1.9	53/2813

*Data are not available beyond 1918–19.

Using data from both Tables 1 and 2, it is possible to derive some measure of Mead's popularity among sociology graduate students. Table 2 indicates that an average of 11% of the registered graduate students in sociology enrolled in one or more of Mead's courses during any academic year. Although there are lows of 7.3% and 5.3% during the 1899–1909 period, there is a clear trend that Mead's courses became increasingly popular, especially in the decade following 1904–09.

Only tentative conclusions may be drawn about Mead's popularity among all sociology graduate students during the last twelve years of his career. The number of sociology graduate students enrolled in Mead's courses between 1919–20 and 1930–31 is a known figure. Excluding 1928–29—the year Mead was on sabbatical and only had two philosophy students—the average sociology graduate enrollment for this period was 7.4. The mean enrollment for a comparable earlier period, from 1908–09 to 1918–19, was 8.1. In absolute terms, Mead's popularity among all sociology graduate students declined after 1918–19. In fact, Mead's decline in popularity was considerably larger than what is reflected in the mean enrollment differences. Although the enrollment of registered graduate students decreased during World War I, it is generally acknowledged that graduate education expanded tremendously in the post-World War I era. Accordingly, it is possible to argue that Mead's popularity among sociology graduate students significantly declined after 1918–19.

While it is not possible to fully substantiate a pattern of declining enrollment for all sociology graduate students, it is possible to establish it for two important subsamples of this population—those students who were subsequently awarded the Ph.D or M.A. degree. Table 3 measures Mead's popularlity among sociology Doctors of Philosophy and students awarded the Master of Arts degree.[7]

Table 3 establishes that Mead's popularity among sociology doctoral students suffered a sharp decline after 1920. Six of the seven students (85.7%) who were awarded the doctorate during the 1915–19 period enrolled in one or more of Mead's courses. However, by the 1925–29 period—the last complete teaching period for Mead—only six of the twenty-six (38.5%) sociology doctoral students were enrolled. A similar pattern of Mead's decreasing popularity characterizes the enrollment of sociology M.A. students. In fact, Mead was never as popular among M.A. students. During his entire teaching career, 43.4% of the doctoral students enrolled in Mead's courses, whereas only 24.4% of the M.A. students similarly enrolled. Thus, the pattern depicts Mead's increasing popularity until around 1920, and thereafter a subsequent decline.

Table 3 also allows for a comparison of Mead's popularity among sociology doctoral students with his popularity among doctoral students in philosophy, psychology, and education. Again, sociology is second only to philosophy. Nearly all philosophy doctoral students had Mead as an instructor, compared to less than half of the sociology doctoral students. However, even with his decline in popularity, far more sociology

Table 3   Number and Proportion of Ph.D.'s and Sociology M.A.'s Enrolled in Mead's Courses, 1894–1935

Year	Sociology (Ph.D.'s)	
	%	N
1894–1899	20.0	2/10
1900–1904	37.5	3/8
1905–1909	28.6	2/7
1910–1914	70.0	7/10
1915–1919	85.7	6/7
1920–1924	68.4	13/19
1925–1929	38.5	10/26
1930–1935	23.1	6/26
Total	43.4	49/113

doctoral students had Mead as an instructor than did students in psychology and education. As we suggested earlier, it is this comparative perspective that makes the enrollment of sociology graduate students in Mead's courses appear distinctive. Not only were there proportionally more sociology doctoral students in Mead's graduate student audience, but, excepting philosophy students, they tended to enroll in greater proportions than students from other departments.

Enrollment
Concentrations of
Sociology Students

Although the evidence suggests that Mead was a comparatively popular teacher among sociology graduate students, the majority did not sample widely from among the range of courses Mead taught.[8] This tendency is demonstrated in Table 4 which reports, in five-year intervals, the proportion of Mead's courses in which one or more sociology graduate students were enrolled. Sociology graduate students enrolled in less than one-third (31.5%) of all courses taught by Mead. Moreover, there is a definite trend that sociology students enrolled in a smaller range of courses after the 1910–14 period. Therefore, paralleling the previously noted decline in Mead's popularity was an accompanying pattern of sociology graduate students enrolling in a narrower range of courses.

Mead first taught a course bearing the title Social Psychology in the fall of 1900. After 1908 he routinely taught Social Psychology. In 1918 he changed the title of this course from Contemporary Social Psychology to

Philosophy (Ph.D.'s)		Psychology (Ph.D.'s)		Education (Ph.D.'s)		Sociology (M.A.'s)	
%	N	%	N	%	N	%	N
100.0	7/7					0.0	0/4
100.0	10/10	100.0	2/2	33.3	2/6	12.5	1/8
100.0	6/6	100.0	9/9	100.0	4/4	6.2	1/16
100.0	13/13	78.6	11/14	50.0	1/2	36.0	9/25
84.6	11/13	50.0	7/14	20.0	3/15	50.0	8/16
83.3	10/12	11.8	2/17	7.9	3/38	22.7	5/22
100.0	22/22	15.8	6/38	5.0	2/40	20.0	7/35
80.0	16/20	5.1	2/39	0.0	0/49	24.0	12/50
92.2	95/103	29.3	40/133	9.8	15/154	24.4	43/176

Advanced Social Psychology. What is important to recognize is that most of Mead's sociology student enrollment was in his social psychology courses. Table 5 readily establishes this concentration of sociology graduate students. In fact, after Mead began teaching Advanced Social Psychology, only twice did this course account for less than half of his sociology student enrollment; Contemporary Social Psychology was scarcely less popular.

Several general conclusions may be drawn from the foregoing discussion. First, it is evident that sociology graduate students provided Mead a continuing source of students for his entire teaching career. Second, their enrollment was of sufficient numbers that only graduate students from Mead's own Department of Philosophy consistently supplied him with more students. Similarly, Mead's popularity among sociology students was exceeded only by philosophy students. Third, although sociology

Table 4   Number and Proportion of all Courses Taught by Mead with Sociology Graduate Students Enrolled, 1894–1931

Year	%	N
1894–1899	35.3	12/34
1900–1904	30.0	9/30
1905–1909	23.3	7/30
1910–1914	42.4	14/33
1915–1919	33.3	13/39
1920–1924	30.6	11/36
1925–1931	26.9	14/52
Total	31.5	80/254

Table 5   Proportion of Sociology Graduate Students Enrolled in Mead's Social Psychology Course Compared to Total Course Enrollment

Academic Year	%	N
1900–1901	50.0	2/4
1902–1903	25.0	1/4
1907–1908	100.0	2/2
1909–1910	90.0	9/10
1911–1912	28.6	2/7
1912–1913	25.0	3/12
1913–1914	100.0	9/9
1914–1915	92.8	13/14
1915–1916	100.0	9/9
1916–1917	52.9	9/17
1917–1918*	25.0	1/4
1918–1919	53.8	7/13
1919–1920	33.3	1/3
1920–1921	66.7	4/6
1921–1922	88.9	8/9
1922–1923	50.0	1/2
1923–1924	85.7	6/7
1924–1925	66.7	2/3
1925–1926	78.6	11/14
1926–1927	66.7	6/9
1927–1928	85.7	6/7
1929–1930	100.0	12/12
1930–1931	90.9	10/11
Total	71.3	134/188

*The title of the course changed from Contemporary Social Psychology to Advanced Social Psychology.

students enrolled in considerable numbers, their selection from among the wide range of courses Mead taught was quite narrow, the majority choosing his social psychology courses. Fourth, Mead's popularity among sociology students declined after 1920. Therefore, to state the obvious, these data clearly establish that the majority of sociology graduate students did *not* enroll in courses taught by Mead. In chapter 9 we offer a plausible interpretation of the myth of Mead's universal popularity.

Graduate Student Recognition

We have shown that the enrollment of sociology graduate students in Mead's courses was far less than the contemporary myth maintains.

Nevertheless, over his lifetime, Mead did have significant numbers of
sociology graduate students in his classroom, especially when he taught
social psychology. An important question, then, concerns Mead's importance to the developing social thought of these students. More generally,
what influence did Mead have on sociology graduate students, including
those who did not enroll or attend his lectures?

Assertions regarding the influence of Mead are numerous (see Smith,
1977: 10–14). We have already called attention to the assertions of
Mead's influence on the development of symbolic interactionism. The
problem in attempting to answer the question of Mead's influence is that
influence is difficult, if not impossible, to establish historically (see Skinner, 1966). Although interpersonal linkages between scholars are frequently regarded as proof of influence, it is important to recognize that
even personal testimony fails to prove influence (Skinner, 1966: 206). In
a sense, then, Mead's influence is not open to historical examination.[9]

If Mead's influence is historically obscure, the same may not be said for
his social recognition. That is, although it may not be possible to determine whether students or other sociologists adopted Mead's ideas, it is
possible to establish whether they extended him recognition. Social recognition (the term "recognition" will hereafter be used interchangeably
with "social recognition") refers to the act of bringing to the attention of
others the name or ideas of a scholar. As Merton (1973) and Hagstrom
(1965) indicate, social recognition is a central feature of science. It is
through such recognition that status is accorded individuals by scientific
communities (Hagstrom, 1965:28). Therefore, we may determine the
extent to which Mead was extended recognition during his lifetime by
examining when, where, and the number of times sociologists brought
Mead's name or ideas to the attention of others. We contend that the
extent of Mead's recognition indirectly provides an index of his "influence."

We begin by examining the extent of Mead's recognition in the doctoral dissertations of sociology graduate students. As the "directed"
end-products of a long educational experience, it would appear that these
scholarly documents are especially sensitive to the feature of social recognition. Two comparative perspectives are provided in this analysis.
First, we examine Mead's recognition in sociology dissertations in relation to his recognition in the dissertations of philosophy, psychology, and
education students. Second, we compare Mead's recognition with the
recognition that sociology students gave to University of Chicago
sociology faculty and selected nonsociology faculty.

Types and
Frequencies of
Dissertation
Recognition

Table 6 presents data on Mead's recognition in the doctoral dissertations of sociology, philosophy, psychology, and education students, from 1895 to 1935. A comparison of these four groups of graduate students indicates that Mead received considerable recognition only in philosophy dissertations (48.9%). He received almost no recognition in the dissertations of psychology and education students.[10] Therefore, recognition in doctoral dissertations, like course enrollment, is highest among philosophy students, followed by sociology students. Mead received recognition in 18.6% of the sociology dissertations.

Table 6   Number and Proportion of Ph.D.'s in Sociology, Philosophy, Psychology, and Education Citing Mead in Dissertations 1895–1935

Year	Sociology		Philosophy		Psychology		Education	
	%	N	%	N	%	N	%	N
1895–1899	14.3	1/7	0.0	0/4				
1900–1904	16.7	1/6	25.0	2/8	0.0	0/1	0.0	0/3
1905–1909	0.0	0/5	100.0	5/5	0.0	0/9	33.3	1/3
1910–1914	22.2	2/9	55.5	5/9	0.0	0/10	0.0	0/2
1915–1919	16.7	1/6	33.3	3/9	20.0	2/10	0.0	0/10
1920–1924	11.1	2/18	75.0	9/12	0.0	0/16	0.0	0/33
1925–1929	19.2	5/26	50.0	11/22	0.0	0/38	0.0	0/39
1930–1935	28.0	7/25	42.1	8/19	0.0	0/38	0.0	0/50
Total	18.6	19/102	48.9	43/88	1.6	2/122	0.7	1/140

Inspection of the rates of sociology recognition from 1895 to 1935 establishes a moderate trend of increasing recognition after the 1920–24 period. After receiving recognition in two of nine dissertations (22.2%) in 1910–14, Mead's recognition decreased to 11.1% in 1920–24. However, there followed a period of increased citation and, by 1930–35, 28.0% of the sociology dissertations cited Mead. The increased recognition for 1920–35 is significant in that it occurred during a period of decreasing student enrollment.

The relationship between student enrollment and subsequent recognition of Mead in doctoral dissertations is illustrated in Figure 1. This graph suggests that the enrollment in Mead's courses was not particularly related to his recognition in sociology doctoral dissertations.[11] In fact, it shows that during the peak of his teaching popularity (1910–24), Mead's recognition was actually declining. Then, as his teaching popularity declined (1920–35), his recognition gradually increased. What the latter trend reflects is that some of Mead's recognition came from students not enrolled in his courses. Four of the doctoral students who recognized Mead after 1930 had not been his students; prior to this time all of Mead's dissertation recognition came from his former students.

Table 7 identifies: the sociology dissertation writers who recognized Mead; the date the dissertation was accepted by the university; and five types of recognition Mead received—(1) personal communication, (2) classroom lectures, (3) named alone, (4) named with others, and (5) articles and writings. An interesting temporal pattern surfaces across the forty-year period under examination. The modal recognition given Mead from 1895 to 1925 was personal communication and references to

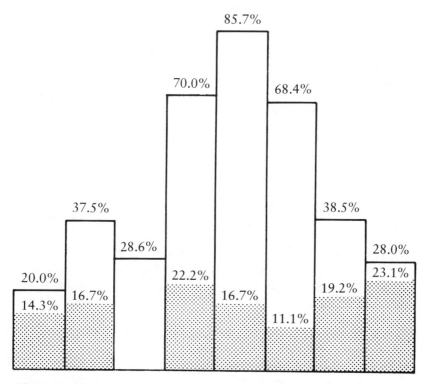

Figure 1 Proportion of Sociology Doctoral Students Enrolled in Mead's Courses
and Citing Him in the Dissertations

Table 7   Types of Social Recognition Provided Mead in Dissertations by Sociology Doctoral Students, 1895–1935

Name of Student and Year of Dissertation	Personal Communication	Classroom Lectures	Named Alone	Named with Others	Articles and Writings
Ellwood, C. A. (1899)	X				
Forrest, J. D. (1900)		X			
Bernard, L. L. (1910)					X
Burgess, E. W. (1913)		X			X
Queen, S. A. (1919)	X				X
Bodenhafer, W. B. (1920)		X	X	X	X
Price, M. T. (1924)		X[1]			
Karpf, F. B. (1925)		X[1]	X	X	X
Krueger, E. T. (1925)					X[2]
Simpson, E. N. (1926)		X	X	X	X
Blumer, H. G. (1928)			X	X	X
Kuhlman, A. F. (1929)					X
Stonequist, E. V. (1930)*					X
Faris, R. E. L. (1931)				X	X
Koshuk, R. P. (1931)*		X[1]		X	X
Quinn, A. Q. (1931)*			X	X	X
Thompson, E. T. (1932)*					X
Cottrell, L. S. (1933)		X[1]			X
Doyle, B. W. (1934)					X[2]

*Not enrolled in Mead's courses.
[1]Stenographic copy of lectures cited.
[2]Recognition in bibliography only.

classroom lectures. From 1925 to 1935 it was predominantly recognition of his articles and writings.[12]

Special attention should be given the "named alone" and "named with others" categories, since these two types of recognition did not occur until 1920. Our interpretation of this finding is that by 1920 the intended audience of the dissertations was expected to be familiar with Mead. For example, to make statements such as, "Readers of Mead will recognize," or "This position is taken by Mead, Cooley, Dewey," is to imply that one's readers are already aware of the scholars, or the ideas, being recognized. Whether the sociologists who read the dissertations were, in fact, aware of Mead is open to question, but doctoral dissertations were written primarily for the Chicago sociology faculty.[13]

The final category of social recognition given to Mead was the citation of his written work, especially his articles. L. L. Bernard was the first sociology student to provide this form of recognition in his 1910 dissertation. As recorded in Table 7, this became the most frequent type of recognition given to Mead. Yet, such recognition must be qualified in two ways. First, among the limited number of students who recognized Mead's articles, only a few articles are cited. Second, the recognition of Mead's articles demonstrates an element of "discovery." Whereas there is usually a delay between publication and recognition by others, what we call "discovery" refers to the considerable lag between the publication of an article by Mead and its subsequent recognition in sociological doctoral dissertations.

Article Citations and
Citation Lags

During his academic career at the University of Chicago, Mead published several articles.[14] Appendix 3 indicates the frequency with which forty selected articles by Mead were cited in sociology doctoral dissertations, three sociology journals, and in books and monographs between 1895 and 1935. The general conclusion drawn from these data is that most of Mead's articles failed to receive recognition from sociologists.

Among the sociology doctoral dissertations, the most frequently cited of Mead's articles (N=7) was "The Genesis of the Self and Social Control," written in 1925. The second most frequently cited articles (N=5) were "A Behavioristic Account of the Significant Symbol" (1922) and "Social Psychology As Counterpart to Physiological Psychology" (1909). The earliest of Mead's articles to receive recognition was his 1903 article, "The Definition of the Psychical." However, most of Mead's articles did not receive recognition. Of the forty selected articles Mead published from 1894 to 1930 (identified in Appendix 3), only 35.1% (fourteen) received citation.

Table 8 shows the relationship between the years Mead's articles were published and their subsequent recognition in the dissertations. It is significant to note that the first citation of Mead's 1903 article, "The Definition of the Psychical," did not occur until 1925 and 1926—a gap of more than 20 years. In fact, only one of Mead's articles was cited in the same year it was published; the average time lag was 5.6 years. The time lag dramatically decreases across the 27-year period in question: during the first 14 years (1903–17) the average lag was 9.3 years; for the last twelve years (1918–1930), the average time lag was 2.0 years. This finding clearly suggests that Mead was not "discovered" by sociology graduate students until the mid-1920s.

Closer examination of the dissertations citing Mead establishes that although most of the dissertations accorded Mead only limited recognition, there are three significant exceptions: the dissertations of Walter B. Bodenhafer (1920), Fay B. Karpf (1925), and Herbert Blumer (1928).[15]

Table 8   Relationship between Year of Article Publication and Mead's Recognition in Sociology Dissertations

Year Published	Year Recognized in Dissertations						Years to First Recognition*
1903			1925 1926				22
1909	1913	1920 1925	1928		1934		4
1910	1913	1925	1928	1931			3
1910	1910		1928				0
1912		1925		1931			13
1913		1925	1928		1933		12
1917			1928				11
1918	1919		1929				1
1922		1925	1928 1931				3
1925		1926	1928	1931	1933 1934		1
1926				1931			5
1929			1930				1
1930				1931			1
1930				1932			2
X̄							5.6

*The average lag in recognition for the period from 1903 to 1917 is 9.3; for the 1918–30 period, the average lag is 2.0.

We previously pointed out that the *AJS* publication of Bodenhafer's dissertation was important in explicating and chronicling the nominalism-realism issue in American sociology. Here we additionally note that Bodenhafer—giving Mead four of the five types of social recognition described in Table 7—was the first sociology graduate student to extend Mead greater recognition. However, Mead's recognition was even greater in the dissertations of Karpf and Blumer, in which both writers devoted special sections to a survey presentation of his theory. Among the sociology dissertations, these are the only two to provide "secondary sources" of Mead's ideas.

Karpf's work, a historical dissertation, is entitled *American Social Psychology and Its European Background* (1925). Blumer's dissertation, *Methods in Social Psychology,* was deposited in 1928. Both dissertations recognize a greater proportion of Mead's articles, including his earliest articles, than do any of the other dissertations.[16] However, the main significance of these two dissertations is that both recognize Mead as an important American social psychologist. The issue here is not whether Mead should have been so recognized, but that he had not previously been afforded this type of recognition in other dissertations.

Citation Frequencies
of Mead versus Other
Chicago Faculty

It is clear that although Mead received only limited recognition from sociology doctoral students during his Chicago years, there is no reason to expect that every sociology dissertation would contain citations of Mead. Therefore, one way to place Mead's recognition in perspective is to consider it in relation to that given to other Chicago faculty.[17] Tables 9 and 10 provide such a comparative perspective by indicating the number and proportion of sociology doctoral students who gave recognition both to Mead and to other Chicago faculty. Both tables also provide a quantitative measure of social recognition by determining the mean number of times a faculty member was cited.[18]

Table 9 establishes that between 1894 and 1935, sociology students gave recognition to a large number of sociology faculty teaching at the University of Chicago. The table also identifies three faculty members who were part of the department as anthropologists.[19] It is in comparison to this group of ten sociology and three anthropology faculty members that we can assess the relative extent of Mead's recognition.[20]

The mean number of citations each of these sociologists received represents one measure of social recognition. Mead received an average of 3.88 citations in each of the seventeen dissertations in which he was given recognition. These means range from 1.25 for Sapir to 8.02 for Park. A difference-of-means test was computed between the recognition given Mead and each of the other sociologists. The results of this analysis suggest that in only three instances was the mean citation given Mead significantly different from the mean citation given other sociologists. The recognition given Park was significantly greater than that accorded Mead ($p<.05$). However, the average recognition of Mead was significantly greater than that given Vincent and Sapir ($p<.05$).

The second measure of social recognition is the proportion of sociology students who recognize both these sociologists and Mead in their dissertations. This measure, unlike that of mean citations, has the advantage of indicating the range of recognition these scholars had among sociology students. It also has the advantage of sharply distinguishing between Mead and the sociology faculty. Mead was cited in 17.2% of the dissertations and thus was accorded more recognition than some Chicago sociologists. However, it is clear that his recognition exceeded only those sociology faculty whom contemporary sociologists generally regard as minor figures. Mead's recognition did not exceed that given to the major

Table 9 Citations of Mead in Sociology Ph.D. Dissertations vs. Citations of Selected Department of Sociology Faculty, 1894–1935

	G. H. Mead		A. W. Small		C. P. Henderson		G. E. Vincent		W. I. Thomas		C. Zeublin	
	no. cit.	n	no. cit.	n	no. cit.	n	no. cit.	n	no. cit.	n	no. cit.	n
1894–1899	3	1	4	3	1	1	1	1	1	1	1	1
1900–1904	4	1	7	3			4	1				
1905–1909			14	3					4	1		
1910–1914	6	2	34	4	15	4	7	3	10	3	1	1
1915–1919	3	1	11	5	3	2	1	1	5	3		
1920–1924	9	2	63	7			4	2	63	12	12	1
1925–1929	15	3	8	3			3	2	78	9	2	1
1930–1935	26	7			1	1			50	13		
Total	66	17	141	28	20	8	20	10	211	42	16	4
Av. no. cit. per diss.	3.88		5.03		2.50		2.00*		5.02		4.00	
Percent of diss. with citations	17.2		28.3		8.1		10.1		42.4		4.2	

[1]Anthropology faculty.
*Significant differences, p < .05

figures: Small, Thomas, Park, Burgess, or Faris. Controlling for time, there is no difference between the recognition given Mead and Ogburn.

Park received recognition in 55.5% of the dissertations examined, Burgess in 46.5%, and Thomas in 42.2%. These three are recognized more than twice as frequently as Mead and considerably more often than any other sociologist. The next highest levels of recognition occurs for Small (28.3%), Faris (25.2%), and Mead (17.2%).

Although many of President Harper's former Yale colleagues felt he would fail to attract a distinguished faculty to a new institution in the heart of the Midwest, they were wrong. Harper was able to recruit many of America's leading scholars to the University of Chicago (Goodspeed, 1916). Many of these scholars received recognition in the dissertations of sociology students. Table 10 compares the recognition given twelve non-sociology faculty with that of Mead. As may be seen, Mead did enjoy some prominence among sociology students. Based on a comparison of the mean number of citations, Mead received significantly more recog-

G. Taylor		R. E. Park		E. W. Burgess		E. Faris		W. Ogburn		F. Starr[1]		E. Sapir[1]		F-C. Cole[1]	
no. cit.	n	no. cit.	n	no. cit.	n	no. cit.	n	no. cit.	n	no. cit.	n	no. cit.	n	no. cit.	n
3	2	4	1												
		8	3	1	1										
3	2	78	14	32	10	2	1	3	3	1	1	3	2		
1	1	141	17	96	14	31	8	4	2	2	1	5	4	21	7
3	2	210	20	120	21	65	16	29	6			2	2	5	1
10	7	441	55	249	46	98	25	36	11	3	2	10	8	26	8
1.43		8.02*		5.41		3.92		3.27		1.50		1.25*		3.25	
7.1		55.5		46.5		25.2		11.1		2.0		8.1		8.1	

nition than his colleague, Edward S. Ames, and more than Veblen in political economy (p < .05). In fact, only Dewey received more citations than Mead in the dissertations.[21]

Mead's prominence is also evident in the proportion of sociology students citing him in comparison to other faculty. Mead's recognition exceeded that given to all but two faculty members—Veblen and Dewey. Although Veblen received the same proportion of recognition (17.2%), we have already indicated that Mead's mean number of citations significantly exceeded Veblen's. However, we regard with some importance the fact that Dewey's recognition exceeded that of Mead's. Not only did Dewey receive a greater number of citations, but he was recognized in twice as many dissertations (33.3%). Dewey's greater recognition in sociology dissertations is consistent with the implications of our earlier textual analysis of Chicago sociological writings.

In our analysis of doctoral dissertations we have provided a dual context for assessing Mead's recognition among sociology doctoral students.

Table 10   Citation of Mead in Sociology Ph.D. Dissertations vs. Citations of Selected Other University of Chicago Faculty, 1894–1935

	G. H. Mead		J. Dewey (Philosophy)		J. H. Tufts (Philosophy)		E. S. Ames (Philosophy)		J. R. Angell (Psychology)		H. Carr (Psychology)	
	no. cit.	n	no. cit.	n	no. cit.	n	no. cit.	n	no. cit.	n	no. cit.	n
1894–1899	3	1	16	3	4	1						
1900–1904	4	1	22	3								
1905–1909			2	1								
1910–1914	6	2	14	2	5	1	1	1	13	4		
1915–1919	3	1	1	1	1	1	3	3				
1920–1924	9	2	18	7	1	1			1	1		
1925–1929	15	3	31	8	2	1	6	2			5	1
1930–1935	26	7	47	8	1	1						
Total	66	17	151	33	14	6	10	6	14	5	5	1
Av. no. cit. per diss.	3.88		4.58		2.33		1.67*		2.80		5.00	
Percent diss. with citations	17.2		33.3		6.1		6.1		5.0		1.0	

*Significant differences, p < .05

As we have just shown, *all* of the prominent sociology faculty received greater recognition than Mead. This is most evident in Park's case, but Small, Thomas, Burgess, and Faris also exceeded Mead's recognition. Our earlier analysis of the dissertations in which Mead did receive recognition also provides a useful base for interpreting the extent of his recognition. Whereas most sociology doctoral students failed to cite Mead, even those who did, cited very few of his articles. However, Mead's recognition did increase after 1925, despite this being a period of declining sociology student enrollment. That Mead's recognition was gradually on the increase is further supported by the fact that a few sociology doctoral students began to "discover" some of Mead's early writings and argue that he was an important American social psychologist.

In spite of Mead's comparative prominence, the most striking observation in our analysis is that Mead's recognition by sociology doctoral students was very limited. It is *only* in relation to other nonsociology

J. B. Watson (Psychology)		L. L. Thurstone (Psychology)		J. H. Judd (Education)		T. Veblen (Polit. Economy)		J. Addams (Hull House)		C. E. Merriam (Polit. Science)		S. Mathews (Divinity)	
no. cit.	n	no. cit.	n	no. cit.	n	no. cit.	n	no. cit.	n	no. cit.	n	no. cit.	n
						2	1						
						1	1			3	1	3	1
				8	2	7	5	6	2			5	2
2	1											2	1
9	2			1	1	4	3	9	4				
4	2	8	5	7	1	4	2	12	3	6	2	1	1
7	1	30	7	2	1	6	5	2	2	11	3		
22	6	38	12	18	5	24	17	31	11	20	6	11	5
3.67		3.17		3.60		1.41*		2.82		3.33		2.20	
6.1		12.1		5.0		17.2		10.1		6.1		5.0	

faculty and to doctoral students from other departments that Mead's recognition appears distinctive. Therefore, we have not only shown that Mead's sociology student enrollment was far less than commonly assumed, but also that his social recognition was significantly smaller than his student enrollment. Certainly there is no evidence in sociology doctoral dissertations to suggest that Mead's "influence" was either enormous or widespread. Although the following chapter will show that Mead was accorded importance by some of his students, it will also establish that during his lifetime Mead was of minor importance in the development of American sociology.

8

The Social Recognition of Mead in American Sociology 1895-1935

One of the many myths surrounding George Herbert Mead is that he published very little during his lifetime. As intimated in chapter 7, such a view is unwarranted. As Fisher and Strauss (1979:9) recently noted, although Mead did not write and publish books, he "published one or more papers virtually every year of his professional life." The point is that sociologists, including those not affiliated with the University of Chicago, had access to Mead's ideas. Consequently, they need not have been Mead's students to have been influenced by his social thought.

In this chapter we examine the extent of Mead's "influence" on American sociology by examining his recognition in sociology journals, books, and monographs. Special attention is given to University of Chicago sociologists and their students to determine whether Mead's name and ideas were introduced to sociology through his sociology students.

Recognition in Sociology Journals

Three journals of American sociology were published during Mead's lifetime. Only the *American Journal of Sociology* was published during the entire period of time under consideration. As the unofficial journal for the American Sociological Society until 1936, this

Chicago-based publication was certainly the premier journal for American sociologists during this early period of American sociology. The journal enjoyed an international readership. Two new journals, *Sociology and Social Research* and *Social Forces*, began publication in 1921 and 1922, respectively. Analyzing these three journals provides one measure of the extent of Mead's recognition within the wider sociological community.

In journals scholars can receive recognition from contributors or from the journal itself. Contributors may provide the five types of recognition previously discussed for dissertations: personal communication, classroom lectures, named alone, named with others, and recognizing the articles and writings of a scholar. In journal-controlled recognition, two new types of recognition are possible: journals may either recognize scholars by publishing their work, or by calling attention to their work through the literature and book reviews.

The *American Journal of Sociology*

Table 11 summarizes the types of recognition given to Mead in the *American Journal of Sociology (AJS)* between 1895 and 1935. From the data, one can conclude that Mead received minimal recognition in *AJS*. On the other hand, the data indicate that most who did give Mead recognition were linked to the University of Chicago.

Charles A. Ellwood, the first to recognize Mead (in 1898–99), was Mead's principal source of recognition prior to 1920. However, because Ellwood only mentioned personal communication with Mead, none of Mead's articles were cited in the *AJS* until the 1920s. Although L. L. Bernard cited an article in 1910–11, it was not until 1920–21 that Mead received several forms of recognition from a single author. That author, Walter B. Bodenhafer, cited Mead's lectures, named him alone, named him with others, and called attention to his written work. The publication of Bodenhafer's articles was a significant point of demarcation in the extent of recognition accorded Mead.[1]

All of the above authors were Chicago-trained sociologists who had enrolled in one or more of Mead's courses. Many of the remaining *AJS* contributors linked to the University of Chicago were from disciplines other than sociology.[2] Significantly, most of Mead's *AJS* recognition came from nonsociologists. In fact, much of his recognition after 1920 came from the psychologist-turned-sociologist, Ellsworth Faris. In Faris's "topical summary" of American social psychology (1926:625), he wrote,

Table 11   Recognition of Mead in the *American Journal of Sociology*, 1895–35

Year	Personal Communication	Classroom Lectures	Named Alone	Named with Others	Articles and Writings	Review of Literature	AJS Writings by Mead	Name of Person Recognizing Mead in a Contributed Article
1895–96								
1896–97								
1897–98								
1898–99	X*							Ellwood**
1899–1900						X	X	
1900–1	X							Ellwood**
1901–2								
1902–3								
1903–4								
1904–5								
1905–6								
1906–7								
1907–8							X	
1908–9	X					X		Craig**
1909–10	X							Ellwood**
1910–11					X*			Bernard**
1911–12				X				Lewis
1912–13								
1913–14								
1914–15						X		
1915–16						X		
1916–17								
1917–18							X	
1918–19								
1919–20								
1920–21		X*	X	X	X			Bodenhafer**
1921–22					X			Kantor**
1922–23						X		
1923–24						X		
1924–25								
1925–26						X	X	Maurer
1926–27		X	X	X	X			Faris**; Taft
1927–28								
1928–29				X				Faris**
1929–30							X	
1930–31								
1931–32	X	X	X	X	X			Smith
1932–33								
1933–34				X				Droba
1934–35								

*Ph.D. dissertation.   **Former graduate student of Mead.

"Basic to the work of a whole group of social psychologists are the articles of Mead."[3] At issue, again, is not whether Mead should have been so recognized, but that he had not previously received such recognition. That this recognition came from the new editor of the *AJS* is deserving of special comment.

The last two authors to recognize Mead during the 1895–1935 period were T. V. Smith and D. D. Droba. Smith wrote an *AJS* article commemorating Mead and was at that time a faculty member in the Department of Philosophy. Interestingly, although Smith had received his Ph.D. in philosophy from the University of Chicago in 1922, we can find no evidence that he ever enrolled in any of Mead's courses. Given the enrollment data on philosophy students, this places Smith in a very unusual position.

Droba's recognition of Mead is noteworthy for a different reason: it occurs indirectly through his recognition of Fay B. Karpf. As Droba (1933:513) states, "Karpf gave us a brief summary of the attitude theories of Faris, Thomas and Mead." The significance of Droba's remarks is his designating a secondary source of Mead's ideas available in Karpf's recently published *American Social Psychology: Its Origins, Development and European Background*—the revision of her 1925 dissertation. (We discuss Karpf's dissertation-turned-book in the next section when we examine Mead's social recognition in texts and monographs.)

We suggested that journals also exercise control over the recognition given scholars. With respect to this type of recognition, Mead published three articles and two book reviews in *AJS*.[4] However, it was in the area of literature reviews that the *AJS* accorded Mead the most recognition. In seven different years his name and ideas were recognized by listing, synopsizing, or reviewing work he had published elsewhere.

It may be seen that, although journal-controlled recognition of Mead increased after 1920, it was never extensive. Prior to 1920, Mead's recognition was confined to an occasional listing of his articles in the journal's section on "literature of interest to sociologists." In contrast, the last three times Mead was recognized, his written work—including two of his most frequently cited articles—was abstracted.[5]

*Sociology and Social
Research* and *Social
Forces*

Table 12 presents the combined results of the examination of Mead's recognition in *Sociology and Social Research* (*SSR*) and *Social Forces* (*SF*) between 1921 and 1935. We will discuss that data separately and then compare Mead's recognition in all three journals.

Table 12   Recognition of Mead in *Social Forces** and *Sociology and Social Research*, 1921–35

Year	Personal Communication	Classroom Lectures	Named Alone	Named with Others	Articles and Writings	Review of Literature	SF & SSR Writings by Mead	Person Recognizing Mead
1921–22								
1922–23								
1923–24								
1924–25						X		
1925–26								
1926–27				X	X			Bodenhafer**; Barnes
1927–28			O	O	O			House; Queen**; Sutherland**
1928–29								
1929–30					O			Bain
1930–31								
1931–32			X	X	X			Bittner
1932–33						X		
1933–34								
1934–35							O	

*Publication of *Social Forces* began in 1922.
**Former graduate student of Mead's.
XRecognition in *Sociology and Social Research*.
ORecognition in *Social Forces*.

The first recognition given Mead in these new journals was "controlled."[6] In 1925, *SSR* abstracted Mead's "The Genesis of the Self and Social Control" in one sentence: "Social control depends upon the degree to which the individuals in society are able to assume the attitudes of others who are involved with them in common endeavors." The first recognition of Mead by a journal contributor also occurred in this journal—in a 1927 article by Walter B. Bodenhafer. During the same year Mead received recognition from two other contributors to *SSR*.

First, Harry E. Barnes recognized Mead by suggesting that Ellwood's interest in functional psychology was partly derived from Ellwood's student days under Mead and Dewey. Second, in the journal's book review section, Mead's name is mentioned as one of the scholars discussed in Christopher J. Bittner's privately published book, *The Development of the Concept of the Social Nature of the Self* (his dissertation written at the State University of Iowa).

The only extensive recognition given Mead in either of these journals appeared posthumously in C. J. Bittner's *SSR* commemorative article, "G. H. Mead's Social Concept of the Self." Oddly, this non-Chicago sociologist bases part of his defense of Mead's importance to social psychology on Mead's extant recognition. Bittner wrote, "Few books in social psychology of real merit have appeared in which Dr. Mead is not quoted."[7]

The final recognition Mead received in *SSR* suggests that Fay B. Karpf's book may have been of some importance in giving Mead recognition. A review of Karpf's book named Mead as one of the scholars she examined.[8]

The first mention of Mead in *Social Forces* came in a 1927 article by Floyd N. House entitled, "Development in the Theory of the Social Personality." During the same publication year Mead received recognition from Stuart A. Queen and E. H. Sutherland—two of his former sociology graduate students—who cite him in a series of articles concerned with experiments in social work interviews and nonverbal gestural communication between social workers and clients. Read Bain was the only other *SF* contributor to recognize Mead. Bain's graduate training at Chicago was limited, and no record of his enrollment in Mead's course(s) was found. Finally, the sole journal-controlled recognition of Mead occurred in 1934–35; among the books listed as received for review was Mead's posthumously published *Mind, Self and Society*. *Social Forces* made no mention of Mead's death; *Mind, Self and Society* was not reviewed.

Composite Analysis of
Journal Recognition

Comparing Mead's recognition in the three journals plainly demonstrates that he received very limited recognition in all of them. Appendix 3 presents the combined results of the frequency of Mead's article recognition in the three journals. Not one of Mead's articles was cited by more than five contributors. Moreover, although half of the forty selected articles did receive recognition, most of this recognition did not occur until the publication of the two commemorative essays in the *AJS* and *SSR*.

The relationship between the year of Mead's article recognition and the year of publication is shown in Table 13. This table shows the extensive lapses between the time one of Mead's articles was published and its subsequent recognition. The mean delay in recognition was 7.8 years. For the 1903–17 period it was 15.4 years; in the 1918–30 period 2.8 years. Only two years are highlighted in this table: 1926 saw the publication of Faris's feature article on American social psychology in which he called attention to six of Mead's articles; and the most distinctive year, 1931, is the year Mead died and was memorialized in *AJS* and *SSR*.

The few scholars who gave Mead recognition were closely linked to the University of Chicago. Thus, as one might expect, Mead was given the most recognition in *AJS* followed by *SSR*. We have already noted Mead's recognition by the editor of *AJS*—Ellsworth Faris. The editor of *SSR* was Emory S. Bogardus—another of Mead's former students. In contrast, *SF*

Table 13   Relationship between Year of Article Publication and Mead's Recognition among Contributors to Three Sociology Journals

Year Published by Mead	Years Recognized in Contributed Articles					Years to First Recognition*
1903					*1931*	28
1909	*1921*	*1922*	*1926*	*1927*	*1931*	12
1910			*1926*			16
1910					*1931*	21
1910	*1910*		*1922*	*1926*	*1931*	0
1912					*1931*	19
1913			*1926*		*1931*	13
1917					*1931*	14
1922			*1926*	*1928*	*1931*	4
1923					*1931*	8
1925			*1926*	*1928*	*1931*	1
1926					*1931*	5
1926					*1931*	5
1929					*1931*	2
1929					*1931*	2
1929					*1931*	2
1929					*1931*	2
1930					*1931*	1
1930					*1931*	1
1930					*1931*	1
$\overline{X}$						7.8

*The average lag in recognition for the 1903–17 period is 15.4; for the 1918–30 period the average lag is 2.8 years.

was edited by Howard W. Odum—a non-University of Chicago Ph.D.
Not surprisingly, Mead received the least amount of recognition in this
journal.

Recognition in Sociology Books and Monographs

General Patterns

The second category of sociological literature that establishes the extent
of Mead's recognition among American sociologists is an availability
sample of 181 books and monographs published between 1894 and
1935.[9] Table 14 reports the number and proportion of writers giving
Mead recognition for this period. As may be seen, nearly one-fourth
(24.3%) of the books and monographs included recognition of Mead.

Table 14   Number and Proportion of Writers Citing Mead in Selected Sociology
Books and Monographs, 1894–1935

Year	% (N)	Number of Books and Monographs
1894–1899	———	6
1900–1904	———	6
1905–1909	16.7 (2)	12
1910–1914	———	4
1915–1919	19.0 (4)	21
1920–1924	15.2 (5)	33
1925–1929	27.8 (15)	54
1930–1935	40.0 (18)	45
Total	24.3 (44)	181

As in the earlier sources examined, the pattern of Mead's recognition was
on the increase, especially after 1920–24. For the last period examined
(1930–35), fully 40.9% of the books and monographs gave Mead recognition. Whereas the very nature of books and monographs encourages more comprehensive treatment of a subject, it is nevertheless important to note that none of the sources previously examined—including
the dissertations of Chicago sociology doctoral students—accorded
Mead as much recognition as these books and monographs. Yet, even
here, it is clear that Mead's recognition was a limited and largely post-
1920 phenomenon.

The type of social recognition given Mead is presented in Table 15.

This table also names those scholars who recognized Mead, and indicates whether they were his former students. Mead received all five types of recognition previously discussed. However, most writers of books and monographs make reference to Mead's articles or writings. The recognition of personal communication or of Mead's classroom lectures is very rare. Not until 1924 did Mead begin to be named alone and named with others.

Although Mead's social recognition was not confined to scholars with close connections to Chicago, Table 15 emphasizes that several do share

Table 15   Type of Social Recognition Provided Mead in Books and Monographs, 1894–1935

Year of Recognition	Personal Communication	Classroom Lectures	Named Alone	Named with Others	Articles and Writings	Name of Person Citing
1905	X					Small
1909					X	Thomas*
1915					X	Ellwood*; King*
1917					X	Ellwood*; Smith
1920					X	Williams
1922					X	Bogardus*
1924				X	X	Allport; Case; Park and Burgess*
1925			X	X	X	Young*; Hankins; Groves
1926			X		X	Bernard*; Bogardus*; Faris*
1927			X		X	Barnard*; Young*
1928					X	Markey; Mukerjee and Nath Sen-Gupta
1929			X	X	X	Hart*; House; Lundberg; Markey; Lasswell*; Smith
1931			X		X	Bogardus*; Childs; Folsom; Bernard*; Young*; Queen*
1932		X	X	X	X	Eubank; Karpf*; Waller
1933			X	X	X	Bain; Cooley, Angell and Carr; Hiller; Reuter* and Hart
1934					X	Bogardus*; Bossard
1935		X			X	Dawson and Gettys; Krueger* and Reckless*; Queen*; Bodenhafer* and Harper; Tuttle; Young*

*Student of Mead's at the University of Chicago.

that distinction. Mead was cited in 44 books and monographs, singly and jointly authored. In 72.7% (32) of the books, one or more of the writers according Mead recognition were either former Chicago graduate students or faculty. In fact, of the 45 social scientists who gave Mead recognition, 35.6% (16) had been students of Mead's.

Articles Cited and
Citation Lags

We have pointed out that most of Mead's recognition in books and monographs called attention to his published work. Appendix 3 indicates which articles were recognized and the frequency of their citation. Mead's 1922 article, "A Behavioristic Account of the Significant Symbol," was the most frequently recognized. Thirteen books cite this article, but several other articles received nearly the same number of citations. Overall, 45.0% of the 40 selected articles identified in Appendix 3 received recognition.

Table 16 presents data on the relationship between the year of article recognition and the date of its publication. The results are consistent with our earlier findings—that Mead's recognition was largely a product of the 1920s, and it was not until 1924 that several of his articles were cited. For example, it was only in 1928 that Mead's 1903 article, "The Definition of the Psychical," was cited. Similarly, some of Mead's 1909–13 articles were not recognized until the 1920s—an average delay in recognition of 10.3 years. Mead's late "discovery" as a social psychologist for sociology is further reflected in the following examination of some of the books in which Mead gained recognition.

Recognition in
Specific Books

The first book recognition given Mead appeared in Small's *General Sociology* (1905). A footnote in Small's text (designed for graduate students) cites Mead as a critical colleague in the field of psychology who perceived no sharp division between psychology and sociology. Mead's second instance of recognition came from W. I. Thomas in his *Source Book for Social Origins* (1909). However, Thomas merely cited in a bibliography Mead's 1906 article on Wundt. Neither Small nor Thomas gave Mead recognition in any of their other books we examined.

We have shown that it was not until 1924 that a single book cited more than one of Mead's articles. Interestingly, the first author to do so was

Table 16   Relationship between Year of Article Publication and Mead's Recognition in Books and Monographs

Year Published				
1903				
1906	*1909*			
1909		*1917*		
1910			*1922*	*1924*
1910	*1915*			*1924*
1910				*1924*
1912				*1924*
1913				*1924*
1915		*1917*		
1917				
1918			*1920*	*1924*
1922				*1924*
1923				
1925				
1929				
1930				
1930				
1930				
1934				
X̄				

*The average time lag in recognition for 1903–17 is 10.3 years; for the 1918–35 period, 2.1 years.

Floyd Allport in his *Social Psychology*—an anomaly in that Allport was never directly affiliated with the University of Chicago.[10] Another non-Chicago scholar, C. M. Case, also accomplished a first by reprinting one of Mead's articles (the 1918 *AJS* article, "The Psychology of Punitive Justice") in his *Outline of Introductory Sociology: A Textbook of Readings in Social Science* (1924). This article was not cited in any of our previously discussed sources.

In 1925 Harry E. Barnes edited *The History and Prospects of Social Science*. In a section on social psychology, Kimball Young (one of Mead's former students) stated, "Mead's papers are scattered in the periodical literature of the last fifteen years. The reader may refer to the following which give the most important materials for social psychology." Young listed four articles: "Social Psychology as Counterpart to Physiological Psychology," "The Mechanism of Social Consciousness," "The Social Self," and "A Behavioristic Account of the Significant Symbol."[11]

In 1928, John F. Markey gave Mead extensive recognition in *The Symbolic Process and Its Integration in Children*. Markey discussed

Year Recognized										Years to First Recognition*
1925	1926	1927	1928	1929	1931	1932	1933	1934	1935	
			1928							25
										3
1925	1926	1927	1928	1929	1931	1932	1933			8
	1926			1929	1931	1932	1933	1934		12
	1926		1928							5
			1928	1929		1932	1933			14
1925			1928			1932	1933		1935	12
1925		1927	1928	1929		1932	1933			11
										2
			1928							11
1925	1926				1931	1932	1933	1934		2
1925	1926	1927	1928	1929	1931	1932	1933			2
		1927	1928							4
		1927	1928	1929		1932	1933		1935	2
				1929		1932				0
						1932		1934		2
									1935	5
					1931					1
									1935	1
										6.4

Mead's theory and cited nine articles, including the first book citation of "The Definition of the Psychical" (1903). Mead gained considerable recognition in Markey's article, "Trends in Social Psychology," which appeared in G. A. Lundberg's *Trends in American Sociology* (1929). Markey's recognition of Mead equalled that of Young. But unlike Young, Markey's brief period of Chicago graduate education did not include enrollment in any of Mead's courses.

The year 1929 saw several significant book citations of Mead. In addition to Markey's, F. N. House spot-lighted Mead in his *The Range of Social Theory*. But perhaps the most salient recognition of Mead in 1929 appeared in *Chicago: An Experiment in Social Science Research,* edited by T. V. Smith and Leonard S. White. In a chapter subsection titled, "The Influence of Mead and Thomas," Harold D. Lasswell (1929:177–78) wrote:

> The study of human personality has an impetus, a tradition, and a more or less distinctive orientation at the University of Chicago, due especially to the influence of George H. Mead and William I.

Thomas. Mr. Mead, who has been a member of the Department of
Philosophy since 1894, has been formulating an inclusive theory of
the development of the self which has drawn the attention of successive University generations to the deep consideration of fundamental
issues. His approach is philosophical, in the sense that his chief preoccupation is with the elimination of the subjective-objective dichotomy from the description of mental processes in relation to sur-
roundings. But his approach is scientific in the sense that his training
included laboratory work in physiological psychology, and that his
speculations have been disciplined and chastened by the procedures
and findings of the natural sciences. Mr. Mead's analysis of stimulus
and response has legitimated the objective position of psychological
acts in the behavior sequence. His account of the rise of the self
through the process of "playing the role of the other" furnishes a
vantage ground from which the statements by Cooley, Freud, Watson, Bechterev, and other representatives of current movements in
sociology and psychology may be surveyed. The unpretentious yet
penetrating influence of Mead is traceable in the work of many
scholars and scientists who have been associated with the University
of Chicago, even though many of them have never been under his
immediate direction, for his ways of thinking have become more and
more the common property of several departments in the institution.

It certainly does not appear that Mead's "influence" was as pervasive as
Lasswell asserts, but it is important to note that by 1929 Mead was for
the first time being recognized as a major figure at the University of
Chicago.[12]

Aside from an occasional summary of his ideas, no book devoted a
section exclusively to Mead prior to his death in 1931. But in 1932 Fay B.
Karpf's *American Social Psychology: Its Origins, Development and
European Background* gave Mead his most extensive recognition during
the period we examined. Karpf's book provided a special section on
Mead's social psychology, and is noteworthy for the two ways in which
Karpf justified her claim that Mead was important to the development of
social psychology. First, she linked Mead's social psychology to that of
Dewey, Thomas, Faris, and others (Karpf, 1932:319). Second, she cited
the prior recognition given Mead by Allport, Bodenhafer, Queen, Young,
Faris, Bogardus, and L. L. Thurstone. (Thurstone, also a former student
of Mead's, is the only scholar we have not previously noted as giving
Mead recognition.) However, Karpf (1932:327) especially notes Faris's
evaluation of Mead's importance by quoting, "To Professor Mead, according to [Faris] 'American scholars are indebted for some invaluable
and wholly unique contributions.'"

What should be emphasized is that Karpf did not choose to justify her inclusion of Mead in her dissertation. Thus, a Chicago dissertation apparently required no justification, but a book on the historical origins of social psychology did. In any case, no such justification was deemed necessary for the inclusion and separate treatment of Ward, James, Baldwin, Cooley, Ross, Dewey, Ellwood, Bogardus, Allport, and Bernard in her book.

Given Karpf's comparatively extensive recognition of Mead, we should pause to consider her evaluation of Mead's articles because, at that time, they were the only widely available source of Mead's writings. In general, she regarded Mead's writings as obscure and unrepresentative of his ideas—hardly the type of comment to send readers hurrying to read Mead. As Karpf (1932:318) stated:

> . . . Mead's influence upon American social-psychological thought
> has been exerted chiefly by way of the classroom and only secondar-
> ily by way of his published writings. The latter are fragmentary in the
> first place and both involved and obscure, and hence limited in their
> appeal, in the second place. A survey of Mead's published discussions
> of social-psychological material would, therefore, be peculiarly in-
> adequate as an index of the importance of his social-psychological
> theory. It is necessary to link these discussions of scattered aspects of
> his theory with his point of view as a whole, and this is to date not
> available in published form. The following summary is accordingly
> based on an unpublished outline of Mead's social-psychological
> theory and on his class presentation of the material, as well as on
> some of his published articles.

A more representative source of Mead's ideas, Karpf (1932:318n) suggested, was "available at the University of Chicago library in manuscript form and to be published shortly." That source is now familiar to many scholars as the sole source of Mead's ideas—his posthumously published *Mind, Self, and Society* (1934). Among the books and monographs we examined, this book was cited only in Dawson and Getty's 1935 revised edition of *An Introduction to Sociology;* their 1929 edition made no mention of Mead. Thus, it is clear that Mead's wide recognition by sociologists did not occur until after the appearance of his posthumously published books, especially *Mind, Self, and Society* (see Sprietzer and Reynolds, 1973).[13]

Conspicuous
Exclusions of Mead
from Sociology Books

To gain a better perspective of Mead's recognition, including his recognition among Chicago sociologists, it is instructive to consider some
of the books and monographs written between 1894 and 1935 in which
Mead received no mention. Doing this makes it easier to appreciate the
limited recognition Mead received in sociology throughout his lifetime.
    Small and Vincent's 1894 An Introduction to the Study of Society is
sometimes regarded as the first sociological text written solely for students. There is no recognition of Mead. Similarly, Mead received no
recognition in Charles Henderson's 1898 Social Elements: Institutions,
Character and Progress. The same is true of the many volumes by Giddings, Ward, or in the major works of Cooley.[14]
    Although Ellwood was one of the first to recognize Mead, he did not
consistently do so. Thus, there is no citation of Mead in his 1913 Sociology and Modern Social Problems.[15] Nor did Ross recognize Mead in his
1916 Social Psychology: An Outline and Source Book. It was only in the
1926 edition of Bogardus's Introduction to Sociology (originally published in 1917) that Mead received recognition. Even in this fourth edition, only one paragraph called attention to Mead's 1910 article, "Social
Consciousness and the Consciousness of Meaning." Bogardus finally
"discovered" one of Mead's articles sixteen years after it had been published.
    There was no citation of Mead in Charles H. Judd's 1918 Introduction
to the Scientific Study of Education. Judd, as we noted in the last chapter,
was on the Chicago faculty as head of the education department. Even
more surprisingly, Mead was not mentioned in Thomas and Znaniecki's
important work of 1918, The Polish Peasant in Europe and America.
    Although it has already been noted that Mead's recognition prior to
1920 was very restricted, even in the later period his social recognition
was limited. Park and Burgess's Introduction to the Science of Sociology
was published in 1921. As we have indicated, Mead was cited in this
classic text, but his lack of prominence might be regarded as an anomaly.
The authors (1924:vi) acknowledged that they were following the
framework of Thomas's Source Book for Social Origins. As a consequence, included in the more than 1,000 pages are numerous reprints of
writings by such Chicago scholars as Thomas, Judd, Watson, Dewey,
Small, and Ellwood. Yet, none of Mead's written work was included
among the source materials. In fact, Mead received only one brief

"named with others" mention, and two of his articles were called to the attention of readers only in the selected bibliography. Similarly, there was no recognition of Mead in the 1925 Park, Burgess, and McKenzie book, *The City.*

Evidence available in this research suggests that Mead was primarily linked to sociology through social psychology. Nevertheless, he failed to receive recognition in Ellwood's 1925 book, *The Psychology of Human Society: An Introduction to Sociological Theory.* William McDougall did not cite Mead in his 1926 *Introduction to Social Psychology.* Moreover, Mead's name is conspicuously absent from Burgess's 1929 *Personality and the Social Group.* Thus, even in books dealing with social psychology and written by sociologists who had been his students, Mead did not consistently receive recognition.

We are now in a position to assess the extent of Mead's recognition among American sociologists during his lifetime and through the year 1935. Our analysis of sociology journals, books, and monographs has established that Mead did receive some recognition and that his recognition increased after the mid-1920s. This pattern of recognition is basically consistent with the pattern we found in sociology dissertations. However, we have also found that, with the exception of a few isolated instances, Mead's recognition was limited and incidental. We must conclude from the analysis of these data that Mead had only minimal "influence" on the development of American sociology during this period.

Notwithstanding the marginal relationship Mead occupied with respect to the development of early American sociology, we have explicated the important part played by Chicago sociologists, especially Mead's students, in extending him recognition. Of special importance, our analysis identified a small number of sociologists and social psychologists who gave Mead considerable recognition. Among the most distinctive of this group we may note Ellwood, Bodenhafer, Young, John F. Markey, Fay B. Karpf, and especially Faris. (In anticipation of chapter 9, we will add Herbert Blumer to this list, although his distinction was found only in the analysis of doctoral dissertations.) Chapter 9 presents a more careful consideration of Mead's historical relationship to Chicago sociology, and, most important, Faris's crucial role in Mead's recognition.

Mead and Chicago Sociology   Recollections of Former Sociology Graduate Students

We have noted the lack of historical work on the development of Chicago sociology. Except for scattered comments, the only monographs to attempt histories of this era are those of Faris (1970) and Carey (1975). Both of these monographs provide insight into different aspects of Chicago sociology. However, neither author systematically questioned Mead's relationship to the evolving organizational structure of Chicago sociology during Mead's long academic tenure in the Department of Philosophy. The following discussion draws upon the memories of former sociology graduate students to augment our previous analyses of this historical relationship.[1]

To better understand Mead's historical relationship to Chicago sociology, we will approach his career as comprising two distinct periods—a pre-1920 and post-1920 period. This time period is not an arbitrary point of division. Not only does it mark the shift from nominalism to realism, and the increasing social recognition given Mead. But this period of time is also closely linked to changes in Chicago sociology signalled by the arrival of Robert E. Park, the return of Ernest W. Burgess and Ellsworth Faris, the departure of W. I. Thomas, and the death of Albion W. Small. It is Mead's differential relationships to these major Chicago sociologists and their students that provide a basis for interpreting his marginality to Chicago sociologists.

Pre-1920 Chicago
Sociology and Mead

In 1892 Small left his position as president of Colby College and, like many other distinguished American scholars, journeyed to the Midwest to help found the University of Chicago. With a recent Ph.D. in history and an interest in sociology, Small became head of the first graduate Department of Sociology in the United States. Yet, it may be appropriate to pose the question, What was Small the head of? That is, what was sociology at this time? As Faris (1970:9) suggests, an answer to this question had not yet been formulated:

> When the Chicago department was founded in 1892, the voices of Ward, Sumner, Spencer, and Giddings were still dominant. Durkheim was just one of the sociological voices abroad. None of the original faculty of the Chicago department was trained in sociology because there had been no department to train them. Thus there was still a large amount of uncertainty about what the task was to be—what sort of sociology was to be created. It was to be nearly thirty years more before their successors could feel confident that they were at last on the true road.

In this section we briefly examine Mead's relationship to the evolving structure of American sociology as it began to take shape at Chicago. The passage of time has made sketching this relationship difficult. However, it does appear useful to note the unsettled state of sociology during this period as a background to the responses these few sociologists made to Mead. The failure of Chicago sociologists to embrace Mead during this period may reflect in part the lack of intellectual direction in sociology and the efforts of this new science to legitimate academically its enterprise. In any case, as we have shown in chapter 6, their theoretical interests and approaches were often contrary to Mead's.

The questionnaire we sent to former graduate students yielded responses from only two sociologists who received their doctorates prior to 1920. Information on one other pre-1920 student was found in Carey's (1975) interviews. Therefore, research on this period is indeed indebted to the foresight of L. L. Bernard, whose life histories included 35 University of Chicago sociology graduate students who had been students prior to 1920.[2] It is this sample of 38 Chicago students, then, that makes it possible to examine Mead's relationship to pre-1920 Chicago sociology.

We begin the examination by considering the enrollment of this sample of graduate students in courses taught by Mead. Second, we consider the extent of recognition given Mead in the life histories collected by Bernard in 1927 and 1928. Finally, to sketch some salient aspects of this relationship, we draw upon the narrative comments in the Bernard life histories, the responses of Queen and Elmer to our questionnaire, and Carey's (1975) interview with Mrs. Howard Jensen.

Enrollment Patterns

One possible challenge to our interpretation of these findings rests on the representativeness of our sample. Baker, Long, and Quensel (1973) posed this question for the entire Bernard sample, but did not resolve it. At issue, of course, is whether the limited number of observations these students made about Mead and Chicago sociologists are representative of the observations that would have been made by the larger student population. The sample includes 22 doctoral students, 4 M.A. students, and 12 students who did not receive graduate degrees in sociology from Chicago. Therefore, these students come from all segments of the graduate student population. More important, it is possible to show that the sample is representative of the larger population with respect to their enrollment in courses taught by Mead.

An examination of this sample's enrollment in courses taught by Mead establishes that 16 of 38 (42.1%) enrolled in one or more courses. This almost equals the proportion (43.4%) of sociology doctoral students enrolled in Mead's courses in the same period (see Table 3, chapter 7). However, we previously noted that graduate students who did not earn the Ph.D. did not enroll in the same proportions as doctoral students. Considering only the doctoral students in this sample, 14 of 22 (63.6%) enrolled in Mead's courses. Many of these were students during the peak of his popularity. Thus, there is no evidence that our sample is unrepresentative of the larger graduate student population. On the contrary, comparative enrollment proportions support the hypothesis that they *are* representative. In any case, these are the only remaining data.

The Bernard Histories

Of special interest to this research are the statements of social recognition given Mead in the Bernard life histories. In the guidelines for writing their life histories, Bernard asked his sample to name those scholars who had intellectually influenced them in their sociological development. He also asked them to differentiate this influence in terms of whether it had been derived from student contacts, writings, and so forth. It is thus possible to obtain a measure of the "influence" Mead generated *while he was still teaching* at Chicago.

Ten of 37 (27.0%) pre-1920 sociology graduate students named Mead as an intellectual influence. All 10 of these students classified Mead as an influential teacher. Therefore, while 42.1% of these students enrolled in courses taught by Mead, only 27.0% named him as an influential teacher; no student named him as influential from any other source. Mead's recognition from pre-1920 students is not sufficient in magnitude to establish him as a major theoretical figure for Chicago sociology graduate students during this early period.[3]

Those sociologists who recognized Mead as an influential teacher were Thomas, Ellwood, Bogardus, Sutherland, Queen, Steiner, Price, Kuhlman, Young, and Bernard.[4] Although several of these were sociologists we have already discussed regarding the recognition they gave Mead in their published writings, only Kimball Young was singled out as giving Mead extensive recognition. The narrative comments of these sociologists suggest the relationship that linked Mead to Chicago sociology prior to 1920.

On January 10, 1928, W. I. Thomas sent L. L. Bernard a revised sketch of his life history (see Baker, 1973). In an accompanying letter, Thomas noted that he was *adding the name of Mead* to those who influenced him. The revised version was apparently not retained by Bernard, because Baker's 1973 publication of Thomas's life history does *not* include recognition of Mead—except in the accompanying letter. What merits emphasis is that Thomas "overlooked" recognition of Mead in the original version.

Thomas was Mead's first sociology graduate student at Chicago, enrolling in three of Mead's courses.[5] Thomas then joined the sociology faculty and remained until 1918. Despite his graduate student contacts with Mead and the later faculty contacts, Thomas's writings gave Mead almost no recognition. Comments of two sociology graduate students who had Thomas as a teacher suggest that he gave Mead only limited recognition in his courses. In fact, recollections of these students suggest that Mead received only limited recognition from *all* of the pre-1920 sociology faculty.

Stuart A. Queen and Manual C. Elmer are the two sociologists who answered our questions regarding Mead's social recognition in the classrooms of sociology faculty. Both Queen and Elmer had been graduate students from 1910 to 1913, although it is not known whether they were enrolled in the same courses at the same time. Only Queen enrolled in courses taught by Mead.[6] What is especially interesting is the apparent inconsistency of their recollections. Queen recalls that Small, Vincent, and Park gave Mead recognition in their classrooms, but that Thomas did so especially. Elmer also reports Thomas giving Mead recognition, but he writes, "Mead was merely mentioned as a promising young man interested in social control thru language and symbols."[7] Elmer does not mention Small, Vincent, or Park. He does, however, suggest that only Henderson gave Mead recognition with any frequency. Queen specifically indicated that Henderson gave Mead *no* recognition.

Despite the inconsistencies in their statements, it appears that Elmer and Queen agree that the recognition Mead received was limited. We suspect that although Mead received recognition, he did not consistently receive it. That is, as Elmer's statement suggests, Mead may have been viewed as a scholar of promise, but not as a scholar who had already made significant contributions. At issue, of course, is not whether Mead had made significant contributions by this time, but that he was not yet receiving consistent recognition for doing so.

Perhaps a few biographical comments about Mead will illustrate this point. In 1894, when Mead arrived at the University of Chicago and Thomas enrolled in the first course he taught, Mead was a young and unaccomplished scholar. He did not have his Ph.D., and he only had three years of college teaching experience.[8] Mead's first article was published this same year. As a point of comparison, Thomas already had a Ph.D. in English Literature and Modern Languages and seven years of college teaching experience (see Thomas, 1966). It is doubtful that Mead's "promise" was compellingly visible to Thomas. However, it is apparent that Mead's *relationship to sociology was at least close enough* that graduate students were occasionally told that he did show promise.

Elmer did not have classroom contact with Mead, but he had heard of Mead while he was a graduate student. He reports that he heard Mead talk on two occasions in 1912.[9] Moreover, Professor Henderson assigned student Elmer the task of writing a synopsis of Mead's 1912 article, "Social Consciousness and the Consciousness of Meaning." Although Elmer does not recall being personally encouraged to enroll in Mead's courses, he does report that Henderson had encouraged both E. E. Eubank and R. D. McKenzie to study with Mead. Queen personally recalls that Small suggested he enroll in Mead's courses. There is, then, evidence that some sociology students received informal encouragement on the part of some sociology faculty to enroll in Mead's courses prior to 1920. It is more certain that *formal encouragement* was provided by the graduate bulletin, which listed some of Mead's courses as appropriate for sociology students.[10]

This formal and informal encouragement to enroll in Mead's courses is reflected in the comparatively high sociology graduate student enrollment during this period. For some of these students, classroom contact

with Mead was sufficiently impressive that they mentioned him in the life
histories they provided Bernard. Bogardus stated, "The third year afforded contacts with Professor George H. Mead and his striking and
profound teaching in social psychology" (Pennsylvania Historical Collections, Pennsylvania State University). Ellwood wrote that Mead had
made a "marked impression on him—although not nearly as marked as
that of John Dewey" (Pennsylvania Historical Collections, Pennsylvania
State University). Others, such as Queen and E. H. Sutherland, simply
listed Mead as an influential teacher.

Mead's impression on sociology graduate students was not always
favorable. Jesse Steiner reported in his life history that Mead had been an
influential teacher, but he also acknowledged that "Professor Mead's
course in social psychology left me cold partly because I was ill prepared
in psychology.... It was not until a couple of years after I had taken
Professor Mead's course that I realized the value of his point of view"
(Pennsylvania Historical Collections, Pennsylvania State University).
L. L. Bernard also reported being less than enthusiastic about Mead's
courses—with the exception of his treatment of Cooley (Pennsylvania
Historical Collections, Pennsylvania State University).[11]

Some of the pre-1920 graduate students reported limited contact with
Mead outside the classroom. Ellwood reported in his life history that
Mead had attended the defense of his dissertation. In the preface to that
dissertation, Ellwood (1901:iv) stated, "To Professor Dewey and his
colleague, Professor Mead, I am indebted for much friendly criticism, but
especially for the philosophic principles which have guided me in analysis
and criticism." Similarly, Queen reports that Mead carefully read and
discussed his dissertation with him as well as offering him several helpful
suggestions for a course that he was taking with Henderson. Although it
is not possible to determine how many pre-1920 sociology graduate
students had contact with Mead outside the classroom, it is apparent that
it occasionally took place.[12]

Students'
Recommendation of
Mead to Other
Students

As important as the question of Mead's recognition by sociology faculty
in the presence of sociology graduate students is the question of whether
students recognized Mead among themselves. In response to this question, both Queen and Elmer recall discussing Mead or hearing others
mention him. Queen recalls, "A group of us, including E. H. Sutherland,

often took walks in Jackson Park, and ate meals together. During these we talked much about Mead's ideas." Elmer recalls E. E. Eubank and R. D. McKenzie mentioning Mead. Both agree, though, that Mead's name was not mentioned any more frequently than some other nonsociology faculty.

There is evidence to suggest that prior to 1920, Mead's reputation as a teacher was spreading to other universities throughout the United States. Queen reports that his decision to go to Chicago was due in part to Mead's presence there. He recalls that he knew Mead was "the outstanding social psychologist of the day." [13] Kimball Young wrote Bernard that "the stimulation to attend Chicago came especially from Joseph Peterson and W. J. Snow, two of my college teachers. Both urged me to be certain to study, among others, with W. I. Thomas, G. H. Mead, and E. S. Ames" (Pennsylvania Historical Collections, Pennsylvania State University). [14] However, Elmer reported that he had not heard of Mead prior to his arrival.

Before they arrived at Chicago, students heard of Mead from varied sources. In Queen's case, it was from a philosophy teacher; in the case of Young, a psychology teacher. However, Carey's (1975) interview with the widow of Howard Jensen suggests that some students heard about Mead from Chicago-trained sociologists. Mrs. Jensen recalls:

> Howard was a student of Victor Helleberg—there at the University of Kansas; Helleberg was much impressed by Dr. Mead at the University of Chicago and influenced Mr. Jensen to go there and take his work under that group of men who were there then. Small and Mead and the group there at the time, but especially Mead. [Special Collections, Regenstein Library, University of Chicago]

Helleberg's name did not appear among those sociologists giving Mead recognition in published writings. Helleberg had, however, been one of Mead's sociology graduate students. [15] What is important here is that some of Mead's pre-1920 sociology graduate students gave Mead recognition in their own university classrooms.

Although Mead may have been a salient personality for some students prior to their studies at Chicago, others did not accord him significance until after they had taken his courses and left Chicago. Jesse Steiner's comments, cited above, are one example. Another such student was Kimball Young. Young was awarded an M.A. in sociology from Chicago in 1918. In his life history he recalled that after a few years of teaching he became interested in psychology and went to Stanford University for the Ph.D. In 1928 he wrote:

Several years devoted to systematic reading and teaching in psychology confirmed my growing belief that academic psychology, both of experimental and textbook variety, failed to describe adequately and explain social behavior. The failure of the mental testers and experimentalists to recognize the importance of cultural and social factors in determining intelligence, habits, and attitudes became increasingly evident. My shift toward sociology at Oregon was a definite and deliberate gesture to attempt for myself a restatement of behavior in terms of both bio-psychological mechanisms and cultural and social conditioning. The influence of Cooley, Mead, and Thomas, especially, became ever more dominant as psychology seemed to bring only partial results in explaining human conduct. [Pennsylvania Historical Collections, Pennsylvania State University]

Young was a student in Mead's 1917 social psychology course, and, as we have shown, he subsequently gave Mead considerable social recognition.

Elmer's recollections allow for a natural transition to our examination of Mead's post-1920 relationship to Chicago sociology. Insightfully, Elmer regards the post-World War I era as the turning point in Mead's recognition:

Mead was sort of an understudy of John Dewey and when Dewey went to Columbia University, Mead pushed ahead. As a matter of fact, it was not until *after World War I,* and after the very tragic publicity of W. I. Thomas and his arrest in a notorious house on Wabash Street,—which resulted in his resignation from the University of Chicago—which everyone knows about but do not mention,—that Mead became really known, and began to do more writing.

Although it is questionable as to what extent Mead was an "understudy" of Dewey, it is certain that he did not "begin to do more writing" after World War I. However, as we have amply shown, it was not until after this time that Mead began to receive recognition for his earlier articles. Therefore, Elmer correctly identifies what might be considered the turning point in Mead's recognition by sociologists, especially at Chicago. There is certainly reason to agree with Elmer on the importance Thomas's departure had for Mead's social recognition. Specifically, it was Thomas's departure that resulted in Ellsworth Faris becoming a member of the department. And with the retirement and subsequent death of Small, Faris became the departmental head and editor of the *American Journal of Sociology,* respectively. As the following discussion indicates, Faris played a very prominent role in establishing Mead's recognition among post-1920 Chicago sociologists.

After nearly three decades of halting intellectual movement, the 1920s ushered in a tremendous burst of research activity in American sociology. Although this change was not confined to the University of Chicago, it was centered there. The change is reflected in Thomas and Znaniecki's *Polish Peasant in Europe and America,* published in 1918, the year Thomas was forced to leave the university. However, it was Park and Burgess who were primarily responsible for the enthusiasm and productivity of sociologists at Chicago during the 1920s. As Carey (1975:159) indicates: "Park and Burgess surrounded themselves with collaborators and students who produced an enormous amount of work and provided for a continuation of their work after they retired. They set guidelines for the work that followed and obtained resources for its continuance."

We turn now to a consideration of Mead's relationship to Chicago sociology during the school's most distinguished period. These data further support our contention that Mead was peripheral to the mainstream of early Chicago sociology. Moreover, because the data base is far more adequate for the post-1920 period, we may state our conclusions more confidently.[16]

Pre-Chicago Sources
of Student Referrals to
Mead

Graduate students entering the sociology department after 1920 came from a wide range of geographical regions and colleges throughout the United States (see Carey, 1975). Only six individuals in the sample had received some or all of their undergraduate education at Chicago. One question posed to those respondents who had received their predoctoral education at institutions other than Chicago was whether they were aware of Mead when they arrived at Chicago and, if so, what was the source and extent of their knowledge. Their responses indicate that a sizable number of sociology graduate students at Chicago may have been aware of Mead when they began their graduate work in sociology.

Twenty Chicago sociology graduate student alumni answered the question of prior awareness. Exactly half of these respondents reported a prior awareness.[17] These limited data suggest that after 1920, Mead was recognized in many institutions of higher education throughout the United States. However, it is more important to establish the source of these students' awareness of Mead and the extent of their knowledge before they arrived.

These respondents were asked whether their undergraduate instructors had been trained at Chicago. Among the 24 individuals who answered this question, 16 (67%) remembered having Chicago-trained sociologists as undergraduate instructors. In fact, these students indicated that it was often these teachers who convinced them that Chicago was the foremost center for the study of sociology in the United States. It is also clear that many of these Chicago-trained sociological mentors were the source of Mead's recognition.[18] Only one former sociology graduate student recalled hearing of Mead exclusively from nonsociology faculty at his undergraduate institution.

Yet, the majority of students who arrived at Chicago to begin sociology graduate work only recognized Mead's name; they knew only that Mead was a Chicago professor. Everett C. Hughes recalls that when he arrived at Chicago he knew "almost nothing" about Mead's ideas. Similarly, Herbert Blumer states that he knew "just the name; nothing to attach any importance to it" (Personal Interview, August 1, 1974). As we pointed out earlier, Blumer had taken an A.B. and an M.A. in sociology, in 1920 and 1921 respectively, with Ellwood at the University of Missouri. He remained at Missouri as an instructor in sociology until 1925, when he began graduate work at Chicago. Leonard S. Cottrell recalls that "Krueger and Reckless mentioned him as influencing Faris, but did not elaborate on Mead's ideas." In fact, what some students heard did not cast Mead in a favorable light. A. R. Mangus states that he had heard Mead "was very abstruse, wordy, difficult to understand." The one known exception to this pattern of limited awareness of Mead was Carroll D. Clark who reports, "Before going to Chicago, I had never met Mead but had read and studied assiduously everything of major consequence he had published." Clark had received his M.A. in sociology from the University of Kansas.

The "Kansas Connection"

In our analysis of the writings of sociologists we identified a group who extended Mead social recognition; in the 1920s a limited number of these gave him considerable recognition. It is reasonable to infer that this same pattern of differential recognition characterized the classrooms of sociologists throughout the United States. As our data establish, prominent among these institutions was the University of Kansas.

The University of Kansas stands out in the responses we received to our question of whether, prior to their arrival at Chicago, students were encouraged to enroll in Mead's courses or read his writings. Seven of 25 (28%) respondents recalled such encouragement; two of these had been Kansas undergraduates. A second and more noteworthy source is that L. L. Redmond, a Kansas-trained sociologist, was the only non-Chicago sociologist in the 258 life histories collected by Bernard to name Mead as influential to his intellectual development.[19] Redmond cited Mead's writings as the source of influence; significantly, the teachers he named as influential were Victor E. Helleberg, Stuart A. Queen, and Curt Rosenow.

Fortunately, Clark's comments specify in some detail the nature of Mead's "Kansas connection." At Kansas, Clark indicates that "Mead was not an obscure figure. He was very much to the fore-front." Clark reports that several of his teachers "had worked very closely and effectively with Mead." Clark named the same faculty as Redmond did—Queen, Rosenow, and especially Helleberg.[20] Helleberg, Clark suggests, was a "disciple of Mead. The term 'disciple' is not too strong because Helleberg was the kind of teacher who, though vastly stimulating, had a tendency to draw students around him almost in a cult." Concerning Helleberg's classroom recognition of Mead, Clark recalls he "had mimeographed for the use of his advanced courses . . . all the articles of Mead that he could get hold of." Included in these was Mead's 1903 article, "The Definition of the Psychical." It appears that Helleberg's recognition of Mead at Kansas may have been exceeded only by Faris's at Chicago.

We can conjecture that Kansas is related to one rather significant incident of Mead's social recognition: Bodenhafer, the first sociologist to give Mead extensive recognition in sociology dissertations and in the *American Journal of Sociology,* received his M.A. in sociology from Kansas in 1915.[21] In any case, as Clark recalls, "One who studied sociology here at the University of Kansas in the 1920s . . . was very likely to be well acquainted with George Herbert Mead—although the subtleties of Mead's complete philosophical and social psychological perspective would not necessarily get to him." Clearly, these circumstances were far different from those experienced by the majority of sociology students at other universities.

Intradepartmental
Referrals

If post-1920 sociology graduate students arrived at Chicago uninformed about Mead, they did not depart with the same lack of awareness. Without exception, every former Chicago sociology student in the sample indicated they heard of Mead after they began their graduate work. As these findings suggest, it is reasonable to assume that during the 1920s and early 1930s, it was impossible for sociology graduate students to avoid hearing others acknowledge Mead.

Much of the research we reported in chapters 7 and 8 focused on the enrollment of sociology graduate students in Mead's courses and their recognition of his written work. We specifically asked former graduate students about two related aspects of these activities. First, in order to discover whether an informal referral process was in operation, we asked if anyone had suggested Mead's courses to them. (In the previous section we pointed out that Mead's courses received official departmental recognition and recommendation.) Second, we asked if any of Mead's articles may have been suggested to them.

With respect to course enrollment, sixteen of twenty-one (76%) of the sample recalled that others recommended that they enroll in Mead's courses. Two kinds of referral sources were identified: most frequently mentioned was the suggestions of fellow graduate students (10 of 16). In fact, Leonard S. Cottrell, Jr., one of the sociologists answering this questionnaire, was specifically named by two different respondents as the graduate student who suggested they enroll in courses taught by Mead. The second source of enrollment suggestions came from sociology faculty. What is significant about this source is that most of the respondents recall only one sociology faculty member making that suggestion: Ellsworth Faris (8 of 16). Other sociology faculty who were each mentioned once were Small, Burgess, and Blumer. The survey of former sociology graduate students repeatedly confirms that Faris played a significant role in the recognition of Mead among sociologists.

Fourteen of 20 respondents (70%) answered affirmatively that others had recommended they read Mead's writings, and nine credited Faris with the recommendation. Blumer was named three times, Burgess twice, and Small, Park, and Ogburn were each named once. Two students recalled that the suggestion came from Mead himself while they were attending his classes. Interestingly, no one reports that fellow graduate students were the source. Perhaps this reflects the fact (argued below) that graduate students did not read Mead very extensively.

Apparently, most sociology graduate students left Chicago having read something by Mead. Among the 21 individuals who responded to a question on this, 17 (81%) reported affirmatively; thus, slightly more reported reading Mead than receiving suggestions to do so. However, the range of their exposure to Mead's writings was very narrow. Guy B. Johnson recalled that his reading of Mead's writings was "very meager" while he was a graduate student. Helen McGill Hughes recalled reading one paper by Mead after hearing him speak before the Sociology Club. Other sociologists reported reading one or two articles. Albert Blumenthal reported the widest selection, recalling that he read "everything that was relevant to social psychology."[22]

We noted above that a large proportion of students received some type of informal encouragement to enroll in Mead's courses. Comparing this to the enrollment records of the respondents in our sample, we see that 39% of these 36 students actually enrolled in one or more of Mead's courses.[23] (This may be compared to the 43.4% enrollment of doctoral students and 24.4% enrollment of terminal M.A. students.) Although only two of these sociologists enrolled in more than one of Mead's courses, all but one enrolled in his Advanced Social Psychology course. What is most significant is that a sizable proportion of our post-1920 sample—61% of the 36 individuals—did not enroll in *any* of Mead's courses. In fact, 22 of 27 (81%) Chicago sociologists in the Bernard sample did not enroll. These proportions are indicative of the general post-1920 decline in enrollment in Mead's courses previously discussed (chapter 7).

The comments of those students who did not enroll help eliminate the contradiction between the actual enrollment figures and the assumptions of many students that all sociology graduate students enrolled at least in Mead's Advanced Social Psychology course. We have established the popularity of this course among sociology students. From our sample, 36.9% enrolled in Social Psychology; however, an additional 28% indicated they audited the course or attended an occasional lecture. Thus, it is possible that although sporadic, the attendance of those students who did not enroll may have been frequent enough to create the illusion that the vast majority of sociology graduate students enrolled in at least this one course by Mead. Evidence from this research finds no support for the myths of universal enrollment and Mead's widespread popularity.

Mead's Limited
Personal Association
with Students and
His Relationship to
Blumer

The responses of this sample also establish that Mead's contact with sociology graduate students was almost exclusively restricted to the classroom. Only three individuals indicated having had any contact with Mead outside the classroom. Norman Haynor reports that he may have had incidental contact with Mead when the latter was president of the Settlement House Board. Robert E. L. Faris, the son of Ellsworth Faris, indicates that the only contact he had with Mead outside the classroom occurred once, when Mead had his entire family over for dinner. However, Faris recalls that he was only fourteen or fifteen years old and that Mead spent the entire evening talking with his father. The one known exception to this pattern of very restricted contact occurred in the case of Herbert Blumer. Nevertheless, Blumer's comments suggest that even his contact was not very frequent.

Blumer's recollections are instructive for two reasons. First, they not only contribute to a construction of the nature of the relationship between Blumer and Mead, but second, they also may be used to suggest the general pattern of contact between Mead and Chicago sociology. As we indicated, Blumer recalls having come to Chicago knowing the name of Mead, but essentially nothing else about him. However, Blumer states that he had Faris as a teacher during his first quarter: "In that course I think I really became familiar with the name Mead and was given some impetus to move in the direction of familiarizing myself with his work." As Blumer recalls, Faris "was very influential in taking his own students—who were students specializing in the area of social psychology inside the Department of Sociology—and directing them toward Mead's course. So, I would say that by all odds, this was the primary link between Mead in philosophy and the people in sociology at that time" (Personal Interview, 8/1/74).

An examination of Mead's grade reports establishes that Blumer enrolled in two of his courses.[24] Blumer recalls taking three or four of Mead's courses. It would appear, therefore, that Blumer was among the sociology graduate students who informally audited an occasional course with Mead. It also appears that Blumer took more courses with Mead than other sociology graduate students of the post-1920 era. However, it was Blumer's contact with Mead as a research assistant that clearly distinguishes his contact from that of the other students. As Mead's research assistant, Blumer recalls getting to know Mead "on a person-to-person basis" (Personal Interview, 8/1/74). It was out of this context that Blumer recalls having occasional intellectual discussions with Mead. For the post-1920 graduate students, Blumer's assessment appears correct: "So far as I know, I was probably the only one outside of philosophy as a graduate student who sort of got into that fairly close relationship with him" (Personal Interview, 8/1/74).[25]

Blumer acknowledges that his memory of the origins of his relationship to Mead has dimmed. He recalls that in part it derived from a paper he wrote for Mead on the development of the self.[26] Blumer recalls Faris telling him that Mead was very much impressed with the paper. Later, Faris directed Blumer's dissertation, and Mead participated in Blumer's oral examination. Blumer joined the sociology faculty upon completion of his doctorate in 1928; he does not report having much interaction with Mead after his graduate days.

In the winter of 1931 Mead asked Blumer to take over his Advanced Social Psychology course. As Blumer recalls the circumstances, "I had a telephone message to visit Mead in the hospital. While I was there he asked me to take over his course on Advanced Social Psychology, which was about three weeks into the quarter" (Personal Communication, 11/17/74). It is noteworthy that Mead approached the sociology staff, for it clearly demonstrates that his relationship was such that he sought and received assistance. However, it is equally significant that Mead appears to have first contacted Faris with the request to teach his course.[27] Given Faris's teaching and departmental commitments, we suspect Faris declined and recommended his younger colleague. Thus, even in the case of Blumer's "special" relationship to Mead, we see a degree of mediation by Faris. Faris appears, time and again, as the primary figure to call to attention of sociology graduate students the name and ideas of Mead— and, in perhaps one case, to call to Mead's attention the name of graduate students.

Faris's Role in Mead's
Popularization in
Relation to That of
Other Faculty

Contemporary sociologists generally associate Mead with the historical development of social psychology. The mention of his name in dissertations, journals, and books suggests that historically this was the case. Accordingly, we asked former sociology graduate students a two-part question. First, we inquired about their enrollment in social psychology courses and, second, about whether their social psychology instructors gave Mead recognition. The responses indicate that most sociology graduate students *had* enrolled in social psychology courses. However, whether they had been exposed to Mead depended upon which department offered the course, and upon the instructor.

Thirty of 36 respondents (82%) who could be classified on the question of social psychology enrollment had taken at least one course. Eighteen of the 30 (60%) identified Faris as the sole instructor in the course. Another 33.0% of the sample also identified him as one of their social psychology instructors. Other sociology faculty listed as social psychology instructors were Park, Blumer, L. L. Bernard, and Edward Sapir. Faculty from outside the sociology department listed as social psychology instructors were Thurstone and Kingsbury (psychology), Lasswell (political science), and Judd (education). The results from this question establish that, with the notable exception of Mead in philosophy, the exposure of sociology graduate students to social psychology was largely limited to courses in their own department.

Most students indicated that Faris was their main source of instruction for social psychology. Similarly, they recall that Faris was the only social psychologist who gave Mead extensive social recognition.[28] In fact, these repeated references to Faris as one who recognized Mead, strongly suggest that after 1920 *no* student taking social psychology with Faris failed to hear about Mead. Several students recall that Faris's recognition of Mead extended to all or most of the courses he taught.[29]

Although Faris had been a pre-1920 student of Mead's, there is minimal information available to illuminate their personal relationship. Faris enrolled in a series of four courses with Mead between 1911 and 1913, receiving the Ph.D. in psychology in 1914. Faris's dissertation is not on deposit with the library at Chicago, but recall that during this period, psychology graduate students were still enrolling in Mead's courses in considerable numbers.[30] Indeed, Kurt Rosenow and J. R. Kantor—the two psychologists we identified earlier for giving Mead recognition in sociology journals—were students during this same period. What is most important is that with the arrival of this psychologist-turned-sociologist to replace the departed Thomas, there was a significant increase in the amount of social recognition given Mead in the sociology department.

Most of the sociologists in this sample did not have Blumer as an instructor because, as a young faculty member, he taught a greater number of undergraduate courses. However, five respondents recall hearing Blumer give Mead recognition in his classroom instruction. One recalls, "Since I took Blumer's course on social psychology soon after he had completed his doctoral dissertation on Mead, the course was primarily a summary of that dissertation." Blumer's dissertation, of course, was not about Mead, but the statement does indicate that Mead was recognized by Blumer. We suggest that the addition of Blumer to the sociology faculty greatly increased Mead's exposure to sociology graduate students.

Fewer and less detailed are the recollections of these respondents regarding Mead's recognition by sociology faculty other than Faris and Blumer. Only 16 students answered this question, 13 (81%) of whom indicated that Mead received limited recognition. They named Burgess as the faculty member who most often recognized Mead (10 of 16), followed by Park (7 of 16), Wirth (3 of 16), Ogburn (2 of 16), and Floyd House (1 of 16).[31] We think that it is of special importance, however, that although Mead's recognition by these faculty was limited, it was generally favorable.[32]

Mead and Park

The previous observations establish the extent of Mead's recognition in the classrooms of sociology faculty. But what of the interpersonal ties between Mead and other faculty members? Although we had anticipated that our sample could provide responses to this question, we were wrong. It appears there was such a sharp separation between the off-campus life of students and faculty that students were simply not in position to make these observations. As a consequence, no student recalls seeing Mead interacting with the sociology faculty.[33]

Two sociologists, however, indirectly establish that a personal relationship did exist between Mead and Park. We will sketch that relationship for three reasons: First, it is simply of interest that Mead and Park may have had a personal relationship. Second, and related to this, it is clear that whatever the relationship, it did not affect Park's recognition of Mead. Third, it is useful to call attention to the faculty's off-campus intellectual life since that life is of potential importance for the understanding of any scholar's intellectual development.

The personal relationship between Park and Mead is described in the recollections of Clarence E. Glick, who indicates that he lived with "Dr. and Mrs. Park during the summer of 1927 in Chicago and for six months in Hawaii (1931–32). Park knew Mead very well and often spoke highly of him as a friend—and bitterly of the treatment Mead received at the University of Chicago toward the end of his life."[34]

For a brief description of the off-campus intellectual life of Chicago

faculty, at least as it pertained to Park, we draw upon the memory of
Everett C. Hughes. Hughes acknowledges that he was not aware of this
life while a graduate student, but became aware of it later as a faculty
member. Although Mead had died by the time Hughes returned to
Chicago, it was during this latter period that Hughes became friendly
with the Parks, Edward S. Ames in philosophy, and Elinor Castle Nef, a
writer and favorite niece of Mead's.[35] Hughes described the intellectual
life of this group and others in the following manner:

> The talk there was sociology and philosophy and definitely influenced
> very much by Mead, Dewey.... I think one should add, in order to
> understand these men, that the talk was very literary. Park was a
> voracious reader of novels and poetry and fed these things back into
> his sociology and into conversation in these circles.

Yet, in spite of Glick's statements, Hughes "cannot say just what Mead's
role was in that circle if he had any."

For our purposes, it is not necessary to establish that Mead participated in Park's intellectual circle. It is sufficient to ascertain that Park
claimed a friendship with Mead, and that Mead seems to have received a
degree of recognition in Park's intellectual circle.[36] Significantly, as evidenced by the textual analysis of Park's writings and student recollections, this relationship did not affect Mead's recognition among
sociologists or sociology graduate students.

The Meadian "Oral Tradition" among Sociology Graduate Students

It is apparent that outside the classroom, sociology graduate students did
not interact with sociology faculty to any great extent. Whatever Mead's
recognition or interaction in these circles, it could not have been very
important to them. As we have shown, inasmuch as Mead did not receive
much recognition by Park or others, either in their classrooms or writings, there is reason to emphasize the importance of Mead's recognition
among sociology students themselves. Nearly all students recall discussing Mead among themselves while they were graduate students. Blumer
places considerable emphasis on Mead's "oral tradition" among his fellow graduate students:

> I think the more accurate way to depict that situation is to say that
> among the graduate students themselves there was more or less the
> tradition being passed on from one generation of students to the

next. A tradition which was centered around the name of Mead which indicated that here was a man of outstanding importance, one who made outstanding contributions, and accordingly, the student in the Department of Sociology whose interests were at all in the direction of social psychology, should, obviously, have contact with Mead and take this particular course I referred to before. [Personal Interview, 8/1/74]

The course Blumer is referring to is, of course, Mead's Advanced Social Psychology. As we have previously indicated, fellow graduate students were the most frequent source of encouragement to enroll in this course. What we may add to this observation is that they discussed Mead's ideas among themselves.[37] Moreover, in response to a question comparing Mead's recognition to that of other Chicago faculty, it is apparent that Blumer's assessment holds: "There was no other person, I think I can state rather safely, who occupied a similar kind of position like that of Mead, in the case of sociology students" (Personal Interview, 8/1/74).

Not all of the student responses indicate Mead was favorably recognized by all graduate students. The previous comments regarding the extent of Mead's recognition in student conversations implied that some students were unresponsive. For example, Nels Anderson recalls hearing about Mead from fellow graduate students, but "not to make me curious about Mead. In my student work I was getting Mead second-hand enough for my needs." Interestingly, part of the myth of Mead's universal popularity may have resulted from the silence of graduate students who neither enrolled nor audited his courses. As Blumenthal insinuated, some students may have been reluctant to challenge the graduate students who gave Mead extensive recognition: "I heard no significant criticism of Mead's ideas by sociology graduate students. His viewpoint was a fetish to so many students that those with misgivings may have been too tactful to publicize them." Silence may have lessened the possibility of interpersonal conflict between graduate students, and thereby helped create an illusion of greater popularity than is revealed in (1) the recollections of these graduate students, (2) the evidence from Mead's sociology graduate student enrollment, and (3) his recognition in dissertations.

The recollections of the students suggest a cycle of Mead's recognition. These students frequently report that they at least knew Mead's name by the time they arrived at Chicago; they definitely recall participating in his recognition after they became graduate students; and finally, they gave Mead recognition in their own teaching careers.

We asked two questions to determine whether Mead received recognition in courses taught by these students after they left Chicago. We asked whether Mead's ideas were incorporated into their social thought, and whether they assigned Mead's published work in their courses. The responses suggest that the cycle of recognition was not broken. However, the responses also establish that a sizable minority did not give Mead recognition after their graduate days at Chicago. The majority of the 23 sociologists who answered the question believe that they did incorporate Mead's ideas into their own sociological thinking. Some suggest that the incorporation may have been indirect and below awareness, but 15 of the 23 (65%) report that they incorporated Mead's social thought. This belief in Mead's influence is far greater than any of our objective analyses have established. Of course, we have not contended that Mead had no influence on Chicago sociologists, but that it was never as pervasive as the contemporary myth asserts.

Of the 15 who answered the question of whether they assigned Mead's writings, 10 report they did—frequently mentioned was Mead's posthumously published *Mind, Self and Society*. Given Mead's contemporary recognition among sociologists, there is reason to suspect that after his death, he continued to receive recognition from Chicago-trained sociologists. Yet, it should be noted that a sizable minority of our sample reported that they did not incorporate any of Mead's ideas into their sociology, and that they did not ask their students to read his published work. Although they recall hearing other Chicago graduate students and faculty give Mead recognition, he did not become significant for them.

This chapter has partially reconstructed the environs of Chicago sociology graduate students and their relationship to Mead. The recollections indicate that Mead did receive both graduate student and sociology faculty recognition throughout his Chicago years, and that recognition continued after his death. Three of the specific aspects of this recognition deserve reiteration. First, it is clear that sociology faculty, both before and after 1920, gave Mead recognition in their classrooms, but, for the majority of these faculty, Mead's recognition was incidental and did not increase in frequency over time.

Second, the turning point in Mead's recognition was causally linked to changes in the sociology faculty. When Faris replaced Thomas, Mead's recognition increased markedly. No faculty member gave Mead as much recognition as did Faris, and, with the addition of Blumer, Mead's social recognition received increased faculty sponsorship. Significantly, there is little evidence that other sociology faculty gave Mead negative recognition.

The third aspect concerns Mead's recognition among sociology graduate students. It appears that there did exist a graduate-student tradition of discussing Mead's ideas, enrolling in his courses, and recommending that other students enroll. A few sociology graduate students were even quite active in their recognition of Mead. Nevertheless, evidence suggests that a majority of students had little or no exposure to Mead, having never enrolled in his courses. Of those few graduate students who had contact with Mead, it was limited to his Advanced Social Psychology course. Therefore, the recollections of these former sociology graduate students indicate that only a small number of students and faculty were especially "influenced" by George Herbert Mead.

10 Retrospect and Prospect | Larger Contexts of the Study

Although inquiry into American sociological theory is an ongoing process, at this point we must pause to formulate some tentative conclusions, reflexively criticize our effort, introduce some unexplored questions, and briefly suggest this book's relevance to contemporary sociological thought. Our remarks consider three general areas: (1) pragmatism and symbolic interactionism, (2) epistemic and methodological complications in reconstructing intellectual histories, and (3) agenda for future research.

The Pragmatists Revisited

Sociologists perennially look to philosophers for answers about the nature of such concepts as symbol, meaning, and consciousness. This is hardly surprising in that these concepts are critical to both sociology and philosophy. But what is perplexing is the selection of philosophers whom sociologists have singled out, as well as the timing of these selections.

A case in point is the recent emergence of ethnomethodology, phenomenological sociology, and assorted varieties of "humanistic" sociology. As Hinkle (1974:112) implies, these subjective-idealist theoretical orientations easily could have revived Cooley, Ellwood, and other American psychical interactionists with whom they are metatheoretically continuous. Yet they trace their roots to such an unlikely source as Edmund Husserl. The theoretical statements of ethnomethodologists and phenomenological sociologists bear only slight resemblance to Husserlian phenomenology (see Bauman, 1973), and it is highly improbable that this dubious "Husserlian connection" would have been made had not Alfred Shutz proclaimed the relevance of Husserl's philosophy to sociology. Inasmuch as Schutz's personal social thought departs from Husserlian phenomenology in both substance and method, his work has not substantiated the claim. Equally questionable is whether the work of Garfinkel (1967) and other ethnomethodologists has followed Schutz's methodology.

Parallels do exist between Schutz's role in ethnomethodology and Blumer's role in symbolic interactionism. Both serve as intellectual brokers between the philosophical master and the emerging sociological perspective or "school" for which the master supposedly supplied the leading principles. Due to the fact that few American sociologists have interest or training in technical philosophy, the brokers must formulate a highly synthetic version of the master's thought which is fit for consumption by the sociologists. Znaniecki's essay, "Schools and Scholars as Bearers of Absolute Truth," is an insightful description of the ways in which schools of thought are created and sustained. Znaniecki (1940:107) stated, "The growth of the knowledge of sacred schools is thus essentially an accumulation of *commentaries* in which superior scholars interpret for the benefit of their contemporaries and successors either the original holy texts or the writings of earlier commentators." Over a period of time, the synthetic formulation gains a life of its own, new terminologies are added, and the "school" drifts farther and farther away from the master's philosophy.

These developments are necessary to the life and growth of the school. And, even though adopting a master philosopher may facilitate the initial organization and legitimation of the school, its members eventually must either loosen ties with the master or must attribute the developed synthetic formulations to the master. At this point, if only members of the school are engaged in writing its history, they may create an intellectual history of the school which conceals the genesis and subsequent expansion of the synthetic philosophy. As the school grows, the broker becomes far more vital to the school than the master. Yet, one must also recognize that the "master connection" supposition has also grown, and the longer it survives, the more it becomes a part of the disciplinary folklore. Once so enshrined, only considerable argumentative persuasion can dislodge it from its lofty status.

This encrustation has already occurred around Mead and is rapidly forming around Husserl.[1] Perhaps the most regrettable consequence of this process is that many second- and third-generation students accept the historical accounts unquestioningly and treat the synthetic formula as a faithful representation of the master's thought. Consequently, the broker's synthetic formula often replaces a first-hand reading of the master's primary texts. As one surveys the mass of literature produced by symbolic interactionists, it is striking how infrequently Mead's (1964) journal articles and papers (*The Philosophy of the Act*) are discussed in depth or even cited.

The orthodoxy of the synthetic formula threatens to stifle the theoretical growth of the school. The synthetic formula often becomes the standard by which dissenting theoretical formulations, alternative interpretations of the master's philosophy, and revisionist accounts of the intellectual history of the school are judged as erroneous. This obviates any appeal to suspend the synthetic formula in order to shift the discourse toward a carefully documented exposition and rigorous reexamination of the texts of the master philosopher and others presumably close to the school. Recent symbolic interactionist textbooks (Handel and Lauer, 1977; Manis and Meltzer, 1978; Kando, 1977; Hewitt, 1979; Charon, 1979; Karp and Yoels, 1979; Lindesmith, Strauss, and Denzin, 1977) all pay homage to the Blumerian symbolic interactionist credo and offer few proposals for new theoretical directions. In response to criticism, members reassert orthodox positions amd generally assume a defensive, conservative stance (Blumer, 1967, 1973, 1977, 1979; Manis and Meltzer, 1978; Lauer and Handel, 1977; Meltzer, Petras, and Reynolds, 1975; Stone et al., 1974).[2]

An intellectual revitalization could come with a genuinely renewed interest in early American sociologists and pragmatists other than Mead. Significantly, John Petras has argued repeatedly that James and Dewey were of substantial importance to the rise of interactionism in American social psychology, but symbolic imteractionists continue to regard Mead as the most salient of the pragmatists for the history of symbolic interactionism. Blumerian symbolic interactionists would find in James a philosopher who was most congenial to their interests and point of view. James's radical empiricism easily could provide a philosophical justification for Blumer's interpretationism and individualism. James's "will to believe" doctrine is consistent with the definitionist conception of reality. And several other Jamesian concepts (e.g., self, functional theory of consciousness, pragmatic truth) are compatible with Blumerian principles. Psychical interactionists will search Mead's writings in vain to find much support for these nominalistic doctrines (see Wilson, 1970:69 n. 13; Zeitlin, 1973).

Fisher and Strauss (1978a:5) recently stated that Mead played a relatively indirect and symbolic role in early Chicago sociology (see also Fisher and Strauss, 1978b, 1979): "Mead played an essentially symbolic role in the department's intellectual history. For although sociologists incorporated various of his concepts into their research, they neither displayed much interest in his thought nor followed his philosophical path of investigating social problems." As far as we have been able to determine, Fisher and Strauss are the only other students of the history of the Chicago sociology department to arrive at this conclusion regarding Mead's intellectual and organizational relationship to the department. It is an idea whose time has come forty years late.

We have shown that the basic principles of Mead's social behaviorism and philosophy of perspectives are entirely contrary to the voluntaristic nomimalist assumptions of the psychical interactionism of Cooley, Thomas, Ellwood, Blumer, and others. In chapter 6, we further argued that despite a mild uprising of social realism spearheaded by Hayes, Faris, and Bodenhafer, the dominant theoretical position of early Chicago sociology was psychical interactionism. Stated differently, Mead's philosophical position ran counter to the mainstream theoretical stance of Chicago sociology. That Mead's thought was peripheral and, indeed, antithetical to this central theoretical movement of Chicago sociology is incongruent with the common assumption that Mead and his courses enjoyed widespread exposure, popularity, and influence among Chicago sociology graduate students. However, having also shown that this assumption is itself a myth, it is clear that Mead was of strictly secondary importance, both intellectually and organizationally, to the development of Chicago sociology.

It is at this point that the arguments presented in Parts One and Two of this book converge toward an overall understanding of Mead's relation to American pragmatism and Chicago sociology. The nominalistic pragmatism of James and Dewey was more aligned with the individualism and liberalism of the American ideology. Consequently, their psychological theory enjoyed far more recognition and notoriety at Chicago and elsewhere (as evidenced in the thought of Cooley, Thomas, Ellwood, Blumer, Park, etc.) than did the social realism of Peirce and Mead. In short, our research challenges—on philosophical and empirical-historical grounds—Mead's alleged centrality to the development of social psychology and sociology at Chicago. Hence our findings suggest that Blumerian symbolic interactionists could construct a far more plausible account of the history and intellectual genesis of their school if they were to trace their intellectual roots to James and Dewey among the pragmatists and to the psychical interactionists among the sociologists.

On the other hand, symbolic interactionists who aspire to be truly *symbolic* rather than psychical may profit from a fresh reading of Mead's works. Meadian social behaviorism contains hypotheses suitable for study in experimental social and physiological psychology which only a few researchers have pursued (Smith, 1971; Cottrell, 1971; O'Toole and Dubin, 1968). On a theoretical level, Mead's philosophy poses many unresolved and interesting problems—such as the I-me relationship— which have been divested of their force through reformulation in the language of the synthetic formula (see Lewis, 1979).

Contemporary American philosophy has witnessed somewhat of a revival of interest in Peirce, a revival that would also benefit sociologists. Peirce's theory of signs offers a sophisticated paradigm for analyzing the variety of sign-vehicles and various mechanisms of signification which have been topics of continuing interest to Garfinkel, Cicourel, and other ethnomethodologists. Of course, the ethnomethodologists would likely raise some objections to Peirce's semiology, but an encounter with Peirce should prove stimulating. Perhaps the fact that Peirce has surfaced in a recent existential sociology reader (Brown, 1977:89–91) is a signal of his discovery by sociologists.[3]

The Neglected Frontiers: Self-Criticisms of the Study

The history of social theory is incomplete and misleading if written as simply the thought of sociologists. Ideas do not respect disciplinary boundaries as reverently as people do. Sociological theory has always been heavily fertilized by developments in other disciplines, especially psychology, philosophy, biology, and economics. Ideally, therefore, a history of American sociological theory should take into account the influences of parallel movements of thought. This is obviously a highly complicated task which is rarely attempted.[4] Perhaps such an ambitious undertaking is best accomplished through a series of related studies. Regarding the social history of American pragmatism and sociology, such a series is now in progress (Mills, 1964; Rucker, 1969; Faris, 1970; Meltzer, Petras, and Reynolds, 1975; and Carey, 1975; Kuklick, 1973; Kuklick, 1977).

The most crucial element which this series largely fails to provide is a clear sense of critical transition points in the history of American pragmatism and Chicago sociology. Our book has attempted to correct this deficiency, but ours is another project which stands far from completion.

Applying Mead's concept of perspective to the present essay, it is clear that our perspective is restricted by our classifications of theorists according to the nominalism / realism criterion. This approach has the advantage of clarifying divergences among the theorists and thereby suggests approximate locations of these critical transition points. Further, it establishes an organizing methodological principle which reduces our task to manageable proportions. However, it must be recalled that the same subject matter can be understood from a multitude of perspectives, and although our perspective may have illuminated certain features neglected by previous studies, there doubtlessly remain other salient relationships which would appear only from alternative perspectives. Thus, the character of any phenomenon is best apprehended when it is scrutinized from a wide range of perspectives. For example, one could approach the same set of theorists with a "conceptual history" methodology by tracing theorists' different orientations toward certain key concepts ("self," "consciousness," etc.). According to this approach, if the classifications of the theorists correspond to the groupings yielded by the nominalism / realism criterion, as we suspect it would, this result would tend to support our claim that one's position on the nominalism/ realism question carries with it implications for a wide variety of other issues.

On another plane, the present essay merges with Hinkle's (1978) study of the metatheoretical orientations of Small, Cooley, Ward, Giddings, Sumner and Keller, and Ross. When this framework is extended to include the post-1935 periods of American sociology, we will have an American history of social theory which classifies and periodicizes all of the major theories and theorists.

In fact, the year 1935 marks a significant development in American academic sociology. It was at about this time that the organizational centrality of Chicago sociology was being formally challenged within the American Sociological Society (Lengermann, 1979). The *American Sociological Review* was born so that the discipline would have a journal less subject to Chicago control than the *American Journal of Sociology* was perceived to be. Herbert Blumer was a strong opponent of the establishment of the *ASR* and the loss of power and prestige it represented to some Chicago sociologists. Interestingly, it was in the aftermath of this political defeat of the Chicago group that Blumer (1937) officially christened and launched his "symbolic interactionism"—a platform from which he sustained attacks against the statistical methodologies and structural-functionalism of Columbia and Harvard, respectively, the strongest university centers of American sociology outside Chicago. This observation highlights another limitation of the present study. We have given little attention to the effects the overall social organization of American sociology had upon Chicago sociology; consequently, we have produced a rather "internalist" account (Carey, 1975). Nothing approaching an adequate *social* history of symbolic interactionism has ever been written. A more open systems approach would have to describe these larger contexts of discourse, some of which are suggested in section 3 below, and establish interactions between the intellectual and organizational settings.

A few cautionary notes should be made concerning the methodology of Part Two. Interpretation of the data on enrollments in Mead's courses and citations of Mead presents us with many epistemological complications. Any college student can testify to the diversity of factors influencing course selection. Explaining the fluctuations in student enrollments in Mead's courses would require information on variables for which data are not available. For this reason, we have been cautious, and we hesitate to make inferences and conjectures. The data themselves are sufficient to show that, for whatever reasons, sociology students were not streaming into Mead's courses in large numbers. For our purposes, further speculation is neither warranted nor necessary to establish our point that Mead was not organizationally central to the sociology program.

Similarly, citation data can be confounding. An author may be cited (or not cited) for as many different reasons as a student may have for electing a given course. Some sociologists of science have used counts of citations and cocitations to infer the existence of Kuhnian scientific community or to argue the scientific "quality" of an oft-cited article. Such inferences are always questionable (see Sullivan, White, and Barboni, 1977). The most defensible (nontrivial) inference one can draw from a citation is that the writer perceives the cited work as relevant to his or her study in at least one of several types of relevance (see Moravcsik and Murugesan, 1975). One may not validly infer that a frequently cited author exerted "influence" on the thinking of the writer. We therefore prefer the term "recognition." The frequency with which an individual receives recognition through citation is, granting our previously mentioned inference, an indication of his / her perceived relevance to the body of research (e.g., dissertations) in which the citations are occurring. In the case of an individual who receives comparatively little recognition from a given community of scholars, it seems to us that those who claim that the individual exerted considerable intellectual influence over the community must assume the burden of proof. The *prima facie* evidence would appear to support the contrary conclusion. Such placement of the burden of proof is doubly justified in the case of Mead where citation data, interview data, and textual analysis afford convergent validity for the contrary hypothesis. This augmentation of citation analysis with interview data constitutes a methodologically sound approach to assessing the impact of a scholar's work upon a given scientific community or speciality (see Small, 1977).

To summarize, we view this book as part of a much larger enterprise. While parts of this broader picture have been coming into focus over the last decade, other parts remain crudely sketched at present. In the following two sections, we outline some of these more indistinct regions.

Some Sociological Implications of the Nominalism / Realism Distinction

We have been content to offer a revisionist intellectual history without attempting a sociological explanation of this history. Historical reconstruction is, however, a necessary precondition to the possibility of raising questions about wider sociological implications of our research. It may now be asked *why* was Mead so peripheral to early Chicago sociology. Why have symbolic interactionists always traced their intellectual roots primarily to Mead instead of to James and Dewey? Why were the social nominalists (James and Dewey) far more renowned both inside and outside of academia in their own times than were the social realists (Peirce and Mead)? Prior to our analysis, there was little basis for even thinking of such questions.

On a more abstract level, a pragmaticist would ask what difference it can make whether nominalism or realism prevails in philosophy, in sociology, or even in society at large. Although we need not say more here about the significance of the nominalism / realism distinction for philosophy and sociology, a brief consideration of the ethical and political implications of the question will point to the larger societal contexts which have influenced the reception of these competing doctrines in sociology, philosophy, and other disciplines.

As reviewed in chapter 1, the centuries-long debate between scholastic nominalists and realists formed the ideological grounds for political contests between the Church hierarchy and dissident elements within the Church. If we elevate the debate beyond these specific theological issues, we see that the medieval doctrinal disputes represent only one instance of a more general and enduring conflict between two ethical-political philosophies. Although it leads to unnecessary logical complications if carried too far, one dramatic way to display these contrasts between the social, political, and ethical outlooks and implications of nominalism and realism is by listing those qualities which tend to characterize each of them. Not every nominalist or realist will evince all of the expected attendant qualities, but the general profile is, nonetheless, valid within limits. The following is a partial compilation of such qualities:

Nominalism	Realism
particular	universal
individualism	collectivism
chance	law
spontaneity	habit
psychologism	sociologism
Darwinism	Christianity
capitalism	communalism
hedonism	altruism
free will	determinism

The reader is invited to compare these profiles to the representative passages from James and Peirce quoted above (p. 151).

Mead's ethical theory is remarkably similar to Peirce's in its general principles, the main difference being that Peirce argued for sociologically based ethics more passionately than did Mead. Unlike James and Dewey, Mead (1934:321) joined Peirce in insisting that the ethical individual is one who internalizes the social attitude (generalized other) into his or her habits of action. But the social attitude must, according to Mead, be taken in its most generalized form. This implies, for example, that the loyal Nazi executioner, even though he acted from the attitude of the generalized other of the Nazi community rather than for some private purpose, nevertheless acted unethically, for his community itself was antisocial with respect to the larger human community. Mead, though less clearly and emphatically than Peirce, conceived of the ultimate ethical agent as one who adopts a social attitude which takes into account not the interests of an isolated individual, group, community, or nation, but rather the future welfare of the human community-at-large. Consequently, the essence of unethical action lies in the pursuit of goals which serve limited, private ends and are opposed or indifferent to the generalized social consequences of the act.

By contrast, the social nominalist insists that the realists' notion of community is nothing more than a reified fictional construct; this notion blinds realists to the natural right of individuals to pursue their own self-interest without violating the rights of others to do likewise. Social Darwinism, an exemplar of nominalist ethics, does not sanction a Hobbesian war of "all against all" in which there are no social norms whatsoever. Rather, as Spencer pointed out, the nominalist will permit whatever minimal institutions of social control (e.g., police) are required to protect each individual's right to life, liberty, and the pursuit of happiness. As noted above, Dewey preferred to state this principle in positive terms, emphasizing that the goal of all social reform should be to enhance each individual's opportunity to express his or her uniqueness and creativity.

Needless to say, the social nominalist ethic has predominated in the United States, especially since the late nineteenth century. It is an ethical perspective ideally suited to a frontier, largely immigrant, capitalist society. In this milieu, one can understand how John Dewey became the "philosopher of America" (Mead, 1964:391), and why he was something of a hero to Ellwood, Park, Thomas, and others at Chicago. It also helps to explain how Mead could be perceived at Chicago as Dewey's "underling"—an image Mead did little to discredit overtly. Finally, it may further suggest how Mead came to be recast by Herbert Blumer as a psychical interactionist in the tradition of Ellwood, Park, Cooley, and Thomas—all of whom seem to have exerted intellectual influence upon Blumer in the 1920s. This, at least, appears to be a plausible implication worthy of further consideration. Being a social realist, Mead was such an anomaly that most Chicago sociologists, including Blumer, were ill-prepared to receive his message.

Another larger implication of our study is that social nominalists and social realists—whether or not they are academic sociologists—make quite different evaluative assessments of their society. One might expect, for example, that a social realist who finds himself in the midst of a social order dedicated to a social nominalist philosophy would look negatively upon that society. This may be viewed as a problem for the sociology of knowledge which is, in principle, amenable to empirical inquiry.

An indication of the *prima facie* plausibility of this hypothesis can be illustrated by a comparison between Peirce and Sorokin. Biographically, these men had little in common except that both were strong theoretical supporters of social realism and equally strong critics of the nominalist moral stance of American society. Peirce frequently expounded his social ethical principle of "evolutionary love" by opposing it to the ideologies of Darwinism and capitalism which, from his viewpoint and much to his distress, were running rampant in America. In a typical passage, Peirce (6.294) declared:

Here, then, is the issue. The gospel of Christ says that progress comes from every individual merging his individuality in sympathy with his neighbors. On the other side, the conviction of the nineteenth century is that progress takes place by virtue of every imdividual's striving for himself with all his might and trampling his neighbor under foot whenever he gets a chance to do so. This may accurately be called the Gospel of Greed.

For Peirce (6.292) this Gospel of Greed can only lead to societal degeneration: "The twentieth century, in its latter half, shall surely see the deluge-tempest burst upon the social order—to clear upon the world as deep in ruin as that greed-philosophy has long plunged it into guilt."

Sorokin can be described as a Peircean sociologist. Not only did he ably defend social realism (e.g., Sorokin, 1947:149–51), but he also shared Peirce's sentiments regarding nominalist ethics. Perhaps this zeal accounts for his untiring efforts in tracing the social consequences of cultural adoption of differing systems of truth amd knowledge. Sorokin (1947:614) perceived the nominalistic social mentality as a product of the empiricist and materialist underpinnings of the "sensate" system of truth and reality. In the sensate culture, eventually the "very boundary line between the true and the false, between right and wrong, disappears, and society finds itself in a state of veritable mental, moral, and cultural anarchy. No society can long exist under these conditions. Either it perishes or it substitutes another system of truth, one sounder and more adequate to its needs."

Thus, Sorokin was as convinced as Peirce that nominalist social orders will ultimately decay from within. Whether there is any truth to these prophecies of doom is of no concern here. Our only interest is in using Peirce and Sorokin to illustrate our tentative hypothesis that social realists and social nominalists each develop their own distinct ethical and political standards by which they judge society and individuals. If this is true to some degree, it opens many new questions for further investigation. In the following section, we explore still other areas for future research.

Agenda for Future Research

Virtually all historical accounts of the development of American pragmatism have excluded in-depth consideration of Josiah Royce. Insofar as Royce was an absolute idealist and philosophical adversary of James and James's pragmatic conception of truth and reality, he certainly cannot be counted as a pragmatist. Nevertheless, Royce was important to the social history of pragmatism due to his personal associations with James, Peirce, and Mead; and it may well be that he was something of a catalyst within the group. Further research is needed to clarify Royce's relationship to the pragmatists and pragmatic philosophy.

Our intellectual history of Chicago sociology (chapter 6) could be expanded to include Bernard, Bogardus, Veblen, and others. More important, our account has given no notice to the Chicago human / urban ecology group (see Faris, 1970:51–81). With few exceptions, such as Park, there was little overlap between the members of this group and the Chicagoans who worked primarily in general theory and social psychology (Small, Hayes, Bodenhafer, Faris, Blumer, etc.). This raises some intriguing questions. How much competition existed between these groups? Could the emergence of the ecologists partially account for the marginality of the social psychology group within the department, and the declining enrollment of sociology students in Mead's courses in the 1920s? Faris (1970) has discretely little to say about the internal politics of the department, but, if the premises of these questions are not purely fanciful, they may be keys to a better understanding of the organizational contexts of Chicago sociological theory, and specifically, symbolic interactionism. Unfortunately, so far as we know, these types of questions have never been addressed to the older Chicago sociologists, and now it is almost too late.

Similarly, no one has systematically constructed a history of the growth of Blumerian symbolic interactionism from 1936 to 1952. Yet this was scarcely a blank period of Chicago scholarship. During this period, such notable sociologists as Lindesmith, Whyte, Turner, Swanson, Strauss, Shibutani, Rose, Becker, Goffman, and Meltzer were Chicago graduate students. Although not all were Blumer's students, an examination of the dissertations of this period should prove to be a rewarding indicator of Blumer's impact upon his progeny and their recognition / interpretation of Mead, Dewey, Cooley, Park, and Thomas.[5] The time is ripe for such a study because thirty years have elapsed since these sociologists left Chicago, and most of them are still living, and thus potentially available for interviews.

Not only is there no fully developed account of Blumerian symbolic interactionism at Chicago during the 1940s and 1950s, there is comparatively little written about the development of the Chicago philosophy department. Rucker's (1969) work is an admirable beginning, but no one has yet provided a history of the Chicago philosophy department comparable to Kuklick's (1977) in depth study of Harvard philosophy.

Of more relevance to our specific interests, the dissertations of the Chicago philosophy·students who worked under Mead have never been collectively analyzed. Yet the philosophers who studied directly under Mead and whose dissertations he supervised were certainly at an advantage to understand his philosophy. Of course, even his philosophical protégés may have misinterpreted his views (as evidenced in numerous other historical cases), but given their proximate relation to Mead, their judgments surely merit our attention. To illustrate our contention, we will briefly discuss two of these dissertations.

One of Mead's students (ill-fittingly named John Locke) wrote a dissertation entitled "The Social Genesis and Character of Universals" (1923). Because the thesis addresses the nomimalism / realism question in depth and was obviously motivated by Locke's commitment to Mead's philosophy, it is an explication of the Meadian concept of "universal" which goes beyond Mead's own discussions of the concept. Following Mead closely, Locke (1923:11–12) argued that our ordinary experience is immediate and thus does not evidence mind. Insofar as an experience arises as an object within a perspective, there is no need to postulate a "mind" or psychical field to contain those secondary qualities which so troubled the British John Locke:

> By accepting an analysis which strips the external world of color and leaves nothing but physical and mechanical elements in the environment, the introspectionist is forced to locate the color of the object in an individual mind or consciousness of an organism. The Behaviorists, on the other hand, whose position is the same as that outlined in this thesis, arrives at an entirely different view. [Locke, 1923:6]

As we argued in chapter 5, the fact that this view removes these qualities from the individual mind and places them within a "consentient set" does not render the universal Platonic, and "in no way makes these objects and their characters subjective and unreal in any experience" (Locke, 1923:9).

Universals enter into conduct by calling out the generalized response that group members make to the object. The general characters of the object are objectively there in the environment which language—and the individual through the use of language—represents in symbols. This is a totally objective phase of experience and therefore involves no Blumerian "interpretations" or psychical interaction. From an evolutionary standpoint, it is of course true that language was—and is—an emerging phenomenon which can be traced through historical stages; but this process generally operates slowly. Certainly, the universals are not constantly being reestablished within every interaction as radical social nomimalists maintain. Little reflection is required to expose the impossibility of a generalized "reality constructionist" doctrine on a dyadic interactionist level. Both the symbols and the characters they signify transcend individual minds, and this latter admission constitutes the heart of the realist position. As Locke (1923:87–88) stated:

> Thus we see that the mental processes in man come back to an ability on his part to call out the universal characters of things which answer to certain generalized responses. Mind then does not build up these universal characters. What mind does is to indicate these characters to an individual when inhibition has set in. These universals are already involved in the conduct or habits of the group.

If, as seems justified, we consider Locke's dissertation an attempted elaboration of a Meadian social behaviorist approach to universals, his thesis corroborates our interpretation of Mead and reveals the contradictions between Mead's theory and psychical imteractionism which we identified in chapters 5 and 6.

Another philosophy dissertation of interest is M. R. Gilbert's thesis, "Theories of Consciousness" (1923). He argued that Dewey was a subjectivist precisely in that he followed James so closely. Commenting on Dewey's *Essays in Experimental Logic,* Gilbert (1923:7) stated, "It is difficult to find any significant difference between this and what James discusses in the chapter on the Stream of Thought."[6] Gilbert (1923:8) further contended that a review of the stages of Deweyan "inquiry" does not leave us "without having the same feeling that we are dealing with an inner, subjectivistic experience." From this, Gilbert (1923:8) concludes[7] that, "In so far as this is true they [James and Dewey] have on their hands the necessity of showing how this 'function' can be effective in reorganizing any other than one's own ideas of *inner* activities."

Other Chicago dissertations offer insights into early American sociology and philosophy as well as reflections on the thought of central sociology and philosophy faculty at the University of Chicago. Although we cannot further pursue those dissertations here, perhaps these examples foreshadow the benefits that await a more thorough and systematic reading of these manuscripts.

More generally, we believe that historians have not utilized the full potential of dissertations as a data base. To be sure, there are special difficulties in the use of dissertations, especially problems related to the student-professor relationship which pervade dissertation work far more than other types of scholarship. However, for answering certain types of historical questions, the student-professor context of the production process may actually be more of an asset than a liability. It may be argued that graduate students, taken collectively, absorb the intellectual milieu from the academic environment. By this statement, we do not mean to imply that students are incapable of independent and novel thought, but rather that as a group, their dissertations tend to address the major problematics and approaches which occupy disciplinary (and faculty) attention. As such, dissertations may expose facets of the intellectual tenor of a university department or even of a discipline for a given period of its history. For these and other purposes, dissertations have historical value which has been largely neglected.

As a final, and perhaps most urgently needed, proposal for future research, the "symbolic interactionism" of the 1960s and 1970s is yet to be placed within a larger metatheoretical framework. Although Meltzer, Petras, and Reynolds (1975:53–82) claim several varieties of symbolic interactionism, including Goffman's dramaturgical approach and Garfinkel's ethnomethodology, Gonos (1977) argues that Goffman is a structuralist rather than a symbolic interactionist. And Zimmerman and Wieder (1970:295) contend that there is a "fundamental break" between ethnomethodology and symbolic interactionism. The differences between these, and related theoretical orientations, will remain in dispute and comparisons will continue to be obscure or unsystematic until the theories are subjected to rigorous metatheoretical analysis and classification.[8]

A reconsideration of the philosophical affinities and differences among the classic American pragmatists and their influence upon the development of early American sociology promises to foster a deeper understanding of early American sociological theory and to provide new perspectives of relevance to current issues of sociological metatheory. This book has outlined some of these results, but our assessments should be taken as early approximations of an ongoing inquiry. We are hopeful that our studies will encourage others to join the quest begun by Mills.

Academic Year	Fall Quarter
1894–95	Logic
	Comp. Psych.
1895–96	
1896–97	Hist. of Ancient
	Philos.
	Comp. Psych.
1897–98	Seminar: Devel. of
	Greek Intelligence
	Philos. of Nature
1898–99	Seminar: Medieval
	Philos.
	Philos. of Nature
1899–1900	Devel. of Greek
	Intelligence
	Adv. Ethics
1900–1	Philos. of Science
	Social Psych.

Appendix 1

Courses Taught by Mead at the University of Chicago, 1894–95 to 1930–31

Winter Quarter	Spring Quarter	Summer Quarter
Comp. Psych. Meth. of Psych.	Ethics Concepts of Matter and Motion	
Comp. Psych. Meth. of Psych.	Logic Concepts of Matter and Motion	Hist. of Modern Philos. Seminar: Hist. of Modern Philos. Seminar: Kant
Seminar: Medieval Philos. Concepts of Matter and Motion	Logic Seminar: Medieval Philos.	
Seminar: Devel. of Greek Intelligence Comp. Psych.	Movements of Thought in the 19th C. Elementary Logic	
Seminar: Medieval Philos. Comp. Psych.	Movements of Thought in the 19th C. Methodology of Psych.	Kant's Critique of Pure Reason Locke, Berkeley, & Hume Hist. of Psych.
Devel. of Intell. in Mid. Ages Comp. Psych.	Logic Movements of Thought in the 19th C.	
Comp. Psych. Philos. of Evolution	Schopenhauer and von Hartman Logic	Movements of Thought in the 19th C. Kant's Cosmogony Psych. of Aesthetics

Academic Year	Fall Quarter
1901–2	
1902–3	Philos. of Science Psych. of Ethics
1903–4	Elementary Psych. Comp. Psych.
1904–5	Elementary Ethics Relation of Ancient Science & Philos.
1905–6	Hist. of Science
1906–7	Hist. of Science
1907–8	Hist. of Science Philos. of Aristotle
1908–9	Hist. of Science Logic of the Soc. Sciences
1909–10	Hist. of Ancient Philos. Logic of the Phys. Sciences
1910–11	Hist. of Ancient Science Ethics
1911–12	Ethics Philos. of Nature Dev. of Thought in the Modern Period

Winter Quarter	Spring Quarter	Summer Quarter
		Movements of Thought in the 19th C. Concepts of Psych. Philos. of the Renaissance
Contemporary Social Psych. Philos. of Evolution	Comp. Psych. Post-Kantian Idealism	
Aristotle's Metaphysics Philos. of Science		Advanced Psych. Kantian Idealism
	Philos. and Modern Science Comp. Psych.	Schopenhauer Comp. Psych. Advanced Psych.
Philos. of Aristotle Hegel's Logic		Kant's Critique of Pure Reason Comp. Psych.
Ethics Logic of Math. Comp. Psych.	Movements of Thought in the 19th C. Indian Philos.	
Descartes and Leibnitz Social Psych.	Modern Logic	
Devel. of Modern Thought Scientific Concepts since Newton Theoretical Comp. Psych.	Ethics Devel. of Thought in the Modern Period	
Metaphysics of Aristotle Social Psych.	Ethics	Hist. of Ancient Science Social Psych.
Mill's Examination of the Philos. of Hamilton Comp. Psych.	Movements of Thought in the 19th C. Logic of the Social Sciences	
Social Psych. Hist. of Modern Philos.	Descartes, Leibnitz, and Newton Logic of the Social Sciences	

Academic Year	Fall Quarter
1912–13	Ethics Social Psych.
1913–14	Ethics Philos. of Nature
1914–15	Ethics Hist. of Scientific Concepts—Ancient
1915–16	Ethics Rationalism and Empiricism
1916–17	Logic of the Social Sciences Ethics
1917–18	Ethics Rationalism and Empiricism

1918–19	Logic of the Physical
	  and Biological
	  Sciences
	Research
	Special

1919–20	Philos. of France Research Ethics

Winter Quarter	Spring Quarter	Summer Quarter
Renaissance Philos. Seminar: Social Consciousness	Movements of Thought in the 19th C. Intro. to the Logic of Hegel	
Hist. of Modern Philos. Seminar: Social Consciousness Social Psych.	Movements of Thought in the 19th C. Aristotle's Metaphysics	
Hist. of Scientific Concepts—Modern Social Psych.	Movements of Thought in the 19th C. Logic of Science	Intro. to Hegel's Logic Problem of Stoicism, Epicureanism, and Later Skepticism
	Movements of Thought in the 19th C. Social Psych.	Greek Science and Philos. Hume
Modern Philos. Social Psych. Research	Logic Movements of Thought in the 19th C. Seminar: Social Consciousness	
Advanced Social Psych. Seminar: Modern Logical Theory and Hegel's Phenomenology	Intellectual Background of the War Seminar: Hegel's Phenomenology	Seminar: Social Consciousness Metaphysics
Philos. of Kant Research Advanced Social Psych.	Movements of Thought in the 19th C. Kant's Critique of Pure Reason Seminar: Social Consciousness	
Aristotle's Metaphysics Advanced Social Psych. Research	Movements of Thought in the 19th C. Seminar: Social Consciousness Research	Research

Academic Year	Fall Quarter
1920–21	Ethics Philos. of Kant
1921–22	Hist. of Greek Philos. Hamilton and Mill
1922–23	Ethics Logic of the Sciences
1923–24	Ethics Aristotle's Metaphysics
1924–25	Ethics Advanced Social Psych.
1925–26	Ethics Aristotle's Metaphysics
1926–27	Ethics Leibnitz
1927–28	Ethics Contemporary Meta- physical Problems
1928–29	Ethics Logic Research

Winter Quarter	Spring Quarter	Summer Quarter
Advanced Social Psych. Philos. of Kant Seminar: Experience and the Self	Hegel's Phenomenology Movements of Thought in the 19th C.	
Modern Philos. Advanced Social Psych.	Movements of Thought in the 19th C. Hume	
Ethics Advanced Social Psych.	Movements of Thought in the 19th C. Relativity from the Standpoint of Pragmatism Hegel's Logic	
Ethics Advanced Social Psych.	Movements of Thought in the 19th C. Problem of Consciousness	
Ethics Hume	Movements of Thought in the 19th C. Philosophies of Eminent Scientists	Advanced Social Psych. Aristotle's Metaphysics
Advanced Social Psych. Seminar: Dewey's Experience and Culture	Movements of Thought in the 19th C. Problem of Consciousness Research	Modern Philos. Contemporary Meta- physical Problems Research
Advanced Social Psych. Philos. of Eminent Scientists Research	Movements of Thought in the 19th C. Hume Special	Movements of Thought in the 19th C. Philos. of Bergson Special
Advanced Social Psych. Hegel's Phenomenology Research	Movements of Thought in the 19th C. Aristotle Research	Movements of Thought in the 19th C. French Philos. in the 19th C.

Academic Year	Fall Quarter
1929–30	Ethics Aristotle's Metaphysics
1930–31	Hume

Winter Quarter	Spring Quarter	Summer Quarter
Advanced Social Psych. French Philos. in the 19th C.	Movements of Thought in the 19th C. Philos. of Eminent Scientists	Special
Advanced Social Psych. Problems of Philos.		

Academic Year	Fall Quarter
1894–95	*Comp. Psych.* Thomas, W. I.*
1895–96	
1896–97	
1897–98	
1898–99	
1899–1900	*Dev.of Greek Intelligence* Tolman, F. L.
1900–1	*Social Psych.* Adams, R. C. Tolman, F. L.
1901–2	

*Designates doctoral students.

Appendix 2

Distribution of Sociology Graduate Students Among Mead's Courses 1894–1935

Winter Quarter	Spring Quarter	Summer Quarter
Comp. Psych. Thomas, W. I.*	*Meth. of Psych.* Thomas, W. I.*	
Comp. Psych. Clarkson, M. A. Mustard, Mary	*Concepts of Matter* *and Motion* Clarkson, M. A. Cummings, A. Mustard, Mary	*Hist. of Modern Philos.* Forrest, J. D.* *Sem. in Kant* Forrest, J. D.*
Sem: Medieval Philos. Forrest, J. D.*	*Sem: Medieval Philos.* Forrest, J. D.*	
Comp. Psych. Park, J. W.	*Movements of Thought* Barnes, F. Park, J. W.	
Comp. Psych. Dunn, A. W. Ellwood, C. A.* Kellor, F. A. Sikes, G. R.		
Dev. of Intell. in Mid. *Ages* Tolman, F. L.		
Comp. Psych. Tolman, F. L.		*Kant's Cosmogony* Pace, M. A.
		Movements of Thought Klink, Jane
		Philos. of the *Renaissance* Brewster, H.

Academic Year	Fall Quarter
1902–3	
1903–4	
1904–5	
1905–6	
1906–7	
1907–8	
1908–9	*Logic of the Soc. Sciences* Bernard, L. L.* Woods, L.
1909–10	*Hist. of Ancient Philos.* Rainwater, C. E.*
1910–11	

275   Distribution of
Students among Mead's
Courses

Winter Quarter	Spring Quarter	Summer Quarter

Social Psych.
Mumford, Eben*

Comp. Psych.
Bergelund, A.
Riley, T. J.*
Woodhead, H.*

Philos. of Aristotle
Townsend, H. S.

Indian Philos.
Dean, J. D.

Social Psych.
Handman, M. S.*
Helleberg, V. E.

*Dev. of Modern
Thought*
House, J. T.*
Varkala, J. P.
Wander, P.

*Dev. of Thought in
Modern Period*
House, J. T.*
Varkala, J. P.
Wander, P.

Comp. Psych.
House, J. T.*

Social Psych.
Bernard, L. L.*
Fenton, F.*
Matzinger, P. F.
Pope, D. I.
Rainwater, C. E.*

Social Psych.
Bogardus, E. S.*
Burgess, E. W.*
Marten, Vella
Sutherland, E. H.*

Comp. Psych.
Pope, D. I.
Wander, P.

Movements of Thought
Queen, S. A.*

*Logic of the Soc.
Sciences*
Pope, D. I.
Swartz, J. V.
Tinney, Mary
Wander, P.

Academic Year	Fall Quarter
1911–12	
1912–13	*Social Psych.* Blachley, C. D.* Queen, S. A.* Thomas, W. A.
1913–14	
1914–15	*Hist. of Scientific* *Concepts—Ancient* Znaniecki, F. W.

Winter Quarter	Spring Quarter	Summer Quarter

Social Psych.
Newberry, Ruth
Wander, P.

*Logic of the Soc.
Sciences*
Durand, Alice
Erickson, J. E.
McElroy, G.
Newberry, Ruth
Thompson, W. S.

Renaissance Philos.
Blachley, C. D.*
Bruder, M.

Movements of Thought
Gilkerson, R.
Wander, P.

*Seminar: Social
Consciousness*
Handman, M. S.*
Queen, S. A.*
Thomas, W. A.
Wander, P.

*Intro. to the Logic of
Hegel*
Handman, M. S.*

Social Psych.
Battacharya, B.
Bruder, V. W.
Clarke, F. S.
Dutt, B. N.
Erickson, J. E.
Holst, B. P.
Leavell, R. H.
Steiner, J. F.*
Wedgeworth, W. A.
Zee, T. Z.

Social Psych.
Blount, M. L.
Carroll, M. R.*
Clark, R. F.
Gable, W. S.
Jacobson, H. A.
Jensen, H. E.*
Lemstrom, A.
McKenzie, R. D.*
Price, M. T.*
Reuter, E. B.*
Stone, R.*
Thomas, E. B.
Zeeb, Frieda

Academic Year	Fall Quarter
1915–16	
1916–17	*Logic of the Soc. Sciences* Burton, E. R. Egartner, Z. T. Sanderson, D.*
1917–18	*Rationalism and Empiricism* Rauschenbush, W.
1918–19	

Winter Quarter	Spring Quarter	Summer Quarter

Social Psych.
Bacon, Margaret
Church, C. C.
Egartner, Z. T.
Kawabe, K.*
Mann, A. R.
McClintock, E.
Park, E. C.
Sanderson, D.*
Thrasher, F. M.*

Social Psych.
Coffman, H. C.
Davis, T. R.
Forrest, E.
Kuhlmann, A. F.*
Northcutt, C. L.
Sizer, J. P.
Weihe, W. H.
Young, E. F.*
Young, K.

*Seminar: Social
Consciousness*
Coffman, H. C.
Kuhlmann, A. F.*

Research
Egartner, Z. T.
Sanderson, D.*
Stone, R. W.*

Advanced Social Psych.
Daniel, F. O.

*Intellectual Background
of the War*
Hartman, G. E.
Wagg, F. E.

Advanced Social Psych.
Bodenhafer, W. B.*
Crane, C. W.
Hartmann, G. E.
Horak, J.*
Niemi, C.
Rossouw, G. S. H.*
Smith, W. C.*

*Seminar: Social
Consciousness*
Bodenhafer, W. B.*
Crane, C. W.
Hartmann, G. E.
Horak, J.*
Young, E. F.*

Philos. of Kant.
Hartmann, G. E.

Academic Year	Fall Quarter
1919–20	
1920–21	
1921–22	
1922–23	*Logic of the Sciences* Shaw, C. R.
1923–24	
1924–25	*Advanced Social Psych.* Hajicek, S. T. Shonle, Ruth*

Winter Quarter	Spring Quarter	Summer Quarter
Advanced Social Psych. Martin, A. H.	*Seminar: Social Consciousness* Rossouw, G. S. H.* Sato, K.	
Advanced Social Psych. Bickham, M. H.* Junek, O. W. Karpf, F. B.* Shaw, C. R.		
Philos. of Kant Sortor, H.		
Seminar: Experience and the Self Young, E. F.*		
Advanced Social Psych. Daniel, W. A.* Kincheloe, S. C.* Krueger, E. T.* Moore, H. D. D. Mowrer, E. R.* Sell, H. B. Williams, A. L. Williams, H. L.	*Movements of Thought* Shaw, C. R.	
Advanced Social Psych. Earl, Anna		
Advanced Social Psych. Barton, O. L. Cell, C. W. Green, L. R. Runeman, A. L. Simpson, E. N.* Wirth, L.*	*Movements of Thought* Hajicek, S. T.	
	Movements of Thought Roper, M. W.*	

Academic Year	Fall Quarter
1925–26	*Aristotle's Metaphysics* Newcomb, R. G.
1926–27	
1927–28	
1928–29	

283 Distribution of
Students among Mead's
Courses

Winter Quarter	Spring Quarter	Summer Quarter
Advanced Social Psych. Blumer, H.* Cook, L. A. Hu, T. Jenkins, F. R. Johnson, E. S. Morrison, W. L. Nordhoff, W. A. Proctor, D. E. Stephen, F. F. Tibbitts, R. C. Yu, C. T.		*Contemporary Meta-* *physical Problems* Morrison, W. L. Overman, L.
Advanced Social Psych. Boyer, P. B. Newcomb, C. S. Newcomb, R. G. Overman, L. Summer, J. E. Voelker, E. W.		*Movements of Thought* Proctor, D. E.
Philos. of Eminent *Scientists* Leiffer, M. H.		
Research Blumer, H.*		
Advanced Social Psych. Becker, H. P.* Carmichael, M. Faris, R. E. L.* Ireland, W. R. Munnich, J. H. Pierson, R. D.	*Movements of Thought* Ireland, W. R.	

Academic Year	Fall Quarter
1929–30	
1930–31	*Hume* Pierson, R. D.

Winter Quarter	Spring Quarter	Summer Quarter

Advanced Social Psych.
Abbassi, M.
Cottrell, L. S.*
Elmendorf, J. B.
Giffen, N.
Guignard, C.
Hall, M.
Hauser, P. M.
Neely, A. E.
Parson, W. R.
Phelps, M. H.
Watkins, M. H.
Wellman, C. H.

Advanced Social Psych.
Blumenthal, A. B.
Dai, B.
Dashen, G. G.
Doyle, B. W.*
Fitchett, E. H.
McGill, K. H.
Merrill, F. E.
Nelson, R. E.
Parrish, C. H.
Severson, A. L.

Year Published
1894
1896
1899
1900
1903
1903–4
1904
1904
1906
1906
1906
1907
1908
1909
1909
1910
1910
1910
1910
1912
1913
1914
1915
1915
1915

Appendix 3

Distribution and Frequency of Article Recognition in Sociology Dissertations, Journals, and Books 1895–1935*

Name of Article	Frequency		
	D	J	B
Herr Lasswitz on Energy and Epistemology			
The Relation of Play to Education			
The Working Hypothesis in Social Reform			
Suggestions toward a Theory of Philosophical Disiplines			
The Definitions of the Psychical	2	1	1
The Basis for a Parents' Association			
Image or Sensation			
The Relations of Psychology and Philology			
Science in the High School			
The Imagination in Wundt's Treatment of Myth and Religion			1
The Teaching of Science in College			
Concerning Animal Perception			
The Philosophical Basis of Ethics			
Industrial Education, the Working-Man, and the School			
Social Psychology as Counterpart to Physiological Psychology	5	5	10
Social Consciousness and the Consciousness of Meaning	4	1	12
The Psychology of Social Consciousness Implied in Instruction			4
What Social Objects Does Psychology Presuppose?		1	
What Social Objects Must Psychology Pre-Suppose?	2	4	6
The Mechanism of Social Consciousness	3	1	8
The Social Self	3	2	10
A Heckling School Board and an Educational Stateswoman			
Natural Rights and the Theory of the Political Institution			
The Larger Educational Bearings of Vocational Guidance			1
The Psychological Bases of Internationalism			

*Sources for this selection of articles may be found in Broyer (1973).

Year Published

1915
1917
1918
1922
1923
1925
1926
1926
1929
1929
1929
1929
1930
1930
1930

Name of Article	Frequency		
	D	J	B
Madison: The Passage of the University of Wisconsin			
Scientific Method and the Individual Thinker	1	1	1
The Psychology of Punitive Justice	2		9
A Behavioristic Account of the Significant Symbol	5	3	13
Scientific Method and the Moral Sciences		1	2
The Genesis of the Self and Social Control	7	5	11
The Nature of the Aesthetic Experience	1	1	
The Objective Reality of Perspectives		2	
A Pragmatic Theory of Truth		1	
Bishop Berkeley and His Message		1	
National-Mindedness and International-Mindedness	1	1	2
The Nature of the Past		1	
Cooley's Contribution to American Social Thought	1	1	2
Philanthropy from the Point of View of Ethics		1	1
The Philosophies of Royce, James, and Dewey in their			
American Setting	1	1	1

1894   "Herr Lasswitz on Energy and Epistemology." *Psychological Review* 1: 172–75.
1896   "The Relation of Play to Education." *The University* [of Chicago] *Record* 1: 140–45.
1899   "The Working Hypothesis in Social Reform." *American Journal of Sociology* 5: 367–71.
1900   "Suggestions toward a Theory of the Philosophical Disciplines." *Philosophical Review* 9: 1–17.
1903   "The Definition of the Psychical." Decennial Publications of the University of Chicago. "First Series" 3: 77–112.
1903–4 "The Basis for a Parents' Association." *Elementary School Teacher* 4: 337–46.
1904   "Image or Sensation." *Journal of Philosophy, Psychology, and Scientific Methods* 1: 604–7.
1904   "The Relations of Psychology and Philology." *Psychological Bulletin* 1: 375–91.
1906   "Science in the High School." *School Review* 14: 237–49.
1906   "The Imagination in Wundt's Treatment of Myth and Religion." *Psychological Bulletin* 3: 393–99.
1906   "The Teaching of Science in College." *Science* 24: 390–97.
1907   "Concerning Animal Perception." *Psychological Review* 14: 383–90.
1908   "The Philosophical Basis of Ethics." *International Journal of Ethics* 18: 311–23.
1909   "Industrial Education, the Working-Man, and the School." *Elementary School Teacher* 9: 369–83.
1909   "Social Psychology as Counterpart to Physiological Psychology." *Psychological Bulletin* 6: 401–8.
1910   "Social Consciousness and the Consciousness of Meaning." *Psychological Bulletin* 7: 397–405.
1910   "The Psychology of Social Consciousness Implied in Instruction." *Science* 31: 688–93.

*Selection taken from Broyer (1973).

1910   "What Social Objects Does Psychology Presuppose?"
Psychological Bulletin 7: 52–53.

1910   "What Social Objects Must Psychology Presuppose?"
*Journal of Philosophy, Psychology, and Scientific
Methods* 7: 174–80.

1912   "The Mechanism of Social Consciousness." *Journal
of Philosophy, Psychology, and Scientific Methods*
9: 401–6.

1913   "The Social Self." *Journal of Philosophy, Psychology,
and Scientific Methods* 10: 374–80.

1914   "A Heckling School Board and an Educational
Stateswoman." *Survey* 31: 443–4.

1915   "Natural Rights and the Theory of the Political
Institution." *Journal of Philosophy, Psychology, and
Scientific Methods* 12: 141–55.

1915   "The Larger Educational Bearings of Vocational
Guidance." In *Readings in Vocational Guidance*,
edited by Meyer Bloomfield (Boston: Ginn), pp.
43–55.

1915   "The Psychological Bases of Internationalism."
Survey 33: 604–7.

1915   "Madison: The passage of the University of Wiscon-
sin through the state political agitation of 1914;
the survey by William H. Allen and his staff and the
legislative fight of 1915, with the indications these
offer of the place the state university holds in the
community." *Survey* 35: 349–51, 354–61.

1917   "Scientific Method and the Individual Thinker."
In *Creative Intelligence: Essays in the Pragmatic
Attitude*, edited by John Dewey et al. (New York:
Holt), pp. 176–227.

1918   "The Psychology of Punitive Justice." *American
Journal of Sociology* 23: 577–602.

1922   "A Behavioristic Account of the Significant Symbol."
Journal of Philosophy 19: 157–63.

1923   "Scientific Method and the Moral Sciences." *International Journal of Ethics* 33: 229–47.

1925   "The Genesis of the Self and Social Control." *International Journal of Ethics* 35: 251–77.

1926   "The Nature of Aesthetic Experience." *International
Journal of Ethics* 36: 382–92.

1927   "The Objective Reality of Perspectives." In *Proceedings of the Sixth International Congress of Philosophy, 1926*, edited by Edgar Sheffield Brightman
(New York: Longmans, Green and Co.), pp. 75–85.

1929   "A Pragmatic Theory of Truth." *Studies in the Nature
of Truth. Berkeley: University of California Publications in Philosophy* 21: 65–88.

1929   "Bishop Berkeley and His Message." *Journal of
Philosophy* 26: 421–30.

1929   "National-Mindedness and International-Mindedness." *International Journal of Ethics* 39: 385–407.

1929   "The Nature of the Past." In *Essays in Honor of John Dewey*, edited by John Coss (New York: Holt), pp. 235–42.

1930   "Cooley's Contribution to American Social Thought." *American Journal of Sociology* 35: 693–706.

1930   "Philanthropy from the Point of View of Ethics." In *Intelligent Philanthropy*, edited by Ellsworth Faris, Ferris Laune, and Arthur J. Todd (Chicago: The University of Chicago Press), pp. 133–48.

1930   "The Philosophies of Royce, James and Dewey in Their American Setting." *International Journal of Ethics* 40: 211–31.

Notes

Chapter One

1. This reference is to volume 1, paragraph 19 of the *Collected Papers of Charles Sanders Peirce*. All references to Peirce will follow this format, according to the style of Peirce's editors.
2. This account is based on DeWulf (1956), Wild (1948:3–35), and Feibleman (1946: 3–28).
3. Abelard then proposed his doctrine of conceptualism which was supposed to represent the middle ground between nominalism and realism. Briefly, conceptualism is the doctrine that universals come to mind as we see resemblance between particulars. Contrary to extreme nominalism, the reference of universals is to a generality; however, the basis of that generality lies in the mind rather than in the external world. Because it refuses to admit the independent reality of universals apart from their being thought, conceptualism is a poorly disguised nominalism. Consequently, it was not, and never has been, a popular position.

Chapter Two

1. The observant reader may have noticed that any actual sign can be given a tripartite name (e.g., "rhematic indexical legisign") which classifies it according to its type within each of the trichotomies (2.264). Peirce eventually distinguished sixty-six types of signs (see Weiss and Burks, 1946). In fact, there seems to be no definite limit to their number. These extended classifications may be of some interest to linguists, but have no immediate relevance to our concerns.

2. For a complete biographical characterization of the Metaphysical Club, see Mills (1964: 84–120).

3. These essays were, "Questions concerning Certain Faculties Claimed for Man" (5.213–63) and "Some Consequences of Four Incapacities" (5.264–317).

4. The early pragmatism has become popularized to the extent that nearly every work on Peirce's philosophy contains a presentation and discussion of the doubt-belief theory of inquiry. Therefore, we will sketch only the barest essentials of that doctrine required for our purposes. Interested readers may consult the references for further details on the early pragmatism.

5. Yet, by not consistently making utterly explicit the assumed scientific and social context of inquiry, Peirce may have allowed the misinterpretation of his position, so clearly evidenced by Dewey's individualistic theory of inquiry. Although this somewhat foreshadows our discussion of Dewey's pragmatism, it is noted here because, ironically, it is plausible to assert that the spirit of Dewey's philosophy contributed to the debates of the Metaphysical Club through the person of Chauncey Wright. Peirce (5.64) recalled that Wright was captivated by the spirit of Darwinism which, in the 1870s, still burst forth in all areas of intellectual life. As we shall discover, individualism and Darwinism go hand in hand in Dewey's epistemology. Dewey perceived knowledge as the individual's adaptive response to an indeterminate situation. If Darwin were an epistemologist, he probably would have concurred. Peirce also recalled that Wright was always present at the club meetings and was an able opponent whom Peirce "used to face to be severely pummelled" (5.12). On another occasion, Peirce wrote that Wright was "an educative influence upon the minds of all of us who enjoyed his intimacy" (5.64). The slight tinge of Darwinism, barely discernible in some passages of

"The Fixation of Belief," could be reasonably attributed to Wright's influence at the time. If such influence did exist, we must be careful not to overstate it, for Darwinism is diametrically opposed to "evolutionary love"—the basic concept of Peirce's cosmology (see 6.293 ff.). In any case, Dewey apparently thought he detected a Darwinian tint in Peirce's theory of inquiry which he welcomed and magnified into a totally Darwinian account of thought and inquiry.

6. See the chronological bibliography of Peirce's writings in the *Collected Papers,* vol. 7, pp. 251–321.

7. However, it would be a serious mistake to interpret this claim as a positivist doctrine; that would render it nominalistic. Extreme positivists, such as Schlick, insist that a concept is meaningful only if it refers to some *singular* sense datum and, therefore, any subject of which it is predicated can be conclusively verified by a single experience. Weak verificationists, such as Ayer, hold that because scientific propositions *are* general, they cannot be conclusively verified, but are nevertheless meaningful. This is a realistic theory of meaning (see Ayer, 1950: 28. See also Ayer's [1950: 144–47] realistic position on the existence of unperceived objects). There is a world of difference between "strong" verificationists— who are nominalists—and the "weak" verificationists—who are confused realists. For the sake of precise classification, it is unfortunate that both groups are indiscriminately called "positivists." Ayer and other weak verificationists, insofar as their criterion of meaning is concerned, have only to acknowledge more explicitly that the meaning of the most common noun (e.g., "pencil") is as general as a scientific law in order to become thoroughgoing Peircean pragmaticists.

Chapter Three

1. This, of course, is an application of James's pragmatic theory of truth. James's pragmatism

is analyzed on pages 75–79, but the relationship between his psychology and pragmatism is noted here simply to foreshadow the
line of exposition we shall follow.

2. These volumes were published together in
1971. References in this section are to this combined edition which Ralph Barton Perry, the
editor, called "the most important of James's
metaphysical writings."

3. Similarly, James's pragmatic theory of truth
and meaning can be understood as a consequence of radical empiricism. James (1970b:
xxxvi) wrote in the preface to *The Meaning of
Truth* (1909): "I am interested in another doctrine in philosophy to which I give the name of
radical empiricism, and it seems to me that the
establishment of the pragmatist theory of truth
is a step of first-rate importance in making radical empiricism prevail."

4. James was not the first to select neutral
monism as the preferred conception of the universe. Spinoza was a skillful defender of the
doctrine. W. P. Montague and other philosophers after James also adopted neutral monism.

5. In his preface to *Pragmatism,* James (1970a:
14) stated that there is no logical connection
between pragmatism and radical empiricism.
This statement was probably added in hopes
that pragmatism would receive a fair trial,
without being associated with other Jamesian
doctrines already considered dubious by much
of the philosophical community. In any event,
we share Wild's (1969: 331) conclusion that the
statement should not be taken seriously.

6. Perry's two-volume anthology is by far the
most authoritative and comprehensive secondary work on James. It explores in detail every
stage of James's life and philosophy. Our extensive use of Perry's commentary in this section is
prompted by his well-deserved reputation as a
peerless expert on James, and by the comparative redundancy of much of the other secondary
analysis of James's philosophy.

7. Durkheim also held that thoughts are impersonal. He wrote, "In a word, there is something

impersonal in us because there is something social in all of us, and since social life embraces at once both representations and practices, this impersonality naturally extends to ideas as well as to acts" (1965: 494). This is only one of many points of convergence between Peirce and Durkheim.

Chapter Four

1. In addition to his long and intense study of Dewey's philosophy, Bentley also studied the works of Peirce, James, and Mead quite thoroughly. In some respects, his grasp of the differences among the American pragmatists was firmer than was Dewey's. His own approach to logic and semiology was much closer to that of Peirce and Mead than to Dewey's. After first reading Dewey's *Logic* in 1939, Bentley wrote to Dewey:

> The difference between my present status and yours, I take it, is something as follows: You have taken the "biological"—or, more broadly, the "naturalistic"—position, given it well-rounded form, and developed the logical process out of it. . . . My development, instead of being made biologically, was primarily made among law-language problems, and I came out of it with a strong bias in favor of direct observations and primary descriptions *across* sets of men. . . . the language-reasoning-symbolization concept construction will only get itself efficiently formulated when it is worked out in a naturalistically social rather than in a naturalistically organic form. [Dewey and Bentley, 1964: 60–61]

Judging from Dewey's response to this letter, it seems that he never fully appreciated the distinction Bentley was making (Dewey and Bentley, 1964: 63–64). This response is consistent with his failure to differentiate Peirce's and Mead's theory of meaning from his own.
2. The Centennial Bibliography (1962) of Dewey's works is itself a sizable volume.

3. A considerable number of books and articles have described and analyzed Dewey's theory. Because our purpose is not simply to add one more to the list, the discussion is confined strictly to matters relevant to the major thesis of this chapter—specifically, the relation of Dewey's instrumentalism to the pragmatisms of James and Peirce. A concomitant interest is to identify the realistic and nominalistic tendencies of Dewey's logic and to reach a final estimate of his implied position on the nominalism/realism question. Consequently, the following sections are not intended as an exhaustive account of Dewey's theory or of the possible criticism of his position.

4. Dewey never identified the metaphysical role that the term "nature" played in his philosophy. In fact, he did not adequately analyze the metaphysical base of his philosophy. To understand Dewey's philosophy, readers must uncover his metaphysics by their own efforts. As Grace C. Lee (1945: 82) noted, Peirce was the only American pragmatist to acknowledge the need for metaphysical analysis. Peirce (1.129) wrote, "Find a scientific man who proposes to get along without any metaphysics—not by any means every man who holds the ordinary reasonings of metaphysicians in scorn—and you have found one whose doctrines are thoroughly vitiated by the crude and uncriticized metaphysics with which they are packed."

5. We can drop the name "Aristotelian," because Dewey's argument extends to all systems of symbolic logic.

6. Note the contrast between this aim and Peirce's concrete reasonableness or James's uninterrupted stream of experience.

7. For example, Dewey wrote, "The readers who are acquainted with the logical writings of Peirce will note my great indebtedness to him in the general position taken" (138: 9n). See also Dewey and Bentley (1949: 208, 255n8).

8. Russell thought Peirce was assuming that future scientists will be more "clever" or that humankind is "perfectible." Anyone who has

carefully studied Peirce knows that his theory of truth rests solely upon (1) realism and (2) the objectivity of scientific method—it certainly does not presuppose any of the dubious sociological prophecies Russell suggests. Russell's comments demonstrate that he had no understanding of the logical relation between Peirce's conception of truth and his doctrine of signs.

9. In this passage and in the chapter concerning the natural evolution of language in *Experience and Nature,* it is abundantly clear that Dewey is taking a position that, in its vocabulary and general form, is very similar to Mead's theories. This raises a priority question concerning which of them was the original architect of this theory of "consciousness." The question is difficult to resolve because of their close contact and because Dewey always confined his statements of intellectual debt to short statements in prefaces and footnotes. Although Mead is never mentioned in *Experience and Nature,* any student of Mead can easily detect many Meadian phrases and concepts in the book or, if Dewey is granted priority, some of Mead's propositions must be credited to Dewey. We further consider this problem in chapter 5.

10. One notable exception to this tendency was Dewey's (1938: 262–63) statement that his theory of inquiry both agrees and disagrees with nominalism, realism, and conceptualism! For Dewey, his theory had limitless versatility.

Chapter Five

1. Arthur Murphy (1901–1962) was basically a Deweyan instrumentalist and a prominent commentator on the philosophies of Dewey, Moore, Whitehead, and Mead. He was the editor of Mead's Carus lectures (*The Philosophy of the Present*). Murphy ranks among the notable American philosophers of the first half of the twentieth century.

2. Although philosophical systems cannot be "defined" in a single sentence, the reader is entitled to a rough approximation of the meaning

of "objective relativism." This doctrine argues that the qualities of experiences are relative to the experiencer's spatial position, cognitive structure, and organic constitution but that this relativity does not entail subjectivism. Intersubjectivity is still possible among all who occupy the same "consentient" perspective (see Mead, 1938: 112). This will become clearer as we progress.

3. For reasons presented in the previous section, we have based this summary on Dewey's (1938) *Logic,* not on the contrary position expressed in parts of *Experience and Nature.*

4. Any material object can be subdivided, and its separate parts will each retain the property of resistance. This process can continue until we are left with nothing but atomic particles. But those particles still occupy space and resist other matter: "In imagination the extended resistant matter of our experience may be indefinitely subdivided without losing the character which it has in experience" (Mead, 1938: 286). Mead, however, was left with the problem of explaining the reality of *relations* in terms of his contact theory of reality, and he was aware of this problem (1938: 208). Unless this refinement were made, he would seem to be a materialist. Reality is a broader category than existence, but Mead's theory of reality fails to provide clearly for this fact. It is a problem of his theory which he never fully resolved.

5. Some may feel that conservatism is dysfunctional in science. In the extreme it may be; but without a fairly high degree of skepticism regarding new theories, progress would be nearly impossible.

6. It is truly amazing that Mead arrived at these three terms which, it may be recalled, are Peirce's three categories. It strongly suggests that Mead (perhaps unknowingly) acquired some ideas from Peirce through conversations with Dewey or James. Mead studied under Josiah Royce, a man who had detailed knowledge of Peirce's philosophy. Thus, Royce was a

further possible indirect link between Peirce and Mead.

7. For example, "If one approaches a hammer, he is muscularly all ready to seize the handle of the hammer" (Mead, 1934: 11).

Chapter Six

1. W. I. Thomas was equally significant when viewed with the benefit of historical hindsight. His position is discussed below.

2. It should be noted that, although Gustav Ratzenhofer had previously introduced the "interests" concept and Small cites Ratzenhofter extensively in his *General Sociology*, Small developed most of his theory independently (Small, 1916: 818–19). In fact, it may be noted that Small (1905: 433) at one point cites Dewey's definition of "interests" rather than Ratzenhofer's.

3. Small (1905: 472n) reported that Mead criticized his theory for presupposing these "interests" rather than admitting that we are not born with interests. Instead, they are acquired through the socialization process. By partially retaining the biological mode of analysis, Small ultimately fell victim to the same error he detected in the Spencerian system. Unfortunately, Small's discussion reveals that he did not grasp the crux of Mead's objection.

4. Historians of American sociology have not given due credit to Small for providing the seeds for the deep structure of the Park/Burgess theory of competition, conflict, accommodation, and assimilation. As one compares the relevant texts, the general similarity is evident.

5. Thomas was not clear or consistent in his use of terminology (see editor's comment in Thomas, 1951: 196 n.4). The key elements in the situational approach are the physical and social objects (norms, roles, etc.), the individual's previous behavioral orientation toward similar settings, and the individual's self-consciousness assessment of these conditions and his/her motives and responses. Thomas

loosely, and often interchangeably, used the terms "wishes," "desires," "attitudes," and "values" to identify these elements.

6. Thomas (1951: 179 ff.) clearly was aware of the contrasts between the dominant personality types of modern and preliterate societies, but he never systematically developed these insights. Such analysis would have pulled Thomas closer to Durkheim's sociologistic interpretation of personality and undercut his own theoretical system.

7. Even Cooley's social commentary is two-edged. He was living through the blatant vulgarities of late nineteenth-century capitalism, and felt some obligation, or at least, desire to comment on the exploits of the capitalist system. But he was not completely sure what he ought to say. Thus, throughout the second half of *Social Organization* the capitalist is portrayed as first hero and then villain (see Cooley, 1962: 138, 140–41, 195–96, 240, 260–61, 296). In the final analysis Cooley's intent seems to have been to defend the capitalist system, if not always the capitalist. To that extent, it is certainly true (and infrequently recognized) that Cooley anticipated much of the Davis-Moore functional theory of stratification and, as Gutman (1958: 256) notes in passing, the rudiments of structural-functionalism itself.

8. Cooley seems to have borrowed the term "self-feeling" from H. M. Stanley, whose work he held in high esteem (Cooley, 1964:170).

9. In criticizing Blumer's psychical interactionist theory of meaning, Stone and Farberman (1967:410) correctly observed that Blumer's formulation "implies a subjective nominalism that reminds us of Cooley's sympathetic introspection, and here we must insist on the *objective* significance of the universal."

10. Blumer (1969a:21n.) identifies Dewey and Mead as major proponents of humanistic pragmatism. Amazingly, Blumer does not mention James. James's pragmatism is infinitely more humanistic than Dewey's or Mead's, but is certainly equalled by Blumer's.

11. Blumer's more empirical writings testify to the vacuity of his "interpretation" concept as an explanatory device. For instance, his experience with union-management relations left him with the impression that "industrial relations may be likened to a vast, confused game evolving without the benefit of fixed rules and frequently without the benefit of any rules" (Blumer, 1947:277–78). Blumer's nominalistic perspective apparently shielded him from seeing the relatively stable structural parameters which set limits upon the activities of the "acting, striving, calculating" individuals who occupied his attention (see Lichtman, 1970:83). Similarly, Blumer's (1969b) article on fashion is theoretically empty, and rests upon circular, question-begging reasoning.

12. It may be surmised that his contact with German thought, especially Simmel's, left a more lasting impression upon Hayes than did Small and Dewey. At any rate, these theorists, along with Schmoller, are cited by Barnes (1948a) as his primary mentors. Having written his dissertation under Small at Chicago in 1902, it is remarkable that he departed so drastically from the early Chicago school.

13. Only a year earlier, Bodenhafer had taken Mead's advance social psychology course as well as Mead's seminar on social consciousness (Smith, 1977:321). Bodenhafer must be recognized, with Faris, as a sociologist who served as a medium through which Mead's thought was introduced to the sociological community during the early 1920s.

14. Park and Burgess (1970:48) also credit Bodenhafer.

15. We shall not consider the role of Burgess in Chicago sociology, because Park was clearly the theoretician of the team (Janowitz, 1970:xiv).

16. There is an interesting problem here for the sociology of knowledge. Frequently, when a scholar enters an intellectual community near one of its major transition points, his or her writings mirror the competing orientations. The exception seems to occur in those cases in which

the scholar becomes immediately and firmly attached to a particular paradigm or theorist. For example, contrast Park's intellectual development with Faris's.

17. Elsner (1972) observed that the dissertation itself, written in German, is practically unknown to American sociologists.

18. Park readily adopted Mead's theory of communication in his 1939 article, "Symbiosis and Socialization." Interestingly, the article makes no reference to Dewey—an uncommon occurrence in Park's writings. It is almost as if Mead had displaced Dewey and Cooley as Park's principal source on the subject. Note that the article was written after 1934, the year *Mind, Self, and Society* was published. Considering these facts, one has to wonder how much Park really knew about Mead's philosophy prior to Mead's death. One would suspect ordinarily that Park would have learned Mead's theory through contact with Faris and students, if not directly, but it remains difficult to imagine how this could have happened without Park making more use of Mead in his writings before this late date. Such use could have provided a firmer social psychology to support his realism drawn from Simmel, Durkheim, and other European scholars. In any event, one must certainly question Matthews's (1977:149) claim that by 1915, "Park had absorbed much of the approach of Mead."

19. Unfortunately, Faris's failure to distinguish clearly between the psychical interactionism of Thomas/Cooley and the social behaviorism of Mead may have contributed to Blumer's failure (as Faris's student) to make this differentiation. If Faris had made the distinction, it is doubtful that Blumer would have conceived of the symbolic interactionist "tradition" in the way he, and others since, have done. Minimally, Blumer's construction of the intellectual history of symbolic interactionism would have required more defense than has hitherto been demanded of it.

Chapter Seven

1. Students identified as visitors have been counted as enrolled students. There were very few of these. The number of students who attended Mead's lectures without formal enrollment remains unknown. The historical sources of these data as well as an expanded methodological discussion may be found in Smith (1977).

2. Because Table 1 is based on the yearly enrollment distribution of students from different departments, it includes students who may have repeatedly enrolled in Mead's courses from one year to the next.

3. Includes 3.0% (44) unclassified graduate students.

4. Appendix 1 provides a listing by title of all the courses Mead taught at the University of Chicago and when he taught them. Appendix 2 is a list of sociology graduate students by name as distributed among Mead's courses. Comparing these two appendixes for the 1929–31 period provides evidence of the deviation in the enrollment pattern of sociology graduate students given their concentration in Advanced Social Psychology.

5. This analysis does not distinguish students who may have been required to enroll in Mead's courses, although such requirements would inflate his "popularity."

6. The greater popularity of Mead among psychology graduate students reflects the fact that it was only after 1914–19 that the proportion of psychology students in Mead's courses began to decline (see Table 1). In addition, psychology, in contrast to the other three departments, experienced a decreasing enrollment which would have contributed to the decreasing proportion of student enrollment in Mead's courses reflected in Table 1. The evidence in Table 2 strongly suggests that Mead was never very popular among education graduate students.

7. It should be pointed out that Table 3 represents Mead's actual popularity and is not an index of popularity as previously discussed.

8. A comparison of Appendixes 1 and 2 indicates the narrow selection made among Mead's courses.

9. Our comparative analysis of selected Chicago sociologists, although showing a limited number of metatheoretical positions similar to that of Mead, does not prove Mead's influence. However, it should be pointed out that the prevalence of divergent metatheoretical positions does suggest an absence of influence.

10. It should be pointed out the psychology and education dissertations generally contained fewer citations than those in sociology and philosophy.

11. Chi square analysis of the relationship between student enrollment and doctoral dissertation recognition supports this interpretation. Although there is a significant relationship $(p < .05, X^2 = 9.52)$, the stength of the relationship is very weak $(\phi^2 = .09)$.

12. Evidence in the dissertations of Price and Karpf suggests that Mead's classroom lectures were also publicly available. That is, these two dissertations suggest that Mead's lectures from his Advanced Social Psychology course were available in the University of Chicago library, from at least 1924, onward.

13. Until 1920 students were expected to publish their dissertations for a wider audience, although the faculty members were both the initial audience and the judges whose muster the student's dissertation had to pass.

14. An excellent bibliography of Mead's writings is available in Broyer (1973).

15. The year 1931 is also distinctive in that the highest number of dissertations citing Mead were completed $(N = 3)$.

16. Karpf's dissertation was subsequently published as a book. We will discuss it further when we examine Mead's recognition in books and monographs.

17. We regard the question of Mead's comparative recognition as the basic comparison to be made between him and the other Chicago faculty, but it would also be of interest to assess

the enrollment of sociology graduate students in Mead's courses in relation to other Chicago faculty. Given the small size of the sociology faculty, we suspect that few sociology graduate students could have avoided enrolling in at least some of the courses taught by the major departmental figures. In addition, the comments of former sociology graduate students suggest that no other nonsociology faculty occupied the status of Mead. As the comparative recognition data will establish, this assessment appears correct, with the possible exception of John Dewey.

18. Sociology and anthropology faculty nearly exhaust the permanent faculty and include all the major departmental figures teaching during Mead's lifetime. Nonsociology faculty were inductively selected from among those receiving citations in the dissertations. Only 99 of the 102 previously examined dissertations were usable and/or available for our comparative analysis. This difference is reflected in a lower proportion of sociology doctoral students giving Mead recognition (17.2%) than what was earlier reported (18.6%).

19. Throughout this discussion and in presenting the results we have not distinguished between sociology and anthropology. A slight degree of inaccuracy has therefore been introduced, because there was some separation (see Diner, 1975). Frederick Starr was a member of the joint department from its very beginning and he did not retire until the academic year 1923–24. Scattered among the dissertations are those of a few anthropology students; inspection of the titles suggests there may have been five. In any case, Starr received the least amount of recognition from students. Upon Starr's retirement, Fay-Cooper Cole joined the faculty, and one year later Edward Sapir assumed teaching duties.

20. None of these faculty enjoyed as long a tenure at Chicago as did Mead. Both Small and Henderson joined the faculty in 1892, but Henderson died in 1915 and Small in 1926. Vincent

and Thomas joined the faculty after their graduate student days, but Vincent left in 1911, and Thomas did so in 1918. Park joined the faculty as a special lecturer in 1913 and Burgess, after completing his Chicago Ph.D. in 1913, returned in 1915. Faris replaced Thomas, and Ogburn did not arrive until 1926. Other faculty members taught for shorter periods of time. Graham Taylor was on the faculty from 1903 to 1906, and Charles Zeublin's faculty tenure was from 1894 to 1907.

21. Harvey Carr also exceeded Mead's recognition, but it occurred in only one dissertation. There was no significant difference between the mean number of citations given Dewey and Mead.

Chapter Eight

1. Several sociology doctoral students had their dissertations published in *AJS*, either as a single article (e.g., Thomas) or, more frequently, as a series of articles (e.g., Ellwood, Bernard, and Bodenhafer). In the case of Ellwood, Bernard, and Bodenhafer, then, recognition of Mead in their dissertations provided him with wider sociological exposure.

2. Wallace Craig was a graduate sutdent in zoology and a former student of Mead's. J. R. Kantor received a Ph.D. in philosophy and had been a student of Mead's. Taft cited Mead's teaching, but no record of his enrollment in Mead's courses was found. For two of the authors, E. H. Lewis and H. H. Maurer, we could neither locate them as students in any of Mead's courses nor as students at the university. However, both were affiliated with the Lewis Institute of Chicago, so there was at least geographical proximity. D. D. Droba was the only author to extend Mead recognition who could not be readily associated with the University of Chicago.

3. Faris called attention to "A Behavioristic Account of the Significant Symbol," "The Genesis of the Self and Social Control," "Social Consciousness and the Consciousness of Meaning," "Social Psychology as Counterpart to Physio-

logical Psychology," "The Social Self," and "What Social Objects Must Psychology Pre-Suppose?"

4. There is some basis for assuming the book reviews were solicited. We strongly suspect that Faris solicited Mead's commemorative article on Cooley. Herbert Blumer indicates that this was a possibility (private communication).

5. The two articles were "A Behavioristic Account of the Significant Symbol" and "The Genesis of the Self and Social Control." A third article was also abstracted, "Scientific Method and the Moral Sciences."

6. Actually, Mead's name first appeared in *SF* during the 1922–23 publication years as one of several scholars listed on the cover page of an advertisement for the *International Journal of Ethics*.

7. Of course, Bittner's qualification that Mead's name appears in books of "real merit" might severely limit the range of books he considered. However, the results of our analysis of Mead's recognition in books and monographs published during this period will establish that Mead had greater social recognition here than he received in sociology journals.

8. That is, the favorable reviews Karpf's book received in *AJS* and *SSR* may have indirectly led sociologists to examine Mead's work after his death.

9. No claim can be made that the availability sample of books and monographs is representative of the total population of sociology books and monographs published. The sample is, however, representative of those used in Odum's (1951) section on the story of sociology through textbooks. The sample of 181 books was drawn from the libraries of the University of Chicago, University of Illinois, and the University of Georgia. A complete list of the books examined is available in Smith (1977).

10. Others citing more than one of Mead's articles, but not giving him extensive recognition during the 1920s, were Park and Burgess (1924) and Bernard (1926).

11. In his *Source Book for Social Psychology*

(1927), Young reprinted "a Behavioristic Account of the Significant Symbol"—the article most often cited in books and monographs (see Appendix 3).

12. Lasswell, a faculty member in the Department of Political Science, had been a graduate student in three of Mead's courses: Logic of the Social Sciences (F, 1922), Movements of Thought in the Ninetenth Century (S, 1923), and Relativity from the Standpoint of Pragmatism (S, 1923).

13. Ironically, Mead's philosophy was not only like Peirce's in substance, but also became widely recognized only after his death. Recall that a similar spurt of interest among philosophers followed the posthumous publication of Peirce's *Collected Papers*.

14. Interestingly, Mead does receive bibliographic recognition in Cooley, Angell, and Carr's *Introduction to Sociology* (1933).

15. Conspicuously, there was no citation of Mead's 1899 *AJS* article, "The Working Hypothesis in Social Reform," in this book or in any of the other sources we have examined.

Chapter Nine

1. Our sample of former University of Chicago sociology graudate students comes from three sources: (1) 32 questionnaire or interview responses collected in 1975 by Smith, (2) 25 interviews conducted by Carey (1975), and (3) 73 life histories collected in the late 1920s by L. L. Bernard. A complete discussion of this combined sample and its availability may be found in Smith (1977).

2. Bernard actually received life histories from 37. However, the two pre-1920 sociologists who responded to our questionnaire, Stuart A. Queen and Manual C. Elmer, also provided Bernard with life histories.

3. In fact, it is possible that even this recognition is somewhat "inflated" by sociologists who overestimated Mead's "influence" on their intellectual development as students. That is, as Mead's status as a scholar increased after 1920,

some sociologists may have retrospectively identified themselves with the "seminal philosopher." This appears to be a plausible interpretation of Thomas' life history inclusion of Mead and deletion of Dewey (see below). Of course, the same may also be true of some post-1920 Chicago sociologists.

4. The comments of Bernard do not come from his life history but from a fragmentary biographical statement he prepared on Charles H. Cooley.

5. Comparative Psychology (F-1894), Comparative Psychology (W-1895), and Methods of Psychology (S-1895).

6. Movements of Thought in the Nineteenth Century (S-1911), Contemporary Psychology (F-1912), and Seminar in Social Consciousness (W-1913).

7. Unless otherwise specified, all quotations here and in the next section are taken from our 1975 questionnaire.

8. It is unknown whether Mead anticipated completing the Ph.D. at this time, but he did not obtain it.

9. One place Mead occasionally spoke was before the Sociology Club. The 1898–99 *Annual Register* reports that Mead, Vincent, Tufts, and Dewey spoke on Baldwin's *Social and Ethical Interpretations of Mental Development*.

10. In the University of Chicago's 1907–8 *Annual Register,* graduate students were informed that the head of the sociology department would give credit for certain courses taken outside the department. The philosophy department was one of the departments mentioned. In the 1912–13 *Annual Register,* mention of specific courses was made, including two of Mead's: Social Psychology and Seminar on Social Consciousness. By 1913–14 the *Annual Register* named both the courses appropriate for sociology graduate students *and* the faculty members teaching the courses. Mead was one of the faculty named. Significantly, the 1919–20 *Annual Register* listed Mead as one of the "instructors in other departments offering courses

in this department." By 1920, then, some of
Mead's courses were being cross-listed in the
sociology department and formal recognition
was given Mead by the faculty. The *Annual
Register* continued to officially recognize Mead
in this manner until 1924–25. Thereafter, there
was a return to simply calling attention to
courses in other departments appropriate for
sociology students. Some of Mead's courses
continued to be listed. The official cooperation
between the Departments of Philosophy, Psychology, and Sociology regarding financial support of graduate students may also have facili-
tated recognition of Mead. Thus, Burgess, Bernard, and Victor Helleberg held fellowships in
the Department of Psychology during the
period Mead was still teaching a number of
psychology courses other than social psychology. E. S. Bogardus and Bernard held fellowships in the Department of Philosophy.

11. The comments of students from the post-
1920 period also establish that Mead was not
universally well received by those who enrolled
in his courses.

12. Other nonclassroom contact with Mead
could have derived from actual involvement in
the Department of Philosophy. Queen reports
minoring in philosophy, and Bernard indicated
he was a member of the Philosophy Club. There
is reason to suspect that such departmental
boundary-crossing became increasingly in-
frequent after 1920.

13. Queen received his undergraduate education at Pomona College in California, and recalls that the person telling him about Mead
was a Chicago philosophy Ph.D. and one of
Mead's former students.

14. We were unable to identify Snow, but Peterson was a former graduate student of Mead's
who was awarded a Chicago Ph.D. in psychology.

15. In 1941 Helleberg privately published a
monograph which, as he stated, "grew out of
the efforts to assimilate and translate the ideas of
George H. Mead and John Dewey so that my

students at the University of Kansas could understand and use them to guide their lives" (Helleberg, 1941: iv). He was a student in Mead's 1908 social psychology course, but did not earn the Chicago Ph.D. Evidence presented in the next section will suggest that Helleberg and the University of Kansas are entitled to a measure of distinction for their recognition of Mead.

16. Data for this section are taken from an analysis of a combined sample of 36 former sociology graduate students generated by our survey and that of Carey (1975). Twenty-six respondents provided systematic answers to our questions. However, where appropriate, we have classified the responses of all 36 respondents. In addition, these data are supplemented by 27 post-1920 life histories provided Bernard in 1927 and 1928.

17. This does not include the five individuals who had been only undergraduates at Chicago. Three of the five report they knew of Mead as undergraduates. No response was given by the other two.

18. Post-1920 students named several of the pre-1920 students—Helleberg, Steiner, Ellwood and Queen—as those who mentioned Mead prior to their arrival at the University of Chicago.

19. Redmond's life history is available in the Pennsylvania Historical Collections, Pennsylvania State University.

20. We indicated the similarity of Queen to Mead, including Queen's minor in philosophy. Likewise, we noted Helleberg's course enrollment and his fellowship in the Department of Psychology. Rosenow was a former student and psychology Ph.D. who had the added distinction of being one of the two doctoral students in psychology to cite Mead in his dissertation.

21. Further support for this possibility is available by recalling Mrs. Howard Jensen's comment that Mead was receiving recognition from Helleberg prior to 1920.

22. Of course, Blumenthal's statement indicates

that he only read a selection of Mead's articles. There is little reason to suspect that sociology graduate students read any more widely than the articles we have seen cited in various sources, and this was clearly a limited portion of Mead's writings. Nevertheless, for a few sociologists, Mead's articles were salient enough that they identified Mead's writings as a source of intellectual influence in the life histories they provided Bernard. Three of the 27 post-1920 Chicago sociology graduate students gave Mead's writings recognition. In fact, Walter Reckless specifically called attention to three articles in a list of material he indicated he was recalling from memory. The three articles were "A Behavioristic Account of the Significant Symbol" (1922), "The Mechanism of Social Consciousness" (1912), and "Genesis of the Social Self and Social Control" (1925). Four other post-1920 sociologists in the Bernard sample named Mead as an influential teacher (14.8%). This compares to the 10 of 37 (27%) pre-1920 Chicago sociologists who claimed Mead as an influential teacher. Consistent with our interpretation of the recognition of Mead's articles, none of the pre-1920 sociologists cited them as influential.

23. The comments of two other respondents indicate that they may have enrolled as undergraduates in courses taught by Mead.

24. Advanced Social Psychology (W-1926) and Research (W-1927).

25. As we have shown, only Queen reports also having had a person-to-person relationship with Mead, but Queen was a pre-1920 student.

26. The paper is in the possession of Blumer with its comments by Mead.

27. "It is possible that Mead may have asked Faris first to take over the course; I have a faint recollection that Faris said something to this effect to me" (Personal Communication with Blumer, 11/17/74).

28. Among faculty outside the sociology department, sociology students recall that only two gave Mead recognition. Cottrell recalls

Lasswell mentioning Mead a few times, and Clark recalls the same for Edward Sapir. However, Blumer has no recollection of Sapir extending Mead recognition.

29. Hughes recalls that Mead's name received "much attention in any course of Faris." Samuel C. Kincheloe used almost exactly the same wording to describe Mead's recognition by Faris. Karpf suggests that her thesis director "interpreted and popularized" the ideas of Mead. One former student recalls, "There used to be a saying among students that if you have taken one course from Faris, you have taken all and all about Mead." Another student suggests Faris depicted social thought in "B.M." and "A.M." terms—Before Mead and After Mead. We tend to agree with Blumer's assessment that "Faris was clearly a student of Mead's in a very profound sense." Among our respondents, only S. C. Ratcliffe reported that in his course with Faris, he did not hear Faris give Mead recognition; Ratcliffe recalls being a student in one of Faris's first courses at Chicago.

30. Faris's dissertation was entitled, "The Psychology of Punishment." Interestingly, this bears a striking surface resemblance to Mead's 1918 article, "The Psychology of Punitive Justice."

31. The comments suggest that Mead's recognition was indeed minimal. Cottrell states that "Burgess made passing and eclectic use of Mead's conception of self and processes of interaction, but not very profound." Clark similarly characterized Burgess and added that Park occasionally mentioned Mead. Commenting on the two of them, Albert Blumenthal states, "Park and Burgess would mention Mead's ideas in a sentence or two without commendation." Although Clarence E. Glick reports that Wirth made occasional reference to Mead, there were no comments to judge the nature and extent of Mead's recognition by House or Ogburn. Only Hughes takes exception to this pattern of recognition by suggesting that Mead was "very much dealt with." Given

the recollections of others, we regard this as highly unlikely and attribute the inconsistency to the passage of half a century.

32. Eighteen of 20 respondents indicated that Mead was universally well received. Blumer suggests that the response to Mead was "favorable across the board" (Personal Interview, 8/1/74). Similarly, Karpf reports that "Mead was held in high regard by students and colleagues." However, there appears to have been some faculty hesitancy at times. Thus, that Ogburn mentioned Mead at all will come as a surprise to some of these sociologists who specifically commented that Ogburn was either hostile to Mead's ideas or seemed to avoid the discussion of him completely. In fact, one student states, "Park didn't think that Mead stuff did you any good. He didn't encourage me to take such stuff with Mead. But the point is that I was very much impressed with Faris and his social psychology." The latter, of course, is consistent with our interpretation of these data. Faris was the only sociology faculty to consistently assert the merits of Mead's social thought.

33. Although R. E. L. Faris and Blumer believe that Mead and Faris were personal friends, neither recalls seeing the two of them interact. In fact, they are of the opinion that Faris was Mead's only sociology friend.

34. The bitter treatment being alluded to is President Robert M. Hutchins's treatment of Mead and the philosophy department. It appears that Mead was intent on leaving Chicago in the fall of 1931 to rejoin Dewey at Columbia University (see Miller, 1973: xxxvii–xxxviii).

35. The papers of Elinor Castle Nef include several letters of correspondence between her and Mead and provide an interesting perspective on Mead's early years at Chicago (Special Collections, Regenstein Library, University of Chicago).

36. It is certain that Mead shared Park's expansive interests and active off-campus intellectual

and social life (see Miller, 1973; Barry, 1968; Deegan and Burger, 1978).

37. Clark recalls that the students he associated with talked at length about Mead. R. E. L. Faris states, "My fellow students valued his social psychology course and discussed it, groping to understand some of the novel ideas." Samuel C. Kincheloe recalls the situation in a similar way: "We discussed Mead in small table 'groups' and then sought to help each other understand him." The fact that understanding Mead was difficult for many sociology graduate students is reflected in the statement of A. R. Mangus who recalls one student saying, "To understand Mead's statements, I must first get him to explain his statement and then I must get someone more knowledgeable than I, to explain his explanation." As Everett Stonequist indicates, "Mead's range was very great—quite beyond many graduate students." In any case, these recollections establish that Mead received recognition among sociology graduate students.

Chapter Ten

1. To complete the labyrinth, some have attempted to encircle *both* Mead and Husserl by making Mead into an honorary phenomenologist (e.g., see Natanson, 1956; Seeburger and Franks, 1978). For a rejoinder to this move, see Miller (1973: 7–9) and Lewis (1978).

2. This posture is particularly evident if, as a case study, one traces the volatile and frequently misguided reactions to Huber (1973).

3. In any case, this is an improvement over the treatment Peirce received in the earlier Douglas reader wherein his concept of the indexical sign is misrepresented (Douglas, 1970: 38, 349).

4. For an example of the scope of such an enterprise, see Foucault (1970). Even Foucault's work is quite incomplete, in that he mainly considers only the intellectual stimuli to disciplinary development.

5. Wiley (1979: 70) observed that symbolic interactionism enjoyed a "second summer"

with the demise of Parsonian structural-functionalism during the 1960s. Parsons was the symbolic target that provided a catalyst for the revival of symbolic interactionism as a major theoretical perspective in American sociology. And Mead, as interpreted by symbolic interactionists, was portrayed as the founding and unifying theorist of the school. Yet it is inconceivable that he could have been cast credibly into this role unless his social realism had been earlier discarded or underplayed.

6. There is some evidence that Mead was receptive to Gilbert's argument. In the Foreword, Gilbert acknowledged, "Too much cannot be said in appreciation of the splendid cooperation which was given by the entire Faculty of Philosophy in the work of preparing the Thesis, and especially of the open mind with which Professor George H. Mead, to whom it was first presented, was willing to consider the opinion of the writer." We know from his own writings that Mead detected the subjectivism of James's psychology, but it is questionable whether he ever saw the essential dependence of Dewey's theory of inquiry upon Jamesian psychology with its attendant subjective phenomenalism.

7. We read Gilbert's statements about James and Dewey very late in our research and were pleasantly surprised to find our interpretation of the James/Dewey pragmatism in a thesis written fifty-five years ago. In those intervening years, few commentators on American pragmatism have displayed Gilbert's grasp of the core philosophy shared by James and Dewey. Most have become lost in the witch's mirror.

8. An excellent discussion and resolution of some of these issue is available in Rock's (1979) recent analysis of symbolic interactionism and its philosophical foundations. Interestingly, Rock traces several of the inconsistencies in symbolic interactionism to the exposure of Chicago sociologists to Simmel's structuralism and pragmatism. In contrast to our view, Rock depicts pragmatism as a unified philosophy. In addition, he argues that Mead always had a key

role in the development of symbolic interactionism, the latter viewed as essentially
synonymous with *all* of Chicago sociology for
the period we have covered. Despite several
conclusions which we regard as dubious, the
book makes important contributions to what
we consider an urgently needed type of research.

References

Allport, G. W.

1943   "The Productive Paradoxes of William James." *Psychological Review* 50:95.
1971   "Dewey's Individual and Social Psychology." In *The Philosophy of John Dewey*, edited by Paul A. Schlipp, pp. 263–90. LaSalle, Illinois: Open Court.

Baker, Paul J.

1973   "The Life Histories of W. I. Thomas and Robert E. Park." *American Journal of Sociology* 79: 243–60.

Baker, Paul J.; Long, Martha P.; and Quensel, Susan W.

1973   "The Pioneers of American Sociology: An Empirical Study." Paper presented at 68th Annual Meeting of American Sociological Association.

Baker, Paul J.; Ferrell, Mary Z.; and Quensel, Susan W.

1975   "Departmentalization of Sociology in the United States, 1880–1928." Paper presented Annual Meeting of American Sociological Association, San Francisco, Calif.

Barnes, Harry E.

1948a   *An Introduction to the History of Sociology.* Chicago: University of Chicago Press.
1948b   "William Isaac Thomas." In *An Introduction to the History of Sociology*, edited by Harry E.

Barnes, pp. 793–804. Chicago: University of Chicago Press.

Barry, Robert M.

1968   "A Man and a City: George Herbert Mead in Chicago." In *American Philosophy and the Future*, edited by Michael Novak, pp. 173–92. New York: Charles Scribner's Sons.

Bauman, Z.

1973   "On the Philosophical Status of Ethnomethodology." *Sociological Review* 21:5–23.

Bergmann, Gustav

1958   "Frege's Hidden Nominalism." *Philosophical Review* 63:437–59.

Bernstein, Richard J.

1960   Introduction to *On Experience, Nature, and Freedom*, by John Dewey, pp. ix–xlvii. New York: The Liberal Arts Press.

Blumer, Herbert

1928   "Method in Social Psychology." Unpublished Ph.D. dissertation. University of Chicago.
1937   "Social Psychology." In *Man and Society*, edited by E. D. Schmidt, pp. 144–98. New York: Prentice-Hall.
1947   "Sociological Theory in Industrial Relations." *American Sociological Review* 12:271–78.
1964   "Collective Behavior." In *Principles of Sociology*, edited by Alfred McClung Lee, pp. 167–222. New York: Barnes & Noble.
1969a   *Symbolic Interaction: Perspective and Method.* Englewood Cliffs, N.J.: Prentice-Hall.
1969b   "Fashion: From Class Differentiation to Collective Selection." *Sociological Quarterly* 10:275–91.
1977   "Comment on Lewis' 'The Classic American Pragmatists as Forerunners to Symbolic Interactionism.'" *Sociological Quarterly* 18:285–89.

1979   "Comments on 'George Herbert Mead and the Chicago Tradition of Sociology.'" *Symbolic Interaction* 2:21–22.

Bodenhafer, Walter B.

1921   "The Comparative Role of the Group Concept in Ward's *Dynamic Sociology* and Contemporary American Sociology." *American Journal of Sociology* 26:425–64, 588–600, 716–43.

Boodin, John E.

1913   "The Existence of Social Minds." *American Journal of Sociology* 19:1–47.
1918   "Social Systems." *American Journal of Sociology* 23:705–34.

Brown, Richard H.

1977   "The Emergence of Existential Thought: Philosophical Perspectives on Positivist and Humanist Forms of Social Theory." In *Existential Sociology,* edited by Jack D. Douglas and John M. Johnson, pp. 77–100, Cambridge: Cambridge University Press.

Broyer, John A.

1973   "Bibliography of Writings of George Herbert Mead." In *The Philosophy of George Herbert Mead,* edited by Walter R. Corti, pp. 243–60. Winterthur, Switzerland: Amriswiler Bucherei.

Butchvarov, Panayot

1966   *Resemblance and Identity.* Bloomington: University of Indiana Press.

Carey, James T.

1975   *Sociology and Public Affairs: The Chicago School.* Beverly Hills: SAGE.

Carnap, Rudolf

1965   "Empiricism, Semantics, and Ontology." In

Meaning and Action, edited by Ernest Nagel
and Richard B. Brandt, pp. 298–305. New
York: Harcourt, Brace.

Charon, Joel M.

1979   *Symbolic Interactionism.* New York: Prentice-
Hall.

Cooley, Charles H.

1930   *Sociological Theory and Social Research.* New
York: Henry Holt and Co.
1962   *Social Organization.* New York: Schocken
Books.
1964   *Human Nature and the Social Order.* New
York: Schocken Books.
1966   *Social Process.* Carbondale and Edwardsville,
IL: Southern Illinois University Press.

Cook, Gary A.

1977   "G. H. Mead's Social Behaviorism." *Journal of
the History of the Behavioral Sciences*
13:307–16.

Coser, Lewis A.

1977   *Masters of Sociological Thought.* 2d ed. New
York: Harcourt, Brace, Jovanovich.
1978   "American Trends." In *A History of Sociologi-
cal Analysis,* edited by T. Bottomore and R.
Nisbet, pp. 287–320. New York: Basic
Books.

Cottrell, Leonard S., Jr.

1971   "Covert Behavior in Interpersonal Interaction."
Proceedings of the American Philosophical
Society 115:462–69.
1980   "George Herbert Mead: A Personal Appreciation." In *Sociological Traditions from Generation to Generation,* edited by Matilda
White Riley and Robert K. Merton. Nor-
wood, N.J.: Ablex Publishing Corp., in press.

Deegan, Mary Jo, and Burger, John S.

1978   "George Herbert Mead and Social Reform: His

Work and Writings." *Journal of the History of the Behavioral Sciences* 14(4): 362–73.

Descartes, René

1969 *The Philosophical Works of Descartes*, vol. 1. Translated by Elizabeth S. Haldone and G. R. T. Ross. Cambridge: Cambridge University Press.

Dewey, John

1903 *Essays in Experimental Logic.* Chicago: University of Chicago Press. [Quotation from Dover Publications edition, n.d.].

1908 "What Does Pragmatism Mean by Practical?" *Journal of Philosophy* 5:85–99.

1910 "The Experimentalist Theory of Knowledge." In *The Influence of Darwin on Philosophy and Other Essays,* by John Dewey, pp. 77–112. New York: Henry Holt and Co.

1916 "The Pragmatism of Peirce." *Journal of Philosophy* 13:709–15.

1922 *Human Nature and Conduct: An Introduction to Social Psychology.* New York: Henry Holt and Co.

1929 *The Quest for Certainty.* New York: G. P. Putnam's Sons.

1938 *Logic: The Theory of Inquiry.* New York: Henry Holt and Co.

1941 "Propositions, Warranted Assertability, and Truth." *Journal of Philosophy* 38:169–86.

1957 *Reconstruction in Philosophy.* Boston: The Beacon Press.

1958 *Experience and Nature.* New York: Dover Publications.

1963 *On Experience, Nature, and Freedom.* New York: The Liberal Arts Press.

1973 "The Development of American Pragmatism." In *The Philosophy of John Dewey,* vol. 1, *The Structure of Experience,* edited by John J. McDermott, pp. 41–58. New York: G. P. Putnam's Sons.

Dewey, John, and Bentley, Arthur F.

1949 *Knowing and the Known.* Boston: Beacon Press.

1964   *John Dewey and Arthur F. Bentley: A Philo-sophical Correspondence, 1932–1951.* Selected and edited by Sidney Ratner and Jules Altman. New Brunswick: Rutgers University Press.

DeWulf, Maurice
1956   *An Introduction to Scholastic Philosophy.* New York: Dover Publications.

Dibble, Vernon K.
1975   *The Legacy of Albion Small.* Chicago: The University of Chicago Press.

Diner, Steven J.
1975   "Department and Discipline: The Department of Sociology at the University of Chicago, 1892–1920." *Minerva* 13:514–53.

Droba, Daniel. D.
1933   "Topical Summaries of Current Literature: Social Attitudes." *American Journal of Sociology* 39:513–24.

Durkheim, Emile
1965   *The Elementary Forms of the Religious Life.* New York: The Free Press.

Dykhuizen, George
1973   *The Life and Mind of John Dewey.* Carbondale, Illinois: Southern Illinois University Press.

Eames, S. Morris
1977   *Pragmatic Naturalism.* Carbondale, Illinois: Southern Illinois University Press.

Ellwood, Charles A.
1901   *Some Prolegomena to Social Psychology.* Chicago: The University of Chicago Press.
1910   "Discussion." *American Journal of Sociology* 15:616–18.

1912   *Sociology in Its Psychological Aspects.* New
       York: D. Appleton and Co.
1917   *An Introduction to Social Psychology.* New
       York: D. Appleton and Co.
1927   *The Psychology of Human Society.* New York:
       D. Appleton and Co.
1933   *Methods in Sociology.* Durham: Duke Univer-
       sity Press.

Elsner, Henry Jr.

1972   Introduction to *The Crowd and the Public and
       Other Essays,* by Robert E. Park. Chicago:
       University of Chicago Press.

Fain, Haskell

1949   "A Comparison of the Theories of Logic of
       John Dewey and Charles Sanders Peirce."
       Master's Thesis, University of Illinois.

Faris, Ellsworth

1926a "Review of Ellwood, The Psychology of
       Human Society." *American Journal of
       Sociology* 32:305–7.
1926b "The Concept of Imitation." *American Journal
       of Sociology* 32:367–78.
1937   *The Nature of Human Nature.* New York:
       McGraw-Hill Book Co.

Faris, R. E. L.

1945   "American Sociology." In *Twentieth-Century
       Sociology,* edited by Georges Gurvitch and
       W. E. Moore, pp. 538–61. New York: The
       Philosophical Library.
1970   *Chicago Sociology 1920–1932.* Chicago: Uni-
       versity of Chicago Press.

Feibleman, James K.

1946   *The Revival of Realism.* Chapel Hill: The Uni-
       versity of North Carolina Press.
1970   *An Introduction to the Philosophy of Charles S.
       Peirce.* Cambridge: The M.I.T. Press.

Fisher, Berenice, and Strauss, Anselm

1978a "The Chicago Tradition and Social Change: Thomas, Park, and Their Successors." *Symbolic Interaction* 2:5–23.

1978b "Interactionism." In *A History of Sociological Analysis,* edited by T. Bottomore and R. Nisbet, pp. 457–98. New York: Basic Books.

1979 "George Herbert Mead and the Chicago Tradition of Sociology." *Symbolic Interaction* 2, no. 1:9–26 (part 1); 2, no. 2:9–20 (part 2).

Fitzgerald, John J.

1966 *Peirce's Theory of Signs as Foundation for Pragmatism.* Paris: Mouton & Co.

Flournoy, Theodore

1917 *The Philosophy of William James.* Translated by Edwin B. Holt and William James, Jr. New York: Holt.

Foucault, Michel

1970 *The Order of Things.* New York: Pantheon Books.

Freeman, Eugene

1934 *The Categories of Charles Peirce.* Chicago: The Open Court Publishing Co.

Garfinkel, Harold

1967 *Studies in Ethnomethodology.* Englewood Cliffs, N.J.: Prentice-Hall.

Geiger, George R.

1958 *John Dewey in Perspective.* New York: Oxford University Press.

Gonos, George

1977 " 'Situation' versus 'Frame'; The 'Interactionist' and 'Structuralist' Analyses of Everyday Life." *American Sociological Review* 42:854–67.

Goodspeed, Thomas W.

1916   *A History of the University of Chicago.* Chicago: University of Chicago Press.
1926   "Albion Woodbury Small." *The University* [of Chicago] *Record* 12:240–65.

Goudge, Thomas A.

1950   *The Thought of C. S. Peirce.* Toronto: University of Toronto Press.

Gutman, Robert

1958   "Cooley: A Perspective." *American Sociological Review* 23:251–56.

Hagstrom, Warren O.

1965   *The Scientific Community.* New York: Basic Books.

Hartshorne, Charles, and Weiss, Paul

1931   Introduction to *Collected Papers of Charles Sanders Peirce,* vol. 1. Cambridge: Harvard University Press.

Haserot, Francis

1950   "Spinoza and the Status of Universals." *Philosophical Review* 64:469–92.

Hayes, Edward C.

1910   "Discussion." *American Journal of Sociology* 15:612–114.
1911   "The 'Social Forces' Error." *American Journal of Sociology* 16:613–25.

Helleberg, Victor E.

1941   *The Social Self: The Star in the Human Comedy, an Evolutionary Social Psychology Sketch.* Lawrence, Kansas. Private Edition.

Hewitt, John P.

1979   *Self and Society: A Symbolic Interactionist Psychology.* Boston: Allyn and Bacon.

Hinkle, Gisela J.

1952   "The 'Four Wishes' in Thomas' Theory of Social Change." *Social Research* 9:464–84.

1974   "Review of Alfred Schutz and Thomas Luckmann, *The Structure of the Life-World.*" *Contemporary Sociology* 3:112–14.

Hinkle, Roscoe C.

1963   "Antecedents of the Action Orientation in American Sociology Before 1935." *American Sociological Review* 28:705–15.

1966   Introduction to *Social Process*, by Charles H. Cooley, pp. xi–lxiv. Carbondale and Edwardsville, IL: Southern Illinois University Press.

1975   "Basic Orientations of the Founding Fathers of American Sociology." *Journal of the History of Behavioral Sciences* 11:107–22.

1978   "Toward Periodization of the History of Sociological Theory in the U.S." *Journal of the History of Sociology* 1:68–89.

1980   *Founding Theory of American Sociology, 1881–1915.* London: Routledge & Kegan Paul.

Hinkle, Roscoe C., Jr., and Hinkle, Gisela J.

1954   *The Development of Modern Sociology.* New York: Random House.

Hofstadter, Richard

1945   *Social Darwinism in American Thought.* Philadelphia: University of Pennsylvania Press.

Hook, Sidney

1939   *John Dewey: An Intellectual Portrait.* New York: The John Day Co.

Howard, Delton T.

1919   *John Dewey's Logical Theory.* New York: Longman's, Green, & Co.

Huber, Joan

1973   "Symbolic Interaction as a Pragmatic Perspective: The Bias of Emergent Theory." *American Sociological Review* 38:274–84.

Igram, P. G.

1976   "Social Holism: A Linguistic Approach." *Philosophy of the Social Sciences* 6:127–41.

James, Henry (ed.)

1920   *The Letters of William James.* Boston: Atlantic Monthly Press.

James, William

1950a   *The Principles of Psychology,* vol. 1. New York: Dover Publications.
1950b   *The Principles of Psychology,* vol. 2. New York: Dover Publications.
1970a   *Pragmatism.* New York: Meridan Books.
1970b   *The Meaning of Truth.* Ann Arbor: University of Michigan Press.
1971   *Essays in Radical Empiricism and a Pluralistic Universe,* edited by Ralph Barton Perry. New York: E. P. Dutton & Co.

Janowitz, Morris

1966   Introduction to *On Social Organization and Social Personality,* by W. I. Thomas, pp. vii–lviii. Chicago: University of Chicago Press.
1970   Introduction to *Introduction to the Science of Sociology,* by Robert E. Park and Ernest W. Burgess. Chicago: University of Chicago Press.

Kando, Thomas M.

1977   *Social Interaction.* St. Louis: the C. V. Mosby Co.

Karp, David A., and Yoels, William C.

1979   *Symbols, Selves, and Society.* New York: J. B. Lippincott.

Karpf, Fay B.

1932   *American Social Psychology.* New York: McGraw-Hill Book Co., Inc.

Kaufmann, Felix

1959   "John Dewey's Theory of Inquiry," *Journal of Philosophy* 56:826–36.

1967   "John Dewey's Theory of Inquiry." In *John Dewey: Philosopher of Science and Freedom,* edited by Sidney Hook, pp. 217–30. New York: Barnes & Noble, Inc.

Kuhn, Thomas S.

1962   *The Structure of Scientific Revolutions.* Chicago: The University of Chicago Press.

Kuklick, Bruce

1977   *The Rise of American Philosophy.* New Haven: Yale University Press.

Kuklick, Henrika

1973   "A 'scientific revolution': Sociological Theory in the United States, 1930–45." *Sociological Inquiry* 43:3–22.

Lauer, Robert H., and Handel, Warren H.

1977   *Social Psychology: The Theory and Application of Symbolic Interactionism.* Boston: Houghton Mifflin Co.

Lee, Grace C.

1945   *George Herbert Mead: Philosopher of the Social Individual.* New York: King's Crown Press.

Lengermann, Patricia M.

1979   "The Founding of the *American Sociological Reveiw:* The Anatomy of a Rebellion." *American Sociological Review* 44:185–98.

Lewis, J. David

1972 "Peirce, Mead, and the Objectivity of Meaning." *Kansas Journal of Sociology* 8:111–22.

1976a "The Classic American Pragmatists as Forerunners to Symbolic Interactionism." *Sociological Quarterly* 17:347–59.

1976b "The Pragmatic Foundation of Symbolic Interactionism." Unpublished Ph.D. dissertation, University of Illinois at Champaign-Urbana.

1977 "Reply to Blumer." *Sociological Quarterly* 18:291–92.

1978 "Reply to Seeburger and Franks." *Sociological Quarterly* 19:348–50.

1979 "A Social Behaviorist Interpretation of the Meadian 'I.'" *American Journal of Sociology* 84:261–87.

Lichtman, Richard

1970 "Symbolic Interactionism and Social Reality: Some Marxist Queries." *Berkeley Journal of Sociology* 15:75–94.

Lindesmith, Alfred R.; Strauss, Anselm; and Denzin, Norman K.

1977 *Social Psychology.* 5th ed. New York: Holt, Rinehart, and Winston.

Lorenz, Gilbert

1961 "A Semantic Analysis of Dewey's Logic: The Theory of Inquiry." Master's Thesis, University of Illinois.

MacKay, Donald S.

1942 "What Does Mr. Dewey Mean by an 'Indeterminate Situation'?" *Journal of Philosophy* 39:141–48.

Manis, Jerome G., and Meltzer, Bernard N. (eds.)

1972 *Symbolic Interaction: A Reader in Social Psy-*

chology. 2d ed. Boston: Allyn and Bacon.
1978 *Symbolic Interaction: A Reader in Social Psychology.* 3d ed. Boston: Allyn and Bacon.

Marcell, David W.

1974 *Progress and Pragmatism.* Westport, Conn.: Greenwood Press.

Matthews, Fred H.

1977 *Quest for an American Sociology: Robert E. Park and the Chicago School.* Montreal: McGill-Queen's University Press.

McDermott, John J.

1968 Introduction. *William James, The Writings of William James,* edited by John J. McDermott. New York: The Modern Library.
1973 Introduction. *The Philosophy of John Dewey,* vol. 1, *The Structure of Experience.* New York: G. P. Putnam's Sons.

McPhail, Clark, and Rexroat, Cynthia

1979 "Mead vs. Blumer: The Divergent Methodological Perspectives of Social Behaviorism and Symbolic Interactionism." *American Sociological Review* 44:449–67.

Mead, George H.

1930 "Cooley's Contribution to American Social Thought." *American Journal of Sociology* 35:693–706.
1934 *Mind, Self, and Society: From the Standpoint of a Social Behaviorist.* Edited, with an Introduction, by Charles W. Morris. Chicago: University of Chicago Press.
1936 *Movements of Thought in the Nineteenth Century.* Edited, with an Introduction, by Merritt A. Moore. Chicago: University of Chicago Press.
1938 *The Philosophy of the Act.* Edited, with an Introduction, by Charles W. Morris, in collaboration with John M. Brewster, Albert M.

Dunham, and David L. Miller. Chicago: University of Chicago Press.

1964   *Selected Writings.* Edited, with an Introduction, by Andrew J. Reck. Indianapolis: Bobbs-Merrill Co.

Meltzer, Bernard N.; Petras, John; and Reynolds, Larry

1975   *Symbolic Interactionism: Genesis, Varieties, and Criticism.* London: Routledge & Kegan Paul.

Merton, Robert K.

1973   *The Sociology of Science: Theoretical and Empirical Investigations.* Chicago: University of Chicago Press.

Miller, David L.

1973   *George Herbert Mead: Self, Language, and the World.* Austin: University of Texas Press.

Mills, C. Wright

1964   *Sociology and Pragmatism.* New York: Oxford University Press.

Moore, Edward C.

1961   *American Pragmatism: Peirce, James, and Dewey.* New York: Columbia University Press.

Moravcsik, Michael J., and Murugesan, Poovanalingam

1975   "Some Results on the Function and Quality of Citations." *Social Studies of Science* 5:86–92.

Morgenbesser, Sidney

1969   "The Realist-Instrumentalist Controversy." In *Philosophy, Science, and Method,* edited by Sidney Morgenbesser, Patrick Suppes, and Morton White, pp. 200–218. New York: St. Martin's Press.

Morris, Charles W.

1934   Introduction to *George H. Mead, Mind, Self, and Society*. Chicago: University of Chicago Press.

1970   *The Pragmatic Movement in American Philosophy*. New York: George Braziller.

Mullins, Nicholas C.

1973   *Theory and Theory Groups in Contemporary American Sociology*. New York: Harper & Row.

Murphy, Arthur E.

1927   "Objective Relativism in Dewey and Whitehead." *Philosophical Review* 36:121–44.

1971   "Dewey's Epistemology and Metaphysics." In *The Philosophy of John Dewey*, edited by Paul A. Schlipp, pp. 193–225. LaSalle, Illinois: Open Court.

Natanson, Maurice

1956   *The Social Dynamics of George H. Mead*. Washington, D.C.: Public Affairs Press.

Nissen, Lowell

1966   *John Dewey's Theory of Inquiry and Truth*. Paris: Mouton & Co.

Novack, George

1975   *Pragmatism versus Marxism*. New York: Pathfinder Press.

O'Connor, D. J.

1952   "Names and Universals." *Proceedings of the Aristotelian Society* 53:173–88.

Odum, Howard W.

1951   *American Sociology: The Story of Sociology in the United States through 1950*. New York: Longmans, Green, and Co.

O'Toole, Richard, and Dubin, Robert

1968   "Baby Feeding and Body Sway: An Experiment in George Herbert Mead's 'Taking the Role of the Other.'" *Journal of Personality and Social Psychology* 10:59–65.

Park, Robert E.

1927   "Human Nature and Collective Behavior." *American Journal of Sociology* 32:733–41.

1939   "Symbiosis and Socialization: A Frame of Reference for the Study of Society." *American Journal of Sociology* 45:1–25.

1972   *The Crowd and the Public and Other Essays.* Edited, with an Introduction, by Henry Elsner. Chicago: University of Chicago Press.

Park, Robert E., and Burgess, Ernest W.

1970   *Introduction to the Science of Sociology.* Chicago: The University of Chicago Press.

Peirce, Charles Sanders

1931–1935   *Collected Papers of Charles Sanders Peirce,* edited by Charles Hartshorne and Paul Weiss. 8 vols. Cambridge: Harvard University Press.

Perry, Ralph B.

1935a   *The Thought and Character of William James,* vol. 1. Boston: Little, Brown and Co.

1935b   *The Thought and Character of William James,* vol. 2. Boston: Little, Brown and Co.

Petras, John W.

1966   "The Genesis and Development of Symbolic Interactionism in American Sociology." Ph.D. dissertation, University of Connecticut.

1968a   "John Dewey and the Rise of Interactionism in American Social Theory." *Journal of the History of the Behavioral Sciences* 4:18–27.

1968b   "Psychological Antecedents of Sociological Theory in America: W. James and J. M.

Baldwin." *Journal of the History of the Behavioral Sciences* 4:132–42.

1970 |"Changes of Emphasis in the Sociology of W. I. Thomas." *Journal of the History of the Behavioral Sciences* 6:70–9.

Piatt, Donald A.

1971 "Dewey's Logical Theory." In *The Philosophy of John Dewey,* edited by Paul A. Schlipp, pp. 103–35. LaSalle, Illinois: Open Court.

Raphael, D. Daiches

1954 "Universals, Resemblance, and Identity." Proceedings of the Aristotelian Society 69:109–32.

Ratner, Joseph (ed.)

1963 *John Dewey, Philosophy, Psychology, and Social Practice.* New York: G. P. Putnam's Sons.

Raushenbush, Winifred

1979 *Robert E. Park: Biography of a Sociologist.* Durham, N.C.: Duke University Press.

Ritzer, George

1975 *Sociology: A Multiple Paradigm Science.* Boston: Allyn and Bacon.

Rock, Paul

1979 *The Making of Symbolic Interactionism.* Totowa, N.J.: Rowman and Littlefield.

Rosenthal, Sandra B.

1969 "Peirce, Mead, and the Logic of Concepts." Transactions of the Charles S. Peirce Society: A Journal in American Philosophy 5:173–87.

Ross, Edward A.

1911 "Discussion." *American Journal of Sociology* 16:641.

Rossides, Daniel W.

1978   *The History and Nature of Sociological Theory.*
        Boston: Houghton Mifflin Co.

Rucker, Darnell

1969   *The Chicago Pragmatists.* Minneapolis: University of Minnesota Press.

Savery, William

1971   "The Significance of Dewey's Philosophy." In
        The Philosophy of John Dewey, edited by
        Paul A. Schlipp, pp. 479–514. La Salle, Illinois: Open Court.

Scheffler, Israel

1974   *Four Pragmatists.* New York: Humanities Press.

Schneider, Herbert W.

1963   *A History of American Philosophy.* New York:
        Columbia University Press.

Schwendinger, Herman, and Schwendinger, Julia R.

1974   *The Sociologists of the Chair.* New York: Basic Books.

Seeburger, Francis F., and Franks, David D.

1978   "Husserl's Phenomenology and Meadian
        Theory." *Sociological Quarterly* 19:345–47.

Singer, Milton

1980   "Signs of the Self: An Exploration in Semiotic
        Anthropology." *American Anthropologist,* in press.

Skinner, Quentin

1966   "The Limits of Historical Explanations." *Journal of the Royal Institute of Philsophy*
        41:199–215.

Skyrms, Brian

1966   *Choice and Chance.* Belmont, Calif.: Dickenson Publishing Co.

Small, Albion W.

1900   "The Scope of Sociology." *American Journal of Sociology* 6:42–66.

1905   *General Sociology.* Chicago: University of Chicago Press.

1916   "Fifty Years of Sociology in the United States." *American Journal of Sociology* 21:721–864.

1921   "Evolution of Sociological Consciousness in the United States." *American Journal of Sociology* 27:226–31.

1924   "Review of Durkheim, Education et Sociologie." *American Journal of Sociology* 29:608. 29:608.

Small, Henry G.

1977   "A Co-Citation Model of a Scientific Speciality: A Longitudinal Study of Collagen Research." *Social Studies of Science* 7:139–66.

Smith, James W.

1952   "Pragmatism, Realism, and Positivism in the United States." *Mind* 61:190–208.

Smith, Richard L.

1971   "Reflexive Behavior: An Experimental Examination of George Herbert Mead's Treatment of Vocal Gestues." Unpublished M.A. Thesis, University of South Carolina.

1977   "George Herbert Mead and Sociology: The Chicago Years." Unpublished Ph.D. Dissertation, University of Illinois at Champaign-Urbana.

Sorokin, Pitirim

1937   *Social and Cultural Dynamics,* vol. 2. New York: American Book Co.

1947   *Society, Culture, and Personality.* New York: Harper & Brothers.

1966   *Sociological Theories of Today.* New York: Harper & Row.

Sprietzer, Elmer, and Reynolds, Larry T.
1973   "Patterning in Citations: An Analysis of References to George Herbert Mead." *Sociological Focus* 6:71–82.

Stone, Gregory P., and Farberman, Harvey A.
1967   "Further Comment on the Blumer-Bales Dialogue concerning the Implications of the Thought of George Herbert Mead." *American Journal of Sociology* 72:409–10.

Stone, Gregory P.; Maines, David R.; Farberman, Harvey A.; Stone, Gladys I.; and Denzin, Norman K.
1974   "On Methodology and Craftsmanship in the Criticism of Sociological Perspectives." *American Sociological Review* 29:456–63.

Stryker, Sheldon
1977   "Two Social Psychologies: Toward an Appreciation of Mutual Relevance." *Sociometry* 40:145–60.

Sullivan, Daniel; White, D. Hywel; and Barboni, Edward J.
1977   "Co-citation Analysis of Science: An Evaluation." *Social Studies of Science* 7:223–40.

Thayer, H. S.
1968   *Meaning and Action.* Indianapolis: The Bobbs-Merill Co.

Thomas, Milton H.
1962   *John Dewey: A Centennial Bibligraphy.* Chicago: University of Chicago Press.

Thomas, W. I.
1897   "On a Difference in the Metabolism of the

Sexes." *American Journal of Sociology* 3:31–63.

1951   *Social Behavior and Personality.* New York: Social Science Research Council.

Thomas, W. I., and Thomas, D. S.

1928   *The Child in America.* New York: Alfred A. Knopf.

Turner, Ralph H.

1967   Introduction to *On Social Control and Collective Behavior,* by Robert E. Park. Chicago: University of Chicago Press.

Veatch, Henry

1954   *Realism and Nominalism Revisited.* Milwaukee: Marquette University Press.

Volkart, Edmund H.

1951   Introduction to *Social Behavior and Personality,* by W. I. Thomas. New York: Social Science Research Council.

Wagner, Helmut R.

1963   "Types of Sociological Theory: Toward a System of Classification," *American Sociological Review* 28:735–42.

Warshay, Leon H.

1971   "The Current State of Sociological Theory: Diversity, Polarity, Empiricism, and Small Theories." *Sociological Quarterly* 12:23–45.

Weiss, Paul

1965   "Charles S. Peirce, Philosopher." In *Perspectives on Peirce,* edited by R. J. Bernstein, pp. 120–40. New Haven: Yale University Press.

Weiss, Paul, and Burks, Arthur W.

1946   "Peirce's Sixty-Six Signs." *Journal of Philsophy* 42:383–88.

Werkmeister, W. H.

1949   A *History of Philosophical Ideas in America.*
New York: The Roland Press Co.

Wild, John

1948   *Introduction to Realistic Philsophy.* New York:
Harper Brothers.
1969   *The Radical Empiricism of William James.*
Garden City: Doubleday & Co.

Wiley, Norbert

1979   "The Rise and Fall of Dominating Theories in
American Sociology." In *Contemporary Issues in Theory and Research,* edited by W. E.
Snizek, E. R. Fuhrman, and M. K. Miller, pp.
47–79. Westport, Conn.: Greenwood Press.

Wilson, Thomas P.

1970   "Normative and Interpretive Paradigms in
Sociology." In *Understanding Everyday Life,*
edited by J. D. Douglas, pp. 57–79. Chicago:
Aldine.

Wolff, Kurt H.

1959   "The Sociology of Knowledge and Sociological
Theory." in *Symposium on Sociological
Theory,* edited by Llewellyn Gross, pp.
567–602. Evanston, Illinois: Row, Peterson
and Co.
1978   "Phenomenology and Sociology." In *A History
of Sociological Analysis,* edited by T. Bottomore and R. Nisbet, pp. 499–556. New
York: Basic Books.

Woodward, James W.

1945   "Social Psychology." In *Twentieth-Century
Sociology,* edited by Georges Gurvitch and
W. E. Moore, pp. 218–66. New York: the
Philosophical Library.

Wrong, Dennis H.

1961   "The Oversocialized Conception of Man in

Modern Sociology." *American Sociological Review* 26:183–93.

Young, Kimball, and Freeman, Linton

1966   "Social Psychology and Sociology." *Modern Sociological Theory,* edited by Howard Becker and Alvin Boskoff, pp. 550–73. New York: Holt, Rinehart and Winston.

Zeitlin, I. M.

1973   *Rethinking Sociology.* Englewood Cliffs, N.J.: Prentice-Hall.

Zimmerman, Don H., and Weider, D. Lawrence

1970   "Ethnomethodology and the Problem of Order: Comment on Denzin." In *Understanding Everyday Life,* edited by Jack D. Douglas, pp. 285–98. Chicago: Aldine Publishing Co.

Znaniecki, Florian

1940   *The Social Role of the Man of Knowledge.* New York: Columbia University Press.

Index

Abelard, Pierre, 293n
adaptation, concept of:
in Blumer's sociology,
173–74; in Dewey's
philosophy, 88, 94,
98, 104, 109, 116; in
Ellwood's sociology,
168–69
Allport, Floyd, 60, 111,
220, 222
*American Journal of
Sociology*, recognition
of Mead, 213, 216
Ames, Edward S., 207,
232, 243
Anderson, Nels, 244
Aquinas, Thomas, 11,
64
argument, 42
Aristotle, 10, 11, 23, 49,
99. *See also* logic,
Aristotelian
attitude, in Mead's
theory, 139, 141, 144,
171–72, 175–77. *See
also* Mead, taking the
attitude of the other
Averroes, 11
Avicenna, 11
Ayer, A. J., 295n

Bain, Read, 215
Baker, Paul J., 160,
228–29
Baldwin, James Mark,
5, 185, 311n
Barboni, Edward J., 253

Barnes, Harry E., 160,
215, 220, 303n
Barry, Robert M., 317n
Bauman, Z., 248
Becker, Howard S., 258
being, in Hegel and
Dewey, 88, 90, 93
Bentley, Arthur, 88,
297n, 298n
Bergmann, Gustav, 16
Bergson, Henri, 84, 85,
118
Berkeley, George, 37
Bernard, L. L., 154,
202, 211, 227, 229,
241, 258, 308–12n,
314n
Bernstein, Richard J.,
88–89
Bittner, Christopher J.,
215, 309n
Blumenthal, Albert, 238,
244, 313n, 315n
Blumer, Herbert, 203,
225, 235, 237,
239–41, 243, 245,
248, 250, 252, 258,
309n, 314–16n; and
the Chicago School,
154; and Dewey's
epistemology, 113; as
father of symbolic
interactionism, 5,
248–49, 252; as psy-
chical interactionist,
161, 172, 179, 184,
250, 256, 259, 302n;